War in Heaven/Heaven on Earth

Millennialism and Society
Series Editor: Brenda E. Brasher
Senior Advisor: Frederic J. Baumgartner (Virginia Polytechnic Institute)

Millennialism and Society had its genesis in the 1996–2002 annual meetings of the Center for Millennial Studies at Boston University. Those meetings brought together an international array of scholars to discuss the texts and traditions of religious revelation or apocalypses concerning the end of the world as we know it, whether in a tumultuous final judgment or a utopian eternal paradise. As apocalyptic texts advance an argument that massive change on earth is possible, even desirable, because it is part of a divine plan, the scholars' goal was to attain a richer, more nuanced understanding of our most ancient ideas of social change, including their influence on societies today.

The series consists of three volumes. Taken together, *Millennialism and Society* as a series represents a sustained effort on the part of this scholarly network to advance our understanding of what is a frequently unruly element of our cultural heritage.

Other volumes in the series:

The End That Does:
Art, Science and Millennial Accomplishment
Edited by: Cathy Gutierrez and Hillel Schwartz

Gender and Apocalyptic Desire
Edited by: Brenda E. Brasher and Lee Quinby

War in Heaven/Heaven on Earth

Theories of the Apocalyptic

Edited by
Stephen D. O'Leary and Glen S. McGhee

Millennialism and Society, Volume 2

LONDON   OAKVILLE

Published by

Equinox Publishing Ltd

UK: Unit 6, The Village, 101 Amies St., London SW11 2JW

US: 28 Main Street, Oakville, CT 06779

www.equinoxpub.com

First published 2005 by Equinox Publishing Ltd.

British Library Cataloguing-in-Publication Data
A catalogue record for this book is available from the British Library.

Library of Congress Cataloging-in-Publication Data
War in heaven/heaven on earth : theories of the apocalyptic / edited by Stephen D. O'Leary and Glen S. McGhee.-- 1st ed.
    p. cm. -- (Millennialism and society ; v. 2)
  Includes bibliographical references and index.
  ISBN 1-904768-87-3 (hardcover) -- ISBN 1-904768-88-1 (pbk.)   1. Millennialism--Congresses. I. O'Leary, Stephen D. II. McGhee, Glen S. III. Series.
  BL503.2.W37 2005
  202'.3--dc22
                              2004030232

ISBN 1-90476-887-3 (hardback)
        1-90476-888-1 (paperback)

Typeset by CA Typesetting, www.sheffieldtypesetting.com
Printed and bound in Great Britain by Antony Rowe, Chippenham, Wiltshire

Contents

Series Foreword

The *Millennialism and Society* series had its genesis in the 1996–2002 Annual meetings of the Center for Millennial Studies at Boston University. Each year, those meetings brought together an international array of scholars to discuss the texts and traditions of religious revelation or apocalypses concerning the end of the world as we know it, whether in a tumultuous final judgment or a utopian eternal paradise. As apocalyptic texts advance an argument that massive change on earth is possible and even desirable, the over-arching scholarly goal of those gatherings was to attain a richer, more nuanced understanding of what some argue are the most ancient ideas of social change.

The series consists of three volumes. *Gender and Apocalyptic Desire* focuses on the significance of sex and sexuality for the apocalyptic traditions, and on gender as a critical framing element within apocalyptic narratives as well as for how apocalyptic narratives have been appropriated. *The End That Does* recounts the myriad cultural contributions that apocalyptic concepts and energies have spawned, from atomic films to rap. The other volume, *War in Heaven/Heaven on Earth*, critically evaluates the variety of theories employed to analyze the persistence of apocalyptic beliefs and activity into the present day. Taken together, *Millennialism and Society* represents a sustained effort on the part of an established scholarly network to advance our understanding of what frequently has been a rather unruly element in our cultural heritage.

None of this would have been possible without the contributions and support of numerous key people and organizations. Richard Landes along with Stephen O'Leary founded the Center. The two provided intellectual depth and rigour to each gathering that challenged the scholars who came to push their critical abilities to maximum effectiveness. Lilly Endowment provided the funds that underwrote most of the costs of each meeting. Boston University provided space, administrative support, and a professional and student population that served as a willing and engaging audience for the various sessions.

The editors for each volume put in long, hard hours, for little reward. Without them, the series would not have made it into the public domain. Thanks go to Glen McGhee, Stephen O'Leary, Hillel Schwartz, Cathy Gutierrez, and Lee Quinby for months of patient work in assembling these volumes. Finally, thanks go to Janet Joyce and the publishing team at Equinox Publishing Limited for their belief in and support of the series.

The *Millennialism and Society* series is dedicated to Richard Landes, the founder of our intellectual feast.

Brenda E. Brasher
Editor in Chief
University of Aberdeen
Scotland

Acknowledgements

The editors wish to acknowledge the support of the Series Editor, Brenda E. Brasher, Senior Advisor, Frederic J. Baumgartner and Richard Landes for their help in bringing this collection to fruition. In addition, the helpful and responsive editorial staff at Equinox Publishing Limited, especially our editor Valerie Hall, deserve ample recognition for their efforts.

Our thanks go to Richard Landes, Beth Forrest, David Kessler, Kristin Solias, David Van Meter and Jennifer Snow for their involvement in the Annual Conferences of the Center for Millennial Studies, Boston University (1996–2002), as well as to all its participants. Funding for these conferences was generously provided by the Lilly Foundation and Boston University. Without these conferences, it would have been impossible to bring together in this volume such a diverse range of articles bearing on theoretical aspects of millennial studies.

Stephen O'Leary is grateful to Richard Landes for his friendship and continuing inspiration, and to the community of scholars whose participation made the Center for Millennial Studies conferences rewarding and exciting in the years before and after the advent of the new millennium. He wishes to thank Glen McGhee for doing almost all of the work in preparing this volume for publication, particularly for the laborious, time-consuming, and mostly thankless (until now) task of compiling, checking, and standardizing the references for each contributor's chapters.

Glen McGhee wishes to acknowledge the constant support of the librarians at Gulf Coast Community College and Lynn Haven Public Library, whose steady flow of interlibrary loan books provided him a necessary vital connection with intellectual currents and source material. Above all, he is thankful for the support of his dear wife, Sharon, without which his participation in this project would not have been possible. He also wishes to warmly thank the contributors to *War in Heaven/Heaven on Earth* for their time and patience, and especially for the opportunity to exchange ideas and views with them regarding millennialism and culture.

Fittingly, and more than just a coincidence (we'd like to think!), the joint editorial chores for this and the other CMS volumes in the *Millennialism and Society* series were initially undertaken at a pair of weekend meetings held at a Colonial-era bed and breakfast in Boston—the former

home of Samuel Sewall, Colonial America's ardent diarist, discerner of signs of the Second Coming, and foremost millennial scholar of his day.
    According to David Smith:

> Samuel Sewall, too often understood today as a charming diarist who measured out almonds to Mrs Winthrop, was the foremost 'scholar' of the idea [that the Indians were descendants of the lost Ten Tribes of Israel] in the colonies, and his *Phaenomena quaedam Apocalytia*...was the most complete and reasoned exegesis of millennialism attempted by any seventeenth-century American. Bolstered by an exhaustive scholarship, Sewall's hopes that American soil would be the most likely place for an imminent New Jerusalem were eagerly attended by Cotton Mather, who was directly inspired by them. In *Theopolis Americana* (1710) Mather acknowledges his indebtedness to Sewall, and we learn that this millennial work was first read in Sewall's house! (David E. Smith, 'Millennial Scholarship in America', *American Quarterly* 17 [1965], 539-40, with the exclamation point in the original.)

Apparently, we were not the only ones scrutinizing apocalyptic texts in Samuel Sewall's house. Likewise, following along the path set by Samuel Sewall before us, and other students of the millennium, the editors sincerely hope that the work presented here will continue to inspire millennial scholars and millennial scholarship in the years to come.

List of Contributors

Albert I. Baumgarten is Professor of Jewish History at Bar Ilan University, Ramat Gan, Israel. He specializes in the study of Judaism in antiquity, with a particular focus on understanding the experience of Jews of the past from a social-scientific perspective. He is the author of *The Flourishing of Jewish Sects in the Maccabean Era: An Interpretation* (Leiden: Brill, 1997), and the editor of *Apocalyptic Time* (Leiden: Brill, 2000).

David Cook is Assistant Professor of Religious Studies at Rice University specializing in Islam. He completed his undergraduate degrees at the Hebrew University in Jerusalem, and received his PhD from the University of Chicago in 2001. His areas of specialization include early Islamic history and development, Muslim apocalyptic literature and movements, historical astronomy and Judeo-Arabic literature. His first book, *Studies in Muslim Apocalyptic*, was published in 2002 by Darwin Press in the *Studies in Late Antiquity and Early Islam* series, followed by *Understanding Jihad* (Berkeley, CA: University of California, 2005) and *Contemporary Muslim Apocalyptic Literature* (New York: Syracuse University Press, 2005).

Ted Daniels is an independent scholar, as well as a writer, editor, photographer and web designer/developer who lives in Philadelphia. He is the author of *Millennialism: An International Bibliography* (New York: Garland Publishing, 1992) and *A Doomsday Reader* (New York: New York University Press, 1999). He holds a PhD in Folklore and Folklife from the University of Pennsylvania. From 1992 to 2002 he was Director of the Millennium Watch Institute and edited and published its newsletter 'Millennial Prophecy Report'. During this period he collected some 750 shelved feet of millenarian and apocalyptic ephemera, which is now housed in the University of Pennsylvania's rare book collection. His collection also includes approximately 15 gigabytes of electronic material on the same topics.

Leslie L. Downing received his PhD in Social Psychology at Southern Illinois University in 1970, and then taught and conducted group dynamics research while on the faculty of the University of Georgia. He is now a Professor of Social Psychology at the State University of New York

College at Oneonta. Dr Downing's research interests have included group decision-making, as in juries, the effects of deindividuation on aggression and helping, and ingroup-outgroup bias. His graduate courses in group dynamics, social influence, and theories of attitude change seek to address the question: What, if anything, can the field of social psychology contribute to understanding the power of groups to induce ideological conversions and extreme commitments of followers? His book in progress, 'Fragile Realities: Conversion and Commitment in Cults and Other Powerful Groups', is used as a text for his courses.

Marc Fonda is the Assistant Director for Strategic Programs and Joint Initiatives at the Social Sciences and Humanities Research Council of Canada. In this role, his primary responsibilities are to develop and promote research and knowledge-transfer programs in partnership with government and non-government agencies to support applied and policy-oriented research. Fonda received his doctorate in the Psychology of Religion/Women in Religion at the University of Ottawa, Canada.

Cathy Gutierrez is an Assistant Professor of Religion at Sweet Briar College in Virginia, USA. She has published on a variety of millennial and esoteric religious movements, particularly in nineteenth-century America, and is currently working on a manuscript about time in American Spiritualism.

Rosalind I.J. Hackett is a Distinguished Professor in the Humanities at the University of Tennessee, Knoxville, where she teaches Religious Studies and Anthropology. She has published widely on new religious movements in Africa ([ed.], *New Religious Movements in Nigeria* [Lewiston, NY: E. Mellen Press, 1987]), religious pluralism (*Religion in Calabar* [Berlin: Mouton de Gruyter, 1989]), art (*Art and Religion in Africa* [London: Cassell, 1996]), and religion in relation to conflict, gender, the media, and human rights (ed. with Mark Silk and Dennis Hoover, *Religious Persecution as a U.S. Policy Issue*, Hartford, CT: Center for the Study of Religion in Public Life, 2000). She is Vice President of the International Association for the History of Religions.

Richard Landes is a Professor of Medieval History at Boston University. His work focuses on the role of religion in shaping and transforming the relationships between elites and commoners in various cultures, in particular demotic religiosity which prizes equality before the law, dignity of manual labor, and access to sacred texts and divinity for all believers. For the past ten years he has directed the Center for Millennial Studies and is now working on two volumes, the first entitled *Heaven on Earth: The Varieties of the Millennial Experience*, and the second, *While God Tarried: Demotic Millennialism from Jesus to the Peace of God*, 33-1033.

Glen S. McGhee is an independent scholar and consultant living in Florida. His masters degree is from Yale Divinity School, and he has degrees in mathematics and philosophy. For the past decade he has been teaching comparative religion, Biblical studies, and American religious history. He is interested in modeling socio-cultural change, social network theory, and the social construction of institutions.

Joel W. Martin is the Interim Dean of the College of Humanities, Arts, and Social Sciences and Costo Professor of American Indian Affairs at the University of California Riverside. He is the author of *Sacred Revolt* (Boston: Beacon Press, 1991) and *The Land Looks After Us* (Oxford: Oxford University Press, 2001) and the editor of *Screening the Sacred* (Boulder: Westview Press, 1995) and other publications.

Daniel C. Noel was a faculty member in the Department of Mythological Studies at the Pacifica Graduate Institute. At the time of his death, 21 August, 2002, he was working on a book about the evolution of belief in America. Among his many publications in the area of religious studies were, *The Soul of Shamanism: Western Fantasies, Imaginal Realities* (New York: Continuum, 1997) and *Approaching Earth: The Search for the Mythic Significance of the Space Age* (New York: Amity House, 1986).

Stephen D. O'Leary is Associate Professor in the Annenberg School for Communication at the University of Southern California. His research focuses on religious communication, rhetorical theory and criticism, and communication ethics. O'Leary is the author of *Arguing the Apocalypse*, a study of the rhetoric of millennialism in American culture (New York and Oxford: Oxford University Press, 1994). Current projects include a historical study of religious media from oral culture to the Internet, and an analysis of the social controversies over new religious movements

David Redles is Assistant Professor of History at Cuyahoga Community College. He received his doctorate in Modern European History at Pennsylvania State University, where he focused on the religious and psychological dimensions of Nazism. He is the author of *Hitler's Millennial Reich: Apocalyptic Belief and the Search for Salvation* (New York: New York University Press, 2005).

Charles B. Strozier is a Professor of History at John Jay College and the Graduate Center, CUNY, and directs the Center on Terrorism at John Jay College. He is also a training and supervising psychoanalyst at TRISP. Strozier has written widely about apocalyptic violence in the last 20 years and is currently engaged in a large interview study of survivors and witnesses of the World Trade Center disaster.

Damian Thompson is an editorial writer with the *Daily Telegram* newspaper in London. He has a PhD in the sociology of religion from the London School of Economics. His book *Waiting for Antichrist: Charisma and Apocalypse in a Pentecostal Church* was published by Oxford University Press in 2005.

John R. Turner taught history at Norwich University until he retired in 2002. Since then he has continued as a commentator on WNCS in Montpelier, Vermont and has maintained a web site which offers discussion of politics, film, television, and literature (www.wordandimageofvermont.com). His book, *Letters to Dalton: Higher Education and the Degree Salesmen*, was published by Word and Image, Vermont, in 2002.

Introduction and Overview

Almost 50 years ago a trio of ground-breaking publications appeared that would leave their indelible impressions on the emergent branch of inquiry that we are now calling millennial studies. Norman Cohn (1957), Anthony F.C. Wallace (1956), and Leon Festinger and his associates (1956), all tendered their unique contributions from diverse fields: history, anthropology and social psychology.[1] Such interdisciplinary diversity, as the present volume amply demonstrates, continues to sustain and characterize millennial studies, the discipline that seeks to understand what really happened when prophecy failed, and the contexts and causes wherever and whenever millenarians and apocalyptic movements have flourished. Much about this fledging field is still uncertain, not the least regarding the future direction it is to take, the problems that are to be considered, as well as other equally important questions, such as the viability of particular theoretical approaches. This, then, is what the present volume seeks to address, and perhaps something more ambitious as well.

For although almost 50 years have passed, the study of new religious movements, millennialism and apocalyptic movements has become increasingly parochial and cloistered, losing much of its early enthusiasm and vitality by forgetting its interdisciplinary roots. The present volume will perhaps serve to bridge these widening gaps. The contributions included here are, for the most part, by presenters at the Center for Millennial Studies Annual Conferences (1996–2002) held at Boston University under the leadership of Boston University medieval historian Richard Landes and the University of Southern California rhetorician Stephen O'Leary. This self-designated theory volume is the second in the *Millennialism and Society* series published by Equinox Publishing Limited.

War in Heaven/Heaven on Earth: Theories of the Apocalyptic attempts to gather under the heading of 'theory' various interdisciplinary approaches to understanding millennialism and its different manifestations. True to the spirit of the seminal conferences themselves, the volume celebrates the diversity of millennial studies at the same time that its millennial focus—or what could be called its millenniocentricism—gives it defining coherence.

Dividing the chapters into three groups, the volume begins in Part I with general considerations and articulates foundational approaches to millennialism and millennial studies. Part II uses case histories to demonstrate the utility of the millennial approach, while Part III moves toward more theoretical or contemporary considerations within the field.

Overview of the Chapters

Ted Daniels begins the volume with a critical reflection on the issue of rhetoric and power that lies at the core of all apocalyptic forms. The essential conflict of Good versus Evil, us versus them, is central to apocalypticism. Armed with this insight into the underlying dynamic of contention, Daniels can effectively be said to deconstruct apocalypticism.

The 'charters' in the title of Ted Daniels' 'Charters of Righteousness' echo anthropologist Bronislaw Malinowski's idea that certain myths serve as 'charters' for group action and social institutions, insofar as they justify that group's particular aims and world-view.[2] For Daniels, such charters point to the unshakeable confidence with which apocalypticists and millennialists espouse their terrestrial ends. These kinds of claims, of course, bring them into conflict with the socio-political *status quo*, and remind us that the struggle for power and control occupies center stage in the unfolding of their respective career paths or trajectories.

Richard Landes' 'Roosters Crow, Owls Hoot' also shares an interest in the dynamic of contention at work in the core of apocalyptic movements and millenarian outbreaks. Even Landes' barnyard characterizations—from the rooster trying to wake everyone up with their message of impending doom, to the wise old owls who try to shut them up—are prime examples of this ongoing struggle, whose prize is far more than political power, but extends to how reality itself is to be perceived.

Landes also proposes a threefold typology which could be considered a road map for classifying millennial groups, one which has the virtue of accommodating their apparent dynamic metamorphic characteristics and range of combinatorial variety. By proposing a dynamic and flexible tri-axial morphology, Landes avoids various problems often associated with static classification systems. For example, he takes great pains to remind us that movements can and do suddenly 'morph' from one type into another (i.e., non-violent to violent). For this reason Landes presents his typology or schema in order to 'locate' groups at particular times in their life cycle. Although he does not engage in cataloging millennial groups, this can be accomplished quite easily, using three spectra: active agency versus passive agency; demotic or anarchical versus authoritarian; and cataclysmic versus gradualistic (see Landes Fig. 1). However, we must leave it to future millennial scholars to map out the trajectories or career paths that various movements take in order to establish likely (or not so likely) outcomes for successful groups

In her chapter on millennialism and literary narrative, Cathy Gutierrez considers both in terms of the formal significance of closure, that is, how they conceive of their respective endings. Both, she finds, share a formal dependence on closure,[3] but the nature of that dependence differs considerably, as does, and just as importantly, its deferral. Thus, how a fictional story ends differs explicitly from the eschatological end of history, that is, the ultimate closure of history. While millennialists foreground the coming of the end of time, they are also caught between the need to defer the very closure they seek to another time somewhere in the future, but must do so without undercutting their overall closural scheme. Lastly, Gutierrez describes how the strategies used to defer millennial closure highlight its interpretive and sense-making aspect—that can also be found in historical interpretation itself, thus showing both to be projects in hermeneutics.

In his chapter, Albert Baumgarten describes four stages characteristic of millennial groups, beginning with circumstances conducive to a group's message being received, and a favorable audience forming. This is followed by an intensive collective search for 'signs of the times' that confirm the message, and perhaps corresponds to what Richard Landes calls 'semiotic arousal', when events are given special meaning and serve to illuminate the group's world-view. The third stage is characterized by the self-reinforcing process of 'upping the ante', or escalating commitment to the group and its goals.[4] Lastly, inevitably, is disconfirmation; when millennial hopes and aspirations collapse into deep disappointments and disillusionment, sometimes resulting in unforeseen or creative developments.

Until now, the rapid spread of early Islam has remained a stubborn mystery to historians and scholars. But in his examination of what he calls the proto-Muslims, David Cook uncovers textual evidence of widespread apocalyptic urgency and millennial aspirations, and presents these as powerful motivational factors for the formation of coalitions among proto-Muslims and Christians, and Jews, and the drive for conquest just before the end of the world. In this millennial and apocalyptic context, participation in *jihad* becomes almost sacramental, and can also be understood as highly favorable to conversion. All but ignored, the importance of the apocalypticism of early Islam is now becoming recognized.

Joel W. Martin's discussion of Native American millennialism, and of the Sioux Ghost Dance in particular, and its historiographic treatment, serves as a much needed corrective and as a propaedeutic for the further study of early American religion, in all its colonial and pre-colonial contexts. In this essay, Martin espouses the interdisciplinary approach, including the use of anthropology, and revisits unresolved issues regarding Native American millennial outbreaks and relative deprivation theory.[5]

David Redles' examination of the subjective reality of early Nazis, through what he calls the 'millenarian lens', will perhaps be the most dramatic demonstration of the utility of the approach advocated here. To the uninitiated, Redles' contribution on Nazi millennialism may very well prove to be revelatory, and the approach taken will certainly have an impact on how future historians conduct their explorations and analyses of modern European history.[6] Brought to bear on such intractable issues as the origins of the Holocaust, the rise of Hitler to power, and the invasion of Russia, Redles' focus renders each more plausible in the apocalyptic millennial context he describes.

But less obvious, and perhaps just as important, is the question of why so many commentators on the modern world, deeply influenced by this period, have been blind to the millennialism swirling around them. Some, such as Martin Heidegger and Carl Jung, as well as others, were, to varying degrees, caught up in it. But even those that were immune to its appeal were notably unable to discern or make sense of the unseen emotions stirring their fellow countrymen and countrywomen to action.[7] Unless this apocalyptic millennialism is taken into account, and the widespread blindness to it is better understood, the intellectual history of modern Europe will remain incomplete, and in need of a thorough rethinking and eventual rewriting.

Next, Rosalind I.J. Hackett recounts the varying analytical perspectives employed in the aftermath of radical Islamic violence in Nigeria, illustrating the challenges that confront researchers grappling with violent outbreaks, particularly when they take religious forms. Focusing on the Maitatsine movement and uprising of 1980, Hackett seeks to locate the Maitatsine uprising in the traditions of other mahdist movements in Nigeria and Sudan, as well as to review the various explanatory discourses and approaches used by those trying to understand these movements. However, since it would seem that each case is itself unique, Hackett agrees with John Hall's position that a single theory linking religion and violence is inappropriate because 'religious violence is embedded in moments of history and structures of culture'.

Marc Fonda's approach to understanding postmodernism and apocalypticism recognizes that the need for renewal and revitalization in the face of genuine crisis must be met, both in terms of cultural renewal or institutional change. It is from this perspective that Fonda considers postmodernism and its underlying connection with apocalypticism, along with the conditions conducive to the rise of post-structuralism in the US. Both, according to Fonda, derive their potential for change from the need for renewal and the hope for a better tomorrow. Whether it is the kind of paradigmatic change described by Thomas Kuhn, or that presented in ancient mythology (*Enuma Elish* and the combat myth generally), or even in feminism, for the outcome and the hope invested in it, they are alike.

Thus, for Fonda the combat myth is 'a reflection of both postmodern and apocalyptic styles of thought: that is, the tendency to do battle with past monsters, and the vision of creating a new and better world'. Others, including Norman Cohn, J.Z. Smith, and Bruce Lincoln, have also revisited apocalyptic themes, literature and movements, to find an underlying dynamic of contention at work, bringing about a subtle rescoping of what Jonathan Z. Smith calls the 'apocalyptic pattern'.[8] Norman Cohn, for instance, now places Zarathustra's version of an earlier combat myth at the very birth of Zoroastrian apocalypticism.[9]

Scattered throughout the writings of the nineteenth-century German philosopher, Friedrich Nietzsche, are criticisms and observations regarding science that John R. Turner discusses in his chapter, 'A Nietzschean View of Millennial Science'. Turner's not so gentle reminder is cautionary and timely, and reveals the underside of popular visions of scientific progress. As Turner says, Nietzsche is 'magically prescient' when it comes to many contemporary issues, and this applies no less to the millennial hopes kindled by a modern faith or belief in the eventual triumph of science.[10]

Glen McGhee points out in his chapter that Leon Festinger and his associates did not just make Mrs Keech and her group of Spacemen-devotees famous. As the originator of social comparison theory and, later, cognitive dissonance theory, Festinger made full use of institutional changes in education following World War II, the legacy and intellectual assets of Kurt Lewin and German Gestalt experimental psychology, as well as the growth in the prestige of scientific rigor, to facilitate the rise of American social psychology. The rapid growth of the graduate student population following World War II, and their interest in investigating social psychology that was otherwise blocked by behaviorism and psychoanalysis, served to enhance the emancipatory promise of the new theory and contributed to its widespread acceptance.

However, Festinger's contributions ultimately led to increasing fragmentation within the field and the seemingly endless proliferation of psychological theories, instead of the greater unity and coherence that was initially anticipated. McGhee argues that contemporary students of

new religious movements and religious history, whether they are historians, sociologists, or anthropologists, or just students of religion and culture,
are likely to disregard, or worse yet, be ignorant of, the accumulated body
of scientific knowledge produced by social psychologists.[11] There is, then,
he says, a great need for dialogue between these scholarly groups. It is,
therefore, entirely appropriate to include next a chapter on the social psychology of commitment and conversion processes.

In his chapter, Leslie L. Downing presents a model for ideological and
religious conversion using René Thom's cusp catastrophe theory. Developed in the late 1960s, the French mathematician's work aspired to transform mathematical modeling in all areas of use.[12] Downing's application is
based on earlier work in social psychology regarding the psychology of
commitment,[13] and uses this in combination with Thom's cusp modeling
theory.[14] The result offers a description of the dynamics of conversion and
extreme persuasion, the kind found in new religious movements and what
Downing calls 'powerful groups'. This is an important example of the kind
of interdisciplinary collaboration that is possible in millennial studies.[15]

Damian Thompson's 'The Retreat of the Millennium' is an exploration of secularizing processes occurring within a believing community,
and is based upon his fieldwork with a large Pentecostal Church in
London during the approach of the Year 2000 (Y2K), the new millennium. Thompson's sociological exploration focuses on the declining sali-
ence of millennial or millenarian belief in this context, what he calls the
'marginalization of the apocalyptic', and uses this observation as a point
of entry into the often heated debate on religious secularization.[16]

Similar issues regarding secularization are considered from a different
perspective in a piece by Daniel Noel that is his account of the apocalypse of modern belief. In what is a stunning and tragic evocation of mass
media dominated contemporary culture, he enumerates the ways in
which these changes serve to undermine and utterly transform traditional
faith. It has about it the air of finality. This was, sadly, to be one of Dan's
last presentations at CMS, his untimely death ending an astonishingly
fruitful and productive career. He is sorely missed, and wanted to see this
particular article published, as it is here. Indeed, Noel's deep concern
regarding the 'stealth' aspect of media anticipates the power of images
demonstrated in the last chapter of the book.[17]

Chuck Strozier completes the volume with a rare and exclusive approach to the apocalyptic: a view from the inside as it were, from within
the destructive power and trauma of Armageddon itself, by taking us to
Ground Zero—not the location in space, but in the experience of those
who were there.[18] His academic background and career focus uniquely

qualify him as a participant observer of the World Trade Center disaster that occurred 11 September, 2001 in New York City. His chapter certainly brings it down to a personal level, and makes it immediate, from the lingering odor of death, to the inconsolable suffering and shock of those he interviews. At the same time, he places the disaster in its apocalyptic contexts, and diagnoses our lack of psychological preparedness, which he then links to the subsequent loss of our sense of invincibility as a nation. Against the background of apocalyptic images of mushroom clouds, collapsing towers, and the rising terrorist threat, he concludes with a somber reflection on the impact that the birth of the atomic age, and its unimaginable destructiveness, has had on our culture and our souls.[19] In so doing, he points to important shifts that have occurred in the modern apocalyptic sensibility that now frames the contemporary situation.

References

Aubin, David, 'A Cultural History of Catastrophes and Chaos: Around the "Institut Des Hautes Etudes Scientifiques", France' (PhD dissertation, Princeton University, 1998).

Aya, Rod, *Rethinking Revolutions and Collective Violence: Studies on Concept, Theory, and Method* (Amsterdam: Het Spinhuis, 1990).

Bigelow, John, 'A Catastrophe Model of Organizational Change', *Behavioral Science* 27 (1982), 26-42.

Brager, George, 'Commitment and Conflict in a Normative Organization', *American Sociological Review* 34 (1969), 482-91.

Burghes, David N., and A.D. Wood, *Mathematical Models in the Social, Management, and Life Sciences* (New York: Halsted Press, 1980).

Cohn, Norman, *The Pursuit of the Millennium* (New York: Oxford University Press, 1957).

—*Cosmos, Chaos, and the World to Come: The Ancient Roots of Apocalyptic Faith* (New Haven, CT: Yale University Press, 1993).

—'How Time Acquired a Consummation', in Malcolm Bull (ed.), *Apocalypse Theory and the Ends of the World* (Oxford: Basil Blackwell, 1995), 21-37.

Festinger, Leon, Henry W. Riecken and Stanley Schachter, *When Prophecy Fails* (New York: Harper & Row, 1956).

Flay, Brian R., 'Catastrophe Theory in Social Psychology: Some Applications to Attitudes and Social Behavior', *Behavioral Science* 23 (1978), 335-50.

Hout, Michael, and Claude S. Fischer, 'Why More Americans Have No Religious Preference: Politics and Generations', *American Sociological Review* 67 (2002), 165-90.

—'O Be Some Other Name', *American Sociological Review* 67 (2002), 316-18.

Jackson, W.T.H., *The Hero and the King: An Epic Theme* (New York: Columbia University Press, 1982).

Kittler, Friedrich, 'The Mechanized Philosopher', in Laurence A. Rickels (ed.), *Looking after Nietzsche* (Albany, NY: State University of New York Press, 1990), 195-207.

Lee, Martha F., 'Apocalypse and Community: Rethinking the Origins of Millennialism', in Martha F. Lee (ed.), *Millennial Visions: Essays on Twentieth-Century Millenarianism* (Westport, CT: Praeger, 2000), 55-67.

Lewis, Bernard, *Wall Street Journal*, 3 February, 2004 A12, citing C-SPAN shortly after 11 September, 2001.

Lincoln, Bruce, 'Apocalyptic Temporality and Politics in the Ancient World', in John J. Collins (ed.), *The Encyclopedia of Apocalypticism* (New York and London: Continuum, 2000), I, 457-75.

Liu, James H., and Bibb Latané, 'Extremitization of Attitudes: Does Thought- and Discussion-Induced Polarization Cumulate?' *Basic and Applied Social Psychology* 20.2 (1998), 103-110.

Malinowski, Bronislaw, *A Scientific Theory of Culture, and Other Essays* (New York: Oxford University Press, 1960).

Martin, Joel, 'Visions of Revitalization in the Eastern Woodlands: Can a Middle-Aged Theory Stretch to Embrace the First Cherokee Converts?', in Michael E. Harkin (ed.), *Reassessing Revitalization Movements: Perspectives from North America and the Pacific Islands* (Lincoln: University of Nebraska Press, 2004), 61-87.

Marwell, Gerald, and N.J. Demerath, III, ' "Secularization" by Any Other Name', *American Sociological Review* 67 (2002), 314-16.

Merkl, Peter H., *Political Violence under the Swastika: 581 Early Nazis* (Princeton, NJ: Princeton University Press, 1975).

Perry, John Weir, 'The Ritual Drama of Renewal', in *idem, Roots of Renewal in Myth and Madness: The Meaning of Psychotic Episodes* (San Francisco: Jossey-Bass, 1976), 79-164.

Renfrew, Colin, and Kenneth L. Cooke (eds.), *Transformations: Mathematical Approaches to Culture Change* (New York: Academic Press, 1979).

Skinner, B.F., *Walden Two* (New York: Macmillan, 1976).

Smith, Jonathan Z., *Imagining Religion: From Babylon to Jonestown* (Chicago: University of Chicago Press, 1982).

Street, Marc D., 'Groupthink: An Examination of Theoretical Issues, Implications, and Future Research Suggestions', *Small Group Research* 28.1 (1997), 72-93.

—'The Effects of Escalating Commitment on Ethical Decision Making' (PhD dissertation, Florida State University, 1998).

Street, Marc D., and William Anthony, 'A Conceptual Framework Establishing the Relationship between Groupthink and Escalating Commitment Behavior', *Small Group Research* 28.2 (1997), 267-93.

Street, Marc D., Chris Robertson, and Scott W. Geiger, 'Ethical Decision Making: The Effects of Escalating Commitment', *Journal of Business Ethics* 16 (1997), 1153-161.

Wallace, Anthony F.C., 'Revitalizing Movements', *American Anthropologist* 58 (1956), 264-81.

—*Revitalizations and Mazeways: Essays on Culture Change,* (ed. Robert S. Grumet; Lincoln: University of Nebraska Press, 2003).

—'Foreword', in *Reassessing Revitalization Movements: Perspectives from North America and the Pacific Islands* (ed. Michael E. Harkin; Lincoln: University of Nebraska Press, 2004), vii-xi.

Zeeman, E.C., 'Catastrophe Theory', *Scientific American* (April 1976), 65-83.

—*Catastrophe Theory: Selected Papers, 1972–1977* (Reading, MA: Addison-Wesley Publishing, 1977).

Notes

1.   The initial publications were: Norman Cohn, *The Pursuit of the Millennium* (New York: Oxford University Press, 1957); Anthony F.C. Wallace, 'Revitalizing Movements', *American Anthropologist* 58 (1956), 264-81; and Leon Festinger, Henry W.

Riecken and Stanley Schachter, *When Prophecy Fails* (New York: Harper & Row, 1956). More recent work by Norman Cohn includes: 'How Time Acquired a Consummation', in Malcolm Bull (ed.), *Apocalypse Theory and the Ends of the World* (Oxford: Basil Blackwell, 1995), 21-37; and his *Cosmos, Chaos, and the World to Come: The Ancient Roots of Apocalyptic Faith* (New Haven, CT: Yale University Press, 1993). The important papers by Anthony Wallace have been collected and republished, and a retrospective volume on his contributions has also been released: Anthony F.C. Wallace, *Revitalizations and Mazeways: Essays on Culture Change,* (ed. Robert S. Grumet; Lincoln: University of Nebraska Press, 2003); and *Reassessing Revitalization Movements: Perspectives from North America and the Pacific Islands* (ed. Michael E. Harkin; Lincoln: University of Nebraska Press, 2004).

2.   Bronislaw Malinowski, *A Scientific Theory of Culture, and Other Essays* (New York: Oxford University Press, 1960), 48-52, 111, 162.

3.   The denouement of a murder mystery, for example, is a final unveiling or *apocalypsis* that shows how all the disparate clues fit together to identify the culprit, no matter how unlikely it may have seemed earlier to the reader. For millennialists, it is the advent of the end of time that gives meaning and coherence to worldly existence.

4.   Concerning the 'escalation of commitment', see n. 15 below.

5.   Concerning relative deprivation, see more recently Joel Martin, 'Visions of Revitalization in the Eastern Woodlands: Can a Middle-Aged Theory Stretch to Embrace the First Cherokee Converts?', in Harkin (ed.), *Reassessing Revitalization Movement*, 61-87. See also: Martha F. Lee, 'Apocalypse and Community: Rethinking the Origins of Millennialism', in Martha F. Lee (ed.), *Millennial Visions: Essays on Twentieth-Century Millenarianism* (Westport, CT: Praeger, 2000), 55-67; and, sadly overlooked, Rod Aya, *Rethinking Revolutions and Collective Violence: Studies on Concept, Theory, and Method* (Amsterdam: Het Spinhuis, 1990).

6.   The contrast in approaches can be startling. Peter H. Merkl, in his *Political Violence under the Swastika: 581 Early Nazis* (Princeton, NJ: Princeton University Press, 1975), uses some of the same source material as Redles, but nowhere in over 700 pages of sociological analysis is apocalypticism or millennialism mentioned. For Redles, on the other hand, these are the defining characteristics by which Nazi political behavior is to be understood.

7.   Consider, for example, the writings of Carl Jung, Thomas Mann, Erich Fromm, Erik Erikson, Wilhelm Reich and Paul Tillich regarding this period in Germany, and their apparent difficulty in recognizing the apocalyptic millennialism that so moved a nation.

8.   According to Smith, 'Enuma elish [Babylonian combat myth and creation saga] establishes clear parallels between Marduk's kingship in heaven and the kingship of Babylon, the creation of the world and the building of Esagila. The opposite would be the case as well. Destroy Babylon or Esagila, neglect Marduk, pervert kingship, and the world will be destroyed… I am not claiming that the ritual of the Akitu festival is an apocalyptic *text*. I am suggesting that it reflects on an apocalyptic *situation*… The *situation* of apocalypticism seems to me to be the cessation of native kingship; the *literature* of apocalypticism appears to me to be the expression of archaic, scribal wisdom as it comes to lack of a royal patron. Indeed, I would suggest further that… [T]he *apocalyptic pattern* [involves the perception] that the wrong king is on the

throne, that the cosmos will be thereby destroyed, and that the right god will either restore proper native kingship (his terrestrial counterpart) or will assume kingship himself...' (Jonathan Z. Smith, *Imagining Religion: From Babylon to Jonestown* [Chicago: University of Chicago Press, 1982], 94. Cited in part by Bruce Lincoln, 'Apocalyptic Temporality and Politics in the Ancient World', in John J. Collins [ed.], *The Encyclopedia of Apocalypticism* [New York and London: Continuum, 2000], I, 468).

A particularly relevant example of this, in which the underlying dynamic of contention can be seen, is Bernard Lewis' comment regarding militant Islam: 'The question people are asking is why they hate us. That's the wrong question. In a sense, they've been hating us for centuries, and it's very natural that they should. You have this millennial rivalry between two world religions, and now, from their point of view, the wrong one seems to be winning.' (*Wall Street Journal*, 3 February, 2004 A12, citing C-SPAN shortly after 11 September, 2001.) This is, to use the phrase of J.Z. Smith, the perception of an apocalyptic pattern.

According to W.T.H. Jackson, this recurrent theme of contention is present throughout the Western epic traditions as well. Typically, what Jackson calls the 'intruder hero' first appears to challenge the King, and is seen as a threat to the standing order, represented by the King and his court. As can be expected, Jackson points out that the epics are consistently deeply pessimistic about the destabilizing and destructive outcomes of this struggle for succession. W.T.H. Jackson, *The Hero and the King: An Epic Theme* (New York: Columbia University Press, 1982).

9. Cohn, 'How Time Acquired a Consummation', 33-34.

10. Nietzsche's epistemological criticism of science can perhaps be viewed as an early but important precursor of today's handful of 'science studies' and sociology of science sub-disciplines. Arguably the newest trend at large campuses, the Science, Technology and Society (STS) rubric now takes in branches of the feminist critique of science, critical theory, the newest developments in the sociology of scientific knowledge (SSK) and the philosophy of technology.

Although Nietzsche is not often remembered as a technological or social innovator, he was an early adopter of the newly invented, but not quite perfected Malling Hansen typing-sphere. In early 1882 he acquired the typing-sphere, which resembled a bubble-headed pin-cushion sprouting keys like toadstools, in order to overcome his difficulties reading and writing that were due to his extreme shortsightedness. But after a brief two-month long infatuation with the new technology, the 'heavy rains of the Riviera spring...left nothing more than meaningless signs on wet paper'. His close friend, Paul Ree, immediately set out to find a replacement, but instead of the requested 'eminent young man', Ree introduced the philosopher to a young Russian woman, Lou von Salomé. Thus began one of the most famous soap operas in modern intellectual history. (See Friedrich Kittler, 'The Mechanized Philosopher', in Laurence A. Rickels [ed.], *Looking after Nietzsche* [Albany, NY: State University of New York Press, 1990], 195-207 [197, 204-205]). There is, however, no evidence that Nietzsche's disappointing experience with the typing-sphere influenced his critique of science in any way.)

11. However, it may well be that psychology itself is not immune to millennialism; for example, B.F. Skinner's utopian novel, *Walden Two* (New York: Macmillan, 1976), which was based on behaviorist psychological principles.

12. The fascinating story of René Thom, the French algebraic topologist and winner of the Fields Medal in 1958, and mathematical catastrophe theory, is ably told by David Aubin in his 'A Cultural History of Catastrophes and Chaos: Around the "Institut Des Hautes Etudes Scientifiques", France' (PhD dissertation, Princeton University, 1998), 782 pages. Helpful introductions to the cusp catastrophe and its applications can be found in: David N. Burghes and A.D. Wood, *Mathematical Models in the Social, Management, and Life Sciences* (New York: Halsted Press, 1980), 247-58; and E.C. Zeeman, 'Catastrophe Theory', *Scientific American*, April 1976, 65-83. Unexplained bimodalism or polarization observed in data sets are sometimes considered possible candidates for further investigation using cusp catastrophe theory. Various attempts have been made to apply catastrophe theory to cultural change (Colin Renfrew and Kenneth L. Cooke [eds.], *Transformations: Mathematical Approaches to Culture Change* [New York: Academic Press, 1979]), organizational change (John Bigelow, 'A Catastrophe Model of Organizational Change', *Behavioral Science* 27 [1982], 26-42), and collective behavior (E.C. Zeeman, *Catastrophe Theory: Selected Papers, 1972–1977* [Reading, MA: Addison-Wesley Publishing, 1977]) as well as attitude change (James H. Liu and Bibb Latané, 'Extremitization of Attitudes: Does Thought- and Discussion-Induced Polarization Cumulate?' *Basic and Applied Social Psychology* 20.2 [1998], 103-110).

13. The understanding that psychological commitment may be considered as a splitting factor first appears in the work of George Brager, 'Commitment and Conflict in a Normative Organization', *American Sociological Review* 34 (1969), 482-91; see also Brian R. Flay, 'Catastrophe Theory in Social Psychology: Some Applications to Attitudes and Social Behavior', *Behavioral Science* 23 (1978), 335-50, here pages 340-41.

14. The basic approach taken here can perhaps be strengthened by considering the 'control factors' as 'conflicting factors', rather than as being orthogonal (see Flay, 'Catastrophe Theory in Social Psychology', 336-37; Burghes and Wood, *Mathematical Models*, 253-54; and Zeeman, *Catastrophe Theory* [1977], 19, 332-33). This would better display the true complementary nature of the control factors. Thus, for example, commitment would be tied more directly to the forces opposing it in the model, much as inertial forces act as friction to oppose a force applied to an object.

15. Another promising but under-utilized area of study in this regard is the 'escalation of commitment' work done over the last few decades by Barry Staw, Irving Janis, and others, regarding ever increasing levels of commitment by a group or individual to an objective that is unlikely to be achieved. Recent results suggest that unethical choices should be considered as a predictable exit strategy for those involved in escalating commitment situations, and that unethical behavior is more likely in those escalation of commitment situations where the locus of control is external, thus confirming previous observations regarding authoritarian groups. (Marc D. Street, 'The Effects of Escalating Commitment on Ethical Decision Making' [PhD dissertation, Florida State University, 1998], 164. See also *idem*, 'Groupthink: An Examination of Theoretical Issues, Implications, and Future Research Suggestions', *Small Group Research* 28.1 [1997], 72-93; Marc D. Street, Chris Robertson, and Scott W. Geiger, 'Ethical Decision Making: The Effects of Escalating Commitment', *Journal of Business Ethics* 16 [1997], 1153-1161; and Marc D. Street and William Anthony, 'A Conceptual Framework Establishing the Relationship between Groupthink and Escalating Commit-

ment Behavior', *Small Group Research* 28.2 [1997], 267-93.) Lastly, it is interesting to generally note that the work done within organizational and management studies on the radicalizing effects of escalation of commitment processes does not appear to be well-integrated into social psychology, indicating the need for interdisciplinary outreach here as well.

16. See, for example, the following exchange between sociologists: Gerald Marwell and N.J. Demerath, III, ' "Secularization" by Any Other Name', *American Sociological Review* 67 (2002), 314-16; Michael Hout and Claude S. Fischer, 'O Be Some Other Name', *American Sociological Review* 67 (2002), 316-18; and Michael Hout and Claude S. Fischer, 'Why More Americans Have No Religious Preference: Politics and Generations', *American Sociological Review* 67 (2002), 165-90.

17. For Noel, the 'stealth' issue is not simply that the History Channel widely disseminates information about history, but rather that people *get* their history from the History Channel. Indeed, over the decades, history and other forms of knowledge have increasingly come to be accessed through a mediating technology, usually visually based, endowing that media with an undelegated authority and credibility. Thus, for example, Liu and Latané report that, 'When bombarded with large amounts of information on a topic, people will tend to see the topic as more important: when they know nothing about the topic, they will think of it as less important' ('Extremitization of Attitudes', 105; see n. 12 above).

18. That the memory of the first atomic bomb detonation in the desert near Alamogordo, New Mexico, on 16 July, 1945, should be summoned in the act of naming the WTC disaster site 'Ground Zero,' points to the merging of these epochal events in the collective psyche. That this connection between the two events has gone largely unnoticed, until now, gives us reason to ponder the uncertainty of the new age ushered in.

19. The personal transformations and upheavals of those Strozier calls 'mystics, artists and psychotics' explicitly correspond to the apocalyptic images and rituals of collective cultural renewal in the life work of John Weir Perry, MD (e.g., John Weir Perry, 'The Ritual Drama of Renewal', in *idem, Roots of Renewal in Myth and Madness: The Meaning of Psychotic Episodes* [San Francisco: Jossey-Bass, 1976], ch. 5, 79-164). Also in this regard, see Joel W. Martin, in the section titled 'Millenarian Initiation', this volume.

Part I
Core Ideas of Millennial Theory

Charters of Righteousness:
Politics, Prophets and the Drama of Conversion[*]

Ted Daniels

Politics

The apocalyptic drama begins when someone says the world is about to be changed in every respect, down to its very physical form. Commonly he or she foretells that nearly everyone will die, or at least suffer, in the process. But there is hope for a tiny number of very special people. They will survive the changes, and afterwards they will be (at least) demigods, who will live forever. Generally speaking, at the end the earth will return to its original condition: paradise.

This kind of prophecy involves a familiar form of belief about the end of human life as we know it. Many religious systems have their own versions of this account, and they all involve destruction of the way things are, a sort of cosmic recycling. Life starts over on a cleansed planet, all things made new and perfect.

Eschatology is generally understood to refer to ideas about last things. Catherine Keller gives a somewhat more nuanced translation of this root word, saying it is best rendered as 'edge', which suggests an important difference.[1] Prophets and commentators refer to apocalypse as The End, but its focus ultimately is always on a new beginning, a sudden shift in the *order* of the world. There's always something beyond the edge for the millenarian believer.

Prophets threaten us with falling stars, titanic earthquakes, famine, pestilence, and wars. One thing accomplished by the mention of Earth Changes, as the New Age calls them, is to manifest the scope and seriousness of the change that is envisioned. Even the fabric of creation becomes a moral player in this titanic and final battle between the forces of good and evil, no matter how they are conceived. In fact it is the order of the world, not the world itself, that will end. This glorious victory will herald the dawn of the millennium, which in Christian theology refers to Christ's final thousand-year reign of perfect peace and justice: a restoration of Paradise.

Perhaps the most generally accepted definition of millennialism is Norman Cohn's. He calls it a type of salvationism: it must be collective, terrestrial, imminent (i.e., to be expected soon and suddenly), total (embodying perfection, not mere improvement), and brought on by a recognized supernatural agency.[2] There is room to argue with some of these points; many apocalyptic movements invoke no supernatural agency, for example, relying instead on conceptions of natural law to legitimize their predictions of change. However, a key point in Cohn's definition, one with which no one I'm aware of has found fault, is that the salvation millennialism invokes is terrestrial. It will happen here, it will involve this world.

Millennialism is not, or not only, a matter of finding an individual heavenly home. It promises rescue from evil, perhaps for everyone, but typically for a small community of believers.

This salvation will happen in time, that is, in this world, not in a hereafter. However, in religious doctrines of apocalypse, it is placed at time's end: the present is always just on the cusp of dissolution into eternity.

All societies have an account of creation, attributed to some superhuman, if not supernatural, force. These accounts of how we came to be all serve to provide a charter for society, a set of basic assumptions, which, in the ordinary course of events, go unquestioned.[3] These cosmologies nearly all propose that the earth was, at its beginning, perfect. Beginnings are sacred, and at that time the world was paradise. Who would worship a God who couldn't make a perfect world?

Yet in every paradise there is a fall. In the myths some event introduces change into paradise and turns it into the world. What brings on this change can be almost anything: sin, a mistake, or mere chance. Ever since whatever-it-was happened, the world has been bad, and life has been hard and painful: close to hell, if not actually hell itself.

Apocalypse promises to redress this turn of events. After evil's destruction, there will be a perfected world. We, or at least the saints, will live out a blissful existence in Eden.

Since paradise is perfect it is incapable of change. Change in perfection can only transform it into something else and something less. The situation of a dweller in paradise confronting change is like that of someone standing at the North Pole: every direction is south and downhill. Perfection can only degrade, and any change in paradise is subversive. Paradise is outside time, but it's never more than a moment long. It always fails, and when it does, it changes to its opposite: hell. In myths of perfection there is no middle ground, no compromise. Paradise, like everything else in the millennium, reflects a precarious shifting polarity.

Secular and political millenarianism are just beginning to attract the kind of analytic attention that has for years been paid to their religious counterparts, in part because the conclusion that millenarianism is inherently political is becoming inescapable. This can be said of religion in general: to the extent that it attempts to govern access to power, and to prescribe its exercise, religion is political.

Martha F. Lee makes much this point in her *Earth First!: Environmental Apocalypse*, where she observes, following Clifford Geertz and others, that political ideology and religious dogma share most attributes in common, other than their purported origins.[4] Both consist of 'basic assumptions' about humanity and its place in the world. The two arenas often remain rigidly separated, especially in their own self-presentations, and frequently come into conflict, but at the analytical level the similarities are striking. Religion and politics are competing gladiators in the arena of opinion, where they also must compete with science. Neither of the latter two makes much reference to spiritual matters and they ordinarily reject any attempt to find it in their texts, but nevertheless all three attempt to provide and govern a social world-view. Lee observes that it is difficult in this environment to classify any given movement with millenarian ideas as either political or religious. I suggest that the attempt be abandoned, in recognition that the two are not ultimately distinct.

Philip Lamy observes that strictly secular millenarian ideas propose a human apocalypse.[5] That is, they rely on purely human agency both as promoters of evil and as ultimate saviors: self-salvation is the best we can hope for in most of the movements he discusses, though there are others where salvation will be collective. Lamy notes that many such secular millenarian movements are closely allied with, if not actually part of, nationalist movements, though the latter have 'purely political' goals in mind.[6] It is not clear what distinction he intends to draw here, since it appears that all apocalypses propose political aims: it is the order of this world that is to be redeemed, and that is a political action, regardless of the nature of the agency that will bring it about. This observation—that millennialism has political aims—is not new. It appears in any number of analytical writings on millennialism and apocalypse, but few if any observers have reached the conclusion that seems to me inescapable: that millennialism is inherently political because it arises from the perception of political evil—the abuse of power—and seeks to remedy it.[7]

The failure to observe the inherently political nature of millenarianism may arise from an unspoken assumption that politics necessarily involves direct involvement in political activity: everything from getting out the vote to staging coups to mailing bombs. Millenarian movements frequently (but by no means invariably) withdraw from the world in an effort to protect their purity from contamination by the world's corruption. They oppose and frequently renounce the world's order, actions which are in fact political. Rejection of politics is political. As with the hermit who rejects society in his isolation, the action of withdrawal condemns that which will not change. Stephen O'Leary's point that millennialism is rhetorical furthers this argument.[8] Apocalypse is an argument about power, and it is not always addressed to its adherents. It may make a proclamation across an ideological divide.

Prophets and Conversion

Almost anywhere you look prophetic careers follow the same trajectory. Prophets begin their lives as sinners, outsiders, disregarded and insignificant people. Then something happens. They undergo some crisis that changes their lives in fundamental and drastic ways. They experience conversion, in a sudden and sometimes shocking way. This conversion is seen, by them and at least some others, as a total and perhaps inexplicable change in their character. Where once the prophet was feckless, perhaps rootless, but in any case a nonentity, now he (they are frequently women) has absolute confidence in himself and the mission he thinks comes directly from god.[9]

The source of this enormous faith in oneself and one's mission may derive from the conversion experience itself, but in many cases it is seen to follow on the experience of a vision in which the prophet is given the mission from a divine or superhuman source whose authority is quite unquestionable. It generally contains instructions on how the prophet is to proceed in accomplishing this divine and enormous task, and absolute assurance that its source is both authentic and infallible in its support of the mission. These experiences combine to provide the prophet with whatever share of charisma he or she may garner from supporters, and contribute greatly to the loathing opponents feel. Charisma is negative as well as positive.

In any case conversion is the prime motif of both the prophet's career in general, and of apocalyptic thinking when the prophet's mission takes that track. To consider one more or less obscure example: at the time of Handsome Lake's first vision (1799) the Seneca Nation had gone from the position of one of the three major powers in northern North America to a rural proletariat in extreme deprivation and hardship in the course of two generations. Alcoholism was rampant, and Handsome Lake suffered heavily from it and other miseries common to his people among whom he was a chief, albeit a despised one.

This was a typical prophetic career. Handsome Lake's alcoholism and other troubles had made him so ill that he was bedridden, and then he had his vision. This seems to have come to him in a coma—his relatives were preparing to bury him when he revived. This apparent resurrection would certainly give him a powerful and immediate charisma. Following this vision and others he became a widely-known and well-respected prophet, and quickly recovered from his ailments, giving up alcohol for the rest of his life and leading his people to do the same, also adopting European farming practices and modes of life while retaining in 'pure' form certain traditional rites and practices.[10]

Handsome Lake's beliefs and practices were apocalyptic. He predicted the destruction of the world in three generations; such delay, by the way is a rarity in apocalyptic prophecy, which typically reports an imminent destruction. If it is not going to involve people alive now, what's the point of listening? Handsome Lake's mission was to forestall this outcome, with the help of three angels and the Great Spirit. Like many other prophets, he at first fell into a grandiose, world-saving pattern of behavior, but later moderated his aims under the influence of another vision. His mission focused on ridding the Seneca of white dominion. It is especially significant that this political aspect of his mission was given to him in a co-appearance of Jesus Christ and George Washington; a marriage of political with religious revolution. His way was intended for his people alone, a way for them to survive and possibly flourish in a radically new social and economic context. Handsome Lake's movement still exists today. He is revered among the Seneca, but his movement, though it envisioned apocalyptic global change, functions, like many others, as a nativist revitalization.

It may be instructive to consider a different prophetic career, where real conversion, like that described for Handsome Lake, seems *not* to have occurred. In seventeenth-century Jerusalem the recognized Jewish prophet Nathan of Gaza declared that he'd had a vision that told him that a wandering holy man named Sabbatai Zvi (1626–1676) was the messiah. Despite Zvi's apparent instability—he seems to have suffered from what is now known as 'bipolar disorder'—and his uncertainty of his own calling, he was widely and almost immediately accepted as the messiah throughout world Jewry, despite opposition from some rabbis. Even Christians applauded this apparent sign of the imminence of the Second Coming.[11]

Zvi made his way from his native city of Smyrna (now Izmir) to Jerusalem, where he attracted a good deal of attention. He had a sound rabbinic education but was prone to ecstatic moments in which he would perform bizarre and unlawful acts. He claimed religious meaning in these performances, some of which he declared to be new rituals.[12] He belonged to a type wholly unknown to Judaism, the holy sinner. From the moment he first became known in Smyrna in 1648 until Nathan had his vision and proclaimed him in 1665, there was literally no one who would have acknowledged him as the messiah. In fact Nathan had to convince Zvi of the authenticity of his mission, for the messiah had grave doubts.

His career was meteoric: in 1666 he went on a mission to Adrianople, the sultan's seat, with the mission of dethroning him and taking over the Ottoman Empire. The sultan had him arrested and offered him a choice between conversion and martyrdom. Zvi took the path of least resistance and became Muslim.

In his mind the choice confirmed his mission, and his supporters were not long in reaching the same conclusion. Zvi, they said, had to become an apostate for the very purpose of bringing on the restoration of the lost sparks of divinity from among the Muslims. He penetrated evil in order to rescue and elevate the sparks.

This was a break with tradition that no one could have anticipated. There was simply no suggestion of anything like it anywhere in either the Talmud or the Torah. But to the believers (as Zvi's followers called themselves) it now appeared that literally everything in the ancient writings foretold and led up to this moment. This was the new Torah of redemption, or rather the old one seen through redemption's new eyes and with its deeper wisdom.

Acceptance of this view was far from unanimous, and most believers fell away and returned to traditional practice. According to Walter Zenner, 'Jews everywhere hid in shame' after Zvi's apostasy.[13] But for those who stayed, there was an uncanny glamour to Zvi and his acts. His movement persisted among them down to the first decades of the twentieth century as quasi-underground heretical sects. Some of them decided that full holiness was only to be found in copying the Messiah. They converted, or pretended to, to whichever was the dominant religion of the country where they lived. There was in this new dogma an implicit but quite logical antinomianism, that is, a justification for acts which, in the traditional system, were condemned as sins.

Leaving the persistent followers aside, this story makes clear the crucial significance of conversion to prophecy. There is no suggestion in the literature I have seen on Zvi that he underwent anything like the change of heart that defines real conversion. He accepted the mantle of the messiah on the word of another, despite his own doubts of his calling. The vision was not his, but Nathan's; he tried to build a career on borrowed charisma, and when the test came he and it both failed.

It might be as well to address the common misconception that the purpose of prophecy is prediction. That is an important aspect of any prophecy, of course, and some commentators have observed that the prophet's charisma is reinforced by the accuracy of his minor predictions. The ultimate one inevitably fails, of course, but that need not damage the prophet's reputation where his followers are concerned. In fact it may enhance his reputation. Apocalypse is full of paradoxes.

To understand this point about the nature of prophecy, we might consider the respective cases of Noah and Jonah. Jonah's commission from God was to 'cry against' the people of Nineveh. He warned them of God's coming wrath, and the Ninevites believed him; they fasted and put on sackcloth, and, at the king's command, turned from sin and violence, in the hope that God would repent. He did, but Jonah was not pleased. He prayed God to kill him in his apparent disgrace and failure. But God sent the parable of the gourd, to teach Jonah what the Ninevites already knew: the value of mercy. If God had set himself absolutely against Nineveh and its 'much cattle', what might have been the purpose of pursuing Jonah to the very belly of the fish in order to send him there? Why give any warning if the city's destruction was inevitable and no repentance might prevent it? But this is precisely what happened in the Genesis version of the Noah story, although Noah received no such commission. There was to be no warning, because the matter of the world's destruction was closed. Only the remnant—Noah's own family—underwent this-worldly salvation through the unmediated agency of God alone. Surely the point of Jonah's reluctant preaching was precisely this: to forestall fulfillment of the prediction.

Another version of the story of Noah presents the converse case of the prophet as a miserable failure. His prophetic commission is detailed in the Qur'an.[14] In that redaction of the story, Noah labored for 'ages' to convince the people of God's anger, but they mocked his every attempt. Finally he called on God to fulfill His wrath. Noah had failed to convince anyone outside his own family (we might wonder if they played along to humor the old man), and the prediction was fulfilled.

These cases bring up the crucial issue of context in relation to prophecy. Nineveh was soaked in wickedness, as the people well knew. Jonah provided the spark that lit the fire of repentance even in the king. In Noah's day things appear to have been going along quite nicely. People were living routine quotidian lives, 'marrying and giving in marriage'; their condition did not warrant listening to a message like Noah's.[15]

It seems superficially that Jonah's mission was in vain. He understood it no better than many of our contemporaries. The point of his activity was to prove the prediction false, and in this he succeeded admirably. Fulfillment of apocalyptic prediction marks a failure of the prophet's mission. Jonah was a successful *prophet* because his *prediction* failed. The people and especially the king of Nineveh believed him, took the correct action, and averted the local apocalypse. Every successful outcome of apocalyptic prophecy takes this form. The prediction is always conditional: it is what will happen unless the people convert, or at least repent, and follow God's will in either case.

These prophecies belong to a class that only an obscure discipline called sociocybernetics seems to have noticed. Everyone is familiar with Robert Merton's 1948 conception of the self-fulfilling prophecy. Less prominent but no less socially real and important is the self-negating prophecy, that is, a prediction whose publication tends to cancel its own fulfillment. Jonah's prediction of doom for Nineveh was obviously such a forecast. Like any good warning, it succeeded only in canceling its own fulfillment.[16] The Year 2000 (Y2K) predictions followed this model. We were told that unless we spent untold millions on updating software there would be a global economic collapse. We spent the money (by some estimates $100 for every human alive) and the catastrophe was averted.

The Drama of Conversion

Given that the prophet has converted (and this conversion is not a mere shifting of allegiance, like St Paul's—his personality remained unchanged, we're told: he had been the most ardent opponent of Christianity and became its chief supporter) it then becomes necessary that he converts others. A prophet with no following is no prophet at all. His vision conveys a message that he must lead others to hear and follow. They have to undergo something like his own conversion, though I know of none who demands of his following the full visionary experience; that would be a dilution of his authority which in nearly every case will be unwelcome, to say the least.

In many if not most cases the process stops there. The prophet and his following continue for the prophet's lifetime, and the movement may continue after the prophet dies, with a successor at the helm. When the vision and its message are apocalyptic, the case is altered. Apocalypse is a special kind of vision.

Apocalyptic prophecy can be conceived as a growing spiral. It begins in the conversion of the prophet, expands to bring that result to the first tiny following, and expands to take in enough people—often the canonical 144,000—to reach a 'tipping point' where evildoers, or at least their ways, can be eliminated with superhuman collaboration.

Stephen O'Leary's study of apocalyptic persuasion makes it clear that Christian apocalyptic is a rhetorical drama proposing a solution to the problem of evil in a world created by a beneficent and omnipotent deity.[17] It is rhetorical in that it seeks to convince listeners of the correctness of its point of view and that their lives will turn out to have meaning, despite all the evidence to the contrary produced by the chaotic torments of history. The nature of that meaning is fundamental: apocalypse tells the believer that his or her presence on the planet will turn out to matter, that is, to make an ultimate difference. The believer is promised a pivotal role in the ultimate drama in which the purpose of existence will finally be revealed.

And, in its promise of ultimate eternal life, it defeats the true core of evil: death. As O'Leary points out, time and evil are of the same substance, if only in that death is the prime marker of time's passage.[18]

Apocalypse is dramatic in that it presents the solution to the problem of evil in history in terms of a struggle between forces of good and evil. Apocalypse is an attempted solution to the problem of theodicy, that is, an attempt to reconcile the notion of an all-good and all-powerful creator with a creation that has room for evil. This is not necessarily a problem in strict logic, but it is a problem in every human society, regardless of what kind of religious tradition it adheres to. Apocalypse shares with all myths the attribute of attempting to reconcile life's inherent contradictions in an explanatory story whose effect is to promote social order.[19] Apocalypse proposes finally to force the world to make sense, to moralize and convert it, and at least some of its human inhabitants, to the holy realm it was originally supposed to be. It proposes transformation of the world (back) into the sacred place it ought to be.

It is necessary to make clear at once that apocalypse is never about the literal end of the world. It never proposes the actual destruction of the physical planet, despite the fact that it may, like the book of Revelation or Handsome Lake's prophecies, make reference to titanic damage to its fabric in the final battle between the forces of good and evil. The only prophecy I'm aware of that comes close to predicting this ultimate destruction is the nuclear winter scenario proposed by Carl Sagan and others, and that only warned of the destruction of life, not the planet itself.[20]

It is clear that the earthquakes, falling stars, tidal waves and other geophysical catastrophes invoked in apocalyptic rhetoric need to be analytically understood as symbols of the cosmic scope of the battle that's envisioned. The world that's going to end in end-of-the-world scenarios is the world as Augustine understood it. His *Civitas Dei* (City of God) put an end to apocalyptic speculations within the Roman Church. Augustine (354–430 CE), responding to this and other heresies in the early church, composed a Christian view of history in which the world was permanently divided between the City of the World and the City of God. Everyone must choose which to ally himself with, God or Satan. The Church represents God's City, while the world, of course, is Satan's. This is the world that needs to end: Satan's irredeemable sandbox, the world of (merely) human power; always corrupt, always unjust, it inflicts untold suffering on the righteous.

The inevitable apocalyptic trope of rejection of earthly power and its incurable corruption can be seen vividly in the book of Revelation itself. The book's purpose was to prepare those churches for the Second Coming and the end of history, which Christians still expected momentarily. The Emperor Domitian's reign (81–96 CE) renewed the persecution of Christians, which persuaded them the time was at hand. John's aim in writing the book was to provide encouragement for his brothers in their time of need.

It was about this time that the book of Revelation was composed, in clear and direct response to those persecutions. There is little doubt that the figure of Antichrist was composed with Nero in mind. Jesus appears as the king on a white horse, with flaming eyes and a sword protruding from his mouth, to strike the nations with his word.

Its author is unknown, though a church tradition ascribes the book to St John the Evangelist. It is generally thought to have been written on the island of Patmos in the Aegean, where its author had been banished by Roman authority 'on account of the word of God and the testimony of Jesus' (Rev. 1.9). Sometime between the years 69 and 96 CE, by the best estimates, the author says he heard 'a loud voice like a trumpet' telling him to 'write what you see in a book and send it to the seven churches, to Ephesus and to Smyrna and to Pergamum and to Thyatira and to Sardis and to Philadelphia and to Laodicea' (Rev. 1.10-11).

John deliberately wrote in an obscure and coded array of symbols in order to conceal his anti-Roman polemic intent from the authorities. It was intended for use in its time, and many of its symbolic referents are no longer understood. Contemporary interpretations vary widely, and none of them are generally accepted. But given its claim to prophetic authenticity, interpreters continue to try to find contemporary applicability of its vivid but obscure symbols.

The book's purpose is clear. It was intended to be a quasi-secret testament of its author's vision, to be read in the Christian churches of his day. It carefully avoids any direct reference to Rome and the identity of the Beast (666 is a coded reference to Emperor Nero, in a kind of *gematria* where letters are assigned numeric values), but in its symbolic encoding and the grotesque monsters that swarm through its pages, it can have left little doubt in its hearers' minds what it referred to.

Ultimately all apocalypse ends in eternal bliss. No matter what use the narrative is put to, it seems unarguable that its audience is invited to identify itself with the faithful, not the beasts of the pit and the sea and their minions, as in Revelation. Yes, we the hearers (the book was originally intended for reading aloud) will shudder at their dreadful fate, and resolve to avoid it, but ultimately we rejoice in salvation as prospective saints. As in any other comic narrative, tragedy looms along the way, but the protagonists always win, and the antagonists always lose. This is necessary, given apocalypse's nature as a moral reconciliation of evil.

O'Leary makes it clear that Revelation's enduring hold on Christian believers (and others) owes as much to its literary strengths and peculiarities as to its canonical status in Christianity.[21] I suggest that much of its endurance as a source of speculation about the timing of the apocalypse can be attributed to the same symbolic coding that assured its deniability at the time of its writing. Its monsters and demons and cloudy dream-like references uniquely combine the attributes of vividness and obscurity in a way that leaves them irresistible to believing analysts of every epoch. In this way at least it shares apparently permanent authority with Nostradamus, whose works have never gone out of print. What can John have meant by the beast with ten horns, and what is the little horn? Who or what is the Whore of Babylon? As encoded references, these questions have no ultimate answer, since they can and have been taken to refer to nearly any conspicuous figure whose power seems mysterious or suspect.

The most vivid figure in Revelation is Antichrist, the great opponent, who occupies the author's attention more than any other character. It is in his attributes and actions that the wickedness of earthly power appears most clearly. Briefly, the Antichrist's story goes as follows: according to prophecy he will appear only when the gospel has been preached to the entire world, and the Jews are gathered once again in Israel.[22] There will be a great 'falling away' of Christians before he is revealed, which some commentators take to refer to the rapture, the snatching up into heaven of the elect to preserve them from the terrors of the tribulation.[23] Antichrist will convince even many believers that he is the Second Coming and reign over the entire world for a period of three and a half years, during which there will be unprecedented peace and harmony everywhere. He will unite all the world's religions into one, in a philosophy based on monism.

All who follow him and accept his mark (666) in their foreheads and their hands, paralleling the *tefillin* orthodox Jews wear at worship, will prosper in this period, for only they will be permitted to buy and sell. In contemporary interpretations of this idea, cash will have been withdrawn from circulation, to be replaced by a sort of debit card, issued only to bearers of the mark, which will be readable by some form of scanner like those used in supermarkets.

This period and the three and a half years following it together will make up the Tribulation, a time of unique suffering for Christians, at first, but finally for everyone, when Antichrist tries to enforce universal worship of himself as God. In this effort Satan and a false prophet will assist him, to make up an unholy triumvirate, a satanic counterpart to the Holy Trinity.

Antichrist will set up an unspecified 'abomination of desolation' in the holy of holies (a parallel to the abomination of Antiochus Epiphanes), inside the rebuilt third Temple of the Jews, in Jerusalem. This is usually taken to refer to a colossal statue of himself, which everyone must worship.

This desecration will provoke an attack on Israel by armies of the North, which Antichrist will defeat, with a coalition of other nations. This will give him unchallengeable power and total despotic rule over the earth, for the short period until the true Christ appears and defeats him for good at Armageddon. He assumes ultimate worldly and spiritual power. He is a political figure and the book of Revelation is a manifesto.

Antichrist is recognizable by his wickedness, that is, his rejection of God and Christ. He is a great liar, and gains allegiance by bribery. Most tellingly for our purposes, he is a 'satanic reformer', one who intends to change 'times and laws' (Dan. 7.25). He may try to change the calendar, and will be the greatest anti-Semite known to history. Though the Jews initially will accept him as their Messiah, they will repudiate his covenant after the abomination of desolation, and Antichrist will then seek to destroy them all.

Apocalypse is always about the powers of the earth and how to overthrow them. Given religious rhetoric like Revelation's it can sometimes be easy to lose sight of this fundamental thing. But the millennium lives to oppose. It always sets up the order of paradise, the once or future state of perfection, in antagonism to the way things are. The millennium reverses the way of the world, and switches the polarity of its moral signs, so that what's good in common sense perception becomes the source of evil. A, if not the, main point of contention between millennial visions and the way the world actually is, is knowledge. The millennial project always wants to uproot, overthrow, and discard the world's way of perception, and especially the knowledge that undergirds its conception of the world. Cosmology itself is a main target of this opposition, and the 'common sense' that's based on it. The drama that apocalypse proposes is nothing less than the world's conversion. As the prophet was converted, so his movement must convert. As they convert, so must the world.

References

Cohn, Norman, 'Medieval Millenarism: Its Bearing on the Comparative Study of Millenarian Movements', in Sylvia L. Thrupp (ed.), *Millennial Dreams in Action* (The Hague: Mouton, 1962), 31-43.

Geyer, Felix, 'Cybernetics and Social Science: Theories and Research in Sociocybernetics', *Kybernetes* 20.6 (1991), 81-92.

Henshel, R.L., 'Credibility and Confidence Loops in Social Prediction', in R.F. Geyer and J. van der Zouwen (eds.), *Self-Referencing in Social Systems* (Salinas, CA: Intersystems Publications, 1990), 31-58.

Keller, Catherine, *Apocalypse Now and Then: A Feminist Guide to the End of the World* (Boston: Beacon Press, 1996).

Lamont, William, *Godly Rule: Politics and Religion, 1603–60* (London: Macmillan–St Martin's Press, 1969).

Lamy, Philip, 'Secularizing the Millennium: Survivalists, Militias, and the New World Order', in Thomas Robbins and Susan J. Palmer (eds.), *Millennium, Messiahs, and Mayhem: Contemporary Apocalyptic Movements* (New York: Routledge, 1997), 93-118.

Lanternari, Vittorio, *The Religions of the Oppressed: A Study of Modern Messianic Movements* (New York: Knopf, 1963).

Lee, Martha F., *Earth First!: Environmental Apocalypse* (New York: Syracuse University Press, 1995).

Long, Theodore E., 'Prophecy, Charisma and Politics: Reinterpreting the Weberian Hypothesis', in Jeffrey K. Hadden and Anson D. Shupe (eds.), *Prophetic Religion and Politics: Religion and the Political Order* (Sociology of Religion Series, 1; New York: Paragon House, 1986), 3-17.

O'Leary, Stephen D., *Arguing the Apocalypse: A Theory of Millennial Rhetoric* (New York: Oxford University Press, 1994).

Pessar, Patricia R., 'Millenarian Movements in Rural Brazil: Prophecy and Protest', *Religion* 12.2 (1982), 187-213.

Redles, David, ' "The Day Is Not Far Off…": The Millennial Reich and the Induced Apocalypse', in Stephen D. O'Leary and Glen S. McGhee (eds.), *War in Heaven/Heaven on Earth: Theories of the Apocalyptic* (London: Equinox Publishing, 2005), 119-41.

Scholem, Gershom G., *The Messianic Idea in Judaism and Other Essays in Jewish Spirituality* (New York: Schocken Books, 1971).

Talmon, Yonina, 'Millenarianism', in *International Encyclopedia of the Social Sciences* (18 vols.; New York: Macmillan/Free Press, 1968), X, 349-62.

Tucker, Robert C., 'The Theory of Charismatic Leadership', *Daedalus* 97 (1968), 731-56.

Turco, R.P., O.B. Toon, T.P. Ackerman, J.B. Pollack and Carl Sagan, 'Nuclear Winter: Global Consequences of Multiple Nuclear Explosions', *Science*, V. 222, no. 4630, December 23, 1983.

Wallace, A.F.C., 'Mazeway Resynthesis: A Bio-Cultural Theory of Religious Inspiration', *Transactions of the New York Academy of Science* Series II, 18.2 (1956), 626-38.

—*The Death and Rebirth of the Seneca* (New York: Alfred Knopf, 1970).

Walzer, Michael, *The Revolution of the Saints: A Study in the Origins of Radical Politics* (Cambridge, MA: Harvard University Press, 1965).

Worseley, Peter, *The Trumpet Shall Sound: A Study of 'Cargo' Cults in Melanesia* (New York: Shocken Books, 1968).

Zenner, Walter P., 'The Case of the Apostate Messiah: A Reconsideration of the "Failure of Prophecy"': *Archives de Sociologie des Religions* 21 (1966), 111-18.

Notes

    *   Portions of this chapter appeared in somewhat different form in my *A Dooms-day Reader* (New York: New York University Press, 1999). I am grateful to the publisher for permission to reprint them here.

    1.   Catherine Keller, *Apocalypse Now and Then: A Feminist Guide to the End of the World* (Boston: Beacon Press, 1996), 20.

    2.   Norman Cohn, 'Medieval Millenarism: Its Bearing on the Comparative Study of Millenarian Movements', in Sylvia L. Thrupp (ed.), *Millennial Dreams in Action* (The Hague: Mouton, 1962), 31-43.

    3.   Stephen O'Leary, *Arguing the Apocalypse: A Theory of Millennial Rhetoric* (New York: Oxford University Press, 1994), 25

    4.   Martha F. Lee, *Earth First!: Environmental Apocalypse* (New York: Syracuse University Press, 1995), 14-15.

    5.   Philip Lamy, 'Secularizing the Millennium: Survivalists, Militias, and the New World Order', in Thomas Robbins and Susan J. Palmer (eds.), *Millennium, Messiahs, and Mayhem: Contemporary Apocalyptic Movements* (New York: Routledge, 1997), 93-118.

    6.   Lamy, 'Secularizing the Millennium', 113.

    7.   My main authority for this point of view is Peter Worseley's observation that a religious movement 'must always, objectively, be *politico-religious*', if only in defining its members' relations with the rest of the world (*The Trumpet Shall Sound: A Study of 'Cargo' Cults in Melanesia* [New York: Schocken Books, 1968], xxxvi). Other sources include Patricia R. Pessar, 'Millenarian Movements in Rural Brazil: Prophecy and Protest', *Religion* 12.2 (1982), 187-213; Michael Walzer, *The Revolution of the Saints: A Study in the Origins of Radical Politics* (Cambridge, MA: Harvard University Press, 1965); Theodore E. Long, 'Prophecy, Charisma and Politics: Reinterpreting the Weberian Hypothesis', in Jeffrey K. Hadden and Anson D. Shupe (eds.), *Prophetic Religion and Politics: Religion and the Political Order* (Sociology of Religion Series, 1; New York: Paragon House, 1986), I, 3-17; Vittorio Lanternari, *The Religions of the Oppressed: A Study of Modern Messianic Movements* (New York: Knopf, 1963); William Lamont, *Godly Rule: Politics and Religion, 1603–60* (London: Macmillan–St Martin's Press, 1969); Robert C. Tucker, 'The Theory of Charismatic Leadership', *Daedalus* 97 (1968), 731-56; Yonina Talmon notes that millenarism is often strongly related to political movements and often becomes itself such a movement ('Millenarianism', in *International Encyclopedia of the Social Sciences* [New York: Macmillan/Free Press, 1968], X, 349-62). More contemporary sources include Lamy, 'Secularizing the Millennium', O'Leary, 'The apocalypse is (among other things) a mythic narrative about power and authority' (*Arguing the Apocalypse*, 55).

    8.   O'Leary, *Arguing the Apocalypse*.

    9.   Secular apocalyptics, Marxism for example, obviously make no reference to god. In these cases the source of inspiration is demoted from the supernatural to the

merely superhuman: the dialectic of history, in Marx's formulation. But the principal of inspiration from a trans-human source is the same.

10. A.F.C. Wallace, 'Mazeway Resynthesis: A Bio-Cultural Theory of Religious Inspiration', *Transactions of the New York Academy of Science* Series II, 18.2 (1956), 626-38. See also Wallace's *The Death and Rebirth of the Seneca* (New York: Alfred Knopf, 1970), 239-66.

11. Gershom G. Scholem, *The Messianic Idea in Judaism and Other Essays in Jewish Spirituality* (New York: Schocken Books, 1971).

12. Scholem, *The Messianic Idea*, 60.

13. Walter P. Zenner, 'The Case of the Apostate Messiah: A Reconsideration of the "Failure of Prophecy" ', *Archives de Sociologie des Religions* 21 (1966), 111-18.

14. Surah, 71.

15. As David Redles' chapter in this volume makes clear, it was exactly the context of the perceived collapse of German civilization in the Weimar Republic that gave Hitler's apocalyptic visions their prophetic and charismatic force.

16. This apparent paradox is discussed in R.L. Henshel, 'Credibility and Confidence Loops in Social Prediction', in R.F. Geyer and J. van der Zouwen (eds.), *Self-Referencing in Social Systems* (Salinas, CA: Intersystems Publications, 1990), 31-58. See also Felix Geyer, 'Cybernetics and Social Science: Theories and Research in Socio-cybernetics', *Kybernetes* 20.6 (1991), 81-92.

17. O'Leary, *Arguing the Apocalypse*, 34-44.

18. O'Leary, *Arguing the Apocalypse*, 32.

19. Paul Ricoeur, quoted in O'Leary, *Arguing the Apocalypse*, 21.

20. R.P. Turco, O.B. Toon, T.P. Ackerman, J.B. Pollack and Carl Sagan, 'Nuclear Winter: Global Consequences of Multiple Nuclear Explosions', *Science*, V. 222, No. 4630, December 23, 1983.

21. O'Leary, *Arguing the Apocalypse*, 64-68.

22. This is a condensation of a generalized fundamentalist Christian version of the story. Other sects differ on the details, but the fundamentalists are the most active believers in this aspect of the millennium myth.

23. There is endless debate on this topic. Will it happen at all, or will Christians lose their faith in the Tribulation? If it does happen, when will it happen? Pre-trib, post-trib, mid-trib, in the jargon of contemporary belief? The Rapture received special prominence in the work of the nineteenth-century divine John Nelson Darby and his doctrine of dispensationalism.

Roosters Crow, Owls Hoot:
On the Dynamics of Apocalyptic Millennialism

Richard Landes

A rooster and a bat were waiting for the light.
The rooster said to the bat, I await the dawn.
But you, why do you want the light?
                                    Talmud Sanhedrin, 98a

The Millennial Perception in Apocalyptic Time

Millennialists view a dramatically different world from the gray complexities we denizens of normal time have come to live with. They pay close attention to human suffering, and its causes, evil, injustice, oppression. The religious among them believe that a benevolent and omnipotent God, or gods, or ancestors, do exist and intervene in the *saeculum*. Among the most common variant, monotheists, a God of Justice and his disciples on earth await his Day of Judgment; he allows evil to flourish as a test. For them the unhappy anomalies that most sweep under their mental rugs, occupy the heart of the matter. God's unwillingness to intervene in history stems not from indifference or incapacity, but from a desire to test us. Then at last, on a great Judgment Day—*Doomsday*—the evil will get their just punishment and the good, their just reward.

   Indeed, so great and dramatic a transformation will take place on this Day, that the world will then enter a wondrous period (conventionally 1000 years—*mille anni, millennium*) of justice, joy, fellowship, and abundance. Here the rapacious social world will turn upside down. Here the lamb shall lie down with the lion *and* get a good night's sleep.[1] Here the weapons of elite dominion—sword and spear—become the tools of honest labor—plowshare and pruning hook. Here people enjoy and share the fruits of their honest labor undisturbed: 'On that day, says the Lord of Hosts, everyone of you shall invite his neighbor to come under his vine and under his fig tree' (Zech. 3.10). Here nations live in peace because they study not war, but peace because, fearing the Lord, they have taken upon themselves the yoke of a heavenly kingdom, to walk in God's paths, to earn their bread by the sweat of their brow, to treat their fellow humans fairly. At its heart, millennialism, certainly the *demotic* millennialism described above, contains a fundamental and profound act of the will, a willingness and a willfulness. Such attitudes of empowerment generally get crushed under the heavy atmospheric pressure of authoritarian societies and their ideologies of submission and passivity. They rarely act peremptorily in public.

Millennialists have a passion for justice. They think they know good and evil well. When they look at humanity, many see not various kinds of peoples, but a few saints and a vast sea of sinners, some redeemable, some (most) not. They see quite clearly who will suffer punishment (above all the abusively powerful), and who will gain reward (those faithful willing to risk all for the kingdom of heaven) at the final Revelation. And they do not believe in compromise. They anticipate the absolute eradication of evil—corruption, violence, oppression—and the wondrous bliss of the just kingdom for the good. The Angel of the Endtime spews out tepidity. 'You are neither hot nor cold, therefore I spew you out', says the angel of Revelation to the church of Laodicea.[2] For millennialists, the gray world of the *corpus permixtum* will—*must*—pass away.

Some of these believers hold that the abuse of power, the use of violence for selfish purposes—in a word, *injustice*—constitutes the greatest of sins, bringing humanly induced suffering into the world. And they look forward to the day when such violence, and all its institutional trappings, will vanish. Thus millennial thinking, however spiritually put, is political thinking. All millennialists hope that commitment to their beliefs will spread far and wide enough to bring about a transformation of the social, *and therefore* the political universe. That is the very essence of millennialism, as opposed to other forms of eschatology: *the just live free in this world*.[3] It might be by and by, but the messianic promise is no pie in the sky. It is a transformation of humanity, an evolutionary leap to a different way of human interaction. To use the language of evolutionary epidemiology, millennialism is a *meme* programmed to spread as far and wide as possible.[4] To use the language of political science, millennialism is a (the first?) revolutionary ideology.[5]

Revolutionary ideologies only begin to appeal to large numbers of people (i.e., the meme only spreads widely) when they feel themselves close to the moment of turning, of transformation. For millennialists, this means apocalyptic time, that process from the moment before one enters the vortex of the eschaton. For a Christian, this means when Jesus returns; for some Jews, messiah; for some Muslims, the mahdi; for the communist, the withering away of the state; for the Nazi, the rule of the master race over the planet; for the Islamist, the rule of Islam over the planet.

The historian only gets to see millennialism when apocalyptic time activates it. But long before he sets his highly trained mind upon the literate precipitation that such apocalyptic movements set in motion, a town, a region, a generation of people have gone into a psychological arena where anything becomes possible, where grown men can cry, life-long enemies can forgive and embrace, and the magical forces of the universe will come to the aid of those who long for help. To people who believe themselves in the midst of apocalyptic time, many things come, many things become possible. Such people bring us saintly men wandering through Europe preaching peace, and warriors with crosses wading in blood up to their horses bridles,[6] believing that *this* was the Day our Lord promised *us*, the day to rejoice therein. To the people who inhabit this apocalyptic time, *we* who read about them so many years later, should not have happened. *We* are their unthinkable universe. And they were quite wrong in thinking so. But just because they were wrong, does not mean they were inconsequential.

For people who have entered apocalyptic time, everything quickens, everything enlivens, everything coheres. They become semiotically aroused —everything has meaning, patterns. The smallest incident can have immense importance and open the way to an entirely new vision of the world, one in which forces unseen by other mortals operate.[7] Everything becomes meaningful, even how one brushes one's teeth. The whole world is watching and millennialists believe that their shots are 'heard around the world'. And all the signs they now can 'read' point in one direction: *now* is the time! Believers commit themselves to this world of transformation, convinced of the superiority of their perceptions, convinced that the uncomprehending mass (including the old elites about to pass away) will either soon join them, or get shredded in the coming cosmic transformation. His or her semiotic arousal leads the believer straight into the apocalyptic vortex.

Such believers have varied careers. Apocalyptic time is always in the offing, although uncertain conditions certainly encourage it. But rarely do they give birth to millennial movements, still more rarely do those movements make a lasting mark on the public consciousness (make it into the record), and still more rarely do millennial movements take power. And of that small minority who do take power, no millennial movement can sustain the hallucination that the new world is indeed messianic for more than a short while. The most sustained period for such episodes of mass delusion generally last less than 20 years to judge by the earliest (Akhenaten) and one of the most recent (Hitler). Faced with such an erratic documentation from movements so short-lived and, in their passing, so reviled, we historians have a decided disadvantage in trying to understand what we deal with. The record is written by people deeply hostile to the millennial actors (Matthew of Münster), or, if not the actors, their (incorrect) apocalyptic expectation (Martin Luther).[8]

The key lies in imagining the beginning (based on extensive ancillary material from anthropology), and then following the dynamics of apocalyptic time as the movement enters into that magical time, takes shape, reaches its height, then handles the terrifying disorientation of acknowledging failure and re-entering normal time—a world they had never imagined would still be there. Here they stand, not glorious apocalyptic prophets commanding the faithful, but ashamed and impotent before the very people they had dismissed with contempt only moments earlier. How do these groups and the individuals within them handle the cognitive dissonance of having embraced prophecy that failed?

Here, among other places, we find the origins of totalitarianism, that uncontrollable urge to hide one's shame by coercing purity, even at the cost of huge numbers of lives. Here the apocalyptic imagination is quite capable of contemplating with enthusiasm the death of over 5 billion people. At their worst, the paranoid messianic emperors like Hitler, Mao, Stalin, Hong Xiu Chang tried to carve the millennium out of the body social over which the forces of the universe have given the true believers the power. One cannot do millennial historiography if one cannot talk about the motivating power of shame.

In order to understand millennial beliefs and their apocalyptic movements, we must become familiar with their fundamental tensions.

The Varieties of Millennial Experience

Eschatology

This notion holds that *at the end* (*eschaton*) of 'time', the Lord will judge the quick and the dead, all together, publicly. This apocalyptic theodicy— the time when the just are rewarded and the evil-doers punished—can give birth to two possible aftermaths:

- an *eschatological* (final) one in which the earthly world is consumed in purifying fires. Rewards in heaven, as with punishments in hell, are final.
- a *millennial* one in which the new world of justice appears on earth and marks a messianic age of abundance and the joy of fellowship.

Eschatological thought tends towards totalism: the conclusion is ultimate and decisive, a closed, final solution. The messiness of earthly existence must itself burn up in the process. This vision of an ultimate solution welcomes zero-sum thinking (dualism), imagining a closed form of redemption: the good in heaven, the evil in hell; the body and all its messy delights, gone, *permanently*. Tertullian's vision of a heaven where the saved got to watch, like on some extensive cable TV, the torments of the damned in all their locations in Hell (which later inspired Dante to visionary poetry) may well represent a high-water mark in millennial *ressentiment*,[9] but it also illustrates the workings of closed (zero-sum) images of redemption. When the body and soul are separated, the very drama of moral existence has been resolved. There is no future, no more tests, no more hopes. The story has ended. Future generations and the open-ended directions in which they might move, no longer have a say in the redemptive process. For the apocalyptic eschatological thinker, this is the End. The game is over.

Millennialism

The millennial option moves in the opposite direction in its search for justice—it needs to happen *in this world*. It is an open challenge to the narrative that says, everybody is morally corrupt, no real change is possible, this is how things *have to* be. It expects that spiritual strength will transform this world by transforming society. By transforming the way people interact, it will bring on a time of justice *here on earth*. Thus millennialism is a form of social mysticism that is deeply politically subversive. A more subversive notion one imagines with great difficulty.

Thus in this chapter, I use the term *millennial* to designate the belief that at some point in the future the world that we live in will be radically transformed into one of peace, justice, fellowship and plenty. This can, but need not, entail a belief in God. The earliest recorded millennial movements all have invoked God or gods. But possibly as early as ancient Greece, and with increasing frequency in the course of the last half millennium (1500–2000 CE), the West has produced and exported a number of secular, indeed atheistic forms of millennialism. Marx's vision of the future, for example, fits all the criteria for demotic millennialism—from the vision of a non-coercive society (the withering away of the state), to the dignity of manual labor ('workers of the world…'), to the radical egalitarianism (renunciation of private property), to the semiotic arousal of reading the signs indicating imminent apocalypse (historical dialectic).

Some historians object to maintaining so capacious a definition for millennialism, and suspect that it is merely a ploy for claiming a whole range of subject matter, suspect that such a definition comes down to including virtually every radical movement in history within the purview of millennial studies. My suggestion is that we are far too early in our research to decide what relevance millennial studies has for these topics or not. Given that most people have never thought about Nazism as a millennial movement—and this includes scholars who know that the Nazis claimed to inaugurate the *tausandjähriger Reich*—it seems a bit early to decide how useful or bloated the term might be. My contention is that by understanding movements that share the simple combination of *a millennial vision of the world transformed, and an apocalyptic belief in that transformation's imminence,* one can make sense of these movements in significant ways. They participate in an unusual and characteristic range of dynamics that are well worth understanding. These movements form a natural grouping of socio-cultural phenomena that cut across all cultures and regions and periods of history. They are still with us. We are in their currents.[10]

Millennial beliefs stand out as particularly important among eschatological beliefs in that they anticipate the rewards of the good times coming *on earth*, in the flesh, within the *saeculum*.[11] As a result millennialism takes on more active forms than other eschatologies since, in these scenarios, the dramatic changes happen in *this* world, *in time*. Thus we find especially strong tendencies towards both social perfectionism and human agency. More cosmic scenarios, on the other hand, those in which only God can effect any significant change, discourage precisely these activist tendencies, and produce *passive apocalyptic scenarios*, whether they are cataclysmic (as in contemporary pre-millennial dispensationalism), or transformative ones (Quakerism after the Restoration in 1660).

Although, therefore, not all millennial beliefs are activist, all secular millennial movements have active apocalyptic scenarios. There is no one but 'us' (however defined) to bring about this transformation. The *secular*[12] dimension of millennialism—its insistence that redemption occurs in the world of time and history, in the *saeculum*—makes it possible for non-theistic versions to emerge, like utopianism and communism. Until the advent of nuclear weapons, cosmic apocalyptic scenarios necessitated a deity.[13]

Thus although millennialism by this definition can cover a very wide range of beliefs and behavior patterns from active to passive, violent to pacifist, all of these patterns relate significantly to one another. When we work with these definitions, we keep company with both the Church Fathers, who despised precisely this 'earthly' element of millennialism, and modern anthropologists who want to study it in all its forms, from the tribal cargo cults of Melanesia to the post-modern cargo cults of UFOs.[14]

Scholars who want to limit millennialism to those seeking radical social change through violence,[15] miss a key dynamic. Individual millennial believers or groups can dramatically change their attitudes towards the 'other' *in* apocalyptic time—peace, violence, reconciliation, extermination—and however radically different they may seem to us, as reported in the documents, they can and often do participate in the same trajectories. The wave of new religious movements we call the 'Protestant Reformation' produced the exceptionally egalitarian and pacifist Anabaptist communities which gave women a prominent role and renounced all forms of coercion. But under the pressures of a public breach of apocalyptic time in 1533 in the town of Münster, they turned to violent, patriarchal and hierarchical behavior.[16] To understand the phenomenon, we need to focus on its key components—a belief in the possibility of radical social change, perfection, in this world (*millennialism*), and an expectation that this revolution is now occurring (*apocalyptic*).

Demotic millennialism represents bottom-up and egalitarian ideals. The inhabitants of the messianic world act justly by choice, and thus there will be no need for government. The Zealots of Jesus' time cried 'No king but God!'—the demotic political formula of monotheism.[17] Demotic millennialists view empire and hierarchy as the incarnation of evil.[18] For them, freedom and justice in the messianic age will abolish all dominion of people over each other, a kind of *holy anarchy* in which the 'saved' behave justly not from fear but from love. Although some forms of demotic millennialism look for a 'unified' population of believers, others involve a multicultural world, where '*nation* does not lift up sword against *nation*', and honest hard-working people enjoy the fruits of their labor regardless of their form of worship.[19]

The danger that these egalitarians run, is what Nietzsche called 'slave morality', that is, the whining argument of the weak that the powerful do not have the right to push them around.[20] Once they take power, their demotic principles, which they only invoked to advance their (weak) case, get jettisoned for the dominating imperative. As the Athenians put it: *Those who can do what they will; those who cannot suffer what they must.*[21] The large numbers of demotic millennial movements that turn into totalitarian adventures (like the Taiping Rebellion or the Communists) reflect precisely the kind of reversal that so many cynics anticipate from the proponents of equality: they only speak of fairness when they are weak, and with power—in millennial cases, absolute power—such discourse rapidly turns to coercive purity.[22]

Hierarchical or imperial millennialism proposes a top-down model of the perfect society. It thus reverses the monotheistic political formula of anarchic millennialism. Rather than 'No king but God', they insist 'One God, one king, one religion'.[23] This scenario views the cosmic battle for the world pitting chaos (evil) against order (good), and calls for the establishment of justice and peace from the top-down, by a hierarchy on earth that mirrors the hierarchy in heaven, with an emperor-messiah, world conqueror who represents God on earth, the image or icon of God on earth.[24] In Christianity this tradition dates back to the time of Constantine, and produces the notion of a 'Last' or messianic Emperor who will conquer the world and bring all within the just confines of true Christianity.[25] This tradition of a final 'world conqueror' who inaugurates the golden age appears in many world historical traditions, including both Buddhism and Hinduism.[26]

Apocalypticism

The millennial vision of a humanity capable of collective transformation and, hence, of the possibility of a just society becomes a discourse of beliefs about time. It interprets the present in terms of the future, and therefore places timing at the center of its rhetoric.[27] If one believes that the great transformation is far off in the future, millennialism tends to have a pacifying effect—it gives meaning to one's sufferings in the long run, but discourages any action in the present. The time is not 'ripe'. If, on the other hand, one believes the transformation is imminent—that is, *apocalyptic*—then one becomes far more active. Then one joins with others and starts revivalist movements, rich in emotion and tears of joy.[28]

The obviously important role of apocalypticism (imminence) in bringing millennialism to light has tended, however, to blind many to the distinction. Indeed most definitions of millennialism including Cohn's, subsume the apocalyptic component under the millennial.[29] But just because it is only when millennialists believe the end is imminent that we can actually *see* the phenomenon in action, this does not mean that when we can not see it in our documents, it is not present. On the contrary, when we attend to apocalyptic beliefs and their inevitable disappointment, we find a richly textured narrative about how once eager public advocates of the eschatological beliefs do their best to disappear after the failure, *ex post defecto*.[30]

Thus, despite key 'common' traits, especially in comparison with those approaches that 'accept' the world 'as is', millennial beliefs take a wide variety of forms. We can profitably divide them into several polar attitudes towards key issues: (1) The *apocalyptic* question: When and how would the millennial transformation come about? (2) the question of agency: Who does what to bring about this transformation? and (3) the *millennial* question: What would the millennial kingdom after look like? In answer to the first question we have cataclysmic versus transformational apocalypticism; in answer to the second, we have a continuum from divine to human agency, human to divine passivity; and in answer to the third, we have authoritarian or hierarchical versus anarchic or demotic millennialism.

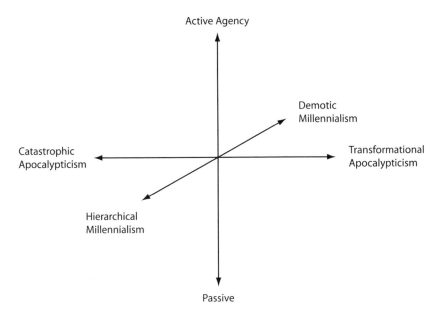

Figure 1. *Apocalyptic and Millennial Variations*

Cataclysmic apocalyptic scenarios foresee enormous destruction preceding the advent of the God's kingdom. They tend to emphasize the depravity of man—most people are damned and must perish before any truly just society can come about. This apocalyptic scenario thus involves staggering levels of violence and destruction—rivers of blood, plague, earthquakes, floods, famines, devastation of war and natural calamity. Religious forms of cataclysmic apocalyptic belief, like modern 'pre-millennial dispensationalism' among American Protestants, tend to emphasize the central role of God and divine agents in bringing about the millennium. In secular varieties, the revolution and the radical transformation of society can only come about through huge destruction, often man-wrought. With people like Michael Bakunin, we encounter a kind of lust for destruction (*libido delendi*) that raises some profound psychological issues.[31]

In these scenarios evil forces control the world either openly or, in many Christian and anti-modern versions, secretly. This latter version, the conspiracist, imagines a world-wide conspiracy that will soon—at the apocalyptic moment—spring its trap and enslave the whole world. The most widespread and familiar form of this belief in the coming of a world in the grip of a totalitarian cabal fears the emergence of a *New World Order*.[32] Modern Protestant 'pre-millennialism' expects Jesus to return *before* the millennium to destroy Antichrist and his agents in the battle of Armageddon, and then to found the kingdom of the saints (millennium). Here humanity has a passive role, largely limited to penitence and preaching: 'Repent, for the kingdom of heaven is at hand'. Heaven's Gate, and many other gnostic apocalyptic approaches, view this physical world as a prison from which we all need to be released, this planet (*saeculum*) as something that will be 'plowed under' at the great transformation. When we imagine the apocalypse as disastrous and speak of Doomsday as a day of terror, we are referring primarily to various manifestations of the cataclysmic millennial scenario.

Transformational apocalyptic scenarios emphasize people's voluntary and peaceful change. A massive collective change of heart, perhaps divinely inspired, brings on the messianic age. Transformational scenarios assume that large numbers of people can transcend their current social paradigms and move into a messianic mode voluntarily—lion lies down with lamb, aristocrats beat their swords into plowshares and their spears into pruning hooks and earn their food by the sweat of their brow. Transformational millennialism tends to foster programs of radical—often unrealistic—social change (peace movements, universal temperance, emancipation, utopian communes); and places great emphasis on educational reforms that create 'new' people (citizens, comrades, believers).

Currently, the most prominent form of transformational millennialism comes from the 'new age' movements set in motion by the millennial wave of the 60s—environmentally harmonized communes.[33] In Protestant circles, transformational millennialism is known as 'post-millennialism' (that is, Jesus comes back *after* his faithful create the millennium on earth), although there are cataclysmic variants of post-millennialism.[34] Historically, transformational (post-)millennialism has contributed to a number of typically American 'reformist' developments—the second Great Awakening, the Civil War, utopian farming and industrial communities (from the Shakers and Amish to the Oneida and Fourier communities), the profession of social work, the civil rights movement, and so on.

Active versus Passive Apocalyptic Scenarios

Both these scenarios vary internally according to the various roles they assign to God and humans in bringing about the transformation. The most passive apocalyptic scenarios are eschatological (because redemption is not in time, there is nothing to change on earth) and cataclysmic (only superhuman forces can effect the necessary destruction). Such scenarios relegate a passive role to humans: they must await God's 'appointed' time, and their task calls for repentance not for social transformation.

Paul apparently embraced such a notion when he called on Christian slaves to accept their status and Christian subjects to accept the rule of the existing powers. It is difficult to imagine Paul expecting slavery and the rule of unjust pagans (especially those of the Roman Empire) as a feature of the coming kingdom. But he does not think that one should expend one's final efforts, just before the return of Christ in power and glory, in resisting a doomed system: 'For you know what hour it is, how it is full time now for you to wake from sleep. For salvation is nearer to us now than when we first believed; the night is far gone, the day is at hand.'[35]

Passive non-millennial scenarios are largely a-political, and tend, therefore, to be more 'respectable' to owls in 'normal time'. But one can certainly find cases of passive transformational and millennial scenarios. Movements that stress individual transformation, meditation, and limited participation in the larger culture—the kingdom of heaven is within—discourage any visible millennial activity, all the while ardently using apocalyptic rhetoric. In certain cases this passive stance can shift to active by holding out millennial goals (e.g., the intellectual vanguard of the revolution).

Active scenarios, on the other hand, place agency in human hands: mankind, perhaps inspired by God, brings about the dramatic events. Most active apocalyptic scenarios at least start out as transformative—human beings, transfigured by God's grace (or that of the historical dialectic), inaugurate the millennial world. All secular scenarios are activist (no God to await), but so are many religious ones. The messianic vision of Isaiah and Micah places the key in the actions of the nations who flow to Jerusalem. But their action consists of accepting the yoke of God's justice, to voluntarily submit to God's kingship. Nations turn to his paths, and they convert the weapons of aristocratic violence (swords and spears) into tools of honest manual labor (plowshares and pruning hooks).[36]

Active apocalypticism, however, tends to prefer cataclysmic variants since they promise more readily tangible results to an impatient enthusiast. With the advent of serious technological empowerment, they have become the most likely apocalyptic scenario of this next millennium. From the revolutions of France, Russia, Germany, and China, to the feverish apocalyptic visions induced by nuclear weapons, we have a growing array of cataclysmic apocalyptic thinking that is vigorously activist.[37] Such groups, starting out small, tend to view the social world as if it were a set of high-pressured tectonic plates where a small but well-aimed explosion can trigger a massive quake (Aum Shinrikyo and the Tokyo subway system). Similarly, bin Laden's blows to the symbols of American power—World Trade Center and Pentagon—were intended to trigger the collapse of America and the beginning of victorious global *jihad*. What they lack in strength, they make up for in enhanced technology and the 'true' understanding of who is good and who is evil.

Now while all these apocalyptic and millennial variants appear to have mutually exclusive traits, this is only the deception of a categorical approach that tries to define a movement by a single set of beliefs. On the contrary, millennialism is a dynamic phenomenon, and in the course of an apocalyptic episode, a movement can literally flip from one extreme to the other. Among the classic cases, we find the Anabaptists who, in the course of their failed millennium at Münster from 1533–1535, went from the most radically pacifist and egalitarian of the new 'Protestant' groups to a violent and authoritarian group (transformational demotic to cataclysmic hierarchical).[38] Inversely, a violently revolutionary group like the Bahai could transform into a radically demotic, transformative millennial religion in the aftermath of their military failure. Indeed, one might suspect that the inevitable disappointment and failure of any apocalyptic group will act as a trip switch to flip it back and forth from active to passive, or, vice-versa, demotic to hierarchic, cataclysmic to transformational. In this paradoxical volatility we may find some of the keys to the strange relationship between millennial vision and violence.[39]

Thus the apocalyptic and millennial variants presented above should be taken not as categories, but as a map of terrain over which millennial groups, in the course of an apocalyptic episode, may travel extensively. So in order to understand the phenomenon in practice, rather than in theory, we must turn to the great 'activator' of millennial hopes—apocalyptic expectations. These convictions of the imminence of transformation drive millennialists out of the closet and into the public arena.

Apocalyptic Expectations: The Disinhibiting Imminent Transformation

The apocalyptic scenario stands firmly in the realm of 'hidden transcripts', and most of us do not even notice the non-apocalyptic millennialists in our very midst. They can live among us invisibly, adapting to our secular world, while nurturing their outrageous hopes. China has a long tradition of 'secret societies' whose centuries-long, possibly millennia-long history is punctuated by apocalyptic outbursts, revolts and revolutions.[40] These believers have accepted the current rules 'under protest' even if that protest is, provisionally, silent. They await eagerly the moment when the rules will change, and change dramatically. In the early-fifth century, a bishop named Hesychius wrote to Augustine in a veiled reproach for his opposition to the widespread apocalyptic expectation of the day: 'The coming of the Lord is to be loved and expected, for it is a great bliss for those who love His coming...'[41] In the mid-nineteenth century, an African-American slave woman put it somewhat more vehemently:

> There's a day a-coming! I hear the rumbling of the chariots, I see...white folks' blood a running on the ground like a river and the dead heaped up that high! O Lord! Hasten the day when the blows and the bruises and the aches and the pains shall come to the white folks... O Lord! Give me the pleasure of living to that day...[42]

James C. Scott has called these sentiments a 'full throated hidden transcript', the most elaborate and all-encompassing of the resentments that people, forced to pretend to like what they hate, tell themselves and their trusted friends in times of unguarded candor.[43] The fact that Aggy had a rich Christian apocalyptic imagination, despite the fact that the slaves' access to Christian beliefs was, in principle, severely restricted, underlines the radical split between public and private discourse. Aggy, like so many other commoners who don't normally count, had access to an oral biblical tradition, far more radical than the one taught in the schools she could not attend.[44] And although Scott does not say so explicitly, it seems implicit in his thesis, that the more violence goes into enforcing the 'public transcript' and its *prime divider*, the more violence fills the apocalyptic visions of its disappearance. The powerful—the *potentes*—often know well that such transcripts exist and have them as targets...

> For then will end the tyranny of kings and the injustice and rapine of reeves and their cunning and unjust judgments and wiles. Then shall those who rejoiced and were glad in this life groan and lament. Then shall their mead, wine and beer be turned into thirst for them.[45]

These are the future rejoicings of people who truly hate their elites, and look forward to their demise.

The elites know about hidden transcripts, but they generally consider such expressions of ill will as acceptable pressure valve releases—*as long as they remain private*. The danger comes when such hidden transcripts go public, when the status quo and its rules are openly challenged. These are moments of great emotion, when public discourse can change dramatically, challenging and even overthrowing the prevailing transcripts.[46] And millennialists are, at heart, people who hope and dream of this day. For them, it is a Day of *pleasure*.

Apocalyptic expectations—the imminence of the Day—provide one of the most powerful dynamics for bringing hidden transcripts—many and loud ones—to the surface. The whole point of public transcripts is that they get *everyone* to pretend that they *voluntarily* accept the current situation. Violence, almost by definition, should not play a visible role in their maintenance, except in specific, often ritually defined conditions (e.g., sacrifice, execution). The public transcript is the very quintessence of *self*-imposed inhibition. And it is the threat of *future* punishment for transgressions that keep people in line. We, denizens of society, learn to inhibit ourselves by accepting this predictable future.[47] But when people believe that the future will be radically different from the past, they become radically uninhibited, at least in terms of the current public transcript. None of the 'normal' threats work to intimidate someone who, to those on the outside, appears literally 'mad'. Nothing frightens the guardians of the public transcript more than such a rogue voice. Of all hidden transcripts, the most dangerous—unless one can ridicule it—is the apocalyptic voice of prophetic vengeance. And most elites generally respond, when they cannot silence it, by exterminating any manifestation of it. We underestimate the significance of hegemonic silence as a strategic response. Insofar as reality is socially constructed and maintained, silence is the most powerful weapon of all.

However frightening to the guardians of order, apocalyptic time is literally a deliverance for millennialists. Convinced that the moment for the great transformation is at hand, they step into a dramatically different universe where the final, cosmic revelation, the final resolution of good and evil, enters the public sphere. Here the 'powers' that rule this world receive their just humiliation, if not eternal punishment. Here 'saints' who have suffered, at least humiliation, at most real pain and even death, at last have their day of vindication. Here all earlier suffering becomes meaningful, all the turned cheeks, the humiliations, the crushing burdens. Here, at last, the millennial believer gets to say a resounding, a cosmic 'I told you so!' Like roosters, apocalyptic believers crow to signal that the long night has passed, and the dawn of the great and terrible Day of Rejoicing is at hand.

Apocalyptic millennialists live in a world overflowing with meaning and purpose. They live at the climax of human and sacred history and have at least a front-row seat, maybe even a speaking role in this ultimate cosmic drama. To them there is no 'chance', no gray zones of suspended meaning. They become semiotically aroused—everything is a sign, every event, a message about the unfolding drama, every encounter, destined.[48] When the signs indicate the final drama, their readers enter apocalyptic semiosis. From the people they meet, to the texts they read, to events that happen around them, everything coheres as part of a huge apocalyptic plan, crystalline in its clarity and glorious in its implications. Sometimes the plan is nefarious—an international conspiracy by the forces of evil to enslave mankind; sometimes benevolent—the dawn of a new age. In any case, whereas it once existed only in the shadows, scarcely discernable, the signs of its advent are now legible, visible, clear to anyone with discernment.

Such semiotic arousal fires the imagination, loosening tongue, hand, body to write, speak, sing, paint, dance the visions, to communicate the good news to as many as possible—those with eyes to see and ears to hear. Thus those in apocalyptic semiosis become the *vocationally aroused*, stepping out of their closets, and into the public arena, burning with enough fervor and conviction that they are ready to forsake the safety of convention, the anonymity of consensus, the protection of mimetic desire in public. Believers who have received this calling burn bridges to their past lives: they give away their wealth, they leave their homes, forsake spouse and family, friendships, jobs and professions. 'If any one comes to me and does not hate his own father and mother and wife and children and brothers and sisters, yes, and even his own life, he cannot be my disciple.'[49] They say things that alienate the powerful and influential, they are capable of both sacred joy (Francis of Assisi) and sacred violence (Hitler). Such behavior is always radical, whether it benefits others—charity both emotional and material—or harms them—violence aimed at eradicating evil. In any case, because the believer has broken with the past, he has made a leap of faith into a future whose advent he or she has *seen* coming.

Living in such a world carries obvious advantages. Believers are true warriors in the battle with evil, the adrenaline flowing, every fiber of their being engaged in their navigation of every last precious moment. They 'live with death on their shoulder'.[50] No longer bound by customary rules, no longer prisoners of conventional expectations, millennialists can explore the world of human possibilities and experiment with their own feelings.

Their imaginations unfettered, they can make connections and intuit relations at levels of that escape most of us pedestrians.

Committed to egalitarian ideals, demotic millennialists are especially imaginative in the field of social relations—generating and embracing new social paradigms that, in some cases, go mainstream (the opposition to slavery in America at the time of the Revolution was from millennialists).[51] This social creativity often places a high value on manual labor (as any egalitarian ethic must) and millennialists often become early adapters of new technology, especially communications technology.[52] Millennialists are prolific in what they do, whether it is art, writing, dance, song, communication. They live in an enchanted and exciting world and they want nothing more than to bring the rest of us into it. Or, if we won't move, bring it to us. And if we still resist, alas, strike us down as the apocalyptic enemy.

But this apocalyptic millennial condition also carries serious disadvantages, many related to its prime occupational hazard—the belief of all such enthusiasts that they occupy the center of the cosmic stage. Hence the central fantasy shared by all apocalyptic believers—they have been chosen by God (or by the fates, destiny, or the dialectic of history) to live at that central turning point in human destiny. Not only 'the whole world is watching',[53] but the whole cosmos is involved. When Mhlakaza, Nongqawuse's uncle, first heard of the vision, he saw in it his vehicle to overcome his attention-starved soul. Taught to preach millennial rhetoric, but turned away by white Christians, he now had a real prophecy. He could and did stride right into the courts of the chieftains and, with their help, lead the people to their redemption, just as had Moses.[54]

This self-image becomes problematic when the millennialist's expectations are disappointed or frustrated, the failure, *defectum*. Here we find a frequent tendency to 'up the ante',[55] like addicts increasing their doses and the potency of the drugs they use to keep themselves 'up'. When the August moon of 1856 did not produce the awaited return of the ancestors, the failure led to an even greater wave of cattle-killing. Semiotic arousal becomes semiotic promiscuity—anything means something and free association becomes an impeccable and convincing system of meaning. Vocational arousal becomes megalomania, in which one stands not merely near or on the stage, but at the very center of the entire drama. In such apocalyptic conditions, not just opposition, but even tepidity becomes an affront, a willful obstacle to the glorious salvation on its way. And megalomania often leads to paranoia, whence the elaborate conspiracy theories that so often populate the minds of millennialists. After all, what is paranoia but the megalomaniac belief that most of the people in the world have nothing better to do with their time than to plot against you? The history of millennialism is littered with the wreckage of groups with leaders who, unable to tolerate the world's enduring imperfection (including their own), preferred to destroy everything they could.[56]

Of course, the idea that one can resolve such emotional distress with a fantasy of a situation in which one is already and will soon be visibly the center of the cosmos has profound conceptual flaws, not the least of which is the inevitable disappointment. Roosters believe that, in the very near future, either God or some cosmic force (extraterrestrials, the dialectic of history, technological breakthroughs) will *publicly* intervene *on their side*, punishing those who scoffed and opposed them, rewarding them and their faithful companions. Evangelical pre-millennialists, for example, currently anticipate an awesome *tribulation* (based on the book of Revelation), a seven-year period of staggering punishment for the billions of sinners (non-believers) on the planet.

There is great irony behind all such thinking. The coming tribulation is not that of the outsiders who cling pitifully to their antiquated notions of a world that goes on tomorrow much as it has today, who scoff at the news and mock the prophet. No, the tribulation will strike the true apocalyptic believer, the rooster, who must confront his or her own failed expectation. This is true, moreover, whether the rooster successfully produces a radical change in this world or not. However much power men like Robespierre, Lenin, Hitler, Mao, Khomeini, or any other 'successful' rooster wields, they always find that humans fail them, that the new citizen, comrade, Aryan, or Muslim who in principle should emerge with the destruction of the forces of evil, fails to materialize. Because roosters are perfectionists—at once their strength and weakness—they cannot be satisfied with partial transformations.

Thus, in a profound sense, the study of millennialism as a historical force is the study of disappointment, and how these most extravagant optimists come to terms with their failed hopes. The results are as extravagant as the hopes, but in a nutshell, the answers that the disappointed millennialists have come up with range from the formation of new religions and the establishment of productive technologically sophisticated communities, to totalitarianism and civil society. The key paradox here is that although millennial prophecies have *always* proven wrong in their apocalyptic expectations, they have rarely proven inconsequential or unproductive. Studies have shown that while pessimists are more often right in predicting the future, optimists accomplish more.[57] Partly that is due to the willingness to take risks; partly to the enthusiasm that optimism brings to a task, partly to a willingness to learn from mistakes. The history of mil-

lennialism reflects such a dynamic—a range of fruitful mistakes, however
nourishing or poisonous. And the history of the most millennial culture in
world history—the West—is that of a long series of interlocking and
unintended consequences that we, retrospectively, like to call progress.

Anti-Apocalyptic Owls: The Nocturnal Wisdom of the Public Transcript

Every force has its contrary, and not surprisingly, a force as volatile and
uncompromisingly hostile to the status quo as apocalyptic expectations
has its implacable enemies. For every rooster crowing on his dunghill that
the great and terrible Day has dawned, there are a dozen owls hooting
from their lecterns that the night is still long, the foxes abroad, the master
asleep, and only damage can come from prematurely awakening the
barnyard. To roosters, they seem like a cross between ostriches with their
heads in the sand, and bats blinded by daybreak. But they have a certain wisdom. They are the guardians of 'normal time'; to them falls the
(self-appointed) task of preventing change from happening too rapidly.
Minerva's owl sees in retrospect, it flies, *ex post defectu*, at dusk.

Whereas roosters like to tell about the emperor's new clothes (those in
authority are fools), owls have a cautionary tale about Chicken Little, who,
with his hysterically apocalyptic reading of a fallen acorn, led the whole
barnyard into the clutches of Foxy Loxy.

There are different kinds of owls:

- reluctant owls—who do not believe the millennium will come
  although they do not like the world as it is (quiet pessimists); and
- aggressive owls—who like the world as it is, and will resist any
  effort to change it, unless it be to their advantage (loud pessimists);
- millennial owls—who believe the millennium will come, but,
  for a variety of reasons, believe that now is not the time (quiet
  optimists).

True owls are, by nature, conservative, anxious of (if not hostile to)
change, especially to rapid change, suspicious of radical new ideas and
approaches. Obviously, most people in the established elite of any culture
tend to be owls. The process is self-selecting. But that is never true of all
of the cultural elite, and societies where the dominant religion promises
an apocalyptic resolution to the current world—Judaism, Christianity, Islam
—tend to produce an unusually high number of roosters *within its own
elites*. *La trahison des clercs* [The treason of the intellectuals]. Therein lies
the key to understanding the exceptional nature of the 'modern West'.

Normally, and especially in prime divider societies, owls dominate public discourse, and one of their jobs is to make sure that roosters do not breach the public transcript. Indeed, so profoundly do they dominate that most roosters never even appear on our documentary screens, although we can suspect they had a more powerful *oral* existence. The documents —writing is a retrospective act—are inherently hostile to apocalyptic discourse; oral speech is especially suited to apocalyptic rhetoric. Owls are representatives not so much of the *status quo*, but of the rules of the current social paradigm. They are powerful and influential precisely because they have played the rules to their own advantage (true of both aristocrats born into positions of power and meritocrats who achieve them). Needless to say, they are not only hostile to new rules, but use the current rules to thwart the introduction of new ones.[58]

Owls have a reputation for wisdom, and in most millennial cases that reputation is well deserved.[59] The vast majority of roosters have, in fact, proposed ludicrous scenarios and equally implausible rule sets. The owls' steady grip provides a most valuable stability since any culture whose elite runs after every (or even every tenth) apocalyptic rumor will not long endure. True, what is now proved was once only imagined; but much that is imagined does not get proved.

Just as roosters have both their strengths and their weaknesses, so do owls. Their main failure inverts the rooster's great strength; that is, they lack imagination and they cling to the current order of things even after it has become dysfunctional. Owls have an almost instinctual response to sweeping ideas or predictions of social mutation—they dismiss them, if necessary with scorn and ridicule. Their attitude is justifiable—you can't jump every time someone says take a conceptual leap. But behind this reflexive response often lies an unwillingness to question the prevailing paradigm. As Kuhn puts it, 'normal scientists' are problem solvers; they know the rules and they pose their problems and seek their solutions according to them.[60] To question the rules disrupts an orderly world and undermines predictable rewards for diligence, for mimetic discourse.[61] And just as the rooster's danger is to fall from exhilaration to megalo- mania, so the owl's danger is to fall from skepticism into negativity, from critical reasoning to clinging to Reason, whether that 'logic' be stoic, scholastic, positivist, or whatever new form the normative paradigm takes. Overall, these seem like mild and venial sins when compared with the colossal crimes of maniacal messiahs. But even these can cause serious and unnecessary culture wars.

Owls and Roosters Interact: Chicken Littles and Ostriches

When roosters crow, the natural tendency of owls is to hear them as 'Chicken Littles'—alarmists whose excessive imaginations have cooked up panic from nothing. Roosters, of course, tend to set off such responses because they, almost from the start of their missions, articulate their insights with the intention of shocking, knocking their listeners loose from their complacent attachment to what the roosters know is a fast fading world. Thus, roosters want and need rapid and energetic responses—this is, after all, for the good of their listeners. They thus have little patience with the slow responses and reasoned skepticism of their owlish reasoners.[62] Thus, just as owls tend to see roosters as Chicken Littles, roosters tend to see owls as ostriches, their heads in the sand, blissfully and tragically unaware of the oncoming stampede. And of course, if one would make oneself heard by someone whose head is in the sand, obviously one must speak louder. And the louder you speak the more incomprehensible and unreliable the speech. So the more shrill the Chicken Little roosters are, then the more unresponsive, the farther down in the sand, do the ostrich owls bury their heads.

What we have here is a failure to communicate, something which, in the course of millennial history has often led to tragic consequences.[63] But it is more than just a well-intentioned failure. It is a lack of understanding on both sides to imagine anything but a zero-sum relationship between roosters and owls. Each sees the other as its nemesis, each works towards eliminating the other. Behind the exuberant embrace of the rooster lies a fanatic passion and a staggering capacity for violent intolerance. And behind the seeming deafness and ridicule of the owls lies a more aggressive defensiveness which, should the rooster persist, can shift from politely ignoring to much more violent objection.[64] The owls, as do the roosters, know full well that were the new message successful, it would spell the end of the old hegemony—cultural, social, political. Owls do not stand poised between listening and ignoring. Most of the time, and throughout most of human history, owls have chosen between ignoring and exterminating. Louder rarely means more success when roosters try and reach owls. Most often it just enrages both further.

The most dangerous situations occur when the rooster crows loudly and attracts an enthusiastic audience of people who grow progressively hostile to the authorities, largely on a diet of resentful private transcripts now become public. The apocalyptic community bathes in the charisma of openly speaking what so many hearts for so long kept locked away in trunks. As long as roosters crow to unresponsive barnyards, owls can mock and ignore. But when roosters gather a large and enthusiastic following, when their claims begin to gain currency strong and wide, the situation becomes intolerable. The high priest Amaziah expresses the owls' reaction to the rooster Amos: 'Amos has conspired against you in the midst of the house of Israel. The land is not able to bear all his words' (Amos 7.10). When owls see a real threat from roosters, they shift from ostrich to hawk, confining roosters to monasteries, prisons and mental hospitals where possible, and where necessary, executing them and massacring their followers. That was certainly the Roman policy around 30 CE. Jesus, no matter how pacifist, a-political, and unthreatening he might have been, would prove intolerable to the Romans merely because of the excitement he aroused. Messiahs, in the pre-modern period, rarely die of natural causes.

The key to millennial movements is neither the roosters, nor the owls, but the audiences. Unlike a political candidate whose following may shake up the electoral calculus, apocalyptic leaders with even a fraction of a percent of an audience, have a weapon of enormous potency. Messiahs exercise immense influence over their followers. Charismatic leaders demand total response, and the rewards of apocalyptic belief are commensurate with the intensity of the commitment.[65] No rhetoric is more powerful than apocalyptic rhetoric, no greater motivation exists in the human repertoire than the belief that ones' every action is crucial to the final destiny of the human race.[66] If the leader can convince his following that God, or the historical dialectic calls for ruthless destruction, there is almost no limit to the damage they can do, trying to save the world by destroying it. And no movement, no matter how big, does not start small. But without the tacit or, still better, warm approval of the public, without the ability to enter the public sphere with apocalyptic proposals and get a hearing, such dedicated troops can do little.

Millennialism brings out the most noble and most base of human behavior, from genocidal rage of Crusaders and Nazis to the extravagant love of a Francis or a George Fox. It continues to operate in this modern age where, having tossed out God from the apocalyptic scenario, we have replaced his immense destructive powers with our own. If we don't understand the appeal, the varieties and the dynamics of millennialism, we don't understand a critical element of one of our own, and other cultures' greatest passions.

References

Alexander, Paul, *The Byzantine Apocalyptic Tradition* (ed. Dorothy de F. Abrahamse; Berkeley, CA: University of California Press, 1985).
Augustine, *Letters* (trans. W. Parsons; New York: Fathers of the Church, 1955).

Baumgarten, Albert I., 'Introduction', in *idem* (ed.), *Apocalyptic Time* (Leiden: E.J. Brill, 2000).

Benz, Ernst, *Evolution and Christian Hope: Man's Concept of the Future from the Early Church Fathers to Teilhard de Chardin* (New York: Doubleday, 1966).

Blake, William, *The Complete Poetry and Prose of William Blake* (ed. David Erdman; Berkeley, CA: University of California Press, 1982).

Bloch, Ruth, *Visionary Republic* (New York: Cambridge University Press, 1985).

Boswell, James, *Life of Johnson*, III (ed. G.B. Hill; rev. L.F. Powell; Oxford: Clarendon Press, 1934–1964).

Brasher, Brenda, 'Semiotically Aroused: Through the Looking Glass of Millennial Studies', (Presented at the Annual Meeting of the Center for Millennial Studies; Boston University, Boston, Massachusetts, 29 October, 2000).

Brodhead, Richard H., 'Millennium Prophecy and the Energies of Social Transformation: The Case of Nat Turner', in Abbas Amanat and Magnus Bernhardson (eds.), *Imagining the End: Visions of Apocalypses from the Ancient Middle East to Modern America* (New York: I.B. Tauris Publishers, 2002).

Cohn, Norman, *The Pursuit of the Millennium* (Fairlawn, NJ: Essential Books, 1957).

—*Cosmos, Chaos and the World to Come: The Ancient Roots of Apocalyptic Faith* (New Haven, CT: Yale University Press, 1993).

Crawford, S.J. (ed.), *Byrhtferth's Manual* (Early English Text Society, Original Series, 177; London: Oxford University Press, 1972).

Daniels, Ted, *Millennialism: An International Bibliography* (New York: Garland Publishing, 1992).

Erdman, David, *Prophet against Empire* (Princeton, NJ: Princeton University Press, 1969).

Fulop, Timothy E., and Albert J. Raboteau (eds.), *African-American Religion: Interpretive Essays in History and Culture* (New York: Routledge, 1997).

Frye, Northrop, *Fearful Symmetry* (Princeton, NJ: Princeton University Press, 1965).

Hall, John R., *The Ways Out: Utopian Communal Groups in an Age of Babylon* (London and Boston: Routledge & Kegan Paul, 1978).

Hill, Charles, *Regnum Caelorum: Patterns of Future Hope in Early Christianity* (Oxford: Clarendon Press, 1992).

Hill, Christopher, *Antichrist in Seventeenth-Century England* (London: Oxford University Press, 1971).

—*Puritanism and Revolution* (London: Panther, 1992).

Josephus, *Josephus: The Complete Works* (trans. William Whiston; Grand Rapids, MI: Kregel Publications, 1978).

Kodera, Takashi James, 'Nichiren and his Nationalistic Eschatology', *Religious Studies* 15 (1979), 41-53.

Kuhn, Thomas, *The Structure of Scientific Revolutions* (Chicago: University of Chicago Press, 1962).

Leib, Franklin Allen, *Behold a Pale Horse* (New York: Forge, 2000).

Levine, Robert, *Vale of Tears* (Berkeley, CA: University of California Press, 1992).

Lifton, Robert J., *Destroying the World to Save it: The Tale of Aum Shin Rikyo* (New York: Henry Holt, 1999).

Lynch, Aaron, *Thought Contagion: How Belief Spreads through Society* (New York: Basic Books, 1999).

Maher, Robert F., 'Tommy Kabu Movement of the Purari Delta', *Oceania* 29 (1958), 75-90.

Mannheim, Karl, *Ideology and Utopia* (London: Routledge, 1936).

Manuel, Frank E., and Fritzie P. Manuel, *Utopian Thought in the Western World* (Cambridge, MA: Belknap Press, 1979).

Mendel, Arthur, *Michael Bakunin: The Roots of Apocalypse* (New York: Praeger, 1981).

—*Vision and Violence* (Ann Arbor: University of Michigan Press, 1999).

Midelfort, Erik, 'Madness and the Millennium at Münster, 1534–35', in C. Kleinhenz and F.J. LeMoine (eds.), *Fearful Hope: Approaching the New Millennium* (Madison, WI: University of Wisconsin Press, 1999).

Naquin, Susan, *Millenarian Rebellion in China: The Eight Trigrams Rebellion* (New Haven, CT: Yale University Press, 1976).

Nietzsche, Friedrich, *On the Genealogy of Morals* (Oxford: Oxford University Press, 1996).

Noble, David, *The Religion of Technology: The Divinity of Man and the Spirit of Invention* (New York: Alfred A. Knopf, 1998).

Oberman, Heiko A., *The Roots of Anti-Semitism: In the Age of Renaissance and Reformation* (Philadelphia: Fortress Press, 1984).

O'Leary, Stephen, *Arguing the Apocalypse: A Theory of Millennial Rhetoric* (New York: Oxford University Press, 1994).

Olsen, Theodore, *Millennialism, Utopia, and Progress* (Toronto: University of Toronto Press, 1982).

Peires, J.B., *The Dead Will Arise* (Johannesburg: Ravan, 1989).

Peterson, Eric, *Monotheismus als politisches Probleme* (Gütersloh: Gütersloher Verlagshaus Mohn, 1978).

Protocols of the Elders of Zion (Chulmleigh: Britons, 1968; [New York: Beckwith, 1920]).

Quinby, Lee, *Anti-Apocalypse: Exercises in Genealogical Criticism* (Minneapolis: University of Minnesota Press, 1994).

Robertson, Pat, *The New World Order* (Dallas: Word Books, 1991).

Scott, James C., *Domination and the Arts of Resistance* (New Haven, CT: Yale University Press, 1989).

Stewart, Pamela, and Andrew Strathern (guest eds.), 'Millennial Countdown in New Guinea' *Ethnohistory* 47.1 (Winter 2000), special issue.

Tai, Hue-Tam Ho, *Millenarianism and Peasant Politics in Vietnam* (Cambridge, MA: Harvard University Press, 1993).

Talmon, Jacob, *The Origins of Totalitarian Democracy* (New York: Praeger, 1960).

Thompson, E.P., *Witness against the Beast: William Blake and the Moral Law* (New York: New Press, 1993).

Thompson, Keith, *Angels and Aliens: UFO's and the Mythic Imagination* (Reading, MA: Addison Wesley Longman, 1991).

Tiger, Lionel, *Optimism: The Biology of Hope* (New York: Simon & Schuster, 1979).

Tucker, Robert, 'The Theory of Charismatic Leadership', *Daedalus* 97 (1968), 731-56.

Wilson, Brian, *The Social Dimensions of Sectarianism: Sects and New Religious Movements in Contemporary Society* (Oxford: Clarendon Press, 1990).

Witherington III, Ben, *Jesus, Paul and the End of the World* (Downers Grove, IL: InterVarsity Press, 1992).

Notes

1.   The joke tells of a zoo-keeper who had a fabulous 'messianic' exhibit where a lion and a lamb shared the same cage. 'How do you do it?' asked an amazed observer. 'Easy', he replied, 'lots of lambs'. Or, as Woody Allen put it, 'the lion lies down with the lamb, but the lamb doesn't get much sleep'.

2.   Rev. 3.16.

3.   The *just* live free in this world. The just *live free* in this world. The just live free *in this world.*

4.   Aaron Lynch, *Thought Contagion: How Belief Spreads through Society* (New York: Basic Books, 1999).

5.   Karl Mannheim, *Ideology and Utopia* (London: Routledge, 1936); Norman Cohn, *The Pursuit of the Millennium* (Fairlawn, NJ: Essential Books, 1957); and Jacob Talmon, *The Origins of Totalitarian Democracy* (New York: Praeger, 1960).

6.   Let's hope the description was a rhetorical exaggeration—it was only splashing that high—rather than an actual event. The rejoicing in blood is a characteristic element of many millennial movements. See the verse of the French National Anthem, *La Marseilleise*: 'Let the blood of our enemies flow in our plowed furrows'.

7.   Jung called this synchronicity. Whether, how or why it happens is not clear; that people think it does unquestionably happens often.

8.   Heiko A. Oberman, *The Roots of Anti-Semitism: In the Age of Renaissance and Reformation* (Philadelphia: Fortress Press, 1984), 120-22.

9.   On Tertullian and *ressentiment*, see Nietzsche, *On the Genealogy of Morals* (Oxford: Oxford University Press, 1996), 15. This desire for vengeance is the opposite of Origen's *heretical[!]* notion that even Satan himself, *a fortiori* all people, will eventually be saved.

10.   See Theodore Olson, *Millennialism, Utopia, and Progress* (Toronto: University of Toronto Press, 1982); and Frank E. Manuel and Fritzie P. Manuel, *Utopian Thought in the Western World* (Cambridge, MA: Belknap Press, 1979).

11.   Often historians, especially historians of theology, use a more restrictive term for millennialism, as, for example recently Charles Hill, *Regnum Caelorum: Patterns of Future Hope in Early Christianity* (Oxford: Clarendon Press, 1992), 1-8. Hill rejects the broader term as I use it here in favor of a more restrictive one, 'full blown chiliasm' [the Greek term for millennialism] he insists, includes all three elements of (1) a temporary period (not necessarily 1000 years); (2) earthly; and (3) messianic [individual deliverers play a key role] (pp. 5-6). If one does not adhere to this specific scenario, he argues, if one denies the interim, temporary millennial period, one 'remove[s] oneself from the millennialist camp' (p. 1, n. 1). Aside from the fact that he is tracing this particular configuration in early Christianity, Hill gives no reason to so restrict the definition. It does, certainly, permit him to argue that not only is millennialism not the dominant ideology of the early Church (contra many, primarily Protestant German historians, *Regnum Caelorum*, 2-4), but that not even the book of Revelation(!) is millennial. His analysis would be far more useful if he had a term for the larger phenomenon, as well as for this subset which he convincingly correlates to other beliefs. If he wishes to define his particular brand of thinking chiliasm, fine, but to so rigidly define it in order to marginalize it does not help us to better understand. Hereafter, I refer to the larger phenomenon of expectation of the kingdom of God *on earth* (Hill's points 2 and 3) as *millennial.*

12.   Here I use the term in Augustine's sense of the time-space continuum, the embodied, the historical. For Augustine, the *saeculum* could *not* be redeemed. There was no earthly millennium of peace, never would be.

13.   See Strozier, this volume.

14. For a sense of the full range of millennial beliefs and the various disciplines that contribute to this field of study, see Ted Daniels, *Millennialism: An International Bibliography* (New York: Garland Publishing, 1992); for a recent discussion of the anthropological dimensions, see the special edition of *Ethnohistory* 47.1, 'Millennial Countdown in New Guinea', (eds. Pamela Stewart and Andrew Strathern; [Winter 2000]).

15. For Charles Hill, the socially disruptive dimension is key (*Regnum Caelorum*, 1 n. 1). This seems to be a widespread tendency among historians, drawn largely from a (possibly superficial) reading of Cohn's *The Pursuit of the Millennium*.

16. Erik Midlefort, 'Madness and the Millennium at Münster, 1534–35', in C. Kleinhenz and F.J. LeMoine (eds.), *Fearful Hope: Approaching the New Millennium* (Madison: University of Wisconsin Press, 1999), 115-34.

17. Josephus, *Antiquities of the Jews* 18.1.6: 'These men agree in all other things with the Pharisaic notions; but they have an invisible attachment to liberty; and they say that God is to be their only Ruler and Lord'. Josephus, *Josephus: The Complete Works*, translated by William Whiston (Grand Rapids, MI: Kregel Publications, 1978), 377.

18. Christopher Hill on the sects of the seventeenth civil war in England. See Christopher Hill, *Antichrist in Seventeenth-Century England* (London: Oxford University Press, 1971). See also, David Erdman, *Prophet against Empire* (Princeton, NJ: Princeton University Press, 1969); and E.P. Thompson, *Witness against the Beast: William Blake and the Moral Law* (New York: New Press, 1993).

19. Obviously, for most anarchic millennialists, certain forms of religiosity, like human sacrifice, do not qualify as 'just'. They have a strong tendency towards iconoclastic thinking.

20. Nietzsche, *On the Genealogy of Morals*. The Nazi use of Nietzsche represents one of the great ironies of history since they represent precisely the kind of self-pitying *ressentiment* at loss of power that Nietzsche denounced.

21. Thucydides, *Peloponnesian War* 5.89.

22. On coercive purity, see Lee Quinby, *Anti-Apocalypse: Exercises in Genealogical Criticism* (Minneapolis: University of Minnesota Press, 1994); on the prediction of reversal with power, see the Athenians to the Melians in Thucydides, *Peloponnesian War* 5.85-116, or, more acidly, by Nietzsche (above, n. 8).

23. Eric Peterson, *Monotheismus als politisches Probleme* (Gütersloh: Gütersloher Verlagshaus Mohn, 1978).

24. Norman Cohn, *Cosmos, Chaos and the World to Come: The Ancient Roots of Apocalyptic Faith* (New Haven, CT: Yale University Press, 1993).

25. Paul Alexander, *The Byzantine Apocalyptic Tradition* (ed. Dorothy de F. Abrahamse; Berkeley, CA: University of California Press, 1985).

26. For Buddhism see Takashi James Kodera, 'Nichiren and his Nationalistic Eschatology', *Religious Studies* 15 (1979), 41-53; Hue-Tam Ho Tai, *Millenarianism and Peasant Politics in Vietnam* (Cambridge, MA: Harvard University Press, 1993). On Hinduism see Robert F. Maher, 'Tommy Kabu Movement of the Purari Delta', *Oceania* 29 (1958), 75-90.

27. Stephen O'Leary, *Arguing the Apocalypse: A Theory of Millennial Rhetoric* (New York: Oxford University Press, 1994), 195-206.

28. Cf. the discussion of Ben Witherington III in *Jesus, Paul and the End of the World* (Downers Grove, IL: InterVarsity Press, 1992), 15-22.

29. Cohn, *The Pursuit of the Millennium*; Talmon, *The Origins of Totalitarian Democracy*; and Brian Wilson, *The Social Dimensions of Sectarianism: Sects and New Religious Movements in Contemporary Society* (Oxford: Clarendon Press, 1990).

30. Josephus describes how the followers of a failed messiah—an Egyptian false prophet—dispersed after his defeat, 'every one to his own home and there concealed themselves'. *Jewish Wars* 2.13.5, in *Josephus*, 482.

31. See Arthur Mendel's brilliant study, *Michael Bakunin: The Roots of Apocalypse* (New York: Praeger, 1981).

32. The *locus classicus* of this is the *Protocols of the Elders of Zion* (Chulmleigh: Britons, 1968; New York: Beckwith, 1920); see its more recent avatars, UFOs, in Keith Thompson, *Angels and Aliens: UFO's and the Mythic Imagination* (Reading, MA: Addison Wesley Longman, 1991); Christian fundamentalist, Pat Robertson, *The New World Order* (Dallas: Word Books, 1991), and Franklin Allen Leib, *Behold a Pale Horse* (New York: Forge, 2000). See above, n. 2.

33. See John R. Hall, *The Ways Out: Utopian Communal Groups in an Age of Babylon* (London and Boston: Routledge & Kegan Paul, 1978).

34. E.g., the post-millennial Reconstructionists, whose cataclysmic scenario made Y2K so attractive to some (Gary North). Chip Berlet has described these groups as 'Calvinism on crack'.

35. Rom. 13.11-12. Paul on slaves, 1 Cor. 7.17-24; on obeying the powers that be, followed by the passage cited above: Rom.13.1-10.

36. Isa. 2.2-4; Mic. 4.1-4.

37. See Christopher Hill, 'John Mason and the End of the World', in *Puritanism and Revolution* (London: Panther, 1992), 290-302; R.J. Lifton, *Destroying the World to Save it: The Tale of Aum Shin Rikyo* (New York: Henry Holt, 1999).

38. Erik Midlefort, 'Madness and the Millennium at Münster', in Christopher Klein-henz and Fannie Le Moine (eds.), *Fearful Hope: Approaching the New Millennium* (Madison, WI: University of Wisconsin Press, 1999), 115-34.

39. Arthur Mendel, *Vision and Violence* (Ann Arbor: University of Michigan Press, 1999).

40. Susan Naquin, *Millenarian Rebellion in China: The Eight Trigrams Rebellion* (New Haven, CT: Yale University Press, 1976).

41. Augustine, *Epistolae* 198 [418 CE], *Letters* (trans. W. Parsons; New York: Fathers of the Church, 1955), IV, 353.

42. Words of Aggy, a southern slave cook quoted in Mary Livermore, *My Story of the War* (Hartford, 1889), cited in James C. Scott, *Domination and the Arts of Resis-tance* (New Haven, CT: Yale Univeristy Press, 1989), 5.

43. Scott, *Domination*, ch. 1. He points out how Aggy had said this not in front of her master (who had just whipped her daughter for a theft she had not committed), but after he left, in the presence of the governess from New England whom she apparently trusted not to tell the master.

44. *African-American Religion: Interpretive Essays in History and Culture* (ed. Timothy E. Fulop and Albert J. Raboteau; New York: Routledge, 1997).

45. *Byrhtferth's Manual* [c. 1011], (Early English Text Society, Original Series, 177; ed. S.J. Crawford; London, 1972), 242, lines 3-9.

46. The term 'hegemonic discourse' refers to the prevailing public transcript. Scott, *Domination*, 70-107.

47. Scott notes astutely that the public transcript not only constrains those below, but also those in the elite whose behavior must conform to expectations in order for them to maintain their position of authority (he analyzes Orwell's 'The Elephant Hunter' in this connection), Scott, *Domination*, 10-11.

48. See Brenda Brasher, 'Semiotically Aroused: Through the Looking Glass of Millennial Studies'. Note, most deeply religious monotheists believe that nothing is coincidental, that God wills everything that happens, and that every event has meaning. The apocalyptic believer, however, takes these signs to indicate imminent transformation, as a call to dramatic change, initially for him or herself, soon for everyone.

49. Lk. 14.26. Even as hyperbole, the passage clearly articulates the break, cf. a milder variant in Mt. 10.37. Other passages have Jesus renouncing his family ('What have I to do with thee?' Jn 2.4) and claiming that those who follow the Lord are his true family, not his birth family. The break with family that the hyperbole suggests seems of a pair with the hostility to Judaism in the same sources (cf. Mt. 12.46-50).

50. 'When a man knows he is to be hanged in a fortnight, it concentrates his mind wonderfully…' Samuel Johnson, quoted by James Boswell, *Life of Johnson* (ed. G.B. Hill; rev. L.F. Powell; Oxford: Clarendon Press, 1934-1964), III, 197, (17 September, 1777).

51. Richard H. Brodhead, 'Millennium Prophecy and the Energies of Social Transformation: The Case of Nat Turner', in Abbas Amanat and Magnus Bernhardson (eds.), *Imagining the End: Visions of Apocalypses from the Ancient Middle East to Modern America* (New York: I.B. Tauris Publishers, 2002); Ruth Bloch, *Visionary Republic* (New York: Cambridge University Press, 1985).

52. Among the many examples, consider Shaker unpatented contributions to American technology; Seventh Day Adventists and Kellog's Cereal and Graham crackers (to bring Americans over to a vegetarian diet); Protestants and the printing press; Nazis and television; see Ernst Benz, *Evolution and Christian Hope: Man's Concept of the Future from the Early Church Fathers to Teilhard de Chardin* (New York: Doubleday, 1966), 121-42; David Noble, *The Religion of Technology: The Divinity of Man and the Spirit of Invention* (New York: Alfred A. Knopf, 1998).

53. Chant of the demonstrators at Chicago in 1968. Cf. the American revolutionary slogan about the onset of the hostilities in Lexington and Concord: 'The shot heard round the world'.

54. On Mhlakaza, see J.B. Peires, *The Dead Will Arise* (Johannesburg: Ravan, 1989) who tracks down his extensive relationships with Christian missionaries and his failed attempts to 'make it' in the world of Christian preaching, 33-36.

55. Al Baumgarten, 'I suggest that there are moments when millennial movements need to "up the ante", by forcing their members to accept risks which will increase solidarity and loyalty. At the simplest level movements "up the ante" in order to take advantage of the bonds established between those who share dangers. [There is also] the common commitment of those willing to take the risk, as opposed to those apos-

tates who refuse: the risk binds those who will share in the imminent blessings, unlike the apostates doomed to perdition. Designating and expelling these apostates also contributes to the sense of solidarity among those who endure.' In Albert I. Baumgarten (ed.), 'Introduction' from *idem*, *Apocalyptic Time* (Leiden: E.J. Brill, 2000), x-xi.

56. The most recent and extraordinary example of this is the NRM the Movement for the Restoration of the 10 Commandments in Uganda (March 2000).

57. Lionel Tiger, *Optimism: The Biology of Hope* (New York: Simon & Schuster, 1979).

58. A good example of this kind of behavior on the part of 'normal' scientists to ignore the anomalies in their paradigm has been outlined by Thomas Kuhn in *The Structure of Scientific Revolutions* (Chicago: University of Chicago Press, 1962).

59. I took the imagery of the rooster from the Talmudic discussion cited as an epigraph to this chapter; but rather than use the bat as its antithesis, I preferred the imagery of the 'wise' owl as my nocturnal animal because the bat seems so invidious, and whether the proud roosters like Reb Simlai like it or not, the historian has to admit that the owls have consistently gotten it right.

60. Kuhn, *Structure of Scientific Revolutions*, ch. 3.

61. Northrop Frye points out, 'pedantry means…that kind of contact with culture which consists in belittling the size and scope of the conceptions of genius, the "nothing but" principle of reading everything on the minimum imaginative level… Imaginative intensity applied to a wrong or inadequate object can be corrected; a deficiency in intensity never can be.' Northrop Frye, *Fearful Symmetry* (Princeton, NJ: Princeton University Press, 1965), 422.

62. For a good example of the dynamics here, see the interesting interaction between Joan of Arc and the French aristocratic military command in the movie *The Messenger* (1999).

63. This dysfunctional relationship was delineated by Blake in the *Marriage of Heaven and Hell* (1796), where the roosters are called energy (desire) and the owls, reason. Substituting the terms works perfectly: 'Indeed it appeared to Reason [the owls] as if Desire [the roosters] was cast out, but the Devil's [rooster's] account is that the Messiah [the owl's savior] fell and formed a heaven [ecclesiastical notions of paradise/the Church] of what he stole from the Abyss [the unfettered mind]'. Plate 5f.; *The Complete Poetry and Prose of William Blake* (ed. David Erdman; Berkeley, CA: University of California Press, 1982), 34.

64. The classic case here is the Canudos community in the backlands of Brazil at the end of the nineteenthth century—c. 14,000 men, women and children wiped out for having the temerity to drop out of an society where they occupied the bottom rungs. See Robert Levine, *Vale of Tears* (Berkeley, CA: University of California Press, 1992).

65. Robert Tucker, 'The Theory of Charismatic Leadership', *Daedalus* 97 (1968), 731-56.

66. O'Leary, *Arguing the Apocalypse*.

The Millennium and Narrative Closure

Cathy Gutierrez

The religious phenomenon of millennialism is counter-intuitive to most people: believers not only expect that the end of the world is at hand, they often desperately desire for that to be the case. The reasons for this sociological reaction to contemporary events are manifold; millennialists are frequently persecuted and almost always ridiculed for their beliefs, and they anticipate to be not only vindicated but also to have their oppressors punished at the apocalypse. The state of the world is often seen as corrupt beyond repair, and its dissolution is not a matter to be mourned but rather a purging of sin to be celebrated. And while often terrifying, the events of the final days are momentous ones that will culminate in the arrival of the messiah and the elimination of suffering for the true believers.

In addition to these sociological and psychological responses to the end of time, I will be arguing that another force is also at work—narrative understanding. Millennialists understand themselves as the protagonists in a plot authored by God, and they not only witness the calamitous events of the last days, it is often their responsibility to usher them in. I will argue that millennialism is a form of religious sense-making; by foregrounding the coming end of time, millennial groups adopt a narrative understanding of history. History itself is seen as having a distinct beginning, middle, and end, with all historical vagaries subsumed into necessary events for the plot of time. The threat of chaos or meaninglessness is conquered, and all suffering is recast as historically necessary and divinely sanctioned. In short, time becomes trustworthy.

Like narrative, millennial systems use the promise of closure as the focusing lens of the present. Closure is anticipated as the end point that will retrospectively make sense of the past and present; events that appeared random or threatening will be recast with new meaning that only the end can confer on them.[1] Unlike narrative, however, the success of a millennial movement is dependent on its ability to continually defer the very closure that is its defining feature in order to survive. Strategies for deferring closure implicate plot and interpretation as well. Millennialism is a reading strategy for history, narrating the one true story of the world. I will delineate two basic chronotypes, or constructions of time, that millennialists tend to follow, what I have termed the 'linear' and the 'mimetic' imaginations of time. The choice of chronotype will govern the behavior of believers to a great extent.

Time and Narrative

For a theory of narrative, the first articulation of time is made by Aristotle in his *Poetics*. While Aristotle is not concerned with time per se, he is concerned with the process of emplotting narrative, which, I argue, is inherently an act of temporalization. Plot is a temporal sequence of events that serves to create a necessary consonance between the beginning, middle, and end. Aristotle writes:

> So then, just as in the other mimetic arts a unitary mimesis is a representation of a unitary object, so the plot-structure, as the mimesis of action, should be a representation of a unitary and complete action; and its parts, consisting of the events, should be so constructed that the displacement or removal of any one of them will disturb and disjoint the work's wholeness. For anything whose presence or absence has no clear effect cannot be counted an integral part of the whole.[2]

By drawing a necessary connection between the sequence of events and the outcome of the plot, Aristotle constructs an understanding of time as it is found in narrative. By focusing on the necessity of coherence between the consecutive events, Aristotle effectively temporalizes narrative: emplotment is the process of creating a unified space of time in which all discrete measurements of time within the narrative can be accounted for as meaningful in relation to the end. In *Time and Narrative* Paul Ricoeur writes of Aristotle,

> Plot was first defined, on the most formal level, as an integrating dynamism that draws a unified and complete story from a variety of incidents, in other words, that transforms this variety into a unified and complete story. This formal definition opens a field of rule-governed transformations worthy of being called plots so long as we can discern temporal wholes bringing about a synthesis of the heterogeneous between circumstances, goals, means, interactions, and intended or unintended results.[3]

This view of narrative time has consequences for the reader of plots: Time is meaningful, and the events in it are never extraneous or random. In *Modern Fiction and Human Time* Wesley Kort discusses time and plot in narrative as investing time itself with epistemic intelligibility. He writes:

> The coherence plot provides is inextinguishable. The result...is that narrative time appears as trustworthy. Events, no matter how painful or unin-

telligible they may seem at first, are part of some larger coherence. This affirmation appears despite the fact that many of the events depicted are disruptive, even violent and traumatic: the loss of continuity with traditional authorities and values, personal dislocation, social fragmentation, and the devastation produced by war. The trustworthiness of time is tested by but finally vindicated in the face of events negatively related to meaning.[4]

While a sequence of events is necessary for the process of temporalization, the events themselves are composed of digressions that complicate the situation as it drives toward closure. These events consist of, for Aristotle, *peripeteia*, or the change of one state of things to its opposite, and discovery, the change from ignorance to knowledge.[5] Contrary to an assumption that *peripeteia* diverts the movement of plot toward closure, these formal requirements for plot are intrinsic to the process of plot itself. The *peripeteia* is the very substance of the movement toward closure and will define the circumstances under which closure is possible. *Peripeteia* consists of diversions within the plot itself away from immediate, premature closure of the central storyline: the plot necessarily has to wander into subplots and episodes within the primary story in order to protract the sense of time for an appropriate narrative crescendo and conclusion. Narrative time is inexorably linked to the intricacy of plot and can be sustained as long as the coherence between the beginning and the end is apparent to the reader.

In *The Sense of an Ending* Frank Kermode argues that these seeming diversions from achieving closure reinforce the reader's dependence on and belief in eventual closure: *peripeteia* requires of the end that it will justify this digression, and thus paradoxically reinforces the belief in the end. Kermode writes:

> *Peripeteia*, which has been called the equivalent, in narrative, of irony in rhetoric, is present in every story of the least structural sophistication. Now *peripeteia* depends on our confidence in the end; it is a disconfirmation followed by a consonance; the interest of having our expectations falsified is obviously related to our wish to reach the discovery or recognition by an unexpected and instructive route. It has nothing whatever to do with any reluctance on our part to get there at all. So that in assimilating the *peripeteia* we are enacting that readjustment of expectations in regard to an end which is so notable a feature of naive apocalyptic.[6]

The chronotype of the *linear*, teleological temporalization found in millennialism is closely related to Aristotle's formal definition of narrative as emplotment. A millennialist movement may posit an understanding of time as having stemmed from an originary point *A* that has now passed to point *B* and is rapidly moving toward eschatological closure at point *C*. As a general feature, either points *B* or *C* or both are understood as being utterly unique in the history of the world; nothing like this situation has ever been seen on heaven or earth previously. As a rule, if that uniqueness is found at point *B*, the movement is utopian. If it is found at point *C*, the movement is apocalyptic.[7]

Thus, linear time connects the past and present with the future in a causal relationship, which, through the deferrals of arriving at the closure of point *C* incrementally invests the closure itself with importance. Linear time as it is found in narrative, however, is not limited to reinforcing and validating the originary beliefs as they are understood by the group—it is also creative and generative of new meaning. In discussing Greimas' theory that the quest narrative aims at restoring a previous order, Ricoeur adds a generative possibility—the quest may not only restore an order, it may also create a new one. Ricoeur argues,

> The test, the quest, and the struggle may not therefore be reduced to the role of being the figurative expression of a logical transformation. The latter is instead the ideal projection of an eminently temporalizing operation. In other words, the mediation realized by the narrative is essentially practical, either, as Greimas suggests, in that it aims at restoring a prior order that is threatened, or in that it aims at projecting a new order that would be the promise of salvation.[8]

Thus, a linear construction of narrative time seeks to make the literary past, present, and future into a coherent whole. The reader's belief that the end will justify and elucidate the present is the sense-making position that not only gives credence to the current *peripeteia* but ironically reinforces and requires digressions from achieving closure. The linear emphasis of this chronotype is in service of creating consonance and meaning. In *Time and the Novel* Patricia Tobin summarizes,

> [L]ineal [sic] decorum pervades the structure of realistic narrative: All possibly random events and gratuitous details are brought into an alignment of relevance, so that at the point of conclusion all possibility has been converted into necessity within a line of kinship—the subsequent having been referred to the prior, the end to the beginning, the progeny to the father.[9]

Narrative time is not only coherent, it is necessary and causal.

The second category, *mimetic* or repetitive chronology, is also generative, albeit in a different manner. The mimetic chronotype indicates the re-playing of a previous historical or textual event with a new outcome.[10] This chronotype enacts a relationship of similarity or appropriation which is a sense-making position with reference to the beginning that is, in the present, finally going to come to its appropriate closure which it failed to do the first time. For example, the Mormons, by appropriating Hebrew Scripture, could view persecution by the American government as necessary and even sacred by associating themselves with the holy trials of the Jewish patriarchs in Babylonian captivity. The chronotype, however, is not only repetitive but also generative of new meaning—the new Moses would reach the promised land and the Mormons would create the utopia divinely conferred on them by superseding the Jews as chosen.

In *Fiction and Repetition* J. Hillis Miller argues that this mimetic model in literature is a metaphoric process. The assimilation of the originary text-world with the contemporary one generates new meaning by an act of resemblance. Miller writes,

> What Deleuze calls 'Platonic' repetition is grounded in a solid archetypal model which is untouched by the effects of repetition. All the other examples are copies of this model. The assumption is such a world gives rise to the notion of a metaphoric expression based on genuine participative similarity or even identity, as when Gerard Manley Hopkins says he becomes Christ, an 'afterChrist', through the operation of grace… The validity of the mimetic copy is established by its truth of correspondence to what it copies.[11]

Miller's argument is especially important in emphasizing that each copy is made from the original that is not diminished by the existence of copies. This form of mimesis is therefore differentiated from the creation of simulacra, which are copies of the copies, and at least in the Platonic schema become increasingly polluted with alloys the farther they are generated from the original. What is missing from Miller's analysis, however, is that the mimetic act of copying is always-already an act of interpretation of the original, and how the original mythos is understood will determine how it is socially or textually repeated to new ends.

In *The Anxiety of Influence* Harold Bloom articulates this process in the case of a poet 'giving birth to his own father', as Bloom borrows from Kierkegaard, in the interpretation of a precursor. Bloom states:

> A poet swerves away from his precursor, by so reading his precursor's poem as to execute a *clinamen* [a creative mis-reading or misprision] in relation to it. This appears to be a corrective movement in his own poem, which implies that the precursor poem went accurately up to a certain point but then should have swerved precisely in the direction that the new poem moves… The poet antithetically 'completes' his precursor, by so reading the parent-poem as to retain its terms but to mean them in another sense, as though the precursor had failed to go far enough.[12]

The mimetic chronotype is not only repetitive but also generative. Narrative or millennialist groups that deploy mimesis, the act of imitating a precursor, do so with a different outcome in mind, an improvement on the original text. The 'return' to a paradisiacal Eden, in which *Endzeit* is *Urzeit*,[13] does not accurately articulate the project of millennialism: the second Eden, promised land, or apostolic purity is different not only in time but also in nature and composition. By constructing the outcome of eschatological change as a return to but also an improvement on the original state, millennialism creates new religious meaning and expressions.

Nonetheless, the mimetic chronotype is as concerned with closure as the linear chronotype is: both seek to make a sensible whole which produces narrative coherence and confers meaning on time and experience. By focusing on the end of time as the locus of religious meaning in the present, millennialists who construct time as mimetic and repetitive interpret the past such that it will cohere with the intended future and the present. The emphasis on closure retrospectively creates the past. In *Reading for the Plot* Peter Brooks articulates this phenomenon in narrative:

> The very possibility of meaning plotted through sequence and through time depends on the anticipated structuring force of the ending: the interminable would be meaningless and the lack of an ending would jeopardize the beginning. We read the incidents of narration as 'promises and annunciations' of final coherence: across the bulk of as yet unread middle pages, the end calls to the beginning, transforms and enhances it.[14]

Religion writ large is implicated in the acts of temporalization and the creation of meaning in relation to time. However, the distinction between the phenomenon of millennialism and the more general acts of temporalization in all religion is a distinction of both depth and purpose. As Ricoeur writes of the novel,

> All fictional narratives are 'tales of time' inasmuch as the structural transformations that affect the situations and characters take time. However, only a few are 'tales about time' inasmuch as it is the very experience of time that is at stake in these structural transformations'.[15]

Millennialism is preeminently a tale about time.

History as Epistemology

While I have made numerous claims about similarities between narrative and millennialism, they are nonetheless clearly different beasts with different functions in the world. Furthermore, it would be too facile to state that narrative is secular millennialism and millennialism, religious narrative: while both strive toward and resist closure, each refers to discrete

concepts. While each is ordered and temporalized, the atoms of information that each orders are radically different.

Novels order fictive but nonetheless recognizable elements; people or
aliens or bunnies encounter challenges that emerge through fictive time
and are resolved in closure. Millennialism orders history as it is perceived
by the group: the elements are predetermined by experience and theological belief. While there is room for choices in that historical schema—
for example, a group may choose Revolutionary America as its point of
origin rather than the apostolic church—the elements that constitute the
past that is driving toward closure are understood as given. Given, however, is not to say objectively true or without a great deal of interpretive
spin: the apostolic church and Revolutionary America are themselves
ordered and sanitized through the imaginative process of making them
originary and most often pure.

This is to say, novels and millennialism do different work, but they do
their works similarly. Novels create chaos and then order it; millennialism perceives chaos and then orders it. Both engender faith in time and
the eventual achievement of appropriate closure. However, the participant's concept of what is at stake in creating this temporal order is
incommensurate.

The distinction is analogous to the difference between fantasy and
memory: neither imaginative project participates in the phenomenologi-
cally 'real', yet both invoke reality by referring to elements which do exist
in it, or at least may.[16] In fantasy, elements of reality are imagined and
then set in motion.[17] I may imagine that I am a Rumanian Countess who
enjoys terrorizing the local opera company. While all of the elements of
this fantasy exist, they do not do so together to the best of my knowledge,
and they certainly do not do so with me as a central player. On the other
hand, if I seek to understand a paralyzing phobia of snakes, I may go to a
therapist who will plumb my memories until a satisfactory explanation is
determined. My memories are no more 'real' than my being a Countess;
however, they can be ordered and interpreted in such a way as to do real
work in the world and perhaps lessen my fear of snakes.

Many novels, of course, participate in the ordering of history and act
as an instrument of knowing about the world. Insofar as this is the case,
these novels refer to reality. However, millennialism necessarily takes this
course, and is understood as divinely sanctioned. Both create meaning in
relation to an end; narrative closure is provisional, however, whereas millennial closure is ultimate.

The heart of the matter is the difference between the forms of temporalization. Novels believe themselves to be about aesthetics or enter-

tainment; millennialism believes itself to be about epistemology. Both structure time into meaningful patterns, but to different ends. Both postpone closure. Novels eventually achieve closure, whereas millennialism as a rule does not. The distinction, I propose, is grounded in the different work that each does: closure is an aesthetic requirement for narrative. The creation of coherence out of chaos dictates that once the aliens have been defeated or the heroine married off, wholeness has been achieved and therefore the chaos, or the very content of the novel, has ended.

Millennialism is denied this possibility because it is an epistemic project; should closure ever be achieved, the millennialist project itself, as a sense-making tool, would become moot. The believer is thus left with irreconcilable options: agree that wholeness has been achieved and then abandon the entire world-view in which this was made possible, or deny that closure has been achieved and maintain the world-view that seeks it. Closure must be postponed because millennialism itself has created an epistemic paradox: history has been ordered as a plot with God as the author. Time is reliable and current difficulties are invested with sacred meaning. Closure will be achieved when the world ends, which, so far, it clearly has not. To abandon the storyline is to abandon the entire structure of epistemology and to run the risk of rendering history and current trials meaningless.

Clearly, the more urgent the millennialism the more likely it is that the epistemological structure will need to be abandoned or revamped. As is the case with the Millerites, who predicted the end of the world in 1843, there were several attempts to postpone closure within the millennialist project first. Following indisputable evidence that the world had not ended as predicted, many followers fell away from the millennialist world-view.[18] Some attempted to rework the millennialist understanding of history and continue to defer closure such that millennialism continued to function as a structure of knowledge about the world. In general, the more immediately expected the millennium is, the more it endangers its own ability to make sense of the world when it has been disproven.[19] As an epistemological tool, millennialism must be rejected or reformulated when it shows itself to be flawed.

The heart of the matter is that millennialism backs its believers into an epistemic corner: history is subsumed into God's plot, events are rendered meaningful and suffering is never random because closure is close at hand. However, closure is hardly ever close at hand, and millennialists must choose between recognizing this and thus destroying their sense-making apparatus or finding ways to defer not only closure but also the expectation of it. The ethos of millennialism itself must perpetuate itself in order to continue making sense of the world.

The experience of time is the locus of millennialism, which in the final analysis appears to me to produce a second paradox: the end of time is understood as a given by millennialists (biblical literalness is the most obvious case). By focusing on that as a fact, millennialists subvert time as closural; by delaying closure in order to keep their epistemology intact, millennialists rebel against the structure of time as closural.

The form that this paradox takes, I propose, is a dialectic between history and imagination. History is of course interpreted; in fact, the entire project of millennialism may be summarized as the interpretation of history as causal and meaningful, and this is an imaginative act. However, it is not understood to be interpreted. It is understood to be self-evident. Millennialism is thus produced in the theoretical naiveté of belief: it attains its force from the obfuscation of the difference between fact and interpretation.

This gap between the given and the interpreted again shares resonances with literary theory. In his discussion of Hegel in *Truth and Method*, Hans-Georg Gadamer argues that the doing of history masquerades as factual and self-evident, when in practice historians treat history as literary artifacts which must be understood on their own terms.[20] He writes:

> Thus the resistance to the philosophy of world history drove history into the wake of philology. Its pride was to conceive the continuity of world history not teleologically, nor in the style of pre- or post-romantic enlightenment, in terms of a final state which would be the end of history, a day of judgment for world history, as it were. But for the historical school there exists neither an end of history nor anything outside it. Hence the whole continuity of universal history can be understood only from historical tradition itself. But this is precisely the claim of literary hermeneutics, namely that the meaning of a text can be understood from itself. *Thus the foundation for the study of history is hermeneutics.*[21]

Thus millennialism, the direct religious analog to the philosophical view of history as a single whole, makes the categorical error of mistaking interpretation for fact. It 'reads' history as meaningful, but fails to recognize that it is reading, which is always-already an act of interpretation. However, it is precisely in the slippage between imagination—which constructs the interpretation of history—and self-evident fact that millennialism may survive and mutate in the face of disconfirmation of the end. The move from millennialism into an established religion, which certainly does not always take place, is based on the success of recognizing that it has posited an interpretation, which, *de facto*, may be wrong.

And here the theoretical constructs provided by plot in narrative acquire real force in the sociological world of lived experience. Many millennialist experiments cannot survive their own expectations of the end of time; the ability to sustain a particular world-view depends on believers' abilities to adapt and defer the expectation of closure. I wish to suggest here a possible model for how some millennialist movements are able to overcome their expectation for ultimate closure. Strategies for delaying closure may result in the understanding that the narrative of time was misperceived. The rationale for overcoming cognitive dissonance may proceed something like this: we believed it to be the case that such-and-thus event signaled the breaking of the sixth seal, but in retrospect we were incorrect. We interpreted that event wrongly. This does not mean that all of our prior interpretations were incorrect, thus rendering our world-view senseless, but rather that we 'read' certain events in such a way as to appear to be fact when they were merely misinterpretations. Furthermore, this does not mean that future events will not factually signal the end of time or the reinstating of our dispensation.

Groups that succeed in making the move from what I am metaphorically calling 'fact' to 'interpretation' have thus cut the Gordian knot of millennialism. Their epistemological structure of the narrative of history may stay intact, although it would be understood to be more provisional and open to mistakes than it would have initially. God may continue to write the plot of history, but its readers are fallible.

Furthermore, this situation may give some insight into why millennialism seems to be such a textually-related event. Not only are concepts of time and the suspension of closure epitomized in narrative, but textuality itself may provide the key to understanding that reading necessarily involves interpretation. Gadamer argues,

> What we mean by truth here can best be defined again in terms of our concept of play. The weight of the things we encounter in understanding plays itself out in a linguistic event, a play of words playing around and about what it meant. Language games exist where we, as learners—and when do we cease to be that?—rise to the understanding of the world.[22]

Millennialists read the world as a narrative and in so doing acquire an interpretation which they believe to be a fact. But the process of reading itself involves linguistic play, an inner-textual experience that may signal the interpretive act as one. The process of creating meaning along the lines of a novel engenders the possibility that the believers will come to view themselves as readers. Thus the dialectic between history and imagination is resolved, and the book of the world may continue to generate new meaning.

References

Anderson, Gary, 'The Garden of Eden and Sexuality in Early Judaism', in Howard Eilberg-Schwartz (ed.), *People of the Body: Jews and Judaism from an Embodied Perspective* (New York: State University of New York Press, 1992), 47-68.

Aristotle, *Poetics* (trans. Stephen Halliwell; London: Gerald Duckworth, 1987).

Bal, Mieke, *Narratology: Introduction to the Theory of Narrative* (trans. Christine van Boheemen; Toronto: University of Toronto Press, 1985).

Bloom, Harold, *The Anxiety of Influence* (London: Oxford University Press, 1966).

Brooks, Cleanthe, *The Well Wrought Urn: Studies in the Structure of Poetry* (New York: Reynal & Hitchcock, 1947).

Brooks, Peter, *Reading for the Plot: Design and Intention in Narrative* (New York: Alfred A. Knopf, 1984).

Festinger, Leon, *et al.*, *When Prophecy Fails* (Minneapolis: University of Minnesota Press, 1956).

Gadamer, Hans-Georg, *Truth and Method* (trans. Joel Weinsheimer and Donald G. Marshall; New York: Continuum, 1996).

Girard, Rene, *Violence and the Sacred* (trans. Patrick Gregory; Baltimore and London: The Johns Hopkins University Press, 1977).

Hume, David, *A Treatise of Human Nature* (ed. L.A. Selby-Bigge; Oxford: Clarendon Press, 1992).

Husserl, Edmund, *The Phenomenology of Internal Time-Consciousness* (trans. James S. Churchill; Bloomington: Indiana University Press, 1964).

Hutcheon, Linda, *A Theory of Parody: The Teachings of Twentieth-Century Art Forms* (New York: Routledge, 1985).

Kermode, Frank, *The Sense of an Ending: Studies in the Theory of Fiction* (New York: Oxford University Press, 1967).

Kort, Wesley A., *Modern Fiction and Human Time: A Study in Narrative and Belief* (Tampa: University of South Florida Press, 1985).

Miller, J. Hillis, *Fiction and Repetition: Seven English Novels* (Boston: Harvard University Press, 1985).

Ricoeur, Paul, *Time and Narrative*, II (trans. Kathleen McLaughlin and David Pellauer; Chicago: University of Chicago Press, 1985).

Rowe, David L., *Thunder and Trumpets: Millerites and Dissenting Religion in Upstate New York, 1800–1850* (Chico, CA: Scholars Press, 1985).

Tobin, Patricia, *Time and the Novel: The Genealogical Imperative* (Princeton, NJ: University of Princeton Press, 1978).

Notes

1.   Narrative closure refers here to the expectation of a story's end, in this case the story of history. It is the expectation, rather than the arrival, of closure that invests trust in the middle of the plot: this process is psychological on the individual level, seen most frequently in religious terms with the inevitability of death, particularly when a final judgment will retroactively determine the meaning of life. It is also sociological on the group level, seen most clearly in religious movements that achieve apocalyptic closure, willingly or not, as was the case with the Branch Davideans or Heaven's Gate. On the theoretical, narrative level, there are many fine works on the transformative effect the expectation of narrative closure has on the reader's experience of

plot, many of which I will discuss below. However, for an excellent starting place, see Mieke Bal, *Narratology: Introduction to the Theory of Narrative* (trans. Christine van Boheemen; Toronto: University of Toronto Press, 1985).

2.   Aristotle, *Poetics*, 1451a30 (trans. Stephen Halliwell).

3.   Paul Ricoeur, *Time and Narrative* (trans. Kathleen McLaughlin and David Pellauer; Chicago: University of Chicago Press, 1985), II, 8.

4.   Wesley A. Kort, *Modern Fiction and Human Time: A Study in Narrative and Belief* (Tampa: University of South Florida Press, 1985), 13.

5.   Aristotle, *Poetics* 1452a21–1452b10.

6.   Frank Kermode, *The Sense of an Ending: Studies in the Theory of Fiction* (New York: Oxford University Press, 1967), 18.

7.   The terms 'utopian' and 'apocalyptic' are not used here as mutually exclusive: it is historically accurate and perfectly possible to conceive of a millennialist movement in which both the present and the future do not resemble anything actualized on earth before.

8.   Ricoeur, *Time and Narrative*, 47.

9.   Patricia Tobin, *Time and the Novel: The Genealogical Imperative* (Princeton, NJ: University of Princeton Press, 1978), 7.

10.   The use of the term 'mimetic' means solely that which is imitative of a prior event or, in fiction, of reality. Value-laden uses of the word 'mimetic', such as those of Rene Girard who locates a drive toward violence in mimesis, are not implied in this work.

11.   J. Hillis Miller, *Fiction and Repetition: Seven English Novels* (Boston: Harvard University Press, 1985), 6.

12.   Harold Bloom, *The Anxiety of Influence* (London: Oxford University Press, 1966), 14.

13.   The formula *Endzeit=Urzeit* is frequently used in academic literature, often in association with messianic movements. This usage appears to me to be fundamentally epistemically flawed: a messiah who ushers in the new Eden will create an Eden with a messiah in it, not the Eden in Genesis. For a typical use of the *Endzeit=Urzeit* construction, see Gary Anderson, 'The Garden of Eden and Sexuality in Early Judaism', in Howard Eilberg-Schwartz (ed.), *People of the Body: Jews and Judaism from an Embodied Perspective* (New York: State University of New York Press, 1992), 47-68.

14.   Peter Brooks, *Reading for the Plot: Design and Intention in Narrative* (New York: Alfred A. Knopf, 1984), 93-94.

15.   Ricoeur, *Time and Narrative*, 101.

16.   For a discussion of the temporal differences between fantasy and memory, see Edmund Husserl, *The Phenomenology of Internal Time-Consciousness* (trans. James S. Churchill; Bloomington: Indiana University Press, 1964), 68-79.

17.   For another classical discussion of the distinction between memory and fantasy, see David Hume, *A Treatise of Human Nature* (ed. L.A. Selby-Bigge; Oxford: Clarendon Press, 1992), especially Book I, 'Of the Understanding'.

18.   For the foundational text on the Millerites, see David L. Rowe, *Thunder and Trumpets: Millerites and Dissenting Religion in Upstate New York, 1800–1850* (Chico, CA: Scholars Press, 1985).

19. However, scholarship has shown that the stronger the disconfirmation of a belief is, the more ardently people will continue to adhere to it. For this argument, see Leon Festinger, *When Prophecy Fails* (Minneapolis: University of Minnesota Press, 1956).

20. Gadamer is critiquing this position in literary theory and it certainly has come to pass that post-structuralist literary theory would not posit that a text can be interpreted merely from itself. This is an historical development from the school of the New Critics, a 1950s phenomenon, which posited that texts should be read in relationship only to themselves. More contemporary literary theory would argue that texts stand in relation to each other and are best understood at the crossroads of those other texts they are in conversation with. For the paradigmatic New Critical argument, see Cleanthe Brooks, *The Well Wrought Urn: Studies in the Structure of Poetry* (New York: Reynal & Hitchcock, 1947); for an excellent example of resonances between texts, see Linda Hutcheon, *A Theory of Parody: The Teachings of Twentieth-Century Art Forms* (New York: Routledge, 1985).

21. Hans-Georg Gadamer, *Truth and Method* (trans. Joel Weinsheimer and Donald G. Marshall; New York: Continuum, 1996), 199. Italics in the original.

22. Gadamer, *Truth and Method*, 490.

Four Stages in the Life of a Millennial Movement

Albert I. Baumgarten

The object of this paper is to generalize about the experience of millennial movements.[1] As part of that process I also intend to restore the intellectual link between the study of millennialism and cognitive analysis. Research into millennial movements and cognitive analysis shared an important juncture almost 50 years ago in the pioneering work of Festinger, Riecken and Schachter.[2] They have since parted ways, in particular as a result of the criticism directed against some of the conclusions of Festinger and his colleagues (see further below). I regard this separation as unfortunate. In my view millennial studies and cognitive analysis are like twins separated at birth in a comedy of errors, each of whom has gone its separate way. They need to be reunited in order to reach a happy intellectual ending, one that allows the greatest possible light to be shed on millennial movements.[3]

The generalizations to follow are not intended as a means of overcoming the diversity of millenarian experience, as reflected in the papers in this volume and elsewhere. Rather, to the contrary, I intend to explicitly embrace the diversity of that experience. I take the acknowledgement that there is no single standard millenarian vision in Judaism, Christianity, Islam or any other major religious tradition as one of the hallmarks of contemporary research on the topic.[4]

I suggest that we focus on four stages or phases in the life of a typical millennial group. The first phase is one of arousal, in which the message of the imminent end gets an audience. There are always people claiming that the end is near, but they are often regarded with disdain.[5] In the terms proposed by Richard Landes, the owls normally drown out the roosters in the barnyard.[6] When the message is dismissed its bearer usually retreats back into his or her 'normal' world, anxious to forget the whole episode.[7] What is special about the formation of a millennial movement is that for a variety of reasons circumstances are such that the millennial message attracts a responsive audience. Mutual validation—which is essential for the continuation of the process—then takes place between the bearer of the message and a community which accepts it as authoritative.[8]

There are many reasons for this heightened receptivity to the millennial message. Sometimes circumstances—success or despair—convince people that the end is near. Sometimes a date pregnant with meaning is critical. At a personal level, one circumstance deserves special mention. As Meeks has noted,[9] people whose place in life has undergone a drastic change, either a sudden rise or an acute fall, are especially aware of a sense of a world out of joint, and hence are unusually interested in a message that preaches that their situation is not anomalous, but part of a larger pattern of imminent cosmic change, soon to transform heaven and earth.

The second stage is the search for the 'Signs of the Times'. As it were, a spiritual radar is turned on to seek confirmation of the millennial message in a variety of contexts, including events of the age, both good and bad (sometimes even good and bad at the very same time),[10] chronological reckonings of different sorts and biblical interpretation. This search proceeds by triangulation: as many different independent lines of argument as possible are developed to confirm the conclusion that the end is in fact near. It is impossible to have too many signs of the times. Indeed, paradoxical as it may seem at first, every sign of the times that is found confirms the belief that the end is near, but also increases the urgency for finding more signs of the times. Heightened belief requires an ever higher level of confirmation.

Here, too, the role of a community in accepting these conclusions is vital,[11] as the search for signs of the times fills an important cognitive need, which requires collective confirmation. The members of virtually every millenarian group are well aware that there have been similar movements in the past, that have all disappointed. They are subject to the comment and criticism of friends and relatives, who fear that they have gone mad (compare the remarks concerning Jesus in Mk 3.21). They need to meet this criticism both to others and for themselves, and argue that 'this time it is for real'. An argument based on triangulation meets this need. Any one argument by itself, in its own terms, might not suffice, but the agreement of a number of independent lines of analysis confirms the inevitability of the imminent end. In this way, almost anything can become a sign of the times if a community agrees to grant it that meaning and incorporates it within its proofs of imminent redemption.

It is at times like these that millenarian enthusiasm has an ability to jump the boundaries of faith communities, arousal in one tradition 'infecting' another, with each community working out the significance of the signs of the times within the context of its beliefs.[12] Thus each group might produce its own set of calculations proving that the end is near, and while these calculations might have a different basis in the separate traditions they would concur that the end is imminent.[13]

For the third stage, I would like to borrow a term from the world of gambling, and designate it as 'upping the ante'. When one player increases the amount bet all the others who wish to remain in the game must increase their wagers as well. 'Upping the ante' thus has important consequences for the other players, and for that reason I prefer the term to other possibilities, such as 'going out on a limb', which can be done in isolation and has no equivalent social implications.

I suggest that there are moments when millennial movements need to 'up the ante', by forcing their members to accept risks which will increase solidarity and loyalty. At the simplest level movements 'up the ante' in order to take advantage of the bonds established between those who share dangers. At a next level is the common commitment of those willing to take the risk, as opposed to those apostates who refuse: the risk binds those who will share in the imminent blessings, unlike the apostates doomed to perdition. Designating and expelling these apostates also contributes to the sense of solidarity among those who endure. On an analogous plane, movements often attract 'floaters' who want to try out membership on their own terms for a period of time. These 'floaters' need to be encouraged to make a definite choice.[14] Alternately, those movements that take care of the needs of their members, feeding, clothing and housing them, may feel abused by 'free-loaders', who must be compelled to make a commitment that will justify the movement's investment.[15] Finally, if the risk involves anti-social or even illegal behavior it unites those who share in the 'crime', as their return to ordinary society is difficult if not impossible. When 'upping the ante' takes this form it may reinforce the anti-nomian tendencies apparent in many millennial movements.

There are a number of reasons why movements may go through a phase of 'upping the ante'. For Festinger and his socially scientific minded colleagues and followers, this may be a response to the minor disconfirmations along the way (which precede the more massive and supposedly decisive disconfirmation later in their experience, such as the death of the founder or the arrival of the 'final' date for redemption with no results)[16] which are a regular feature of the life of many millenarian groups. These minor disconfirmations create a need to demonstrate loyalty to the message in spite of the disappointment.[17] Stark and Bainbridge, by contrast, might point to the elusive promises made by leaders of such groups.[18] 'Upping the ante' is necessary in order to hold out a goal which recedes into the distance so as to serve as an on-going focus of commitment. A structuralist analysis, such as that favored by Mary Douglas, would stress the weak nature of leadership in groups of this sort, leading to inevitable competition within the group and tension between members. In order to control this danger and prevent defection, the greatest threat of all, measures must always be taken to assure the faithfulness of members.[19]

'Upping the ante' can take many different forms, that strike an outside observer as ranging from the most benign to the most extreme examples of anti-rational behavior. Propagandizing, revealing the messianic secret, or setting a date for the end are all examples of more benign versions of 'upping the ante'. The accepted sanctity of a widely revered holy place (such as Jerusalem) can also play such a role. Thus when a group moves the focus of its activities to such a center it raises the stakes, as what happens at a locus of sanctity is of greater significance than what happens in some peripheral settlement.[20] At other times, 'upping the ante' can be very anti-rational: a movement may provoke the authorities, go out to face an overwhelming military force, encourage its members to sell their property, not to plant or harvest their crops, or even to jump int the sea, expecting it to part as for the Israelites at the Exodus.

As part of 'upping the ante' some sacrifice of individual identity for the sake of commitment to the movement may also be demanded. The extent of this sacrifice may vary, from a change of lifestyle within the original social context, to the transfer of private property to the group, to transferring one's commitment from the biological family to sectarian brothers (in matters of commercial life, family arrangements such as marriage, education of children, and divorce, or in plans for burial). In more extreme instances, believers may be asked to abandon their original social context to live in the new communal setting, to sacrifice their sexual identity (celibacy), or even to commit suicide.

The consequences of a successful 'bet on the millennium' can be far-reaching. The reinforcement it provides that the end is truly at hand can change the way one lives (see the preceding paragraphs) and yield a certainty that is resistant to almost any sort of disconfirmation. Assured that millennial time is in effect, all possibilities seem realistic. Individuals and movements feel empowered to seek and achieve at a higher level than ever (in a sense, 'upping the ante' once more, so that the cycle spirals upward, feeding on itself), and attain success more regularly.

The last phase, disconfirmation and its aftermath, has been the subject of much research. As we have learned, we need to be careful lest we overstate the absolute decisive nature of disconfirmation as it appears to an outsider.[21] An insider, by contrast, may avoid the conclusion by reinterpretation, mythologization, spiritualization, invoking the idea that the failure is a delay intended to test the faithful, or scapegoating, to mention only a few among a variety of other means.[22] The ante is sometimes raised even higher: the presumed messiah now dead had, in fact, been resurrected.[23] The New Testament supplies at least two examples: as discussed more fully below, some people believed that John the Baptist had been resurrected as Jesus, while the belief that Jesus' disciples found an empty grave and that if Jesus was not in the grave he must be somewhere in the divine realms, is fundamental to Christianity.[24] At an even greater extreme, divine status may be claimed for the messiah who seems to have failed.[25] Paradoxically, from the perspective of the outsider, for the insider, 'disconfirmation' can even become the most important mark of truth: the messianic 'failure' was all part of the original plan of salvation, from the outset. Hope once raised is not so easily quashed; the pleasures of living in millennial time are not easily relinquished. It is remarkable just how powerful faith can be, and how resistant to disconfirmation.[26] Sometimes, a prophecy of the end, which has long since been disconfirmed by our standards can re-emerge anew generations later.[27]

Nevertheless, in most recorded examples, the disillusion ultimately proves decisive, and groups must make the transformations necessary to re-enter normal time. Experience must now be re-interpreted in light of what has happened,[28] but these difficult moments may also be ones of great social creativity, as the vision of a new world to come (held in times of expectation of imminent upheaval) does result in change in the bad old world which has remained. Millennial hopes remove many of the restraints of the imagination because the ordinary means of repression of new ideas are less effective at times of millennial excitement, and the hope of the dawn of a new world allows possibilities thus far inconceivable to seem feasible. A new social order can be imagined as one arranged very differently than in the past, hence creativity can flourish at these times, and dreams of a new heaven and a new earth experienced in millennial time may come to shape normal time in new ways, so that many unanticipated consequences may ensue.[29]

As in all previous phases, the consent of the community to the interpretation is crucial, and may lead to experimentation with several notions until one agreed understanding is fixed. Accordingly, this is a time when factionalism may be rife (perhaps as much as in the period when hopes of imminent redemption are high, although for other reasons).[30] Some disappointed members defect as a result of disconfirmation. In both ancient and modern examples those who desert the faith are likely to be denounced by those who remain.[31] If those who leave first are members with a lower level of commitment, the remnant will be composed (on the whole) of those whose commitment level was higher. The experience of defection can push that remnant to demand even higher proofs of loyalty, thus reinforcing the extremist tendencies of the group. For those who do leave the moment of departure is important for their relative status in their own eyes. Whenever that decision was taken by any individual, all those who left before were traitors and all those who left afterwards were fools.[32]

The message may also mutate and take new forms, as I believe was the case when Herod Antipas ordered the execution of John the Baptist. The latter's disciple, Jesus, set out to promulgate the teaching of his master, perhaps even re-doubling his efforts as proof that his faith had not been shaken.[33] Yet, in the process, Jesus discovered his own role as miracle worker and healer. Thus, from first to last, Jesus of the gospels claimed to be continuing the work of his master (see Mk 1.14-15 and 11.29-33). Nevertheless, the disciple's activity, in fact, transformed that of his teacher. We have no account of John ever performing a miracle during his lifetime (cf. the explanations of the miracles performed by Jesus as due to his being the *resurrected* John, Mt. 14.2. Mk 6.14, 16; see also Jn 10.41: the living John 'gave us no miraculous sign'). Jesus also taught a new central ritual, the eucharist (as opposed to baptism, which enters only through the back door in the New Testament, Mk 16.16; compare Mt. 28.19). Under the circumstances it is not surprising that Jesus was criticized for acting so differently from his predecessor, for not fasting, Mk 2.18-22.[34] Perhaps Jesus justified his revision of John's message by means of the argument that the law and prophets were no longer binding as a consequence of the death of John (Mt. 11.11-15; Lk. 16.16). When a new wave of imminent expectation of redemption now focused on Jesus came to an abrupt end on the cross, new mutations of hope emerged, ultimately to lead to the birth of a new religion, neither Greek nor Jew (Gal. 3.28), a third race of mankind.[35]

Viewed from a long-term perspective, then, most disconfirmed millennial movements do not survive as distinct entities. Sooner or later they leave the stage of human history. We should not overstate the case against Festinger. Disconfirmation is real and has an impact that should not be denied. Nevertheless, for the few examples of such groups that successfully negotiate disconfirmation, remain attractive and continue to recruit and grow,[36] disconfirmation can prove to be a source of flourishing on a scale otherwise unimagined.[37] One example of such an outcome may be early Christianity.[38]

One final conclusion is that in analyzing the phases of millenarian groups, one must be sensitive to the various forms faith can take, appropriate to the different social and economic positions of members of these movements.[39] Millennial hopes are not the exclusive province of the dispossessed. We must learn to recognize the triumphalist and elitist varieties as well.[40] Millenarian hopes sometimes trickle from the top down, as well as rise from the bottom up among Jews, Christians and Muslims. There are, as it were, two entrances to the waiting room in which those who believe in imminent redemption congregate. Over one entrance is inscribed the notice that the downtrodden enter here. The other entrance is reserved for the victorious, convinced that they are marching with God to the glorious finale. While their dreams of the end may differ, in accordance with their circumstances, what unites these believers is at least as important as what divides them. Indeed, a group may shift from a triumphalist millennialism to one of despair, or vice versa, in the flicker of an eye.[41] Once one enters the waiting room, remaining there may be more important than the validity of the reason for which one came in, in the first place.

In conclusion, millennialism is one of the most powerful forces for change in social experience. It derives part of its power from its ability to convince believers in the certainty of a vision of a perfect and just world soon to replace the imperfect world we know. As that vision is variable it can suit groups of different sorts without difficulty: the dream can be suited to almost every dreamer. As that vision is malleable it can adapt to changing circumstances of the most diverse variety and still remain persuasive, at least to some.

References

Baeck, Leo, 'Das dritte Geschlecht', in Albert H. Friedlander, *et al.* (eds.), *Leo Baeck Werke, Band 4: Aus Drei Jahrtausenden, Das Evangelium als Urkunde der jüdischen Glaubensgeschichte* (Gütersloh: Gütersloher Verlaghaus, 2000), 228-34.

Balch, Robert, 'When the Light Goes out Darkness Comes: A Study of Defection from a Totalist Cult', in Rodney Stark (ed.), *Religious Movements: Genesis, Exodus, and Numbers* (New York: Paragon House, 1985), 11-63.

Baumgarten, Albert, *The Flourishing of Jewish Sects in the Maccabean Era: An Interpretation* (Leiden: E.J. Brill, 1997).

—'The Pursuit of the Millennium in Early Judaism', in Graham N. Stanton and Guy G. Stroumsa (eds.), *Tolerance and its Limits in Early Judaism and Early Christianity* (Cambridge: Cambridge University Press, 1998), 38-60.

—'The Role of Jerusalem and the Temple in "End of Days" Speculation in the Second Temple Period', in Lee I. Levine (ed.), *Jerusalem: Its Sanctity and Centrality to Judaism, Christianity and Islam* (New York: Continuum Press, 1999), 77-89.

Baumgarten, Albert I. (ed.), *Apocalyptic Time* (Leiden: E.J. Brill, 2000).

Berger, David, 'The Rebbe, the Jews and the Messiah', *Commentary* (September 2001), 23-30.

Burridge, Kenelm, *New Heaven, New Earth: A Study of Millenarian Activities* (Oxford: Basil Blackwell, 1969).

Cohen, Isaac, *Puritanism and the Rise of Modern Science* (New Brunswick/London: Rutgers University Press, 1990).

Douglas, Mary, and Gerry Mars, 'Terrorism: A Positive Feedback Game', *Human Relations* 56 (2003), 763-86.

Douglas, Mary, and Steven Ney, *Missing Persons: A Critique of Personhood in the Social Sciences* (Berkeley, CA: University of California Press, 1998).

Festinger, Leon, Henry W. Riecken and Stanley Schachter, *When Prophecy Fails: A Social and Psychological Study of a Modern Group that Predicted the Destruction of the World* (New York: Harper & Row, 1964).

Filoramo, Giovanni, 'The Case of Davide Lazzaretti', in Baumgarten (ed.), *Apocalyptic Time*, 363-72.

Fried, Johannes, 'Awaiting the Last Days: Myth and Disenchantment', in Baumgarten (ed.), *Apocalyptic Time*, 283-304.

Gager, John G., *Kingdom and Community: The Social World of Early Christianity* (Englewood Cliffs, NJ: Prentice-Hall, 1975).

Gorenberg, Gershom, *The End of Days: Fundamentalism and the Struggle for the Temple Mount* (New York: The Free Press, 2000).

Gruenwald, Ithamar, 'From Sunrise to Sunset—on the Nature of Eschatology and Messianism in Judaism', in *The Messianic Idea in Jewish Thought—A Study Conference in Honour of the Eightieth Birthday of Gershom Scholem Held 4–5 December 1977* (Jerusalem: Israel Academy of Sciences and Humanities, 1982 [Hebrew]), 16-36.

Hill, Christopher, *The World Turned Upside Down—Radical Ideas during the English Revolution* (Harmondsworth: Penguin, 1975).

—*The English Bible and the Seventeenth-Century Revolution* (Harmondsworth: Penguin, 1994).

Hunt, William, *The Puritan Moment* (Cambridge, MA: Harvard University Press, 1983).

Lamont, William, *Godly Rule: Politics and Religion 1603–60* (London: Macmillan, 1969).

Landes, Richard, 'Lest the Millennium Be Fulfilled: Apocalyptic Expectations and the Pattern of Western Chronography', in Werner Verbeke, Daniel Verhelst and Andries Welkenhuysen (eds.), *The Use and Abuse of Eschatology in the Middle Ages* (Leuven: Leuven University Press, 1988), 137-211.

Landes, Richard, 'On Owls, Roosters and Apocalyptic Time: A Historical Method for Reading a Refractory Documentation', *Union Seminary Quarterly Review* 49 (1996), 41-65.

Lewis, Bernard, 'An Apocalyptic Vision of Islamic History', *Bulletin of the British School of Oriental and African Studies* 13 (1950), 308-338.

Meeks, Wayne, *The First Urban Christians: The Social World of the Apostle Paul* (New Haven, CT: Yale University Press, 1983).

Merton, Robert, 'The Unanticipated Consequences of Purposive Social Action', *American Sociological Review* 1 (1936): 894-904.

O'Leary, Stephen, 'When Prophecy Fails and When it Succeeds: Apocalyptic Prediction and the Re-entry into Ordinary Time', in Baumgarten (ed.), *Apocalyptic Time*, 341-62.

Penton, Michael, *Apocalypse Delayed* (Toronto: University of Toronto Press, 1985).

Qimron, Elisha, and John Strugnell, *Discoveries in the Judean Desert X, Qumran Cave 4: V—Miqsat maase ha-Torah* (Oxford: Oxford University Press, 1994).

Ravitzky, Aviezer, *Messianism, Zionism and Jewish Religious Radicalism* (Chicago: University of Chicago Press, 1996).

Reeves, Mary, and Warwick Gould, *Joachim of Fiore and the Myth of the Eternal Evangel in the Nineteenth Century* (Oxford: Clarendon Press, 1987).

Scholem, Gershom, *Major Trends in Jewish Mysticism* (New York: Schocken Books, 1961).

—'Towards an Understanding of the Messianic Idea in Judaism', in *idem, The Messianic Idea in Judaism and Other Essays on Jewish Spirituality* (New York: Schocken Books, 1971), 1-36.

Smith, Morton, 'What is Implied by the Variety of Messianic Figures?', *Journal of Biblical Literature* 78 (1959), 66-72.

Stark, Rodney, 'How Sane People Talk to the Gods: A Rational Theory of Revelation', in M. Williams, C. Cox and M. Jaffee (eds.), *Innovation in Religious Traditions—Essays in the Interpretation of Religious Change* (Berlin and New York: W. de Gruyter, 1992), 19-34.

—*The Rise of Christianity: A Sociologist Reconsiders History* (Princeton, NJ: Princeton University Press, 1996).

Stark, Rodney, and William Bainbridge, 'Of Churches, Sects and Cults: Preliminary Concepts for a Theory of Religious Movements', *Journal for the Scientific Study of Religion* 18 (1979), 117-31.

—'Networks of Faith: Interpersonal Bonds and Recruitment to Cults and Sects', *American Journal of Sociology* 85 (1980), 1376-395.

—*A Theory of Religion* (New Brunswick: Rutgers University Press, 1996).

Stroumsa, Gedaliahu, 'Comments on Charles Hedrick's Article: A Testimony', *Journal of Early Christian Studies* 11 (2003), 147-53.

Szubin, Adam, 'Why Lubavitch Wants the Messiah Now: Religious Immigration as a Cause of Millenarianism', in Baumgarten (ed.), *Apocalyptic Time*, 215-240.

Notes

1.   For a discussion of the sense in which I use the term 'millennial' see A.I. Baumgarten, *The Flourishing of Jewish Sects in the Maccabean Era: An Interpretation* (Leiden: E.J. Brill, 1997), 153-56. As I employ the terms, the most general term is eschatological, which pertains to a belief in the end of days. Millennial movements are a sub-category, whose special quality is the belief that the end is at hand. This belief in an imminent end has social consequences, that is, the ability to change individual and group behavior. Messianic movements are a different sub-category. They specify that eschatological redemption will take place as the result of the activity of a human figure. Some messianic movements are also millennial (that is, the savior is already present or soon to appear/return) others are not. In non-millennial messianic groups the coming of the messiah may be expected hundreds of years hence, thus the belief has little or no social consequences. Thus messianic beliefs are not necessarily millennial. Apocalyptic, as I would employ the term, is the designation of a genre of literary works. These works contain revelations, often but not necessarily focusing on the end of days. On the use of terms compare R. Landes, 'Lest the Millennium Be Fulfilled: Apocalyptic Expectations and the Pattern of Western Chronography', in W. Verbeke, D. Verhelst and A. Welkenhuysen (eds.), *The Use and Abuse of Eschatology in the Middle Ages* (Leuven: Leuven University Press, 1988), 205-208.

2.   L. Festinger, H. Riecken and S. Schachter, *When Prophecy Fails: A Social and*

Psychological Study of a Modern Group that Predicted the Destruction of the World (New York: Harper & Row, 1964 [1956]).

3.   In this synthesis I focus less on how members of these groups behave when they believe the end is nigh, as the general conclusion has been well put by others. See, e.g., K. Burridge, *New Heaven, New Earth: A Study of Millenarian Activities* (Oxford: Basil Blackwell, 1969), 167: 'Knox's remarks concerning the alterations of scandal and rigorism characteristic of enthusiastic movements are not simply good history. The two go together, are integral parts of a transition process in which the new rules are still experimental and uncertain… It could be argued that orgies of sexual promiscuity…and the high idealism often connoted by the release from all desire are polar opposites. But the fact remains that both meet in precisely the same condition: that of no obligation.'

4.   See the essay that turned scholarship on ancient Judaism and Christianity, at the very least, in that direction, M. Smith, 'What is Implied by the Variety of Messianic Figures?', *Journal of Biblical Literature* 78 (1959), 66-72. For an analysis of the variety of millenarian beliefs from another perspective, see G. Scholem, 'Towards an Understanding of the Messianic Idea in Judaism', in *idem*, *The Messianic Idea in Judaism and Other Essays on Jewish Spirituality* (New York: Schocken Books, 1971), 1-36. Maimonides is the most prominent example of Scholem's rational messianism. Note that even in Maimonides' thought, in which the utopian element is at a bare minimum, and the continuation of the natural world as we know it at a maximum, the change to ensue at the end of days remains miraculous. Unlike all change in the unredeemed world, which ultimately proves to be reversible, this change is permanent. There will be no going back to the 'bad old days'.

The overlap between the conclusions argued by Smith and those elaborated by Scholem is not accidental. The extensive intellectual collaboration between these scholars was lifelong. It went back to Smith's youth, when he was seconded as assistant to Scholem when the latter came to New York in 1938 to deliver the lectures that were later published as *Major Trends in Jewish Mysticism*. See G. Scholem, *Major Trends in Jewish Mysticism* (New York: Schocken Books, 1961), ix. See further G.G. Stroumsa, 'Comments on Charles Hedrick's Article: A Testimony', *Journal of Early Christian Studies* 11 (2003), 147-53.

5.   They are told to 'take a Physic', and are usually regarded as medical cases. See, e.g., C. Hill, *The English Bible and the Seventeenth-Century Revolution* (Harmondsworth: Penguin Books, 1994), 243.

6.   R. Landes, 'On Owls, Roosters and Apocalyptic Time: A Historical Method for Reading a Refractory Documentation', *Union Seminary Quarterly Review* 49 (1996), 41-65.

7.   Compare what happens to contemporary sufferers of the 'Jerusalem Syndrome'. Enthused by their visit to the holy land, these tourists begin to act strangely, regularly believing they are biblical figures, but no one pays attention and they remain marginal. When they become dangerous (usually only to themselves) they are hospitalized, and the policy is to put them on the plane back home as quickly as possible. Returning home the victims of the 'Jerusalem Syndrome' are those most anxious to forget the whole embarrassing story.

8. R. Stark, 'How Sane People Talk to the Gods: A Rational Theory of Revelation', in M. Williams, C. Cox and M. Jaffee (eds.), *Innovation in Religious Traditions—Essays in the Interpretation of Religious Change* (Berlin/New York: W. de Gruyter, 1992), 19-34, esp. 28-29.

9. W. Meeks, *The First Urban Christians: The Social World of the Apostle Paul* (New Haven, CT: Yale University Press, 1983), 172-74. From this perspective, I consider it no accident that so many of the protagonists involved in the contemporary dispute over the Temple Mount have experienced great changes in their lives. See the excellent description of the leading figures in this controversy by G. Gorenberg, *The End of Days: Fundamentalism and the Struggle for the Temple Mount* (New York: The Free Press, 2000). In my opinion, the colorful background of the actors in this drama, as described by Gorenberg, is more than just good journalism.

10. See the concluding lines of 4QMMT (C20-22), as published by E. Qimron and J. Strugnell, *Discoveries in the Judean Desert X, Qumran Cave 4: V—Miqsat maase ha-Torah* (Oxford: Oxford University Press, 1994): 'we recognize that some of the blessings and curses have come about that are written in the book of Moses. And this is the end of days, when they will return upon Israel forever.' As the blessings and curses are not specified, modern scholars can only speculate what they might have been. For a modern equivalent in which simultaneous blessings and curses were seen as proof of imminent redemption see A. Ravitzky, *Messianism, Zionism and Jewish Religious Radicalism* (Chicago: University of Chicago Press, 1996), 107.

11. The community always plays an essential validatory role. Britain of the seventeenth century was a time when many radical religious groups were present, and in which confidence in the priesthood of all believers replaced the specialized educated priest as the authorized interpreter of the Bible. Nevertheless, it was the congregation which guaranteed the validity of interpretation, and served as a check on individualist absurdity. See C. Hill, *The World Turned Upside Down—Radical Ideas during the English Revolution* (Harmondsworth: Penguin Books, 1975), 95. See also W. Hunt, *The Puritan Moment* (Cambridge, MA: Harvard University Press, 1983), 121.

12. This ability to jump from one community to another is one of the marks of a successful innovation or notion. When different groups take up the same notion this is proof of its high utility.

13. In the year 2000, at a time when Christian expectation was high due to the turning of the millennium, some Jewish groups proposed a chronology of salvation based on the year 5760, the count in the traditional Jewish calendar. The world will become pure (i.e., eschatologically redeemed) in the year whose number is equal to the content of water in a traditional Jewish immersion pool. That pool contains a minimum of 40 *seahs* of water and each *seah* is equal in volume to 144 eggs: $40 \times 144 = 5760$.

14. Baumgarten, *Flourishing*, 51-55.

15. R. Stark, *The Rise of Christianity: A Sociologist Reconsiders History* (Princeton, NJ: Princeton University Press, 1996), 174-76; Baumgarten, *Flourishing*, 64-66.

16. An example of such minor disconfirmations in the recent case of Lubavitch would be the series of illnesses suffered by the Rebbe in his final years.

17. Festinger, Riecken and Schachter, *When Prophecy Fails*, 8-21.

18. See the discussion of the example of Scientology (not quite a millennial movement, but one modeled on psychotherapy in promising personal salvation, but nevertheless a good example of 'upping the ante') in R. Stark and W.S. Bainbridge, 'Of Churches, Sects and Cults: Preliminary Concepts for a Theory of Religious Movements', *Journal for the Scientific Study of Religion* 18 (1979), 127-28. In more abstract terms, see also R. Stark and W.S. Bainbridge, *A Theory of Religion* (New Brunswick: Rutgers University Press, 1996), 273-75.

19. M. Douglas and S. Ney, *Missing Persons* (Berkeley, CA: University of California Press, 1998), 145-53. See also M. Douglas and G. Mars, 'Terrorism: A Positive Feedback Game', *Human Relations* 56 (2003), 763-86.

20. See A.I. Baumgarten, 'The Role of Jerusalem and the Temple in "End of Days" Speculation in the Second Temple Period', in L.I. Levine (ed.), *Jerusalem: Its Sanctity and Centrality to Judaism, Christianity and Islam* (New York: Continuum Press, 1999), 77-89. Thus millennial movements often issue a challenge to the authority of the established leadership of their time and place. Such a challenge is far more powerful when delivered at a major sanctuary. In ancient Jewish terms this may help explain why Jesus was crucified after having preached at the sole Jewish sanctuary in Jerusalem, and not as a result of his activity in the Galilee.

21. See in particular S. O'Leary, 'When Prophecy Fails and When it Succeeds: Apocalyptic Prediction and the Re-entry into Ordinary Time', in Baumgarten (ed.), *Apocalyptic Time*, 341-62.

22. From among many studies of this topic see the insightful treatment of the topic by I. Gruenwald, 'From Sunrise to Sunset—on the Nature of Eschatology and Messianism in Judaism', *The Messianic Idea in Jewish Thought—A Study Conference in Honour of the Eightieth Birthday of Gershom Scholem Held 4–5 December 1977* (Jerusalem: Israel Academy of Sciences and Humanities, 1982 [in Hebrew]), 18-36.

23. The contemporary Lubavitch belief in the living messianic status of their dead Rebbe has generated the joke that there is a police guard around the Rebbe's tomb because there have been death threats.

24. The evidence for the belief in a resurrected Jesus is much more abundant than that for John, but this may be due to the nature of our sources on John, almost all Christian, that saw John as a potential rival to Jesus, whose claims must be minimized (see further below n. 34).

25. In addition to the obvious Christian case note the contemporary Lubavitch movement. Some believers are claiming divine status for the Rebbe. See D. Berger, 'The Rebbe, the Jews and the Messiah', *Commentary* (September 2001), 23-30, esp. 28-29.

26. This is a point where the pioneering work of Festinger, Riecken, and Schachter is most vulnerable and most in need of modification. The authors of *When Prophecy Fails* viewed disconfirmation virtually entirely as perceived by outsiders—as decisive, totally erasing any remnant of hope, and as a death blow to a millennial movement. These conclusions simply do not stand the test of examination in the light of experience (see above, n. 21; O'Leary observes that even in the case of 'Lake City' examined by Festinger and his colleagues, the movement did not disband in the aftermath of absolute disappointment; some believers remained stalwarts and their commitment became even stronger as time went on). I would note, as merely one example in

addition to the many others, that there are supposedly 30,000 believers in the messianic status of Sabbatai Zvi still living in Turkey, over three hundred years after this figure converted to Islam and died.

27. The on-going fascination in Europe with the thought of Joachim of Fiore is an excellent example of the recurring interest in millennial prophecy, long after its original context had passed, when it should have been considered long dead and irrelevant. See, for example, M. Reeves and W. Gould, *Joachim of Fiore and the Myth of the Eternal Evangel in the Nineteenth Century* (Oxford: Clarendon Press, 1987). For another example of old prophecies revived and reinterpreted long after their original time see B. Lewis, 'An Apocalyptic Vision of Islamic History', *Bulletin of the British School of Oriental and African Studies* 13 (1950), 308-38. The refounding of the Lazzaretist church in 1953, based on the theosophical-gnostic prophecies of two women (Lazzaretti himself had been killed August 18, 1878 and only a small group of followers kept his memory alive) is another example of revival of ideas long after their original context was gone. This revival was effective despite the fact that the message of Lazzaretti himself was rooted in the intellectual and social world of the nineteenth century. On these aspects of Lazzarettism see G. Filoramo, 'The Case of Davide Lazzaretti', in Baumgarten (ed.), *Apocalyptic Time*, 363-72.

28. Richard Landes compares the written record which may result to an account of the 'Emperor's New Clothes', as written by the courtiers. Of course they would not have written that they were fooled by the wicked tailors. Similarly, the authors of written accounts of millennial excitement, who know the end of the story, write from the perspective of disappointment and do not authentically express feelings and expectations when hopes for redemption were high.

29. See the classic study of R.K. Merton, 'The Unanticipated Consequences of Purposive Social Action', *American Sociological Review* 1 (1936), 894-904. That principle is brilliantly illustrated in less formal terms by the charming Frank Capra film, *A Wonderful Life*. The hero, George Bailey, has no idea of the effect he had on the world, and of the unintended consequences of his actions, until the 19-minute sequence in which Clarence the Angel, saving George from suicide in order to get his wings, shows George what a horrible place the world would have been without him.

The aftermath of disconfirmation is a prime time for unanticipated consequences. One example of such an unanticipated consequence would be the rise of modern science in Britain pioneered by men who themselves were believers in the millennial dream. This conclusion, first suggested by Merton himself in his doctoral thesis, in 1938, has since been widely discussed. See I.B. Cohen (ed.), *Puritanism and the Rise of Modern Science* (New Brunswick and London: Rutgers University Press, 1990); and J. Fried, 'Awaiting the Last Days... Myth and Disenchantment', in Baumgarten (ed.), *Apocalyptic Time*, 283-304.

30. To quote Richard Landes, once again, when hopes are high, as well as in the wake of disappointment there is no baseless hatred: all resentment against dissidents is justified as they may be about to cause a failure of hope or are already accused of being responsible for it.

31. For one ancient example see 1QpHab 7.5-14 where those who kept the faith when the end was delayed in coming are praised in contrast to those who weakened. For a modern example see the discussion of the Jehovah's Witnesses and of their

periodic crises and schisms in response to repeated failed prophecy of the end. See M.J. Penton, *Apocalypse Delayed* (Toronto: University of Toronto Press, 1985).

32. See R. Balch, 'When the Light Goes Out Darkness Comes: A Study of Defection from a Totalist Cult', in R. Stark (ed.), *Religious Movements: Genesis, Exodus, and Numbers* (New York: Paragon House, 1985), 11-63.

33. The nature of the relationship between John and Jesus was a matter of great sensitivity. The early phase of Jesus' life as a disciple of John was apparently a fact so widely known that it could not be denied. Yet this aspect of the life of Jesus suggested that Jesus was somehow inferior to John. This conclusion was awkward once a movement developed around the messianic role of Jesus, and even more awkward as believers in the special status of John remained active, at least in the generation of the first disciples of Jesus (Acts 18.24–19.7). Under these circumstances it is no accident that the New Testament placed a declaration in John's mouth, even before meeting Jesus, that he was merely the precursor of someone greater to come (Mk 1.7-8 and parallels). If this proclamation was authentic it might have meant that John understood himself not as the messiah, but as forerunner of the messiah. As Christians elaborated these ideas, however, John himself recognized that he was not fit to baptize Jesus. Rather, Jesus should baptize him (Mt. 3.13-15), thus making John himself testify to the higher status of Jesus.

34. Cf. Mt. 11.18-19 and Lk. 7.33-35 where Jesus and John were compared, but the comparison was made by Jesus and hence, obviously, was not intended to be unfavorable to him. Rather, it is a critique of the age: no matter what one does one is criticized. John neither ate nor drank, so he was suspected of being possessed. Jesus ate and drank, so he was called a glutton, a friend of tax gatherers and sinners.

35. See L. Baeck, 'Das dritte Geschlecht', *Leo Baeck Werke,* Band 4: *Aus Drei Jahrtausenden, Das Evangelium als Urkunde der jüdischen Glaubensgeschichte* (Gütersloh: Gütersloher Verlaghaus, 2000), 228-34.

36. The process of recruitment—in particular as analyzed by R. Stark and W.S. Bainbridge, 'Networks of Faith: Interpersonal Bonds and Recruitment to Cults and Sects', *American Journal of Sociology* 85 (1980), 1376-395—is such that under proper circumstances it may not be harmed by disconfirmation. Thus, if Lubavitch hassidim continue to recruit successfully in spite of (or better, as a result of) the death of their candidate for Messiah, they may be an example of the importance of social networks in recruitment that transcends whatever doctrine the new believer ultimately accepts. Disconfirmation may turn out to be an unanticipated blessing for them, as it was for the early Christians. See further A. Szubin, 'Why Lubavitch Wants the Messiah Now: Religious Immigration as a Cause of Millenarianism', in Baumgarten (ed.), *Apocalyptic Time,* 215-40.

37. Note the concluding musings of Festinger, Riecken and Schachter, *When Prophecy Fails,* 233, who speculate on what might have happened if the movement in 'Lake City' had been skillful proselytizers: 'Their ideas were not without popular appeal, and they received hundreds of visitors, telephone calls and letters from seriously interested citizens, as well as offers of money (which they invariably refused). Events conspired to offer them a magnificent opportunity to grow in numbers. Had they been more effective, disconfirmation might have portended the beginning, not the end.'

38. See especially John G. Gager, *Kingdom and Community: The Social World of Early Christianity* (Englewood Cliffs, NJ: Prentice-Hall, 1975), 39-49.

39. W. Lamont, *Godly Rule: Politics and Religion 1603–60* (London: Macmillan, 1969).

40. See further A.I. Baumgarten, 'The Pursuit of the Millennium in Early Judaism', in G. Stanton and G. Stroumsa (eds.), *Tolerance and its Limits in Early Judaism and Early Christianity* (Cambridge: Cambridge University Press, 1998), 38-60.

41. See Ravitzky, *Messianism, Zionism*, 193-206.

Part II
Approaches to Millennial History

The Beginnings of Islam as an Apocalyptic Movement

David Cook

The Early Ecumenical State of Islam

The importance of the development of Islam in the land of Syria during the seventh and eighth centuries has frequently been under-appreciated by scholars seeking to divine what the nature of the new faith was during this crucial period. According to the traditional Muslim historical interpretation, Arab tribesmen swept out of the Arabian Peninsula shortly after the death of the Prophet Muhammad in 632. Within the short time span of 10–15 years they conquered the lands of Syria, Iraq, Egypt and Persia, halving the territory of the ancient Byzantine empire based in Constantinople, and bringing the Sasanian Persian empire to a close. These tribesmen were inspired by the faith of Islam, and according to the Muslim interpretation of events, given divine aid to judge these two evil empires. The Byzantines and the Sasanians had engaged in a pointless war previous to the Muslim invasion lasting some 25 years and destroying nearly the entire region.

This interpretation, relying as it does upon divine intervention in human affairs, has not been well received by western scholars, who have offered more mundane interpretations. These range from the climatic changes, which apparently resulted in the desiccation of the Arabian peninsula (which according to this interpretation led to the exodus of tribesmen from the region), to the superior military tactics of the Bedouin against the trained armies of the Byzantines and Sasanians. Upon reviewing these western theories, one must honestly say that by comparison the theory of divine intervention still sounds more plausible. However, the above interpretations do not exhaust the possibilities for explaining how early Islam developed and why it conquered much of the classical world and the Iranian plateau. In order to work towards a theory, one must first examine the religious foundations of early Islam, and the nature of the energy feeding it. Because it is difficult to know what precisely the first Muslims believed, although most probably their beliefs differed from the normative Islam of the eighth century onwards, we will refer to the Muslims of the seventh century as 'proto-Muslims'.

We will start with the Qur'an, the revelation given to the Prophet Muhammad, and the one Muslim document universally acknowledged as dating from the early-seventh century. Reading the Qur'an, it is difficult to believe that the Prophet Muhammad truly thought in terms of founding a new faith. The text speaks more of reminding its audience of essential truths rather than bringing an entirely new ideology to the fore (Qur'an 88.21: 'Remind [the people] for you are only one who reminds' among many examples). Therefore, in a quest for the ideological birth-point of Islam, we must seek out those more ecumenical attitudes in the earliest Muslim religious literature and seek to bridge the gap between the pan-monotheistic message of the Qur'an and the aggressive spirit of the *jihad* as revealed in this early literature and the inscriptions preserved from the seventh century. For example, in the Qur'an,

> Say: 'O People of the Book [Jews and Christians], come to an equitable word between you and us, that we worship none but Allah, do not associate anything with Him and do not set up each other as lords besides Allah' (Qur'an 3.64).

This seems to be a most straightforward vision of the monotheism proclaimed in the Qur'an; the desire to build bridges, at least with the majority Christian population of the region. This verse is, of course, one among many other verses which have opposing viewpoints, yet it is significant by virtue of the fact that it is cited frequently in early documents sent from the proto-Muslims in embassies. The effort to build bridges with the Christians is stated more categorically in Qur'an 5.82:

> You will find the most hostile people to the believers to be the Jews and the polytheists; and you shall find the closest in affection to the believers those who say: 'We are Christians'. For among them are priests and monks, and they are not arrogant.

It is clear that the ecumenical basis is a belief in one God, which, although seemingly denied in the Qur'anic attacks upon the doctrine of the Trinity, still allows the very real possibility that Christians and, as we shall see, Jews as well, have a place in the pan-monotheistic creed being created. In the text of the Qur'an, the word used to describe the new community of faith is the word *mu'min* (believer), which is used dozens of times. The community was one of believers in the one God, whose belief was to be purified by the revelation of the Qur'an. By contrast, the words *muslim* or *islam* are only used adjectivally; that is, to describe the condition of a person who is submissive to God.

Although the revelation of the Qur'an ceased with the death of the Prophet in 632, the continued preaching of this message can be traced in many early traditions that have been preserved. Many of these traditions are associated with the Syrian Muslim community and have been preserved in collections such as that of al-Tabarani (d. 971), which tells us of this reality:

> I [Muhammad] was commanded to fight people until they say 'there is no god but God', and when they have said it, their lives and their property are protected from me, solely because of it (*illa bi-haqqihi*), and judgment upon them is in the hands of God.[1]

Those who are familiar with the tenets of Islam as they were to develop during the following three centuries will recognize the statement 'there is no god but God'—it is the first half of what would become the Muslim confession of faith 'There is no god but God and Muhammad is His messenger'. However, in this early version of that statement, the only element required is the basic profession of monotheism, which can be stated by both Jews and Christians as well as Muslims. Apparently the primacy of Muhammad's revelation was not important at this early stage. Indeed, we have documented evidence of Christians who are identified as Christians speaking the above confession of faith in a formal setting, using precisely this formula and being accepted *as* Christians.

> A Christian man began to speak [at the funeral of Hajjaj b. Yusuf, the viceroy of Iraq during the end of the seventh/beginning of the eighth centuries], and said: 'I bear witness that there is no god but God, and Salma b. Shayban[2] [the sub-governor of the region] will bear witness that Muhammad is the Messenger of God'. Then he began to speak [formally] and spoke well.[3]

Although there is no such parallel evidence for Jews, the probability is that they would have had a far less difficult time stating a confession which is very similar to the *shema* `: 'Hear O Israel, the Lord our God, the Lord is one God' (Deut. 6.4), which is said by Jews every day a number of times.

But the proto-Muslims went much further than this in their ecumenical outlook towards Christianity. Scholars of comparative religions have long noted that there is no evidence of any Christian polemics against Islam during the seventh and early-eighth centuries—a most uncharacteristic silence from a community, which had long specialized in polemic, apologetic and heresiography. When the first polemics do appear—from the pen of St John of Damascus, who was apparently a highly placed government functionary of the Umayyad dynasty—they insist upon declaring Islam (or the religion of the Saracens) a Christian heresy. Although this characterization can be interpreted in reductionist terms or as a simple misunderstanding, given the fact of the early Muslim literature, it may well have been simply a genuine indication of the Christian perception of the proto-Muslims.

The evidence for proto-Muslim attempts to find common ground with Christians also includes an inordinate focus upon the person and the mission of Jesus, even above and beyond his place in the Qur'an. (One should, however, note that this exaltation of Jesus has never compromised upon the absolute Muslim rejection of his divinity.) From early Syrian collections of religious material, cited by the great historian of the city of Damascus, Ibn `Asakir (d. 1171), we actually find confessions of faith in which Jesus is given more space than Muhammad:

> Whoever bears witness that there is no god but God—alone without any associate—and that Muhammad is His servant and His Messenger, and that Jesus is the servant of God and the son of His handmaiden (*ama*), and His Word which He cast upon Mary and a Spirit from Him, that paradise is true and hell, it is obligatory for God to let him enter whichever of the eight gates of paradise he wishes.[4]

It is very likely, in fact, that in this particular tradition the element of Muhammad's role is a later insertion by writers concerned with the position of Jesus in this confession of faith—for we have epigraphic evidence in which Jesus is mentioned alone in confessions of faith which are clearly from proto-Muslims—but even with the Muhammadan element present, the position of Jesus is striking.

Thus, the idea of 'belief' is separated from the idea of 'Islam'. The Believers, as they called themselves at this early period, were an ecumenical group, which sought to bring into its fold all who believed in God and the Last Day (a very frequent formula appearing in the Qur'an and the earliest Muslim religious literature). Their society is characterized by the following tradition, cited by Ibn Wahb al-Qurashi (d. 812) in one of the earliest collections that came from Egypt, which is reminiscent of the Sermon on the Mount (Mt. 5–7):

> 'You will never enter paradise until you believe, and you will never believe until you love one another (*tahabbu*), and make peace widespread between yourselves, loving one another, and not one of you will ever believe until his neighbor is secure from his injustices'. They said: 'O Messenger of God, what is *islam*?' He said: 'It is when the *muslimun* are at peace from his [the *muslim*'s] tongue and hand'. They said: ' [Then] what is belief?' He said: 'Those whom *ahl al-islam* have given surety over their blood and their possessions'.[5]

Most scholars who have tried to define the words *islam* or *muslim* have started from the evidence in the Qur'an. This evidence, however, is so contradictory that it is impossible to come to a single conclusion as to the meaning of these words. Therefore, assuming as we have that *islam* and *muslim* were not the primary designations of the community of proto-Muslims, we must turn to the early *hadith* literature to see how these words are used for a definition. There we find that these words are universally defined as people being at a state of peace with one other. Tradition after tradition reveals that these two facets of the early proto-Muslims, paradoxically, existed side by side. From other traditions we find that these *mu'minun* or Believers took as their foundation the statement that 'there is no god but God', while those who would eventually be called Muslims emphasized their absolute commitment to internal peace within the community. These proto-Muslims were at peace with God and with fellow human beings who believed in God and the Last Day (Qur'an 48.16), but at war with those who denied these basic realities. Belief during this proto-Muslim period is more of a personal and ecumenical quality, while *islam* belongs to the field of action, oftentimes fighting external enemies. With this understanding of the ideology of the proto-Muslims, and their ecumenical attitude toward Christians focused upon the figure of Jesus, let us now discuss the messianic kingdom which they sought to promote.

The Reality of the Apocalyptic Kingdom of the Umayyads

Jesus is not only a bridge between the early Muslims and the Christians in the confessional sense, but one of the most prominent figures in the apocalyptic future—he was the first Mahdi, the Muslim messiah. Although in the centuries following, as the polemical relationship between Islam and Christianity became ever more acrimonious, Jesus' position was diminished, it is clear that at this early time, Jesus is the one who is to usher in the messianic kingdom and the ultimate unity between the monotheistic faiths as described in the previous section. From the earliest collection of apocalyptic traditions in Islam, that of Nu`aym b. Hammad al-Marwazi (d. 844), we read:

> The Mahdi, Jesus, will send to fight the Byzantines…and he will remove the *tabut al-sakina* (probably the Ark of the Covenant) from a cave in Antioch. In it is the Torah which was revealed by God to Moses, and the Gospel which God revealed to Jesus. He will judge between the people of the Torah according to their Torah and between the people of the Gospel by their Gospel.[6]

Jesus' role is first of all a martial one: he is to defeat the Byzantines, slay the Antichrist and bring the conquests to a close. But he is simultaneously going to be an ecumenical messiah; each community of monotheists will continue to adhere to its own revelation, and not be converted to proto-Islam.

The sense of ecumenism is augmented by the presence not only of physical enemies such as the Byzantines as we will see, but by spiritual enemies such as the Antichrist. During the Umayyad period we find a number of instances where prominent figures in the society were accused of being the Antichrist, and some only barely escaped this accusation with their lives. Whereas in Muslim apocalyptic tradition as it later developed the figure of the Antichrist is clearly identified as a Jew, it is significant that during the more ecumenical proto-Muslim period only one of the six identifiable Antichrist scares involves a Jew. Apocalyptic expectations at this period did not identify the Jew as Other; as we will see it made an effort to include them.

This early sense of apocalyptic ecumenism is graphically described by the Muslim version of the Parable of the Workers (Mt. 20.1-16), again from al-Tabarani's collection of Syrian traditions:

> Your [length of] staying comparative to the communities previous to you is like that of between the afternoon prayers and the setting of the sun. The people of the Torah were given the Torah and worked with it until the middle of the day, then they could not [anymore], and were given *qirats* [as their wage]. The people of the Gospel were given the Gospel and worked with it until the mid-day prayer, and then they could not [anymore], and were given *qirats* [as their wage]. Then you were given the Qur'an, and you worked with it until the sun went down and were given double the *qirats*. The people of the Torah and of the Gospel said: 'Lord, these have less work and more wage [given to them]!' He said: 'Have I cheated you in your payments in any way?' They said: 'No'. He said: 'This is My bounty, given to whomever I wish'.[7]

Although this is basically a fair paraphrase of the New Testament parable, there are differences. For one, the version in Matthew lists a total of five groups hired throughout the day, and not only three, nor, of course, are they given the overt identifications as in this tradition. Second, the New Testament version is clearly designed to show the bounty of God towards his servants, to change their feelings from having been cheated by a hard task-master to generosity towards their fellow-workers. Although the original is eschatological, lacking the identifications given in the proto-Muslim version, it does not have any immediate consciousness of the end of the world. The proto-Muslims clearly saw themselves as working just before the end of the world, the rightful recipients of God's bounty, worthy to stand with the other previous faiths on an equal footing. But, crucially, this story does not deny God's reward to the Jews and the Christians, that this reward is deserved and will be given at the end of the world, as later Islamic doctrine would do—nor is this predicated in any way upon their reception of the message of Muhammad. Indeed, if there is an element of unworthiness among the three groups, it is on the part of the Muslims themselves. Their *sole* reason for receiving the same wage as the earlier groups did is the arbitrary decision of God, not the result of their own actions.

Nor was the judgment of the end to be long delayed. There are a large number of dateable apocalyptic predictions still extant in the early Muslim religious literature indicating that the proto-Muslims expected the world to come to an end either during the year 70/689–690 or during the year 100/717. The fact that these predictions are still available in such quantities long after the obvious disconfirmation discrediting the original prediction demonstrates the belief in this date and its power within the community. From the early (ninth century) *History of Daraya* (a town just outside Damascus), we read:

> A man came to the Messenger of God [Muhammad] and asked: 'O Messenger of God, what is the length of prosperity (*rakha'*) for your community?' He did not answer anything and the man asked three more times without receiving an answer, so the man turned away and then the Messenger of God said: 'Where is the questioner?' and he turned back. He said: 'You have asked me about something that no one in my community has ever asked about[8]—the length of the prosperity of my community is 100 years' and he said it two or three times, and then the man said: 'O Messenger of God, is there a principality [to appear] or a portent or a sign?' He said: 'Yes, swallowing up by the earth, earthquakes, and release of the bound demons upon the people'.[9]

According to this and many other similar traditions the end was not delayed until long after the Prophet's passing. It is odd, however, that the above tradition specifies that the Prophet had never been asked about the end of the world previously, as there are numerous instances in the Qur'an where he is asked precisely this question. If one compares the great pushes to conquest with the dateable predictions indicating the imminent end of the world, there is a striking correlation. Apparently the proto-Muslims believed themselves to have been allotted a bare 70 or 100 years in order to accomplish the goals of conquering the world, reforming and unifying belief in one God, and passing a messianic kingdom to Jesus who would rule it until the Last Judgment.

Part and parcel of this messianic kingdom was the construction of the Dome of the Rock in Jerusalem on the site of the First and Second Temples, which was destroyed in 70 CE. This structure, which is the earliest Muslim monument still standing today, possesses some of the earliest inscriptions in Arabic which are identifiably Muslim. These inscriptions are largely citations from the Qur'an and consist in their entirety of statements about Jesus, frequently attacking the doctrine of the Trinity and according Jesus the position of a prophet. Once again, this focus upon Jesus is striking. Though Trinitarian Christians in the final analysis see these inscriptions as an attack upon Christianity as a whole, it may very well be that the original intent was instead to focus upon purification of Christianity from the principal offensive element in the eyes of the early Muslims—the divinity of Jesus—and at the same time to focus upon Jesus as the man who would establish the messianic kingdom for both Christians and Muslims in the immediate future.

Nor were Jewish expectations ignored in this building. It is clear that Jews served in the Dome of the Rock for some 50 years after its construction as part of those venerating the site. From a very early tradition preserved in the literature in praise of Jerusalem by a local collector (al-Musharraf b. al-Murajja', fl. tenth century), the Umayyad builder of the Dome, `Abd al-Malik, is actually compared to King David:

> Ka`b found written in one of the books: 'Jerusalem—which is Bayt al-maqdis—and the Rock is called the Temple: I[10] will send to you My servant `Abd al-Malik who will build you and decorate you. I will return to Bayt al-maqdis its earlier dominion, and I will crown you with gold, silver and coral, and I will send My people to you, and I will place My Throne upon the Rock. I am the Lord God, and David is the king of the Banu Isra'il.'[11]

It is clear that in this early Muslim tradition, the position of `Abd al-Malik is that of a renewer. What is he renewing? Most probably a type of the Third Temple, remembering that the Jews during the Byzantine-Sasanian war of 602–628 had made an effort to rebuild this structure after Jerusalem fell to the Sasanians in 614. The Muslim apocalyptic literature speaks extensively of the Temple implements—such as the Table of shewbread, the altar, Ark of the Covenant and the Tablets of the Ten Commandments, among many other items—and indicates that the early Muslims felt that the purpose of the conquests was to find these elements, either in Rome or in Constantinople, and return them to Jerusalem where the Mahdi Jesus could use them in the worship of the true God.

In fact, much of the fighting of the first century of Islam is interpreted by the early apocalyptic literature in terms of vengeance for the destruction of the Temple in Jerusalem. About the future taking of Constantinople in Nu`aym's collection of apocalyptic prophecies, we find:

> I [Ka`b al-Ahbar] have heard that [the destruction of] Constantinople is in return for the destruction of Jerusalem, since she [Constantinople] became proud and tyrannical, and so is called 'the haughty'. She [the city] said: 'The throne of my Lord is built upon the waters, and I [the city] am built upon the waters'. God promised punishment [for it] on the Day of Resurrection, and said: 'I will tear away your decoration, and your silk, and your veil, I will leave you when there is [not even] a rooster crowing in you, I will make you uninhabited except for foxes, and unplanted except for mallows, and the thorny carob, I will cause to rain down upon you three [types] of fire: fire of pitch, fire of sulfur, and fire of naphtha, and I will leave you bald and bare, with nothing between you and the heavens. Your voice and your smoke will reach Me in the heavens, because you have for such a long time associated [other deities] with God, and worshipped other than Him.

> Girls who will have never seen the sun because of their beauty will be deflowered, and none of you who arrive will be able to walk to the palace (*balat*) of their king [because of the amount of loot]—you will find in it the treasure of twelve kings of theirs, each of them more and none less than it [the one before], in the form of statues of cows or horses of bronze, with water flowing on their heads—dividing up their treasures, weighing them out in shields and cutting them with axes. This will be because of the fire promised by God which will make you hurry, and you will carry what of their treasures you can so you can divide them up in al-Qarqaduna [Chalcedon].[12]

This prophecy is reminiscent of the fall of Babylon the Great in Revelation 18; and the fall of Tyre in Ezekiel 28 (where we have a very similar quotation in v. 2: 'In the pride of your heart you say: I am a god; I sit on the throne of a god in the heart of the seas'). But the punishments described are mostly those from Revelation and show the religious nature of the purification being promised to the evil city of Constantinople. It is hardly surprising, therefore, that the proto-Muslims mounted two major expeditions to attack the city and very nearly conquered it. The above tradition brings us to the last part of the early Muslim ideology: the redemptive nature of the fighting.

The Centrality of *Jihad* as a Spiritual Exercise

Clearly *jihad* was a major part of the proto-Muslim belief. Fighting was what enabled the proto-Muslims to conquer unimaginable tracts of territory, and forced the peoples around the Mediterranean basin and the Iranian plateau to take the previously despised tribesmen seriously. This fighting is closely connected to the apocalyptic aspirations of the proto-Muslims as we have detailed above. Taken from the earliest surviving book of *jihad*, that of `Abdallah b. al-Mubarak (d. 797), who lived most of his life in Syria, we read:

> Behold! God sent me [Muhammad] with a sword, just before the Hour [of Judgment], and placed my daily sustenance beneath the shadow of my spear, and humiliation and contempt on those who oppose me, and who-ever imitates a group is [numbered] among them.[13]

This concise theological statement is one of the most important early traditions gathering together under one heading the elements the proto-Muslims found to be important. The Prophet is pictured as sent by God with a sword and a spear, just before the Day of Judgment. This is a blunt statement that clearly indicates the method through which proclamation of the new revelation to the world was to be made. The belief in God's personal intervention on the side of the early Muslims is clear throughout the literature—here the believer is promised victory, because God has already decreed humiliation and contempt for the opponents of Islam. In early Islam, it is clear, the fighting was not only the method of proclama-tion, but also the means by which the individual believer was redeemed.

> Yazid b. Shajara [commander of the Muslim army under Mu`awiya, 661–680] said: 'Swords are the keys to paradise; when a man advances upon the enemy, the angels say: 'O God, help him!' and when he retreats, they say: 'O God, forgive him!' The first drop of blood dripping from the sword brings forgiveness with it for every sin…[14]

In other words, the practice of *jihad* was roughly equivalent in its redemptive and salvific qualities for the early Muslim as the doctrine of the cross was for the Christian. Indeed, we find interspersed throughout the literature statements such as 'only the sword wipes away sins'—almost certainly a response to the equivalent Christian statement 'only the cross wipes away sins'. Even the Arabic words sound very similar.

The fighting was in and of itself a spiritual exercise that bound dis-parate groups together.

> Abu Misbah al-Himsi said: While we were traveling in the land of the Byzantines, during a summer raid led by Malik b. `Abdallah al-Khatha`mi, the latter passed by Jabir b. `Abdallah who was walking and leading his mule. Malik said to him: 'O Abu `Abdallah, ride, for God has granted you a mount'. Jabir said: 'My mount is fine; I am not in need of it. I heard the Messenger of God say: "Whoever dusts their feet in the path of God [*jihad*], God will protect him from hell".' Men leapt from their mounts—never was a day seen with more [soldiers] walking [than that one].[15]

This tradition shows the intensity of the belief in the coming Judgment and the essentially spiritual nature of the fighting during this early period. There is every reason to believe, from the Syrian religious literature, that much of what would later come to be known as 'Islam' was actually developed in the atmosphere of the army camps and on the way to the battlefield. The literature is replete with such situations, questions being asked, problems being solved and models of conduct being developed literally on the war-path. Although it is impossible to know exactly how many of the fighters entered the army sincere Muslims—since it is apparent that Christians, Jews, Zoroastrians and other religious groups fought alongside the early Muslims—one must hazard the guess that on the basis of this literature, the religious indoctrination was intense and it is very likely that those who did not believe at the beginning of a campaign did so by the end. The connection to apocalyptic prophecies is also strong. Commanders like Maslama b. `Abd al-Malik (who conducted most of the raids against the Byzantines during the early-eighth century) are said to have listened to apocalyptic prophecies concerning the fall of Constantinople and then go on raids.[16] Other commanders conducted discussions concerning the Antichrist, the Mahdi and Jesus, and sometimes were even accused of being the Antichrist! Although it is inaccurate to say that conversion to Islam was induced at the point of a sword, part of the formation of the early community was the result of the 'total war' attitude of the Umayyad regime. Rightly Khalid Yahya Blankinship called the proto-Muslim time 'the Jihad state'.

Conclusions

The elements of the successful early Muslim coalition with Jews and Christians are clear. They include a willingness to acknowledge them both as monotheists as long as their belief was pure (and the Christians did not overemphasize the divine nature of Jesus), a fulfillment of both of the Jews' and the Christians' messianic aspirations and joint warfare to bring in the messianic age. If one might have thought that the Christians would have hesitated to collaborate with non-Christians against the Christian Byzantine empire, the proto-Muslims seem to have effectively neutralized that threat. Christians fought alongside the Muslims, prominent Orthodox Christian families such as that of St John of Damascus served in lofty governmental capacities willingly and ably to the ultimate detriment of their co-religionists in Byzantium, and there is little evidence that the Christian population ever served as a fifth-column for the Byzantines. This unity was an absolute necessity for Syrian proto-Islam, given the minority situation of the proto-Muslims, who had to stick together at all costs or they would simply be swallowed up. For example,

> We [the Muslim troops] came from the land of the Byzantines returning [from battle]; when we had left Hims going towards Damascus we passed by a cultivated place which is near Hims—about four miles—at the end of the night. When the monk who was in the cell heard our speech, he came up to us and said: 'Who are you all?' We said: 'People from Damascus, coming from the land of the Byzantines'. He said: 'Do you know Abu Muslim al-Khawlani?' We said: 'Yes'. He said: 'When you come to him, greet him with the peace, and inform him that we find him in the Holy Books as a companion of Jesus son of Mary'.[17]

The monk sees a spiritual kinship with the 'Muslim' Abu Muslim al-Khawlani, who was a very prominent religious figure close to the caliph, and even states outright that in the messianic future when Jesus returns that Abu Muslim will be a part of Jesus' retinue. So, too, we find Jews and Muslims establishing common ground while speaking about the end of the world and the judgment which is about to occur, such as the extensive citation in early Muslim apocalyptic literature of the messianic vision of Isa. 11.6-8 'the lion shall lie down with the lamb' and so on.

The apocalyptic side of the ecumenical equation was represented in everything the proto-Muslims did—their sense of mission, their aggressiveness towards the Byzantines, their desire to punish the latter for their sins, the rebuilding of the Temple (the Dome of the Rock) and other holy buildings. Although it is clear that unlike the later `Abbasids, the Umayyads did not take formal messianic titles as part of their regnal names, they were perceived by the population in these terms and may have used these perceptions to further the legitimacy of their rule, and even to some extent guide their policies. The fact that they used the broadest messianic themes (justice, fair distribution of wealth, a peaceable ecumenical kingdom, etc.) tells us that these concepts were aimed not solely at the proto-Muslims, but at the Christian population, and the much smaller Jewish population as well.

More and more students of Islam are coming to realize that the energy and power required by the conquests was actually supplied by a belief in the imminent end of the world. This belief was common throughout the region of the Mediterranean basin and Iraq where both Christians and Jews composed numerous apocalypses at this time. Christians noted that seven centuries had elapsed between the death and resurrection of Jesus—a number with a great many symbolic connections—and that apparently God had judged the Christian Byzantine empire for its numerous failings. Jews were caught up in their perpetual dreams of the liberation of Jerusalem from Christian rule, and the possible rebuilding of the Temple. There is good evidence that these expectations were exploited by the early Muslims both to mobilize support and to win converts. The apocalyptic foundation of Islam is clear from the Qur'an, from the numerous predictions and prophecies in the early literature, from the doctrine of *jihad*, from the ecumenical spirit of the Believers, and from the rule of peace they sought to extend throughout the known world during the first century of their existence.

References

`Abdallah b. al-Mubarak, *Kitab al-jihad* (Beirut: n.p., 1971).

Abu `Amr al-Dani, *Sunan al-warida fi al-fitan* (Riyad: Dar al-`Asima, 1995).

Abu Ya`la al-Mawsili, *Musnad* (Damascus: Dar al-Ma'mun, 1986).

Abu Zur`a, *Ta'rikh Abi Zur`a al-Dimashqi* (Beirut: Dar al-Kutub al-`Ilmiyya, n.d.).

al-Awza`i, `Abd al-Rahman, *Sunan* (Beirut: Dar al-Nafa'is, 1993).

Bashear, Suliman, *al-Muqaddima li-l-ta'tarikh al-akhir* (Jerusalem: n.p., 1984).

—'Muslim Apocalypses', *Israeli Oriental Studies* 13 (1993), 75-99.

al-Bukhari, Muhammad b. Isma`il, *Sahih* (Beirut: Dar al-Fikr, 1991).

al-Daraqutni, *al-Mu'talif wa-l-mukhtalif* (Haydarabad: n.p., n.d.).

al-Dhahabi, *Siyar a`lam al-nubala'* (Beirut: Mu'assasat al-Risala, 1985).

Griffith, Sidney, 'The First Christian *Summa Theologiae* in Arabic', in Ramzi Bikhazi and Michael Gervers (eds.), *Conversion and Continuity* (Toronto: Pontifical Institute of Mediaeval Studies, 1990), 15-31.

Ibn Abi al-Dunya, *Ahwal* (Giza: Maktabat al-Yasir, 1993).

Ibn Abi Shayba, *Musannaf* (n.p., n.d.).

Ibn `Asakir, *Ta'rikh madinat Dimashq* (Beirut: Dar al-Fikr, 1995–99).

Ibn Bishran, *Amali* (Riyad: Dar al-Watan, 1997).

Ibn Mansur, *Sunan* (Beirut: Dar al-Kutub al-`Ilmiyya, n.d.).

Ibn Wahhab al-Qurashi, *Jami`* (Riyad: Dar Ibn Jawzi, 1997).

al-Khara'iti, *Makarim al-akhlaq* (Beirut: Dar al-Fikr, n.d.).

al-Khawlani, *Ta'rikh Daraya* (Benghazi: n.p., 1984).

Kister, M.J., '…illa bi-haqqihi…', *Jerusalem Studies in Arabic and Islam* 5 (1984), 33-52.

—'Do Not Assimilate Yourselves…', *Jerusalem Studies in Arabic and Islam* 11 (1990), 321-53.

al-Madini, *Naddara Allah amran* (Beirut: Dar Ibn Hazm, 1994).

al-Marwazi, Nu`aym b. Hammad, *Fitan* (Beirut: Dar al-Fikr, 1993).

al-Murajja', Musharraf b., *Fada'il Bayt al-Maqsis wa-l-Sham* (Shafaram: n.p., 1995).

al-Sa`di, *Hadith `Ali b. Hajar al-Sa`di* (Riyad: Maktabat al-Rushd, 1998).

al-Sulami, `Iqd al-durar fi akhbar al-muntazar* (Zarqa': n.p., 1989).

al-Tabarani, *al-Mu`jam al-kabir* (Baghdad: Wizarat al-Awqaf, 1985).

al-Tabarani, Sulayman b. Ahmad, *Musnad al-Shamiyyin* (Beirut: Mu'assasat al-Risala, 1996).

al-Tamimi, Muhammad b. Ahmad, *Mihan* (Beirut: Dar al-Gharb al-Islami, 1988).

al-Zuhri, `Ubaydallah b. `Abd al-Rahman, *Hadith* (Riyad: Adwa' al-Salaf, 1998).

Notes

1.   Sulayman b. Ahmad al-Tabarani (d. 971), *Musnad al-Shamiyyin* (Beirut: Mu'assasat al-Risala, 1996), IV, 167 (no. 3017), versions are I, 90 (no. 129), 372 (no. 645), IV, 130 (no. 2916); Muhammad b. Isma`il al-Bukhari (d. 870), *Sahih* (Beirut: Dar al-Fikr, 1991), I, 14 (no. 25); `Ubaydallah b. `Abd al-Rahman al-Zuhri (d. 991), *Hadith* (Riyad: Adwa' al-Salaf, 1998), I, 207-208 (nos. 165-66); and see M.J. Kister, '…*illa bi-haqqihi.*'.. *Jerusalem Studies in Arabic and Islam* 5 (1984), 33-52 for a discussion of all of the variants; also Suliman Bashear, *al-Muqaddima li-l-ta'rikh al-akhir* (Jerusalem: n.p., 1984), 397.

2.   He is said to have been the commander of the *shurta* (security forces) in the region of Bahrayn.

3.   Ibn `Asakir (d. 1171), *Ta'rikh madinat Dimashq* (Beirut: Dar al-Fikr, 1995–99), XXXVII, 170; for other formal *shahadas* in the presence of al-Hajjaj, Muhammad b. Ahmad al-Tamimi (d. 944), *Mihan* (Beirut: Dar al-Gharb al-Islami, 1988), 211; and for Christians in `Ali's army, see Ibn Abi Shayba (d. 835), *Musannaf* (n.p., n.d.), XII, 266-67 (no. 12784). Sidney Griffith, 'The First Christian *Summa Theologiae* in Arabic', in Ramzi Bikhazi and Michael Gervers (eds.), *Conversion and Continuity* (Toronto: Pontifical Institute of Mediaeval Studies, 1990), 15-31, details the fact that by the second century many Christians hid their faith behind bland monotheistic formulae that were basically Muslim.

4.   Ibn `Asakir, *Ta'rikh*, XLVII, 378-80, XXIX, 354; and compare XII, 330 (which purports to be a letter of Muhammad to the bishop of Ayla); and `Abd al-Rahman al-Awza`i (d. 771), *Sunan* (Beirut: Dar al-Nafa'is, 1993), 30-31 (nos. 43-47).

5.   Ibn Wahhab al-Qurashi (d. 812) , *Jami`* (Riyad: Dar Ibn Jawzi, 1997), I, 318 (no. 218); and compare Ibn Bishran (d. 1038), *Amali* (Riyad: Dar al-Watan, 1997), 26 (no. 3); al-Madini (d. 944), *Naddara Allah amran* (Beirut: Dar Ibn Hazm, 1994), 21-28, 57; al-Khara'iti (d. 939), *Makarim al-akhlaq* (Beirut: Dar al-Fikr, n.d.), I, 410-11; Abu Ya`la al-Mawsili (d. 919), *Musnad* (Damascus: Dar al-Ma'mun, 1986), VII, 199 (no. 4187).

6.   Nu`aym b. Hammad al-Marwazi (d. 844), *Fitan* (Beirut: Dar al-Fikr, 1993), 220.

7.   Al-Tabarani, *Musnad al-Shamiyyin*, IV, 224 (no. 3142); and compare the following version, 'A likeness of you among the previous communities is between the afternoon prayers and the setting of the sun. A likeness of you and the Jews and the Christians is like a man who hired workers and said: "Who will work for the wage of a *qirat* until the middle of the day?" The Jews and the Christians did so until the middle of the day for the wage of a *qirat*, and then he said: "Who will work from the afternoon prayers until the setting of the sun for two *qirats*—for double the wage?" and the Jews and Christians became angry. They said: "We worked more and earned less!" He said: "Have I cheated you of what you deserved?" They said: "No". He said: "This is my bounty which I give to whomever I wish"' (al-Tabarani, *Musnad al-Shamiyyin*, IV, 144 [no. 2955]).

8.   It is difficult to take this statement seriously, since the Qur'an itself (7.187, 33.63, 45.32, 79.42) records people asking about the Hour, and the *hadith* literature is full of these sort of conversations (e.g., Abu Ya`la, *Musnad*, V, 144-45 [no. 2758],

VI, 313 [no. 3631], VII, 104 [no. 4049]; al-Sa`di [d. 858], *Hadith `Ali b. Hajar al-Sa`di* [Riyad: Maktabat al-Rushd, 1998], 192-93; and Suliman Bashear, 'Muslim apocalypses' *Israeli Oriental Studies* 13 [1993], 75-99).

9.   Al-Khawlani (fl. ninth cen), *Ta'rikh Daraya* (Benghazi, 1984), 98; Ibn `Asakir, *Ta'rikh*, LVIII, 461; these last bound demons are unknown to me from other Muslim apocalyptic literature—however, see Rev. 16.13-14; although they may be alluded to in Ibn Abi al-Dunya (d. 894), *Ahwal* (Giza: Maktabat al-Yasir, 1993), 61; and compare al-Daraqutni (d. 995), *al-Mu'talif wa-l-mukhtalif* (Haydarabad, n.d.), II, 616.

10.   Apparently God is speaking.

11.   Musharraf b. al-Murajja', *Fada'il Bayt al-Maqsis wa-l-Sham* (Shafaram, n.p., 1995), 63-64 (n. 50).

12.   Nu`aym, *Fitan*, 284; and compare the variants in Abu `Amr al-Dani (d. 944), *Sunan al-warida fi al-fitan* (Riyad: Dar al-`Asima, 1995), III, 1125 (no. 605); al-Sulami (d. 1261), `*Iqd al-durar fi akhbar al-muntazar* (Zarqa': n.p., 1989), 285 (no. 339); and al-Musharraf b. al-Murajja', *Fada'il*, 231-32 (no. 342).

13.   `Abdallah b. al-Mubarak (d. 791), *Kitab al-jihad* (Beirut: n.p., 1971), 89-90 (no. 105); al-Awza`i, *Sunan*, 360 (no. 1165); Ibn Abi Shayba, *Musannaf*, XII, 349 (no. 13056); and see Bashear, 'Muslim Apocalypses', 76ff., esp. 80; and M.J. Kister, 'Do Not Assimilate Yourselves...', *Jerusalem Studies in Arabic and Islam* 11 (1990), 321-53.

14.   Ibn Abi Shayba, *Musannaf*, V, 301; and compare Ibn al-Mubarak, *Jihad*, 117; Ibn `Asakir, *Ta'rikh*, LXV, 220, and the full speech by Yazid is recorded on 230-31.

15.   Ibn al-Mubarak, *Jihad*, 44-45; compare Abu Ya`la, *Musnad*, II, 242 (no. 944); Ibn `Asakir, *Ta'rikh*, XVIII, 117; and Ibn Mansur (d. 841), *Sunan* (Beirut: Dar al-Kutub al-`Ilmiyya, n.d.), II, 155-56 (nos. 2401-402).

16.   Al-Tabarani, *al-Mu`jam al-kabir* (Baghdad: Wizarat al-Awqaf, 1985), II, 38 (no. 1216).

17.   Ibn `Asakir, *Ta'rikh*, XXVII, 232; al-Dhahabi (d. 1347), *Siyar a`lam al-nubala'* (Beirut: Mu'assasat al-Risala, 1985), IV, 13 (this is a little odd since al-Khawlani is said to have died in Byzantine territory: Abu Zur`a [d. 891], *Ta'rikh Abi Zur`a al-Dimashqi* [Beirut: Dar al-Kutub al-`Ilmiyya, n.d.], 64 [no. 221]).

Before and Beyond the Sioux Ghost Dance:
Native American Prophetic Movements and the Study of Religion*

Joel W. Martin

Within the study of religion, the Sioux Ghost Dance is the exemplar of Native American prophetic movements. It is the religious revolt and millenarian movement most familiar to scholars of religion in America, who invariably invoke it in discussions of Native American religions.[1] Although the Sioux Ghost Dance surely deserves serious attention, its persistent status as privileged example limits the way students of religion understand and interpret Native American movements.

Fixation upon the Sioux Ghost Dance encourages students of Native American religion to remain unversed in the many insurgencies of colonial history. The foregrounding of the Sioux Ghost Dance deflects attention from earlier Native American religious revolts that are equally significant for the study of religion in America, Native American religions, and cultural contact. For just the Eastern Woodlands, these include the Creek millenarian movement of 1813, the Shawnee prophetic movement of 1805, the Delaware revolt of 1763, the Yamasee war of 1715, the Powhatan revolts of 1644 and 1622, and many others that historians continue to uncover.[2] Rather than ignore these movements, or assume that they are adequately represented by the Sioux Ghost Dance, scholars of religion should seek to recover their history and meaning.

A Discourse of Disappearing Indians

If the neglect of other Native American religious revolts were merely a matter of scholarly oversight, we could accomplish this project of recovery through a kind of historiographic affirmative action. Unfortunately, we deal not with an accidental shadow-zone in our knowledge system, but with a significant intellectual aporia. The gap in our knowledge concerning Native American religious revolts results from our discourse on Native American religions, which *resists imagining Native American religions in creative contact with history*. This means that our scholarship discounts historical movements in which Native American religions demonstrated resiliency, improvisation and/or 'non-traditional' assimilation in contact with Europeans or Africans. The study of religion valorizes only what looks like 'traditional' Native American spirituality, pristine forms of religion uncontaminated by incoming religions and peoples. This purist preference is evident in at least two ways: (1) the canonical status given to the book *Black Elk Speaks*, and (2) the way surveys of religion in America include Native American religions in their beginning chapters, but nowhere else.

In recent important textbooks on religion in America, Native American religions are typically treated in an early chapter, often the first chapter.[3] Such placement has the salutary effect of acknowledging the chronological priority of Native American religions in America. However, by placing Native American religions only at the beginning of the work, these textbooks, as diverse as they are in methods and intents, all imply at a formal level that these religions belong only at the beginning of the story of religion in America. Although the contents of that initial chapter may explicitly affirm the richness, creativity, and persistence of Native American religions,[4] the very form of these books conveys to readers a different, if not contradictory, message. Native Americans appear 'before the whites', but then vanish as the texts progress to treat Europeans[5] or African newcomers.[6] Thus, these books, despite their authors' best intentions, can imply that Native Americans disappear from history. The idea of 'disappearing' Native Americans is directly present in the contents of the extremely popular primary source, *Black Elk Speaks*. Nicholas Black Elk's story, as told by John G. Neihardt, powerfully involves readers in some of the intense struggles of a Lakota man born in 1863. Although *Black Elk Speaks* is an extraordinary narrative that deserves reading and rereading, the book does not necessarily provide an accurate portrait of Black Elk or his religion. On the contrary, it gives a highly selective and romantic vision of the man and his religious life. As William Powers argues, Neihardt communicated only the 'traditional' side of Black Elk's story, the side that confirmed European American expectations regarding Native American religions.[7] At the time when Neihardt interviewed him, Nicholas Black Elk had served the Catholic church as a catechist for two decades and was a godfather for more than 125 people. Nicholas Black Elk's devotion to Catholicism was deep and longstanding, yet Neihardt minimized it. Readers of the 'autobiography' encounter a man who fitted the image of a pure traditionalist and was far less a Christian than was the real Nicholas Black Elk.

Given the bias of Neihardt's representation, we must inquire why among all books by and/or about Native Americans this romantic autobiography has become the preferred text of scholars and teachers. Why has *Black Elk Speaks* become 'the most influential book ever published on American Indian religion'?[8] Could the book be so popular in part because the text supports the idea of 'disappearing' Native Americans? As the publisher's frontispiece states: *Black Elk Speaks* relates 'the magnificent primitive drama no people can ever live again'. With its tragic tone, painful descriptions of human suffering, melancholic musings on the Sioux Ghost Dance, systematic suppression of Black Elk's participation in Christianity, and sad ending in which the protagonist laments for the death of his people, the autobiography suggests that Native American religions and peoples were tragically incompatible with modernity. The way its contents seemingly confirm the suppositions and claims of our reigning discourse surely has helped make *Black Elk Speaks* a canonical text for the study of religion.

Our academic discourse advances regularities of inclusion and exclusion that discount the ability of Native American religions to change in response to history. Rather than mere oversight, this discursive system itself, the kinds of Native American religious expressions it magnifies, the canon of texts it selects, and the sort of readings it authorizes, prevent deeper academic contact with histories of innovation, transformation, and resiliency. Consequently, the full recovery of the history of radical Native American religious movements requires much more than remedial historical research; it presupposes disciplinary and discursive self-criticism and should evoke new interpretative experiments.

The Function of the Ghost Dance

We can initiate the needed self-criticism by concentrating upon a crucial node in the entire discursive system, the Sioux Ghost Dance. In the discourse of the contemporary study of religion, the Sioux Ghost Dance inevitably stands for a long series of revolts that emerged in other cultural contexts, times, and places. This practice is problematic, particularly as we realize that it does not foreground the entire Ghost Dance movement. That movement extended all across the West and included many groups well before the Sioux.[9] However, our reigning discourse fixates narrowly upon the Sioux 'outbreak' of 1890 and the massacre at Wounded Knee. Moreover, the Sioux Ghost Dance is all too often described in pejorative language that does not grapple with the movement's internal dynamics and motivations. Weston LaBarre describes the Sioux Ghost Dance as a 'grotesque', 'pathological' movement and blames it on shamanistic influence. According to LaBarre, shamans are usually childlike, insane, and effeminate, and the Sioux Ghost Dance emerged when 'frightened and infantilized' people accepted the 'paranoid' visions of 'psychotic' shamans.[10] Amanda Porterfield repeats, though less harshly, some of the key themes of LaBarre's interpretation of the Sioux Ghost Dance:

> A similar incident occurred during the Sioux 'outbreak' of 1890, which was triggered by the religious fervor of the Ghost Dance. At the massacre of Wounded Knee, many Indians wore Ghost Dance shirts on which pictures of visions of the spirit world were drawn. The wearers believed the shirts would make them invulnerable to the bullets of the U.S. Army. Although the Army's overreaction [sic] to the Ghost Dance was the precipitating cause of the massacre, the delusion of invulnerability promoted by the shamanism of the Ghost Dance helped many Indians to an early and violent death.[11]

As with LaBarre, this description tends to portray the Sioux Ghost Dance as a kind of mental contagion ('religious fervor'). The movement appears to be a form of irrationalism ('delusion') fostered by false prophecy ('shamanism') that made the Sioux complicit in their own massacre.

In his signal revisionist work, Raymond DeMallie argues persuasively for a different understanding of the Sioux Ghost Dance.[12] DeMallie focuses on the symbolic expressions of the Dance, and shows that the Sioux Ghost Dance was a religious movement that had clear resonances with, and deep roots in, the Sun Dance of the pre-reservation buffalo days. Participants in the Sioux Ghost Dance drew upon the pre-existing ritual forms and mythic meanings of their religious tradition. They did not abandon their tradition in an act of desperation. DeMallie's work seriously questions interpretations that equate the Sioux Ghost Dance with psychosis or view it as a religious aberration. His work alerts us to the way scholarship has been shaped by a particular and powerful discourse. By valorizing an incomplete version of the Sioux Ghost Dance, this discourse has excluded other Native American movements and short-circuited consideration of the discursive, interpretive, and political problematics their study would evoke.

An Interdisciplinary Approach

To move beyond these representations and exclusions and toward more inclusive histories and interpretations scholars of religion must immerse themselves more deeply in original historical research and broaden the range of movements considered. This project will require scholars of religion to draw upon a variety of approaches to the data, including those of other branches of the humanities and social sciences.

A Social Scientific Typology of Native American Movements

David F. Aberle provides scholars with a very useful typology of Native American religious movements. Aberle's typology does not try to define and accommodate the manifold labels that scholars have variously applied to these movements, nor does it rely on terms such as 'nativistic', 'reform', 'cargo cult', 'crisis cult', 'acculturational cult', 'utopian community', 'revival', 'messianic', 'millenarian', 'chiliastic', 'eschatological' or 'revitalization'.[13] Rather, Aberle uses two basic categories to establish his typology: (1) 'transformative' movements, which seek total change in the social order, and (2) 'redemptive' movements, which seek total change, but at an individual level. This simple typology enables Aberle to make meaningful distinctions between movements such as the Sioux Ghost Dance and the Peyote religion. The former is interpreted as a transformative movement and the latter as a redemptive movement.[14] Applying this typology, Joseph Jorgensen has provided an illuminating interpretation of the modern Sun Dance as a redemptive movement.[15] Unfortunately, few scholars have attempted to study the other category of movements delineated in the typology—transformative movements.

Native American movements that sought 'total change to the total social or natural order' have been strangely neglected.[16] Only two transformative movements have managed to gain significant scholarly attention and secure a prominent place in the discourse of religious studies: the Sioux Ghost Dance and Handsome Lake's Movement of 1799–1815.[17]

We have reviewed the prominence of the Sioux Ghost Dance in our discourse. We need now account for the visibility of Handsome Lake's movement. Handsome Lake's movement was creative, historically important, and deserves serious study. However, Handsome Lake's movement was not typical of other major prophetic movements in the Eastern Woodlands. Where many other prophets spurned dependency upon Europeans and rejected Christian symbols, Handsome Lake sanctified Christian European values and ways of life. Could this explain in part why the movement is attractive to religious studies' scholars? The Handsome Lake movement provides the discipline's discourse with a useful foil to set against the Sioux Ghost Dance. By juxtaposing a successful Handsome Lake movement and a tragic Sioux Ghost Dance, the discourse implicitly celebrates accommodation and condemns resistance. Most important, by focusing upon these two movements and persistently yoking them together,[18] the discourse blocks consideration of a whole range of movements. In this excluded middle range, we find a rich diversity of transformative movements that did not always end so tragically, but did demonstrate innovation and inspire deep anti-colonial resistance.

Revisionist American History's Contribution

Over the past few decades, American historians have documented with vigor and detail the histories of Native American peoples.[19] Historians also have begun the important work of studying Native American prophetic movements.[20] Such scholarship helps us appreciate the power, creativity, and originality of these movements by acknowledging their great frequency. Well before the Sioux Ghost Dance, Native American peoples engaged in large-scale and dramatic movements of prophecy and rebirth. We have already mentioned several significant examples from the Eastern Woodlands. In addition, among the indigenous peoples who faced Spanish invaders in the Southwest, a prophetic resistance movement arose in 1616 among the Tarahumaras in the great Tepehuan revolt. In Spanish mission provinces in the Southeast, an important religious revolt shook the Guale missions from 1576 to 1585 and again in 1597, followed by similar revolts in Apalachee in 1647 and Timucua in 1656.

The critical comments of the Chibcha Indians of what became Colombia clearly indicate that a pattern of spirit-based revolt extends back to the first half of the sixteenth century. In 1541, their leader rejected the Spanish peace offer, saying,

> You desecrate the sanctuaries of our gods and sack the houses of men who haven't offended you. Who would choose to undergo these insults, being not insensitive? Who would not omit to rid himself of such harassment, even at the cost of his life? Note well the survivors who await you, to undeceive you that victory is always yours.[21]

As the timing of most of these movements reveals, full-fledged prophetic movements almost never occurred in the initial encounter between Native Americans and Europeans. Rather, they emerged after several generations of either direct or indirect contact. They emerged most often within the kind of unequal and exploitative relations that characterized full-fledged colonialism. Several of these movements, particularly the later ones in the Eastern Woodlands, occurred in a context in which Native American groups experienced a severe depletion of marketable game and a rapid loss of land to Europeans. Game depletion and land loss were concerns explicitly and prominently addressed by prophets among the Delawares (Neolin), Ottawas (The Trout), Shawnees (Tenskwatawa) and Creeks (Hillis Hadjo) as well as the Senecas (Handsome Lake). For instance, in 1763 the great Delaware prophet Neolin revealed that the Master of Life had told him,

Ye have only to become good again and do what I wish, and I will send back the animals for your food… As for those [British] that come to trouble your lands, drive them out, make war upon them… Send them back to the lands which I have created for them and let them stay there.[22]

The apparent link between painful contact experiences and the timing of these movements might tempt us to assume the former caused the latter. Indeed, this is the conclusion of some social scientists (LaBarre; Aberle), who assert that contact produced among Native Americans a bitter experience of deprivation, 'a negative discrepancy between legitimate expectation and actuality, or between legitimate expectation and anticipated actuality, or both'.[23] Frustrated and threatened, the victims of negative economic and political experiences, Native American groups responded to innovative prophets, radically transformed their cultures, and sometimes rebelled.

This kind of explanation is problematic for several reasons. It ignores the fact that these negative experiences were practically ubiquitous, experienced by almost all Native Americans. Thus, the theory cannot explain why other groups that suffered comparable deprivation did not revolt. Additionally, deprivation theory focuses so narrowly on negative experiences that it neglects to consider that these movements may have been motivated by positive experiences, visions, and hopes, some derived from the contact context, others springing from renewed connection with tradition. This does not minimize the suffering caused by contact, but affirms that these movements may not have been solely fueled by *ressentiment* or loss of cultural coherence. Colonialism may have been a necessary precondition of these movements, but colonialism and the deprivation that colonial relations produced were probably not the only causes.[24] In addition to the experience of land loss and game depletion, we should also call attention to the impact and power of new visions, visions discerned through ecstatic contact with spirits of water, earth, and sky and amplified in communal discussions.

In contrast to deprivation theory, this approach affirms the full humanity of Native Americans by assuming that they were actors in history rather than merely victims. They not only reacted and rebelled against colonialism, they also innovated tradition and initiated new ways of life within the world created by contact. As James Merrell[25] asserts in his studies of the Catawba Indian experience in colonial South Carolina, contact brought Native Americans just as surely as it brought Europeans and Africans into a 'new world'. Merrell counsels historians to think of 'a "world" as the physical and cultural milieu within which people live and a "new world" as a dramatically different milieu demanding basic changes in ways of life'.[26] Because of contact with European diseases, the Catawbas experienced severe demographic losses. Because of contact with European traders, the Catawbas acquired livestock and poultry, steady supplies of very useful materials, tools, and weapons (iron, cloth, glass, firearms), as well as novel luxuries (silk, rum). Because of conflicts with European settlers and armies, the Catawbas lost most of their land and retained only a small reservation in Carolina. In short, because of these and other experiences brought about by contact, the Catawbas had to learn how to survive in 'a dramatically different milieu demanding basic changes in ways of life'. Along with Africans and Europeans, the Catawbas entered a 'new world'.

New Religious Worlds

Merrell invests a great deal of significance in the metaphor of 'a new world'. He believes that it provides a narratively powerful way of linking the story of Native Americans with the stories of Europeans and Africans in America. Since all of these peoples found themselves in a new world, he argues, historians can no longer fail to integrate Native American history with the rest of American history. Whether or not Merrell's metaphor will alter historiography in the ways he hopes remains to be seen.[27]

Yet the metaphor gives rise to thought, and might fruitfully be taken up in the study of religion to foster a fresh perspective upon Native American religious movements. Merrell's metaphor could be blended with William Paden's image of different religions as inhabiting and constructing different life worlds.[28] Scholars of comparative religion have the task of studying and comparing the plurality of 'religious worlds'.[29]

Blending the perspectives of the colonial historian James Merrell and the historian of religions William Paden, we can argue that the new world entered by Native Americans was also a new 'religious world', a generative locus in which new gods revealed themselves, and old gods were rediscovered; a creative time when new systems of purity displaced old ones, and new myths and rites arose. This new religious world emerged when various 'primordial' religious worlds—Aboriginal, African, and European—were fused by contact, colonialism, and capitalism. Learning how to think and live in this new world along with its various inhabitants constituted a great religious project for every people in this world, and this project found one of its earliest and most original expressions in Native American transformative movements. In these movements, Native Americans engaged new prophecies, dances, and stories to find and forge new religions and new religious identities suited to the transforming realities of colonial and modern contact.

Divining the Path

Cognizant that tribal tradition alone could not provide adequate orientation participants in these movements considered multiple options and energetically borrowed ideas and forms of non-native neighbors (including Christians) and other Native American groups (often from a great distance). The Delawares of 1760, the Shawnees of 1805, the Creeks of 1813, and the Sioux of 1890 used a wide range of cultural resources. From Europeans, they appropriated Christian ideas about the sacred book and the savior.[30] From other Native American groups, they borrowed purification practices. Of course, as they innovated, they took pains to insure that the new religious forms meshed well with traditional indigenous forms. Among the Delawares and Shawnees, the Christian ascent to heaven was correlated with the shaman's sky journey. The Sioux Ghost Dance clearly resembled the old Sun Dance. In all of these movements, the participants were rigorously concerned with divining gestures and disseminating representations of a 'path' that would lead to a meaningful future for themselves and their children. These kinds of divination emerged from traditional shamanistic travels as well as new kinds of pan-Native American contact and organizing the dissemination process employed rumors, speeches, new dances, and 'books'.

Since their historical experiences were partly negative, the divination of this path included and developed a sharply focused analysis of the specific social and economic practices that jeopardized the people's future. Prophetic shamans explicitly attacked commerce that led to economic dependency, consumption of alcohol, disruption of clan relations, and land cessions.[31] They linked disregard for the ancestors with a sterile or counter-productive fascination with 'white' ways. In many cases, especially among the Native American groups still powerful because of numbers or territory, the movement rose to the level of a thoroughgoing critique of colonialism. At this point these movements manifested themselves as politically revolutionary.

In almost all these revolts, the critique of colonialism began at home with self-critique. This self-critique brought to consciousness major ways in which the people had collaborated with colonialist forces. In some of these revolts, it was not just collaborative practices that were criticized and rejected, but particular people. In the Delaware, Shawnee, and Creek revolts, prophets verbally and sometimes physically attacked the indigenous insiders who had accepted and were imposing a 'white' understanding of civilization upon their own people. For example, the Creek prophets demanded the assassination of 'all the Chiefs and their adherents who are

friendly to the customs and ways of the white people'.[32] As these prophetic movements gained popular support, there came into ever sharper
focus a class of Native American people who had betrayed their people.
These traitors appeared to be 'red people' when judged by clan ties and
culture, but with the advent of prophetic discourse it became possible to
specify precisely how their collaboration with colonialist forces jeopardized the people's future. These traitors, many of them chiefs, had agreed
to land cessions, delivered their own people over to European American
agents for justice, or had personally profited from their mediating position
in the rum/fur/skin trades, but failed to redistribute the wealth in accord
with the mainstream ethic.[33] Within the millenarian movement, these
chiefs were for the first time unmasked and named 'malicious enemies'.
They were not scapegoats randomly selected, but a class of internal enemies identified through critical vision. Violent attacks on these enemies
appeared early and ferocious in both the Shawnee and Creek revolts and
relatively late and small-scale in the Delaware prophetic movement.[34]

This self-purge signals that these movements were very much concerned with internal developments and dynamics, not just with responding to 'external' pressures. Among the Shawnees and Creeks, for instance,
the prophets' greatest passion was not to vilify European Americans, but
to identify and purge those natives who had betrayed tradition in order to
pursue personal wealth. In these cases, we must reverse Marxist theory
and assert with Edward P. Thompson that it was struggle that gave rise to
class consciousness. 'People find themselves in a society structured in
determined ways...they experience exploitation...they identify points
of antagonistic interest, they commence to struggle around these issues
and in the process of struggling they discover themselves as classes, they
come to know this discovery as class-consciousness.'[35] Out of the profound spiritual struggle to secure and incarnate a viable identity in their
new world, violent and unprecedented class conflict often ensued within
these transformative movements. In sum, attacks on colonial collaborators
were the indigenous modes for articulating and deepening an emerging
consciousness of class inequalities.

The internal struggle, which sometimes became civil war, demonstrated yet again that transformative movements were movements in
which Native Americans reclaimed their power to shape their own
future as they saw fit, in accord with their understandings of power(s).
For participants in these movements, history was understood not from
the perspective of passive victims confronting a monolithic and inevitable invasion. Rather, they affirmed that their situation was partly their
responsibility by asserting that their situation resulted from the action of

traitors within, traitors who had neglected traditions or, even worse, had actively advanced colonialist forces. Highly charged with a millenarian spirit, the prophets asserted that these traitors could be vanquished by the active intervention of a new kind of anti-colonial warrior, a dancer guided by fresh contact with the sacred. Their millenarian perspective acknowledged that the European American invasion had created the conditions for new kinds of identities, but it asserted even more vigorously that the people must now decide to walk the road to destruction, which would result from passive accommodation, or the 'red' road evoked by conscious and critical resistance and informed by spiritual interpretation. Millenarian prophets called people to imagine the outlines of, and participate actively in, the creation of a post-colonial future. Colonialism may have pushed, but even more important, the sacred *pulled* Native American peoples into a new religious world.

Millenarian Initiation

Though terms such as class consciousness, colonialism, and anticolonialism imply a political reading, we should not lose sight of the way these movements remain concerned with spiritual issues and organized as spiritual processes. Here we can demonstrate more fully how the study of religion will contribute to, and perhaps even criticize, the works of revisionist historians. Revisionist historians do a superb job of uncovering primary sources and recovering details of everyday life.[36] However, because they do not employ comparative perspectives developed in the study of religion, they tend not to examine religious forms such as myth, ritual, and symbol, and they generally underestimate the importance of these forms in Native American societies and popular movements. This is especially problematic, for within colonial Native American societies the political was tightly intertwined with the religious. The interpretation of Native American transformative movements as rites of passage makes this interrelation clear.

Coined by Arnold van Gennep in 1908, the term 'rites of passage' has gained enormous importance in anthropology and the study of religion. Unfortunately, the scope of the term's application has been constricted in a significant way. In contemporary scholarship, rites of passage means first and foremost ceremonies that mark momentous transitions in the life of the individual, 'birth, adulthood, religious membership, marriage, death'.[37] Scholars usually do not think of *collective* social movements as rites of passage. Because such usage goes against the grain of contemporary practice, it needs to be defended logically and empirically. The late Victor

Turner[38] provided the germ of such a defense in one of his final writings. He reminded us that Van Gennep delineated two categories of rites of passage: '(1) Rites that accompany the passage of a person from one social status to another in the course of his or her life, and (2) Rites that mark recognized points in the passage of time (new year, new moon, solstice, or equinox)'. Turner continued, 'The term has come to be restricted…to the former type, which are now sometimes called "life-crisis rites"'. Significantly, Turner was 'not in agreement with this [restriction]', and did not let it constrain his use of the term 'rites of passage'. Rather, he applied the term to a very rich array of social phenomena, including collective historical movements.

In his study of the liminal or transitional phase of rites of passage,[39] Turner remarked that millenarian movements bear striking homologies to rites of passage. If the traditional rite of passage is connected to crises in the human life-cycle, the millenarian movement is connected to phases of history that impose great changes upon people. Both rites of passage and millenarian movements enable their participants to reduce internal differences and increase solidarity (*communitas*). Further, rites of passage and millenarian movements require participants to perform actions symbolizing that they are betwixt and between ordinary social states (liminality). Homologies such as these led Turner to conclude that millenarian movements 'are essentially phenomena of transition'.[40]

Following Turner's lead, we can examine Native American millenarian movements as rites of passage—specifically, ceremonies of collective initiation—performed on a grand scale. Although this line of interpretation has not been so explicitly stated before, some students of millenarian movements have implied it. In his discussion of Native American 'new relions', Sam Gill notes that these movements enabled groups from many different backgrounds to recognize a common identity.[41] Outside of the American context, Peter Worsley finds something similar in his important study of Melanesian 'cargo' cults. Worsley finds that these movements 'weld previously hostile and separate groups together in a new unity'.[42] What needs to be emphasized in the case of Native American movements is that this 'welding' of previously separate groups came about as a result of a process that very much resembled an initiation ceremony. To be sure, it may have been an initiation ceremony on an unusually large scale, displaying a great degree of improvisation, and fusing itself more openly with a political agenda, but it is nonetheless recognizable as a rite of passage experienced on a collective level.

Employing this perspective, we would expect careful study of these movements to reveal that homologies exist between them and pre-existing rituals, either indigenous or imported. For example, initiation rituals or annual rites of renewal may have informed the structure, symbolism, and timing of these movements. Though these and other possible homologies warrant a level of review much greater than can be provided in this brief article, we can at least allude to one of the more striking parallels. Consider a single aspect of these movements, the concern for purification. This drive expressed itself in varied forms. Classical forms included withdrawal into the wilderness, vision-seeking and sacred dances. Innovative forms included destruction of the signs, symbols, and carriers of colonialist civilization (looting, pillaging, burning, wrecking, assassinating). In their quest for purity, the Delaware militants advocated not only that the people 'quit all Commerce with ye White People' but also practice sexual abstinence and a new diet that included the use of an emetic beverage imported from the Southeast.[43] Delaware, Shawnee, Cherokee, and Creek prophets urged their people to abandon European clothing and dispense with ornaments of silver and brass, glass and beads, and other trade goods. Delaware and Creek warriors attempted to rely less upon guns, and more upon bow and arrow. Participants in several of these movements performed many violent acts, killing chiefs and slaughtering livestock.[44] Led by prophets, the Creeks killed and consumed cattle, hogs, and fowl belonging to friendly chiefs and European American traders. Even more significant, the Creek rebels killed their own hogs and cattle, leaving much meat to rot, and then abandoned their corn fields. At the height of this particular movement, it appeared that the prophetic faction was determined to 'destroy every thing received from the Americans'.[45]

To European American observers, acts of renunciation performed by the Delawares, Shawnees, Cherokees, and Creeks seemed purely destructive, purely negative, and completely inexplicable. European American eyewitnesses were incredulous: 'One thing surprises me they have totally neglected their crops and are destroying every living eatable thing... They are daily persevering in this mode of destruction.'[46] Nevertheless, although acts of destruction inaugurated many of these movements, the great majority of these movements were oriented toward something beyond destruction.[47] Within these movements, acts of destruction, purification, and withdrawal were necessary, but they were necessary as a kind of prelude, an opening phase within a larger transformation drama. As in most rites of passage, purification was oriented toward a higher subsequent phase and a new kind of status. In these movements, diverse Native American groups ritually rejected dependence upon European Americans and symbolically affirmed a new status of pan-Native American identity.

In doing so, they were not simply re-assuming an old identity that had been forgotten, although their prophets claimed that was precisely what they were doing. Rather than focusing upon their commonalities, pre-contact Native Americans must have been most conscious of the plethora of highly diverse religious, linguistic, political, social, and cultural forms that divided them into a great number of ethnic groups. Though many of these groups were linked by broad cultural commonalities, complex political arrangements, and significant trade networks, the emphasis was probably upon difference, not commonality. The situation changed dramatically when these diverse peoples were collectively misnamed 'Indians' and then reconstructed as colonized subjects within a world-system dominated by European nation-states. Though ethnic differences did not diminish, and intertribal conflicts did not cease, very deep and widespread cultural and religious commonalities could not help but become more apparent. As diverse Native American peoples found themselves linked by unprecedented types and levels of trade and more rapid forms of transportation, many groups engaged in 'talks' and attempted to unify their political strategies. As they found their economies revolutionized, land bases threatened, and cosmologies challenged as a result of contact with the invaders, it was almost inevitable that a self-conscious pan-Native Americanism would emerge. Prophetic movements recognized this prospect most vigorously and dramatically. In these movements, prophets beckoned diverse peoples to put aside their differences and forge a new common identity. The Ottawa prophet urged Native Americans 'to cultivate peace between your different tribes, that they may become one great people'. Tecumseh, a Shawnee chief, argued that 'all the lands in the western country was the common property of all the tribes'. His brother, the Prophet, affirmed that 'no sale was good unless made by all the tribes'.[48] A Creek prophet said, 'If the red people would unite nothing could withstand them'.[49]

In justifying pan-Native Americanism, several prophets employed a theory of racial polygenesis.[50] Developed by Native Americans during the eighteenth century, this theory held that 'red' people were fundamentally different from 'white' people. Drawing upon this theory, the Shawnee prophet argued that 'the Great Spirit did not mean that the white and red people should live near each other'. In a similar vein, a Cherokee prophet said: 'You yourselves can see that the white people are entirely different beings from us; we are made of red clay; they, out of white sand'.[51] Thus, the prophets asserted that pan-Native Americanism was grounded ontologically. In their view, diverse peoples could unite and hold onto their lands by identifying themselves as 'red people' in opposition to 'white people'.

Signifying Difference

The study of these movements may lead to an important reformulation of Van Gennep's portrayal of initiation.[52] Van Gennep's analysis presupposes a stable society to which the initiand returns in order to assume a well-defined adult status. But for the colonized person undergoing millenarian initiation, no traditional reintegration is possible. Because society under colonialism is always already distorted, millenarian initiation, unlike traditional initiation, cannot terminate in the assumption of a whole or self-same identity. No return to the ordinary world is possible. Rather, if it is to cancel the negativity of colonialism, the initiation process must grant to the initiand actions, words, and meanings that signify an irreducible difference from the identity that the colonial order has imposed or desires to impose upon him/her. Colonizing 'writing' must be overpowered by oppositional writing that is at once more primordial and post-colonial. Furthermore, if the post-colonial movement is to reach significant numbers of people, its leaders must devise strategies for transmitting and preserving this vital difference through time and across space.

Prophets and participants symbolized, disseminated, and embodied *difference* through a variety of means. Prophets developed innovative strategies, including the production of pictographic 'books' or 'maps' and carved 'prayer sticks' to communicate core meanings to wider constituencies.[53] In several significant Native American religious revolts, the prophets and the initiated attached crucial importance to learning new bodily gestures, especially new sacred dances. In 1811, for instance, when several Great Lakes prophets traveled to the Southeast to enlist the support of Chickasaw, Choctaw, Cherokee and Creek Indians, they not only related the shamanistic visions of the Shawnee prophet, they also taught converts 'The Dance of the Indians of the Lakes'. More than any other ceremonial act, belief, or practice, dancing 'The Dance of the Indians of the Lakes' distinguished those Southeastern Indians who joined the Shawnee inter-tribal movement from those who remained friendly with European Americans. Rebels performed this imported dance at ritual executions of friendly chiefs, and before battles. They even performed it during battles in the face of cannon. Of course, the Sioux Ghost Dance movement also centered upon a dance that came from outside, from Native American peoples far to the west. This suggests that one of the vital ways to symbolize a pan-Native American identity was to borrow an expressive practice from a group perceived to be more distant from and less dependent upon European Americans. As we study these movements more fully, our method will necessarily move beyond simple historiography to employ

disciplines and approaches devoted to the study of aesthetic, phenomenological, and literary forms, for it was through gesture, symbol and rhetoric that these movements communicated pan-Native American difference.

Prospects for Comparative Study

Closer study of Native American transformative movements will expand
and deepen knowledge of Native American religions, and it will also open
up interesting opportunities for comparative studies. Since these movements were movements responding to modern contact, scholars will want
to compare them with important forms of cultural innovation practiced by
other New World populations such as European American communitarian
movements, African American slave revolts, and other forms of 'popular'
religion.[54] Though their cultural differences were great, Native American,
African American, and European American populations in the eighteenth
and nineteenth centuries were unavoidably involved in a common economic world-system, faced tremendous changes in traditional orders,
including crucial shifts in gender relations, political organization, demographic profile, and kinship systems. By comparing the religious responses
of Native Americans, European Americans, and African Americans, we
will more fully appreciate how the contact situation imposed common
challenges and inspired very diverse responses. By performing cross-cultural comparisons within the American context, we will make Native
Americans less exotic and further bring the story of their creative responses to the contact experience into the story of religion in America.

Since these Native American transformative movements were responses to colonialism, their study will also encourage comparison with
movements in other colonial contexts. They will be fruitfully compared
and contrasted with millenarian movements, cargo-cult activities, and
millenialist developments in Africa, South America, Melanesia, and early
modern Europe.[55] Native American transformative movements may also
be productively juxtaposed with other forms of cultural politics and
resistance from what is now known as the Third World. The parallels
between Native American prophetic movements and subaltern resistance
in India[56] and the Iranian Revolution[57] are most striking and warrant much
more detailed exploration.

Finally, since these movements took place during a period when
modernity was nascent, they should be juxtaposed with subsequent
religious movements, including various forms of fundamentalism,[58] that
have emerged in the context of fully-developed modernity. Such a
comparison might lead to a theory capable of relating types of religious
movements to various phases in the history of capitalism. Such a theory

would enable an important interdisciplinary dialogue to occur between scholars of religion and neo-Marxist economists, historians, and culture critics.[59]

References

Aberle, David F., *The Peyote Religion among the Navaho* (Chicago: Aldine Publishing, 1966).

Albanese, Catherine, *America: Religions and Religion* (Belmont: Wadsworth, 1981).

Axtell, James, 'The Ethnohistory of Early America: A Review Essay', *William and Mary Quarterly* 35 (1978), 110-44.

—*The European and the Indian: Essays in the Ethnohistory of Colonial North America* (New York: Oxford University Press, 1981).

Bak, János M., and Gerhard Benecke (eds.), *Religion and Rural Revolt* (Manchester: Manchester University Press, 1982).

Berkhofer, Robert, *The White Man's Indian: Images of the American Indian from Columbus to the Present* (New York: Knopf, 1978).

Brotherston, Gordon, *Image of the New World: The American Continent Portrayed in Native Texts* (London: Thames & Hudson, 1979).

Brown, Jennifer, and Jacqueline Peterson, *The New Peoples: Being and Becoming Métis in North America* (Lincoln: University of Nebraska Press, 1985).

Burkhalter, Sheryl L., and Frank E. Reynolds, 'Privileging the Periphery: Reflections on Religious Studies and the Liberal Arts', *Criterion* 26.2 (1987), 2-6.

Burridge, Kenelm, *Mambu: A Melanesian Millennium* (New York: Humanities Press, 1960).

—*New Heaven, New Earth: A Study of Millenarian Activities* (New York: Schocken Books, 1969).

Carmack, Robert M., 'Ethnohistory: A Review of its Development, Definition, Methods, and Aims', *Annual Review of Anthropology* 1 (1972), 227-46.

Carmody, Denise, and John Carmody, *Exploring American Religion* (Mountain View, CA: Mayfield Publishing, 1989).

Cobb, R.C., *The Police and the People: French Popular Protest, 1789–1820* (Oxford: Clarendon Press, 1970).

DeMallie, Raymond J., 'The Lakota Ghost Dance: An Ethnohistorical Account', *Pacific Historical Review* 51 (1982), 385-405.

—*The Sixth Grandfather: Black Elk's Teaching to John G. Neihardt* (Lincoln: University of Nebraska Press, 1984).

Diacon, Todd Alan, 'Capitalists and Fanatics: Brazil's Contestado Rebellion, 1912–1916' (PhD dissertation, University of Wisconsin-Madison, 1987).

Dowd, Gregory Evans, 'Paths of Resistance: American Indian Religion and the Quest for Unity, 1745–1815' (PhD dissertation, Princeton University, 1986).

Drinno, Richard, *Facing West: The Metaphysics of Indian Hating and Empire-Building* (New York: Times Mirror, 1980).

Fabian, Johannes, *Time and the Other: How Anthropology Makes its Object* (New York: Columbia University Press, 1983).

Fausz, Frederick, 'Patterns of Anglo-Indian Aggression and Accommodation along the Mid-Atlantic Coast, 1584–1634', in William Fitzhugh (ed.), *Cultures in Contact* (Washington, DC: Smithsonian Institution, 1985), 225-67.

Fields, Karen, *Revival and Rebellion in Colonial Central Africa* (Princeton, NJ: Princeton University Press, 1983).

Ford, Richard, *Journal of Pontiac's Conspiracy, 1763* (Detroit: Speaker-Hines Printing Company, 1983).

Galloway, Patricia (ed.), *The Southeastern Ceremonial Complex: Artifacts and Analysis* (Lincoln: University of Nebraska Press, 1989).

van Gennep, Arnold, *The Rites of Passage* (trans. Monika B. Vizedom and Gabrielle L. Caffee; Chicago: University of Chicago Press, 1980 [1960]).

Gill, Sam, *Native American Traditions: Sources and Interpretations* (Belmont: Wadsworth, 1983).

—'Native American Religions', in Charles H. Lippy and Peter W. Williams (eds.), *Encyclopedia of American Religious Experience: Studies of Traditions and Movements* (New York: Charles Scribner's Sons, 1988), 137-56.

Gilsenan, Michael, 'Approaching the Islamic Revolution: Akhavi and Fischer', *Merip Reports* 102 (1.12) 1982, 29-30.

Guha, Ranajit, *Elementary Aspects of Peasant Insurgency in Colonial India* (Delhi: Oxford University Press, 1983).

—*Subaltern Studies: Writings on South Asian History and Society*, III (Oxford: Oxford University Press, 1984).

Hawkins, Benjamin, *Letters, Journal, and Writings of Benjamin Hawkins* (ed. C.L. Grant; Savannah: The Beehive Press, 1980).

Hill, Christopher, *The World Turned Upside Down* (New York: Viking, 1971).

Hooglund, Mary, 'Religious Ritual and Political Struggle in an Iranian Village', *Merip Reports* 102 (1.12) 1982, 10-17.

Hunter, Charles E., 'The Delaware Nativist Revival of the Mid-Eighteenth Century', *Ethnohistory* 18 (1971), 39-49.

Jameson, Fredric, *The Political Unconscious: Narrative as a Socially Symbolic Act* (Ithaca, NY: Cornell University Press, 1981).

—*The Ideologies of Theory: Essays 1971–1986* (Minneapolis: University of Minnesota Press, 1988).

Jennings, Francis, *The Invasion of America: Indians, Colonialism, and the Cant of Conquest* (Chapel Hill: University of North Carolina Press, 1975).

—'A Growing Partnership: Historians, Anthropologists, and American Indian History', *Ethnohistory* 29 (1982), 21-41.

Jorgensen, Joseph, *The Sun Dance Religion: Power for the Powerless* (Chicago: University of Chicago Press, 1972).

—'Religious Solutions and Native American Struggles: Ghost Dance, Sun Dance and Beyond', in Bruce Lincoln (ed.), *Religion, Rebellion, Revolution: An Interdisciplinary and Cross-cultural Collection of Essays* (New York: St. Martin's Press, 1985), 102-10.

Kenney, James, (ed. John W. Jordan), 'Journal of James Kenney, 1761–1763', *The Pennsylvania Magazine of History and Biography* 37 (1913), 1-47, 152-201.

LaBarre, Weston, *The Ghost Dance: Origins of Religion* (New York: Doubleday, 1970).

Lankford, George E. (ed.), *Native American Legends: Southeastern Legends* (Little Rock: August House, 1987).

Lawrence, Bruce B., *Defenders of God: The Fundamentalist Revolt against the Modern Age* (San Francisco: Harper & Row, 1989).

Lincoln, Bruce, *Religion, Rebellion, Revolution: An Interdisciplinary and Cross-cultural Collection of Essays* (New York: St Martin's Press, 1985).

Lippy, Charles H., and Peter W. Williams (eds.), *Encyclopedia of American Religious Experience: Studies of Traditions and Movements* (New York: Charles Scribner's Sons, 1988).

Long, Charles H., *Significations: Signs, Symbols, and Images in the Interpretation of Religion* (Philadelphia: Fortress Press, 1986).

Mandel, Ernest, *Late Capitalism* (London: Verso, 1978).

—*Long Waves of Capitalist Development: The Marxist Interpretation* (New York: Cambridge University Press, 1980).

Martin, Joel, *Sacred Revolt: The Muskogees' Struggle for a New World* (Boston: Beacon Press, 1991).

McLoughlin, William G., *The Cherokee Ghost Dance: Essays on the Southeastern Indians, 1789–1861* (Macon, GA: Mercer University Press, 1984).

Meinig, Donald, *The Shaping of America: A Geographical Perspective on 500 Years History, Atlantic America, 1492–1800*, I (New Haven, CT: Yale University Press, 1986).

Merrell, James, 'The Indians' New World: The Catawba Experience', *William and Mary Quarterly*, 3.41 (1984), 537-65.

—*The Indians' New World: Catawbas and their Neighbors from European Contact through the Era of Removal* (Chapel Hill: University of North Carolina Press, 1989).

Mooney, James, *The Ghost Dance Religion* (Washington: Bureau of Ethnology, 1896).

Morrison, Kenneth, *The Embattled Northeast: The Elusive Ideal of Alliance in Abenaki-Euramerican Relations* (Berkeley, CA: University of California Press, 1984).

Nandy, Ashis, *The Intimate Enemy: Loss and Recovery of Self under Colonialism* (Delhi: Oxford University Press, 1983).

Neihardt, John G., *Black Elk Speaks: Being the Life Story of a Holy Man of the Oglala Sioux* (New York: Washington Square Press, 1972 [1932]).

Paden, William E., *Religious Worlds: The Comparative Study of Religion* (Boston: Beacon Press, 1988).

Porterfield, Amanda, 'Shamanism: A Psychosocial Definition', *Journal of the American Academy of Religion* 55 (1987), 721-39.

Powers, William K., 'Review of *The Sixth Grandfather* by Raymond J. DeMallie', *Ethnohistory* 33.1 (1986), 121-23.

—'When Black Elk Speaks, Everybody Listens', *Social Text* 8.2 (1990), 43-56.

Ruether, Rosemary, and Rosemary Skinner Keller (eds.), *Women and Religion in America: The Colonial and Revolutionary Periods, a Documentary History*, II (San Francisco: Harper and Row, 1983).

Quaife, Milo Milton, *The John Askin Papers* (Detroit: Detroit Public Library, 1931).

Salisbury, Neal, *Manitou and Providence: Indians, Europeans, and the Making of New England, 1500–1643* (New York: Oxford University Press, 1982).

Sheehan, Bernard W., 'Indian-White Relations in Early America: A Review Essay', *William and Mary Quarterly* 26 (1969), 267-86.

Spicer, Edward H., *Cycles of Conquest: The Impact of Spain, Mexico and the United States on the Indians of the Southwest, 1533–1960* (Tucson: University of Arizona Press, 1962).

Stefanco-Schill, Carolyn, 'Guale Indian Revolt: Anti-Colonialism in the Old South', *Southern Exposure* 12.6 (1984), 4-10.

Thompson, Edward P., 'Eighteenth-Century English Society: Class Struggle without Class', *Social History* 3.2 (1978), 133-65.

Thrupp, Sylvia (ed.), *Millennial Dreams in Action: Studies in Revolutionary Religious Movements* (New York: Schocken Books, 1970).

Thurman, Melburn Delano, 'The Delaware Indians: A Study in Ethnohistory' (PhD dissertation, University of California, Santa Barbara, 1973).

Trigger, Bruce C., *The Children of Aataentsic: A History of the Huron People to 1660* (Montreal: McGill-Queen's University Press, 1976).

Turner, Victor W., *The Ritual Process: Structure and Anti-Structure* (Chicago: Aldine Publishing Company, 1969).

—'A Few Definitions', in *The Encyclopedia of Religion* (ed. Mircea Eliade; New York: Macmillan and Free Press, 1986), XII, 386.

Vizenor, Gerald, *The People Named the Chippewa: Narrative Histories* (Minneapolis: University of Minnesota Press, 1984).

Wallace, Anthony F.C., 'Revitalization Movements', *American Anthropologist* 58 (1956): 264-81.

—*The Death and Rebirth of the Seneca* (New York: Knopf, 1970).

Waselkov, Gregory, and Brian M. Wood, 'The Creek War of 1813–1814: Effects on Creek Society and Settlement Pattern', *Journal of Alabama Archaeology* 32.1 (1986), 1-24.

Waselkov, Gregory, Peter H. Wood and Thomas Harley (eds.), *Powhatan's Mantle: Indians in the Colonial Southeast* (Lincoln. University of Nebraska Press, 1989).

White, Richard, *The Roots of Dependency: Subsistence, Environment, and Social Change among the Choctaws, Pawnees, and Navajos* (Lincoln: University of Nebraska Press, 1983).

—'The "Middle Ground" for Indians in the Great Lakes', in *Overcoming Economic Dependency, Occasional Papers in Curriculum Series*, No. 9 (Chicago: The Newberry Library, 1989).

Williams, Peter, *Popular Religion in America* (Carbondale: University of Illinois Press, 1989).

Williams, Raymond, *The Country and the City* (New York: Oxford University Press, 1973).

—*Marxism and Literature* (New York: Oxford University Press, 1977).

Wolf, Eric, *Europe and the People without History* (Berkeley, CA: University of California Press, 1982).

Worsley, Peter, *The Trumpet Shall Sound: A Study of 'Cargo' Cults in Melanesia* (London: McGibbon & Kee, 1968).

Wright, J. Leitch, *The Only Land They Knew: The Tragic Story of the American Indians in the Old South* (New York: Free Press, 1981).

Notes

    *   Permission to reprint this essay from *Journal of the American Academy of Religion* Vol. 59.4 (1991), 677-701 has been given by the American Academy of Religion. This essay is a revised version of papers given at the American Academy of Religion Convention in 1988. The American Studies Association Convention in 1989, and the Faculty Colloquium of the Department of Religion at the University of Pennsylvania in 1991. I would like to thank Phyllis Rogers, Ines Talamantez, Mary Farrell Bednarowski, Catherine Albanese, Kenneth Morrison, Amanda Porterfield, Stephen Dunning, and Robert Kraft for their comments. I especially thank Jane Marie Pinzino for her careful reading of this essay in all of its stages. Portions of this essay appear in *Sacred Revolt: The Muskogees' Struggle for a New World* (Boston: Beacon Press, 1991).

    1.   Catherine Albanese, *America: Religions and Religion* (Belmont: Wadsworth, 1981), 36; Amanda Porterfield, 'Shamanism: A Psychosocial Definition', *Journal of the American Academy of Religion* 55 (1987), 721-39, 735; and Peter Williams, *Popular Religion in America* (Carbondale: University of Illinois Press, 1989), 33.

    2.   J. Leitch Wright, *The Only Land They Knew: The Tragic Story of the American Indians in the Old South* (New York: Free Press, 1981); Gregory Evans Dowd, 'Paths of

Resistance: American Indian Religion and the Quest for Unity, 1745–1815' (PhD dissertation, Princeton University, 1986); Charles E. Hunter, 'The Delaware Nativist Revival of the Mid-Eighteenth Century', *Ethnohistory* 18 (1971), 39-49; Melburn Delano Thurman, 'The Delaware Indians: A Study in Ethnohistory' (PhD dissertation, University of California, Santa Barbara, 1973); Frederick Fausz, 'Patterns of Anglo-Indian Aggression and Accommodation along the Mid-Atlantic Coast, 1584–1634', in William Fitzhugh (ed.), *Cultures in Contact* (Washington, DC: Smithsonian Institution, 1985), 225-67; Edward H. Spicer, *Cycles of Conquest: The Impact of Spain, Mexico and the United States on the Indians of the Southwest, 1533–1960* (Tucson: University of Arizona Press, 1962); Carolyn Stefanco-Schill, 'Guale Indian Revolt: Anti-Colonialism in the Old South', *Southern Exposure* 12.6 (1984), 4-10.

3.   Albanese, *America*; Denise Carmody and John Carmody, *Exploring American Religion* (Mountain View, CA: Mayfield Publishing Company, 1989); Rosemary Ruether and Rosemary Skinner Keller (eds.), *Women and Religion in America: The Colonial and Revolutionary Periods, a Documentary History*, II (San Francisco: Harper & Row, 1983); Williams, *Popular Religion in America*; and Sam Gill, 'Native American Religions', in Charles H. Lippy and Peter W. Williams (eds.), *Encyclopedia of American Religious Experience: Studies of Traditions and Movements* (New York: Charles Scribner's Sons, 1988), 137-56.

4.   Albanese, *America*; and Sam Gill, *Native American Traditions: Sources and Interpretations* (Belmont: Wadsworth, 1983).

5.   Charles H. Lippy and Peter W. Williams (eds.), *Encyclopedia of American Religious Experience: Studies of Traditions and Movements* (New York: Charles Scribner's Sons, 1988); Carmody and Carmody, *Exploring American Religion*, and Ruether and Keller, *Women and Religion in America*.

6.   Williams, *Popular Religion in America*; and Albanese, *America*.

7.   William K. Powers, 'When Black Elk Speaks, Everybody Listens', *Social Text* 8.2 (1990), 43-56.

8.   John G. Neihardt, *Black Elk Speaks: Being the Life Story of a Holy Man of the Oglala Sioux* (New York: Washington Square Press, 1972 [1932]), 43.

9.   Joseph Jorgensen, 'Religious Solutions and Native American Struggles: Ghost Dance, Sun Dance and Beyond', in Bruce Lincoln (ed.), *Religion, Rebellion, Revolution: An Interdisciplinary and Cross-cultural Collection of Essays* (New York: St Martin's Press, 1985), 102-10.

10.   Weston LaBarre, *The Ghost Dance: Origins of Religion* (New York: Doubleday, 1970), 41-43, 107, 229-31.

11.   Porterfield, 'Shamanism', 735.

12.   Raymond J. DeMallie, 'The Lakota Ghost Dance: An Ethnohistorical Account', *Pacific Historical Review* 51 (1982), 385-405.

13.   Anthony F.C. Wallace, 'Revitalization Movements', *American Anthropologist* 58 (1956), 264-81, 264 and LaBarre, *The Ghost Dance*, 43.

14.   David F. Aberle, *The Peyote Religion among the Navaho* (Chicago: Aldine Publishing Company, 1966), 315-23.

15.   Joseph Jorgensen, *The Sun Dance Religion: Power for the Powerless* (Chicago: University of Chicago Press, 1972).

16.   Jorgensen, *The Sun Dance Religion*, 7.

17. Anthony F.C. Wallace, *The Death and Rebirth of the Seneca* (New York: Knopf, 1970).

18. See Williams, *Popular Religion in America*, 26-34, and Albanese, *America*, 36.

19. James Axtell, *The European and the Indian: Essays in the Ethnohistory of Colonial North America* (New York: Oxford University Press, 1981); Jennifer Brown and Jacqueline Peterson, *The New Peoples: Being and Becoming Métis in North America* (Lincoln: University of Nebraska Press, 1985); Patricia Galloway (ed.), *The Southeastern Ceremonial Complex: Artifacts and Analysis* (Lincoln: University of Nebraska Press, 1989); Francis Jennings, *The Invasion of America: Indians, Colonialism, and the Cant of Conquest* (Chapel Hill: University of North Carolina Press, 1975); James Merrell, *The Indians' New World: Catawbas and their Neighbors from European Contact through the Era of Removal* (Chapel Hill: University of North Carolina Press, 1989); Neal Salisbury, *Manitou and Providence: Indians, Europeans, and the Making of New England, 1500–1643* (New York: Oxford University Press, 1982); Bruce C. Trigger, *The Children of Aataentsic: A History of the Huron People to 1660* (Montreal: McGill-Queen's University Press, 1976); Gregory Waselkov, Peter H. Wood and Thomas Harley (eds.), *Powhatan's Mantle: Indians in the Colonial Southeast* (Lincoln: University of Nebraska Press, 1989); Richard White, *The Roots of Dependency: Subsistence, Environment, and Social Change among the Choctaws, Pawnees, and Navajos* (Lincoln: University of Nebraska Press, 1983), and Wright, *The Only Land They Knew*.

20. Dowd, 'Paths of Resistance'; William G. McLoughlin, *The Cherokee Ghost Dance: Essays on the Southeastern Indians, 1789–1861* (Macon, GA: Mercer University Press, 1984), and Richard White, 'The "Middle Ground" for Indians in the Great Lakes', in *Overcoming Economic Dependency, Occasional Papers in Curriculum Series*, No.9. (Chicago: The Newberry Library, 1989).

21. Gordon Brotherston, *Image of the New World: The American Continent Portrayed in Native Texts* (London: Thames & Hudson, 1979), 48.

22. Milo Milton Quaife, *The John Askin Papers* (Detroit: Detroit Public Library, 1931), 15.

23. Aberle, *The Peyote Religion*, 323; see also LaBarre, *The Ghost Dance*.

24. Jorgensen, *The Sun Dance Religion*, 8.

25. James Merrell, *The Indians' New World* and *idem*, 'The Indians' New World: The Catawba Experience', *William and Mary Quarterly*, 3.41 (1984), 537-65.

26. Merrell, *The Indians' New World*, 538.

27. The weakness of Merrell's argument is that it does not provide an integrative perspective (cf. Donald Meinig, *The Shaping of America: A Geographical Perspective on 500 Years History, Atlantic America, 1492–1800*, I [New Haven, CT: Yale University Press, 1986]) nor advance a theoretic framework (cf. White, *The Roots of Dependency*, 1983) capable of articulating the historical forces bringing various Atlantic societies into contact. Merrell's argument relies too much upon metaphor and not enough upon metonymy.

28. William E. Paden, *Religious Worlds: The Comparative Study of Religion* (Boston: Beacon Press, 1988), 52-65.

29. Paden, *Religious Worlds*, 53.

30. Exemplified most clearly in the Delaware prophetic movement with its 'Indian Bible', the Book or the absence of the book (and literacy) appears also in the pro-

phetic discourse of the Creek prophets (cf. Joel Martin, *Sacred Revolt: The Muskogees' Struggle for a New World* [Boston: Beacon Press, 1991]).

31. For an example of how these themes were united, see Pontiac's charge (Richard Ford, *Journal of Pontiac's Conspiracy, 1763* [Detroit: Speaker-Hines Printing Company, 1983], 30-32).

32. Benjamin Hawkins, *Letters, Journal, and Writings of Benjamin Hawkins* (ed. C.L. Grant; Savannah: The Beehive Press, 1980), 652.

33. Martin, *Sacred Revolt*; and Thurman, 'The Delaware Indians', 163-65.

34. Hunter, 'The Delaware Nativist Revival', 47.

35. Edward P. Thompson, 'Eighteenth-Century English Society: Class Struggle without Class', *Social History* 3.2 (1978), 133-65, 149.

36. Axtell, *The European and the Indian*; White, *The Roots of Dependency*; and Salisbury, *Manitou and Providence*.

37. Paden, *Religious Worlds*, 113.

38. Victor W. Turner, 'A Few Definitions', in *The Encyclopedia of Religion* (ed. Mircea Eliade; New York: Macmillan and Free Press, 1986), XII, 386.

39. Victor W. Turner, *The Ritual Process: Structure and Anti-Structure* (Chicago: Aldine Publishing Company, 1969), 94-112.

40. Turner, *The Ritual Process*, 112.

41. Gill, *Native American Traditions*, 144-45.

42. Peter Worsley, *The Trumpet Shall Sound: A Study of 'Cargo' Cults in Melanesia* (London: McGibbon & Kee, 1968), 228.

43. James Kenney, (ed. John W. Jordan), 'Journal of James Kenney, 1761–1763', *The Pennsylvania Magazine of History and Biography* 37 (1913), 1-47, 152-201, (188).

44. James Mooney, *The Ghost Dance Religion* (Washington: Bureau of Ethnology, 1896), 668; McLoughlin, *The Cherokee Ghost Dance*, 146; Waselkov, Wood, and Harley, *Powhatan's Mantle*, 189-94, and Dowd, 'Paths of Resistance', 172, 296.

45. Hawkins, *Letters*, 652.

46. Hawkins, *Letters*, 656.

47. Acts of destruction were often important in millenarian movements outside of North America as well. In Burridge's interpretation, these acts serve as a kind of 'hinge' between two social orders. 'Destruction of crops, livestock and other means of gaining a livelihood, through which men and women express and discharge their obligations to each other, represent or symbolize the millenium… No rules and new rules meet in the prophet who initiates the one whilst advocating the other' (Kenelm Burridge, *New Heaven, New Earth: A Study of Millenarian Activities* [New York: Schocken Books, 1969],165-66).

48. Dowd, 'Paths of Resistance', 635, 628.

49. Hawkins, *Letters*, 666.

50. McLoughlin, *The Cherokee Ghost Dance*, 253-61, and George E. Lankford (ed.), *Native American Legends: Southeastern Legends* (Little Rock: August House, 1987), 140-41.

51. Dowd, 'Paths of Resistance', 631, 709-10.

52. Arnold van Gennep, *The Rites of Passage* (trans. Monika B. Vizedom and Gabrielle L. Caffee; Chicago: University of Chicago Press, 1980 [1960]), 65-115.

53. Mooney, *The Ghost Dance Religion*, 666-68, 694-97.

54. Williams, *Popular Religion in America*.

55. Karen Fields, *Revival and Rebellion in Colonial Central Africa* (Princeton, NJ: Princeton University Press, 1983); Todd Alan Diacon, 'Capitalists and Fanatics: Brazil's Contestado Rebellion, 1912–1916' (PhD dissertation, University of Wisconsin–Madison, 1987); Worsley, *The Trumpet Shall Sound*; Kenelm Burridge, *Mambu: A Melanesian Millennium* (New York: Humanities Press, 1960) and *idem*, *New Heaven, New Earth*; Sylvia Thrupp (ed.), *Millennial Dreams in Action: Studies in Revolutionary Religious Movements* (New York: Schocken Books, 1970); Christopher Hill, *The World Turned Upside Down* (New York: Viking, 1971); and János M. Bak and Gerhard Benecke (eds.), *Religion and Rural Revolt* (Manchester: Manchester University Press, 1982).

56. Ranajit Guha, *Elementary Aspects of Peasant Insurgency in Colonial India* (Delhi: Oxford University Press, 1983) and *idem*, *Subaltern Studies: Writings on South Asian History and Society*, III (Oxford: Oxford University Press, 1984).

57. Michael Gilsenan, 'Approaching the Islamic Revolution: Akhavi and Fischer', *Merip Reports* 102 (1/12) 1982, 29-30, and Mary Hooglund, 'Religious Ritual and Political Struggle in an Iranian Village', *Merip Reports* 102 (1.12) 1982, 10-17.

58. Bruce B. Lawrence, *Defenders of God: The Fundamentalist Revolt against the Modern Age* (San Francisco: Harper & Row, 1989).

59. Ernest Mandel, *Late Capitalism* (London: Verso, 1978), and *idem*, *Long Waves of Capitalist Development: The Marxist Interpretation* (New York: Cambridge University Press, 1980); Eric Wolf, *Europe and the People without History* (Berkeley, CA: University of California Press, 1982); Raymond Williams, *The Country and the City* (New York: Oxford University Press, 1973) and *idem*, *Marxism and Literature* (New York: Oxford University Press, 1977); and Fredric Jameson, *The Political Unconscious: Narrative as a Socially Symbolic Act* (Ithaca, NY: Cornell University Press, 1981) and *idem*, *The Ideologies of Theory: Essays 1971–1986* (Minneapolis: University of Minnesota Press, 1988).

'The day is not far off...':
The Millennial Reich and the Induced Apocalypse

David Redles

'The day is not far off', Hitler told a journalist in 1931, 'when we shall be living in great times once more.' Hitler, furthermore, wanted the reporter to spread the good word, explaining that 'what we now need is that intelligent writers should make clear to the citizens of Germany the historic turning point at which Germany stands today. We are on the threshold of a unique epoch in our history.'[1] This essay will discuss the Nazi belief, shared by many leaders and Old Guard followers alike, that Germany had reached a turning point of world historical significance, a time from which a millennial New Age would be born from the chaos of Weimar. To achieve the Millennial Reich, Hitler believed that the eschatological conflict between Aryan and Jew had to come to a 'Final Solution' (in all its apocalyptic connotations).[2]

Weimar Apocalypse

The chaos of post-war Weimar Germany was experienced by many individuals who became Nazis as a time of apocalypse. Street fighting between the extreme left and the extreme right, political assassinations, seemingly endemic unemployment, a devastating hyperinflation followed by an equally crippling depression, combined with what for many Germans was a cultural decay of unparalleled proportions, all fused together and collapsed any sense of order. Many individuals who would convert to Nazism interpreted this period as not simply hard times, but in apocalyptic fashion, as a total 'collapse' of German civilization. Viewing the world through a millenarian lens, many early Nazis believed that Germany was at best threatened by 'enslavement', and more frequently, 'annihilation'. Weimar was a time, then, of salvation or destruction. One Old Guard Nazi, as the early converts referred to themselves, described World War I and the post-war chaos with common millenarian imagery of darkness and light, and a social inversion blamed on the Jewish bogey man:

Barely 18 years old, I went to the field to defend our homeland against a world of instigating enemies. Twice I was wounded. Then in November 1918 the Marxist revolution broke out—dark thunderclouds descended

over Germany that for 15 years allowed no rays of light and no sunshine
upon the earth. In Germany everything went upside down. The Spartacists,
clothed in sailor's uniforms, devastated and destroyed everything they
could lay a finger on. The Jew rose to the pinnacle.[3]

The fear of social fragmentation exhibited by the above Nazi was commonly voiced. Germany appeared fractured by class, religion, age and
gender.[4] The following description of post-war Germany by a veteran
turned department store salesman exhibits the tendency of many Nazis
to see the chaos as resulting from social fragmentation. The creation of
German unity through the coming of a *Führer* [literally 'leader', but with
pronounced messianic overtones] appeared to be his only salvation:

> A new Germany appeared before the eyes and one felt the moral decline
> of a formerly strong nation. Marxist false teaching had caused the Volk,
> already in the broadest circles, to forget the concept of national honor.
> Then came the madness of the Marxist revolt of November 9, 1918 and
> with it the final collapse of the German nation. Party quarrels and
> squabbles fragmented the Volk. Always standing upon a national basis, I
> made a spiritual search for an unknown power that embodied the notion
> of a national and social Germany. Standing amidst the maddening struggle
> of self-sacrifice in a life of sales, this vision grew stronger and stronger. The
> faith was certain in me that only a strong personality could vanquish the
> hate and strife through a national and social greatness.[5]

This man, and many other Germans, found their savior in Adolf Hitler,
who gave voice both to their apocalyptic fears and their desires for salvation. In an early speech of 1922, entitled *Die 'Hecker' der Wahrheit!*
('The "Agitator" of Truth'), Hitler prophesied on the impending apocalypse, and Germany's choice between slavery and annihilation at the hands
of the Jewish-Bolsheviks, or victory and salvation for Aryan humanity if
they followed National Socialism:

> There are only two possibilities in Germany! Do not believe that the Volk
> will wander everlasting in the midst of compromise! It will devote itself first
> to the side that has prophesied on the consequences of the coming ruin
> and has steered clear of it. Either it will be the side of the left: then God
> help us, that leads us to the final corruption, Bolshevism; or it is the side of
> the right, which is resolute…it allows no compromise. Believe me, the
> German Volk lost this World War because it believed it was invincible, and
> had not grasped that there is allowed on this earth only victor and slave.
> And here it is precise—this powerful, great contest can be reduced to but
> two possibilities: either victory of the Aryans or its extermination and
> victory of the Jews.[6]

A Historic Turning Point

Perched on the edge of this abyss, the Nazis believed that Germany, and indeed, Aryan humanity in general, had reached a historic turning point. The old order had collapsed, requiring the appearance of a new order (a new construction of reality). The notion that mankind had reached a historic turning point was a constant theme of Hitler's throughout his career. Alfred Rosenberg, in a work written during the height of the chaos, likened this turning point to those that ushered in the Renaissance and the Enlightenment, a time of 'decline and rebirth'. According to Rosenberg it was a rebirth into a 'new synthesis of life', not simply a new form of government, but inner spiritual transformation, concluding: '[T]oday we are all inwardly experiencing a collapse, and we have a deep longing for a new form of life'.[7]

Old Guard Nazis shared this sense of living at a time of a world turning point, a period when the existence or annihilation of Germany was at stake. Jakob Hoffmann stated: 'I always believed a union of the best forces of Germany must bring about a turning point in order to save Germany from chaos'.[8] Wilhelm Scherer, described what he termed 'a world-historical epoch' this way:

> a presentiment arose in me that only revolution must follow, like one that the glorious history of Germany had not yet experienced. Yes, like one world history had not yet, till now, produced. Germany put into effect a world turning point, brought about by our Führer, his movement, and many of our best who had sacrificed their sacred blood.[9]

Similarly, another early Nazi stated '[W]e are thankful to our Creator to be able to live in this age', while yet another proclaimed that 'the greatest fortune that could befall me was the circumstance that I was born into a time like no other...'[10] Finally, Arno Belger, a local propaganda leader from Halle, described this 'world turning point' in language reflective of his role within the movement:

> An overstrained, spiritually hollow age drew to its close, as antiquated and decaying liberalistic social orders and forms collapsed into themselves. Europe breathed with difficulty under the stifling nightmare of that Uncertain yet Inescapable which was summoned by the shot at Sarajevo as a purifying bath of steel closed upon the civilized world, and so produced the pre-condition for the evolution of the new man of community.[11]

This apocalyptic turning point marked the death of one age and the birth of a millennial New Age—the Third Reich.[12]

Rebirth and the Dawn of the Millennial New Age

Rosenberg's notion that out of the collapse of civilization there is rebirth, is a significant and recurrent element of Nazi millennialism. For many Nazis, the death of their world necessitated the birth of a new world. According to Hitler, it was the Nazis mission to help finish off the dying old world so that the new one could be born. As he explained to an early associate:

> That is precisely the most profound secret of the entire revolution we are living through and whose leadership it is our mission to seize: that there has to be overthrow, demolition, destruction by force! The destruction must be meaningful, not senseless, as under Bolshevism. And it can only become meaningful if we have understood the goal, the purpose, the necessity.[13]

Hermann Rauschning remembers Hitler saying roughly the same thing: 'They regard me as an uneducated barbarian. Yes, we are barbarians! It is an honorable title. We shall rejuvenate the world! This world is near its end. It is our mission to cause unrest.'[14] While Rauschning, and many later historians, took such statements as proof of Hitler's essential nihilism, he and they missed the central point that Hitler saw Nazi violence as hastening the birth of the New Age, the millennial Third Reich. Violence for the Nazis was redemptive, a vehicle for cleansing the earth and thereby saving it.[15]

Old Guard Nazis likewise believed in the coming New Age. In fact, it was the Nazis themselves who heralded the dawn of the New Age. Ernst Röhm exclaimed: '[T]he time in which we live, in which a world has collapsed in a roar and a young world struggles for life and light, will be designated by later generations as the birth of a New Age'.[16] Old Guard Nazi Karl Hepp described the Weimar period as the collapse that presaged the dawn of a New Age:

> A world was forever submerged, and there was something new in the Becoming. A spiritual unrest had seized the world and especially the German people, and permitted men to experience the labor pains of a New Age. I also was strongly possessed by the inner unrest of the New Age.[17]

One early Nazi clearly tied this New Age to an imminent German world domination, achieved for the salvation of humanity:

> Today I am proud, as a co-fighter under the gifted leadership of our Adolf Hitler, to have stepped over the threshold of a New Age. I am also proud to have been able to co-fight in the shaping of German men into National

Socialists and to have been able to assist in the achievement of a National
Socialist Greater Germany of freedom, power and prosperity, which one
day in the future will take over the leadership of all people for the welfare
of all humanity. That was my dream for all these long years and it will find
its fulfillment.[18]

The Mission of the Chosen

The belief in a turning point placed a holy mission upon the shoulders of
Hitler and his disciples. This emphasis on a historic mission awaiting the
Aryan, and thus German, people, is an important and frequently occurring element of Nazi millennialism. In *Mein Kampf* Hitler repeatedly refers
to a 'truly high mission' given to Germany by the 'Almighty', 'Providence',
or 'the Creator'. In Hitler's apocalyptic cosmology this mission required
Aryans to purify themselves in order to reach a stage of biological and
spiritual perfection, thereby achieving a state of god-like capabilities,
ruling the earth as god-men as in ancient times:

> Human culture and civilization on this continent are inseparably bound up
> with the presence of the Aryan. If he dies out or declines, the dark veils of
> an age without culture will again descend on this globe.
>
> The undermining of the existence of human culture by the destruction of
> its bearer seems in the eyes of a volkish philosophy the most execrable
> crime. Anyone who dares to lay hands on the highest image of the Lord
> commits sacrilege against the benevolent creator of this miracle and
> contributes to the expulsion from paradise.
>
> And so the volkish philosophy of life corresponds to the innermost will of
> Nature, since it restores that free play of forces which must lead to a con-
> tinuous mutual higher breeding, until at last the best of humanity, having
> achieved possession of this earth, will have a free path for activity in
> domains which will lie partly above it and partly outside it.
>
> We all sense that in the distant future humanity must be faced by problems
> which only a highest race, become master people and supported by the
> means and possibilities of an entire globe, will be equipped to overcome.[19]

If Hitler alone perceived this sense of mission it could explain only his
personal motivation. However, this sense of mission was shared by many
of his followers. Hitler's personal mission became a shared mission of all
Germans, and by extension, all Aryans. For these Germans, struggling for
Hitler's so-called 'great idea' played a crucial role in their personal sote-
riological mission. Psychologically, it provided a renewed sense of self-
worth and meaning in their lives. One man remarked that '[I]t is, however,
an up-lifting feeling to have taken part in the holy struggle for Germany's

greatness under the Führer and its savior Adolf Hitler'.[20] Another explained that 'for me the essential point is that I may say: "You have, through your struggle, helped the Führer to take the leadership of the German Volk in his hands at the right time, and thereby guard it from destruction!"'.[21]

Hitler delegated this mission to his loyal disciples. Willi Martin recalled a Hitler speech befitting of a prophet and messiah of the Endtime:

> That the Führer had suffered spiritually, we saw in his immensely serious features. However, his words were for us a source of power. These words gave us new courage and resolution for the coming struggle-years. And he admonished us of our mission, and said to us with prophetic words that we, if he could count on us, would obtain an impetus of immense dimensions that would form our battalion into a regiment, this regiment into a division, and this division into an army corps—then the entire Volk would be captured. Thereafter our enthusiasm knew no bounds. And this enthusiasm was for us also the loyalty to this man, who alone had, in the last hour, mastered Germany's fate and had taught us about the future.[22]

It was not by mere chance the Nazis found themselves in such times. Hitler explained: 'We have been chosen by Fate as witnesses of a catastrophe which will be the mightiest confirmation of the soundness of the volkish theory'.[23] Gregor Strasser believed that the Nazis were endowed with the eternal spirit necessary to achieve the millennium:

> There is, however, only one 'right' spirit, only one spirit with a constructive viewpoint; that is the spirit of eternal nature, animated by man, the image of God. It is our strong belief and our deep knowledge that this spirit is in us, in the idea of National Socialism, so that this spirit and no other will build the Millennial Third Reich.[24]

The 'Satanic Jew' and the Soteriology of Race

The progenitors of the apocalyptic chaos, so the Nazis fervently believed, were the Jews. Nazi anti-Semitism was no mere aspect of their ideology, rather was the nucleus around which their apocalyptic racism revolved. Insight into the Nazi millennial world-view can be glimpsed from a relatively obscure early propaganda piece entitled *Bolshevism from Moses to Lenin: Dialogue between Hitler and Me*.[25] This brief work was a stylized conversation between Hitler and his mentor Dietrich Eckart, published in 1924, a few months after Eckart's death, while Hitler was in Landsberg composing *Mein Kampf*.[26] In it Eckart attempts to reveal the hidden history of the Jews and their alleged desire, not simply for world domination, but for world annihilation. The German reader of the time was clearly meant to see the loss of World War I and the subsequent post-war chaos as the product of this same 'hidden force'.

The work uses a pseudo-scholarly approach, with citations to various standard anti-Semitic statements by a host of literary and historical figures. More importantly however, and this is typical of Nazi propaganda then and later, *Bolshevism from Moses to Lenin* also utilizes Jewish sources, primarily the Old Testament and the Talmud (questionably analyzed and translated) to seemingly unmask the Jews.[27] For example, the Book of Esther is explained as a Purim festival 'murder' of 75,000 Persians. It is an event, Eckart writes, that 'no doubt' had 'the same Bolshevik background'. The Egyptian expulsion of the Jews described in Exodus is used to justify the Nazi desire to expel Germany's Jewish population.[28] Ignoring the bounds of time (a deliberate technique to show the eternal nature of the Jewish drive to world domination and annihilation), Eckart likens the alleged Jewish manipulation of the Egyptian rabble or 'Bolshevik horde' to the calls for Liberty, Equality and Fraternity which ignited the French Revolution, thereby implying that Jews used these catchwords of democracy to rile up the mob once again to murder the racial elites. This same implication is later attached to the supposed Jewish role in the Russian and German Revolutions of 1917 and 1919.

Bolshevism from Moses to Lenin concludes with a discussion of the Russian Revolution and the alleged torture deaths of thousands of Russian priests as well as the deliberate death of thirty million Russians by starvation and disease all by the hands of Jewish Bolsheviks.[29] The convergence of the Russian Revolution, the German loss of World War I (and the subsequent chaos of post-war Weimar), and an obscure reference to the *Protocols of the Elders of Zion* [the Kaiser's Dream], are cited as proof that the final attempt of the Jews at world domination is at hand. But it is not simply slavery at the hands of Jews that is being prophesied here. The continuing references to Jewish extermination of non-Jews is deliberate, and from an apocalyptic standpoint, crucial. The pamphlet ends with Hitler discussing the 'final goal' to which the Jew is instinctively 'pushed'.

> Above and beyond world domination—annihilation of the world. He believes he must bring the entire world down on its knees before him in order to prepare a paradise on earth... While he makes a pretense to elevate humanity, he torments it into despair, madness and ruin. If he is not commanded to stop he will annihilate all humanity. His nature compels him to that goal, even though he dimly realizes that he must therefore destroy himself... To be obliged to try to annihilate us with all his might, but at the same time to suspect that that must lead irrevocably to his own destruction. Therein lies, if you will: the tragedy of Lucifer.[30]

Even if we are to take these to be solely the words of Eckart, Hitler expressed exactly the same explanation of Bolshevism and its 'Jewish' origins. Indeed, in *Mein Kampf*, which is dedicated to Eckart, it is a recurrent theme of Hitler's that the Jews were promised in the Old Testament not eternity in the heavenly New Jerusalem, but dominion of the temporal earth. It was to this end that the Jew conspired. Hitler explains that his historical research led him to question whether or not

> inscrutable Destiny, perhaps for reasons unknown to us poor mortals, did not with eternal and immutable resolve, desire the final victory of this little nation. Was it possible that the earth had been promised as a reward to this people which lives only for this earth?

Later in the book, Hitler, speaking of these alleged Jewish machinations, states: '[F]or the higher he climbs, the more alluring his old goal that was once promised him rises from the veil of the past, and with feverish avidity his keenest minds see the dream of world domination tangibly approaching'. This situation would lead to the fulfillment of the 'Jewish prophecy—the Jew would really devour the peoples of the earth, would become their master'.[31] The end result of 'Jewish doctrine of Marxism' would be the literal end of the world:

> As a foundation of the universe, this doctrine would bring about the end of any order intellectually conceivable to man. And as, in this greatest of all recognizable organisms, the result of an application of such a law could only be chaos, on earth it could only be destruction for the inhabitants of this planet. If, with the help of his Marxist creed, the Jew is victorious over the other peoples of the world, his crown will be the funeral wreath of humanity and this planet will, as it did thousands [millions in later editions] of years ago, move through the ether devoid of men.[32]

Hitler continued this theme in his unpublished second book where he states, exactly as in *Bolshevism from Moses to Lenin*:

> The Jewish international struggle will therefore always end in bloody Bolshevization—that is to say, in truth, the destruction of the intellectual upper classes associated with the various peoples, so that he himself will be able to rise to mastery over the now leaderless humanity… Jewish domination always ends with the decline of all culture and ultimately of the insanity of the Jew himself. Because he is a parasite on the peoples, and his victory means his own end just as much as the death of his victim.[33]

The Aryan–Jewish conflict was, quite literally, interpreted as an eschatological war. Hitler defined Marxism as a 'poison' deliberately produced by the Jewish 'prophet' Karl Marx, 'in the service of his race', to bring about the 'swifter annihilation of the independent existence of free nations on this earth'.[34] The final battle would come in a fight to the death with

Jewish-Bolsheviks. In his first important speech after leaving Landsberg prison in 1925, Hitler explained that the Nazi aim was

> clear and simple: Fight against the satanic power which has collapsed Germany into this misery; Fight Marxism, as well as the spiritual carrier of this world pest and epidemic, the Jews... As we join ranks then in this new movement, we are clear to ourselves, that in this arena there are two possibilities; either the enemy walks over our corpse or we over theirs.[35]

A year later, Hitler reiterated that 'there is going to be a final confrontation, and that will not come in the Reichstag but in an overall showdown which will result in the destruction of either Marxism or ourselves'.[36] It was the Nazis' mission, therefore, to prepare Germany for this impending final conflict. Using imagery taken from Revelation 12, Hitler exclaimed:

> It is our mission to forge a strong weapon—will and energy—so that when the hour strikes, and the Red dragon raises itself to strike, at least some of our people will not surrender to despair. I myself represent the same principles that I stood for a year ago.

> We are convinced that there will be a final showdown in this struggle against Marxism. We are fighting one another and there can be only one outcome. One will be destroyed and the other be victorious.

> It is the great mission of the National Socialist movement to give our times a new faith and to see to it that millions will stand by this faith, then, when the hour comes for the showdown, the German people will not be completely unarmed when they meet the international murderers.[37]

This notion of the satanic power of the Jews is no mere rhetorical device for Hitler. When Hitler stated in *Mein Kampf* that, 'the personification of the devil as the symbol of all evil assumes the living appearance of the Jew', he meant it literally that the Jew was the force of evil and destruction in the world.[38] This dualism was a central part of Nazi ideology. In his report written for the Nuremberg trials in 1946, SS Major Dieter Wisliceny, Adolf Eichman's deputy, wrote that Nazi anti-Semitism was based on the 'mystical-religious conception that sees the world as governed by good and evil forces'. The Jews were the 'evil principle', and

> against this world of evil the race-mystics placed the world of good, of light, embodied in blond, blue-eyed people, from whom alone all culture-creating and state-building forces emanate. Now both of these two worlds were alleged to be positioned in a permanent struggle, and the war of 1939, which Hitler had begun, represented only the final altercation between these two powers.[39]

The battle lines were thus drawn. Two opposing forces faced one another; the forces of good and evil, creation and destruction, order and chaos, form and formlessness, God and Satan. Only one force could prevail. It was the mission of Nazism to ensure that Aryan humanity was victorious. World history had reached a turning point of eschatological significance, and the Nazis believed that they, indeed all Aryans, were chosen by higher powers to defeat the agents of annihilation. It was only a matter of time.

The War of Extermination as an Induced Apocalypse

On 30 January 1939, with Europe on the brink of world war, Hitler gave his yearly speech to the Reichstag commemorating his assumption of power, and with it, the dawn of the millennial Third Reich, the Final Reich. He assumed his role as End time prophet, stating

> Quite often in my life I have been know as a prophet and was mostly laughed at. In the time of my struggle for power it was primarily the Jewish people who responded to my prophecies with laughter… I believe that the ringing laughter of Jewry in Germany meanwhile is now stuck in their throats.
>
> I will today again be a prophet: if international finance Jewry within and without Europe should succeed in plunging the peoples yet once again in a world war, then it will result not in the Bolshevization of the earth and thereby the victory of Jewry, but rather the annihilation of the Jewish race in Europe.[40]

The linking of the war with a threat to exterminate the Jews is important. Hitler would return to his prophecy a number of times during the course of the war, and after the Final Solution was underway. Not unimportantly, Hitler, and various Nazi publications, misdated the prophecy to 1 September, 1939, when the Nazis invaded Poland and began World War II. The final struggle against the Jews was inextricably tied to the war itself, for it was the same conflict.

During his 30 January speech the following year, with the coming invasion of the Soviet Union already decided, Hitler returned to his prophecy on the extermination of the Jews if an 'all-out war' should break out, concluding that 'the coming months and years will demonstrate that I will be seen to have been correct'.[41] A year later, only ten days after the attendees at the Wannsee Conference formally began to plan the extermination of all the Jews of Europe, Hitler again returned the prophecy, stating:

We are clear to ourselves that the war can end only with either the Aryan peoples exterminated, or that Jewry will vanish from Europe. I have already spoken about it on September 1, 1939 in the German Reichstag—and I am careful not to make rash prophecies—that this war will not go as the Jews envisage it, namely that the European Aryan peoples will be exterminated, rather that the result of this war will be the extermination of Jewry. For the first time that true old Jewish law will be employed: an eye for an eye, a tooth for a tooth... And the hour will come when the most evil world enemy of all time will have played out its role of the last millennium.[42]

In his New Year message of 1943, following a year that saw the extermination camps erected in Poland and the industrial murder of Jews begun, Hitler yet again returned to his prophecy, proclaiming quite openly:

I said that the hope of international Jewry, that it would destroy the German and other European peoples in a new world war, will be the biggest mistake Jewry has made in thousands of years—that it will destroy not the German people but itself—and about that there is today no doubt.[43]

This belief that World War II was the long-prophesied coming war of extermination was a deeply held tenet for many Nazis and soldiers alike. Acknowledging the importance of such a belief in an imminent apocalyptic struggle between Aryans and Jews does not necessarily mean, that the Nazis ever had a set plan or program to exterminate the Jews.[44] The belief does, however, contain within its own internal logic the *possibility* of its eventual actualization. In other words, if you believe that now is the time, that *the* turning point in world history is at hand, one in which the age old struggle of good and evil, order and chaos, God and Satan, Aryan and Jew, is to be settled once and for all—and just as importantly, if you believe that you have been divinely chosen to take part in this eschatological battle—it is not surprising that you may find yourself in exactly the prophesied scenario, a war of extermination. And in fact many millennial movements have done just that. It is, in many ways, a classic case of cognitive dissonance—what do you do when you face the reality that *the* End or some correlate to *the* End, such as the dawn of the millennial New Age or the outbreak of the apocalyptic final battle, does not occur?[45] Some millennial movements dissipate, some simply re-date the Endtime, and some movements move away from millennialism entirely. But occasionally millennial movements respond to cognitive dissonance by pushing rapidly forward, creating, consciously or unconsciously, exactly the scenario necessary to induce the apocalypse—Waco, Jonestown, Aum Shinrikyo, the Solar Temple, Heaven's Gate—typify this possibility.[46]

By maneuvering Germany into a two front war before Germany was prepared for such a total conflict, Hitler found himself in the apocalyptic war of extermination that he expected, although certainly not exactly as he had planned. Stalingrad is an important event in this regard. The apparent fulfillment of Hitler's many prophecies during his career—concerning his own ascension to power, of Germany's coming rebirth, and certainly the lightning quick victories early in the war all seemed to validate his oft-mentioned 'inner voice'.[47] However, with Stalingrad, Providence's fortune seemed to have abandoned Hitler. But the millennial vision did not collapse. In fact, it became more pronounced. For instance, eschatological pronouncements about the coming miraculous *Endsieg* came with regularity from Hitler, Himmler, Goebbels, Wehrmacht Officers and Front soldiers alike. The demonization of Jews, and the blaming of war on them, likewise increased at the same time that they were in reality being annihilated.

Consequently, with Operation Barbarossa, the invasion of Russia, the true war of extermination began. Not surprisingly, its apocalyptic rendering likewise increased. On the verge of launching the Russian campaign, Hitler explained to his generals the reasons for and objectives of the coming 'colonial tasks' (from notes made by General Halder on 30 March, 1941):

> Two world views battle one another. Annihilating judgment over Bolshevism, the same asocial criminality. Communism immense danger for the future. We must move away from the standpoint of soldierly camaraderie. The communist is not a comrade before and is not a comrade after. It is a question of a war of extermination.

> Struggle against Russia: extermination of the Bolschevistic Commissars and the communist intelligentsia… The struggle must be waged against the poison of decomposition [a Nazi euphemism for the Jews]. That is not a question of the rules of war.[48]

This conception of the Eastern campaign as an apocalyptic war of extermination was subsequently put forth in propaganda aimed at the troops. A pamphlet entitled 'Germany in the Final Battle with the Jewish-Bolshevik Murder-System', given to propaganda officers as part of the 1941 information campaign 'Führer Commands, We Follow', included this solemn proclamation by Hitler to his soldiers (the information officers were told to 'push this'):

> As we at this time enter upon this greatest Front in world history, then it takes place not only on the supposition that it will produce the final settlement of the great war, or to protect the at present bewildered countries

[the newly conquered territories], but rather to save the entire European civilization and culture.

The pamphlet then went on to define Bolshevism, 'the demonic invention of our time', in this way:

> This system of chaos, annihilation, and terror was invented by Jews and is led by Jews. It is the action of the Jewish race. World Jewry attempts through subversion and propaganda to bring together the uprooted and lesser race elements to accomplish this war of extermination against everything positive, against people and nation, against religion and culture, against order and morality. The aim is the production of chaos through world revolution and the establishment of a world state under Jewish leadership.[49]

The apocalyptic war of extermination was not only promulgated to the soldiers through Nazi propaganda. German army officers did their part, translating Hitler's earlier conception of the Eastern war into their own apocalyptic construction. On 2 May, 1941 Panzer Group 4 commander Colonel-General Hoepner not only described the coming Eastern war in apocalyptic terms, but used the war's eschatological significance to call for the utmost barbarity—to counter the perceived threat of annihilation with a 'total annihilation of the enemy':

> The war against the Soviet Union is an essential component of the German people's struggle for existence. It is the old struggle of the Germans against the Slavs, the defense of European culture against the Muscovite-Asiatic flood, the warding off of Jewish Bolshevism. This struggle must have as its aim the demolition of present Russia and must therefore be conducted with unprecedented severity. Both the planning and the execution of every battle must be dictated by an iron will to bring about a merciless, total annihilation of the enemy. Particularly no mercy should be shown toward the carriers of the present Russian-Bolsheviks system.[50]

Could the eschatological imagery embedded in such an order simply reflect rhetorical license, designed to motivate the troops and nothing else? Perhaps, however, they followed exactly the historical and social perceptions held by the Nazis since the beginning of the movement. They followed Hitler's prophecy and his war directives. They followed Nazi propaganda sheets read to the troops. Hitler's prophesied war of extermination, therefore, seemed to have been fulfilled. More importantly, the message got through to the troops. Most of the soldiers of the *Einsatzgruppen* (the special forces assigned to kill partisans and Jews), as well as the *Wehrmacht* (the regular army), grew up in the Nazi millennial Reich. Their school books and other cultural media continually prepared them for the

coming war against the Satanic Jews and their sub-human foot soldiers—
all in the service of their heaven-sent savior Adolf Hitler. The apocalyptic
propaganda continued throughout the war, coming, as was seen, from
both the Nazis and their own officers. We have only to look at the letters
of soldiers in the *Einsatzgruppen* and in the *Wehrmacht* to see that the
millennial world of evil Jewish-Bolsheviks and their minions the Russian
sub-humans, locked in apocalyptic battle with Germany, the force of
order, was accepted by many of those charged with fighting the final war.

Writing to his wife in September 1942, Karl Kretschmer, a member of
Einsatzkommando 4a, conceptualized the war as a battle with Jewry for
the existence or non-existence of the German race:

> We are fighting this war today for the very existence of our *Volk*. Thank God
> that you in the homeland do not feel too much of it. The bombing raids,
> however, have shown what the enemy has in store for us if he had the
> power. Those at the front experience it at every turn. My comrades literally
> are fighting for the existence of our *Volk*. They are doing the same that the
> enemy would do [to us]. I believe that you understand me. Because this in
> our view is a Jewish war, the Jews are primarily bearing the brunt of it. In
> Russia, wherever there is a German soldier, the Jews are no more.[51]

Another *Einsatzkommando* attempted to justify his actions by blaming
the pre-war demonization of the Jews, noting that the millennial peace
could only be achieved with the extermination of the Jews. He explained
that

> …it was hammered into us, during the years of propaganda, again and
> again, that the Jews were the ruin of every Volk in the midst of which they
> appear, and that peace would reign in Europe only then, when the Jewish
> race is exterminated. No one could entirely escape this propaganda..[52]

Like other German soldiers, he found that the Nazi demonization of the
Jewish-Bolsheviks was confirmed by 'much of what we experienced in
Russia'.[53]

Other letters reveal cases of soldiers who, while committing horrible
crimes themselves, inverted reality, perceiving the victim to be the true
beastly murderer. The alleged atrocities, perhaps not ironically, are similar
to those described by Eckart in *Bolshevism from Moses to Lenin*. Therefore
as the war got worse, so did the demonization of the Jew. In July 1942
one soldier wrote home and explained that

> the great task which is imposed on us in the struggle against Bolshevism lies
> in the annihilation of eternal Jewry. If one sees what the Jews have pro-
> duced here in Russia, one can more than ever understand why the Führer
> began the struggle against Jewry. What sorrows would have come over our
> Fatherland if these beast men had maintained the upper hand?

This soldier then went on to describe his frustration in not being able to fight the enemy in the open, only to have to deal with partisans, 'furtive rabble', roaming around at night plundering and murdering. After one such night, he reports, a comrade was found murdered. This was not interpreted as being simply a partisan killing, but rather, as this soldier conceptualized it:

> He was cut down from behind. That can only be the Jew who stands behind these crimes. The crack-down that thereupon took place indeed yielded an entirely splendid success. The population themselves hate the Jews as never before. They now realize they bear all the blame. This struggle must lead to the most extreme limits and we will fight to the end so that this world will find eternal peace.[54]

Besides blaming the mythic 'eternal Jew' for the partisan killing, this soldier further mythologized the death as symptomatic of the Jewish innate criminality, thereby justifying the mass murders, possibly involving indigenous Ukrainians, alluded to in the conclusion. Moreover, the annihilation of the eternal Jew is once again conceptualized as bringing the eternal peace of the Nazi millennium. For these soldiers the blame for the mass destruction, starvation, and horrendous death tolls that they saw around them lay, not with the Russians, the Germans nor even with the reality of modern warfare. Rather they found the culprit in that same 'hidden force' of history seen in *Bolshevism from Moses to Lenin*. The Nazi millennial myth had become reality. In other words, belief in the apocalyptic fantasy became something of a self-defining principle. The horror of the war on the Eastern Front, with its extreme barbarity and loss of human life, with half-starved civilians now eerily resembling the beastly sub-humans of Nazi propaganda wandering about a war-torn landscape like something out of Heironymous Bosch, transformed the conflict into the very apocalyptic war of extermination that Hitler had prophesied for 20 years. The millennial fantasy that provided Hitler, his inner circle, and many Old Guard Nazis with a sense of meaning and direction, not to mention a heightened sense of self-worth, now through the hell of modern warfare provided Hitler's soldiers with the meaning and self-perception needed to withstand and comprehend the constant suffering around them—theirs and their victims'. In other words, faith that one was fighting in a holy war of apocalyptic significance legitimated one's own suffering, as well as justified the suffering imposed on others. The barbarous and often criminal actions of SS and *Wehrmacht* soldiers were transformed into a sacred struggle for existence and universal salvation.

References

Abel, Theodore, *The Theodore F. Abel Collection* (Hoover Institute Archives, Stanford, CA, n.d).

—*Why Hitler Came into Power* (Englewood Cliffs, NJ: Prentice Hall, 1938).

Bärsch, Claus-Ekkehard, *Die politische Religion des Nationalsozialismus* (Munich: Wilhelm Fink Verlag, 1998).

Bartov, Omer, *Hitler's Army: Soldier's, Nazis, and War in the Third Reich* (New York: Oxford University Press, 1992).

Berndt, A.I., and Oberst Wedel (eds.), *Deutschland im Kampf* (Berlin: Verlagsanstalt Otto Stollberg, 1943).

Broszat, Martin, 'Enthüllung? Die Rauschning-Kontroverse', in *idem, Nach Hitler: Der Schwierige Umgang mit unserer Geschichte* (Munich: Oldenbourg, 1987), 249-51.

Buchbender, Ortwin, and Reinhold Sterz (eds.), *Das andere Gesicht des Krieges: Deutsche Feldpostbriefe, 1939–1945* (Munich: C.H. Beck, 1982).

Calic, Édouard, (ed.), *Secret Conversations with Hitler* (New York: John Day, 1971).

Cohn, Norman, *Warrant for Genocide: The Myth of the Jewish World Conspiracy and the Protocols of the Elders of Zion* (London: Serif, 1996).

Dawidowicz, Lucy, *The War against the Jews 1933–1945* (New York: Bantam, 1986).

Denny, Ludwell, 'France and the German Counter-Revolution', *The Nation* 116 (1923), 295-97.

'Deutschland zum Endkampf mit dem jüdisch-bolschewistisch Mordsystem angetreten', (National Archives Microfilm Collection, Records of the National Socialist German Labor Party, T81, serial 890, roll 672).

Die alte Garde spricht (Washington, DC; Library of Congress, 1936).

Diewerge, Wolfgang, (ed.), *Deutsche Soldaten sehen die Sowjet-Union* (Berlin: W. Limpert, 1941).

Domarus, Max, *Hitler, Reden und Proklamationen, 1932–1945* (Würzburg: Schmidt, 1962–63).

Eckart, Dietrich, *Der Bolschewismus von Moses bis Lenin: Zwiegespräch zwischen Adolf Hitler and Mir* (Munich: Hoheneichen-Verlag, 1924).

Engelman, Ralph Max, 'Dietrich Eckart and the Genesis of Nazism' (PhD dissertation, University of Michigan, Ann Arbor, 1971).

Esh, Shaul, 'Eine neue literarische Quelle Hitlers? Eine methodologische Überlegung', *Geschichte in Wissenshaft und Unterricht* 15 (1964), 487-93.

Festinger, Leon, Henry W. Reiken and Stanley Schachter, *When Prophecy Fails: A Social and Psychological Study of a Modern Group That Predicted the Destruction of the World* (New York: Harper & Row, 1956).

Flanagan, Thomas, 'The Third Reich: Origins of a Millenarian Symbol', *History of European Ideas* 8 (1987), 283-95.

Friedländer, Saul, *Nazi Germany and the Jews* (New York: HarperCollins, 1997).

Goldhagen, Daniel Jonah, *Hitler's Willing Executioners: Ordinary Germans and the Holocaust* (New York: Knopf, 1996).

Hänel, Wolfgang, *Hermann Rauschnings 'Gespräche mit Hitler'—Eine Geschichtsfälschung* (Ingolstadt: Zeitgeschichtlichen Forschungsstelle Ingolstadt, 1984).

Hitler, Adolf, *Adolf Hitler Reden* (ed. Ernst Boepple; Munich: Boepple, 1925).

—*Die Rede Adolf Hitlers in der ersten grossen Massenversammlung bei Wiederausrichtung der Nationalsozialistischen Deutschen Arbeiter Partei* (Munich: Franz Eher, 1925).

—*Mein Kampf* (Boston: Houghton-Mifflin, 1971).

—*Hitler's Secret Conversations, 1941–1944* (New York: New American Library, 1953).

—*Hitler's Second Book: The Unpublished Sequel to Mein Kampf* (ed. Gerhard Weinberg; trans. Krista Smith; New York: Enigma Books, 2003).

Lane, Barbara Miller, and Leila J. Rupp (eds. and trans.), *Nazi Ideology before 1933: A Documentation* (Austin: University of Texas Press, 1978).

Ley, Michael, and Julius H. Schoeps (eds.), *Der Nationalsozialismus als politische Religion* (Bodenheim: Philo, 1997).

Maurach, Reinhard, 'Expert Legal Opinion Presented on Behalf of the Defense'. 'U.S. v. Ohlendorf et al'. *Trials of War Criminals before the Nüremberg Military Tribunals under Control Council Law No. 10. Nüremberg, October 1946–April 1949*, IV (Washington: U.S. Government Printing Office, 1949–1953).

Messerschmidt, Manfred, *Die Wehrmacht im NS-Staat: Zeit der Indoktrination* (Hamburg: R.V. Decker, 1969).

Moeller van den Bruck, Arthur, *Der Dritte Reich* (Hamburg: Hanseatische Verlagsanstalt, 1931).

Nolte, Ernst, 'Eine früher Quelle zu Hitlers Antisemitismus', *Historische Zeitschrift* 192 (1961) 584-606.

Peukert, Detlev J.K., *The Weimar Republic: The Crisis of Classical Modernity* (trans. Richard Deveson; New York: Hill & Wang, 1987).

Plewnia, Margarete, *Auf dem Weg zu Hitler: Der 'völkische' Publizist Dietrich Eckart* (Bremen: Schünemann, 1970).

Poliakov, Leon, and Josef Wulf (eds.), *Das Dritte Reich und die Juden: Dokumente und Aufsätze* (Berlin, Arani-Verlags-GmbH, 1955).

Rauschning, Hermann, *The Voice of Destruction* (New York: Putnam, 1940).

Redles, David, 'Heaven's Gate and the Induced Apocalypse', *Clio's Psyche* 4 (1997), 1-5.

—*Hitler's Millennial Reich: Apocalyptic Belief and the Search for Salvation* (New York: New York University Press, 2005).

Rhodes, James M., *The Hitler Movement: A Modern Millenarian Revolution* (Stanford, CA: Hoover Institution Press, 1980).

Rose, Paul Lawrence, 'Talmudic Scholarship in the Stab-Rosenberg's "Institute for Research into the Jewish Question" '. Paper delivered at the 113th Annual meeting of the American Historical Association.

Rosenberg, Alfred, *Die Spur des Juden im Wandel der Zeiten* (Munich: Deutscher Volks-Verlag, 1920).

—*Die völkische Staatsgedanke: Untergang und Neugeburt* (Munich: Deutschvölkische Verlagsbuchhandlung, 1924).

Schieder, Theodor, *Hermann Rauschnings 'Gespräche mit Hitler' als Geschichtsquelle* (Opladen: Westdeutscher Verlag, 1972).

Schram, Percy Ernst (ed.), *Kriegstagebuch des Oberkommando der Wehrmacht (Wehrmachtführungstab) 1940–1945*, II (Frankfurt am Main: Bernard & Graefe, 1961–1965).

Schreiner, Klaus, 'Messianism in the Political Culture of the Weimar Republic', in Peter Schäfer and Mark Cohen (eds.), *Toward the Millennium: Messianic Expectations from the Bible to Waco* (Leiden: E.J. Brill, 1998), 311-61.

Snyder, Louis L., *Hitler's Third Reich: A Documentary History* (Chicago: Nelson-Hall, 1981).

Wagener, Otto, *Hitler—Memoirs of a Confidant* (ed. Henry Ashby Turner Jr; trans. Ruth Hein; New Haven, CT: Yale University Press, 1985).

Wessinger, Catherine (ed.), *Millennialism, Persecution, and Violence: Historical Cases* (Syracuse: Syracuse University Press, 2000).

Weinberg, Gerhard L., 'Germany's War for World Conquest and the Extermination of the
    Jews', *Holocaust and Genocide Studies* 10 (1996), 119-33.
Wistrich, Robert, *Hitler's Apocalypse: Jews and the Nazi Legacy* (New York: St Martin's
    Press, 1985).
Zenner, Walter P., 'The Case of the Apostate Messiah: A Reconsideration of the "Failure of
    Prophecy"', *Archives de Sociologie des Religions* 21 (1966), 111-18.

Notes

1.   Édouard Calic (ed.), *Secret Conversations with Hitler* (New York: John Day,
1971), 21.

2.   As Lucy Dawidowicz remarked, ' "Final" reverberates with apocalyptic promise,
bespeaking the Last Judgment, the End of Days, the last destruction before salvation,
Armageddon. "The Final Solution of the Jewish Question" in the National Socialist
conception was not just another anti-Semitic undertaking, but a metahistorical program devised with an eschatological perspective. It was part of a salvational ideology
that envisaged the attainment of Heaven by bringing Hell on earth.' In Lucy Dawidowicz, *The War against the Jews 1933–1945* (New York: Bantam, 1986), xxxvi. For
more on the millennial and apocalyptic nature of Nazism see my book, *Hitler's
Millennial Reich: Apocalyptic Belief and the Search for Salvation* (New York: New York
University Press, 2005). Two unjustly ignored works that dealt with some of the
themes discussed below are James M. Rhodes, *The Hitler Movement: A Modern Millenarian Revolution* (Stanford, CA: Hoover Institution Press, 1980), and Robert Wistrich,
Hitler's Apocalypse: Jews and the Nazi Legacy (New York: St Martin's Press, 1985).
Recent German scholarship focusing on the world-view of Nazi elites has reasserted
the essentially religious nature of movement. See Claus-Ekkehard Bärsch, *Die politische Religion des Nationalsozialismus* (Munich: Wilhelm Fink Verlag, 1998), and
Michael Ley and Julius H. Schoeps (eds.), *Der Nationalsozialismus als politische Religion* (Bodenheim: Philo, 1997).

3.   The Spartacists were German communists active in Munich. Many were sailors
from the disbanding German navy. This quotation can be found in *The Theodore Abel
Collection* (Hoover Institute Archives, Stanford, CA, n.d.). This collection contains 580
short autobiographies of early Nazis gathered by Abel in 1933 and sociologically
interpreted in his book *Why Hitler Came into Power* (New York: Prentice Hall, 1938).
This quotation is from Abel #35, p. 1. The metaphors of darkness and light and social
inversion and the localizing of blame for chaos on a perceived Other, in this case the
Jews, are typical of the Nazi apocalyptic mentality. The Abel Collection, as with *Die
alte Garde spricht*, discussed below, provides an invaluable source for analyzing the
subjective world of Old Guard Nazis. One set of autobiographical remembrances was
collected by an American scholar in 1933 and the other by the Nazis themselves in
1937–1938. Despite the differing origins of the collections, both reflect similar experiences and interpretations. They are thoroughly millennial concerning the times and
the evolution of the Nazi movement and, regarding the role of Hitler, completely
messianic. However, it could be questioned whether or not the sentiments of the
authors, mostly looking back on events which took place some five to fifteen years
earlier are descriptions of actual experiences or some sort of agreed upon constructed
memory (such as the genre of 'witnessing' literature common to conversion experi-

ences). Certainly something of the latter process has taken place, for as the Nazis compiled their movement's history, as seen in their *Hauptarchiv*, they clearly placed it within an eschatological time scheme. But this only strengthens the argument for interpreting Nazism as a millennial movement. For the construction of memory and history using apocalyptic symbolism points to the construction of a new perception of reality that is at the heart of what I have termed the apocalypse complex. See my *Hitler's Millennial Reich*. Therefore, even a symbolically homogenized retelling of the Hitler conversion experiences tell us something of the psychology involved, regardless of whether or not the events happened exactly as Nazi memory and history portray them. Moreover, there is more to these memories than apocalyptically filtered hindsight. For instance, we know that Hitler and other Nazi ideologues, from their earliest speeches, spoke in apocalyptic terms. We are left with two possibilities: Either the Nazi elites promoted an apocalyptic and millennial world-view, but their followers failed to respond at that time and only a decade later gave voice to the apocalyptic in their reconstruction of memory and history; or these minor Nazis heard the voice of the apocalypse at that time, responded accordingly with a genuine conversion experience and then accurately reported this experience in their autobiographical sketches. I find the latter possibility much more convincing. Moreover, evidence for a simultaneous rhetor/listener apocalyptic relationship does exist. For instance, Ludwell Denny, in 'France and the German Counter-Revolution', *The Nation* 116 (1923), 295, reported that Hitler's followers viewed him as 'prophet and savior'. So while the mythic construction of memory and history is a factor, so too is the importance of the actual Nazi conversion experiences and the millennialism that pervades the movement and its followers.

    4.   For more on social fragmentation see Detlev J.K. Peukert, *The Weimar Republic: The Crisis of Classical Modernity* (trans. Richard Deveson; New York: Hill & Wang, 1987).

    5.   Abel #70, 1-2. Messianism was in the air, so to speak, during the Weimar era. See Klaus Schreiner, 'Messianism in the Political Culture of the Weimar Republic', in Peter Schäfer and Mark Cohen (eds.), *Toward the Millennium: Messianic Expectations from the Bible to Waco* (Leiden: E.J. Brill, 1998), 311-61.

    6.   Adolf Hitler, *Adolf Hitler Reden* (ed. Ernst Boepple; Munich: Boepple, 1925), 17. All translations are mine unless otherwise noted.

    7.   Alfred Rosenberg, *Die völkische Staatsgedanke: Untergang und Neugeburt* (Munich: Deutschvölkische Verlagsbuchhandlung, 1924), 33.

    8.   Found in *Die alte Garde spricht*, a four volume typescript collection of short autobiographies of early Nazis commissioned by Rudolf Hess in 1936. Two sets of this collection, with minor differences between the two, are housed at the Library of Congress (Washington, DC). This quotation is from volume II, Jakob Hoffmann, page 1. Hereafter citations to this collection will appear as *DAGS*, volume #, author, page #.

    9.   *DAGS*, II, Wilhelm Scherer, 12.

   10. Abel #468, 1; Abel #20, 1.

   11. Abel #33, 1.

   12. The term Third Reich most likely came to the Nazis through the Strasser brothers and their association with Arthur Moeller van den Bruck, who, writing in the apocalyptic year of 1923, described the coming 'Third Kingdom' this way: 'It is an old

and great German conception. It arose from the collapse of our first Reich. It was fused early on with expectations of a millennial Reich. Yet always there lived within it a political conception which aimed to the future, not so much upon the end of times, but upon the beginning of a German epoch in which the German Volk will fulfill its destiny on earth.' *Der Dritte Reich* (Hamburg: Hanseatische Verlagsanstalt, 1931), 6. On the millennialism inherent in the term Third Reich see Thomas Flanagan, 'The Third Reich: Origins of a Millenarian Symbol', *History of European Ideas* 8 (1987), 283-95.

13. Quoted in Otto Wagener, *Hitler—Memoirs of a Confidant* (ed. Henry Ashby Turner Jr; trans. Ruth Hein; New Haven, CT: Yale University Press, 1985), 44-45.

14. Quoted in Hermann Rauschning, *The Voice of Destruction* (New York: Putnam, 1940), 244. Rauschning's reliability has been questioned, but I am in agreement with Theodor Schieder that he can be used, albeit with care (as should be the norm with any source). See Schieder, *Hermann Rauschnings 'Gespräche mit Hitler' als Geschichtsquelle* (Opladen: Westdeutscher Verlag, 1972). Wolfgang Hänel has since cast doubt on Rauschning's authenticity in *Hermann Rauschnings 'Gespräche mit Hitler'—Eine Geschichtsfälschung* (Ingolstadt: Zeitgeschichtlichen Forschungsstelle Ingolstadt, 1984). I am unconvinced by Hänel's rather narrow argument, as was Martin Broszat. See Broszat's 'Enthüllung? Die Rauschning-Kontroverse', in his collected essays *Nach Hitler: Der Schwierige Umgang mit unserer Geschichte* (Munich: Oldenbourg, 1987), 249-51. It is true that such stylized accounts of Hitler's monologues, whether as recorded by Martin Bormann or as remembered by Dietrich Eckart, Hermann Rauschning, or Otto Wagener are often viewed by historians with skepticism. If they are taken to be exact transcripts of Hitler's diatribes then this view is understandable. However, if read collectively, as differing accounts and interpretations by various individuals of similar Hitler 'prophecy sessions', where the messianic *Führer* laid bare his vision of the past, present and future, then such sources are indispensable for understanding the subjective reality of the Nazi millennial worldview. Therefore, these Hitler conversation sources must be read as a group, with the historian looking for consistent themes and inconsistent interpretations. The consistencies should be interpreted as not being the exact words of Hitler, but rather accurate reflections of Hitler's world-view. The inconsistencies can be attributed to the vagaries of memory as well as to the subjective interpretations of the remembered conversations by the various individuals who produced them. Hermann Rauschning's *The Voice of Destruction* and Otto Wagener's *Hitler: Memoirs of a Confidant* are good examples of this latter usage. One is by a man, Rauschning, who once believed in Hitler and then lost faith. His account of Hitler speaking was meant to reveal to the world the madman who controlled Germany. Wagener's account of conversations from around the same time as Rauschning's is by a man who never lost faith in Hitler, and saw himself as a keeper of the Grail, whose notes on Hitler's pronouncements were treasured as the words of a prophet. That both accounts, by two men on opposite ends of the Hitler cult, betray a strikingly similar messianic and millenarian Hitlerian world-view, demonstrates the veracity and usefulness of these sources. The differences, for instance regarding Hitler's view of Christianity (Rauschning remembers Hitler as a staunch anti-Christian nihilist, and Wagener a mystic Christian a la *Parzival*), reflect each author's interpretation of Hitler's pronounce-

ments. These sources are not therefore useless or misleading, but simply different accounts of similar experiences.

15. For this reason Saul Friedländer quite properly uses the phrase 'redemptive anti-Semitism' to describe Nazi violence towards the Jews. Discussed in *Nazi Germany and the Jews* (New York: HarperCollins, 1997), esp. 73-112.

16. Quoted in Rhodes, *The Hitler Movement*, 59.

17. *DAGS*, I, Karl Hepp, 2.

18. Abel #62, 9.

19. Adolf Hitler, *Mein Kampf* (Boston: Houghton-Mifflin, 1971), 214.

20. Abel #70, 3.

21. *DAGS*, III, Balzer, 2.

22. *DAGS*, II, Willi Martin, 17.

23. Quoted in Rhodes, *The Hitler Movement*, 60.

24. Quoted in Barbara Miller Lane and Leila J. Rupp (eds. and trans.), *Nazi Ideology before 1933: A Documentation* (Austin: University of Texas Press, 1978), 94.

25. Dietrich Eckart, *Der Bolschewismus von Moses bis Lenin: Zwiegespräch zwischen Adolf Hitler and mir* (Munich: Hoheneichen-Verlag, 1924). This work was compiled from notes after Eckart's death. On the usefulness of this source for an understanding of Hitler's basic view on Jews see Ernst Nolte, 'Eine früher Quelle zu Hitlers Antisemitismus', *Historische Zeitschrift* 192 (1961), 584-606. Margarete Plewnia, in *Auf dem Weg zu Hitler: Der 'völkische' Publizist Dietrich Eckart* (Bremen: Schünemann, 1970), esp. 94-112, is less convinced about Hitler's role in this work, as is Shaul Esh, 'Eine neue literarische Quelle Hitlers? Eine methodologische Überlegung', *Geschichte in Wissenshaft und Unterricht* 15 (1964), 487-93. However, while both works are certainly correct in stating that Eckart is the author, I think both undervalue the central point as to the nature and function of this source. The fundamental question is whether the work provides useful insight into the Nazi world-view, and this it most certainly does. For more on Eckart see Ralph Max Engelman, 'Dietrich Eckart and the Genesis of Nazism' (PhD dissertation, University of Michigan, Ann Arbor, 1971).

26. Hitler later said of Eckart, 'He shone in our eyes like the polar star... At the time, I was intellectually a child still on the bottle.' Quoted in Adolf Hitler, *Hitler's Secret Conversations, 1941–1944* (New York: New American Library, 1953), 222.

27. This built upon the work of Alfred Rosenberg, who in the pages of Eckart's periodical *Auf gut Deutsch* and in his own book *Die Spur des Juden im Wandel der Zeiten* (Munich: Deutschvölkische Verlagsbuchhandlung, 1920), attempted to fuse the Talmud and the notorious forgery *The Protocols of the Elders of Zion* in order to 'expose' the Jews. This tendency to use Jewish sources to 'reveal' their true nature continued after the Nazis assumed power. Discussed by Paul Lawrence Rose in 'Talmudic Scholarship in the Stab-Rosenberg's "Institute for Research into the Jewish Question"', paper delivered at the 113th Annual meeting of the American Historical Association.

28. Eckart, *Der Bolschewismus von Moses bis Lenin*, 7-8.

29. This is another interesting charge, as the Nazis later would determine that some 30-40 million Slavs would have to be starved for German resettlement to be suc-

cessful. See Gerhard L. Weinberg, 'Germany's War for World Conquest and the Extermination of the Jews', *Holocaust and Genocide Studies* 10 (1996), 126.

30. Eckart, *Der Bolschewismus von Moses bis Lenin*, 49-50.

31. Hitler, *Mein Kampf*, 64, 313, 452.

32. Hitler, *Mein Kampf*, 65.

33. Adolf Hitler, *Hitler's Second Book: The Unpublished Sequel to Mein Kampf* (ed. Gerhard Weinberg; trans. Krista Smith; New York: Enigma Books, 2003), 231.

34. Hitler, *Mein Kampf*, 382.

35. Adolf Hitler, *Die Rede Adolf Hitlers in der ersten grossen Massenversammlung bei Wiederausrichtung der Nationalsozialistischen Deutschen Arbeiter Partei* (Munich: Franz Eher, 1925), 8.

36. Louis L. Snyder, *Hitler's Third Reich: A Documentary History* (Chicago: Nelson-Hall, 1981), 51.

37. Snyder, *Hitler's Third Reich*, 52.

38. Hitler, *Mein Kampf*, 324.

39. As found in Leon Poliakov and Josef Wulf (eds.), *Das Dritte Reich und die Juden: Dokumente und Aufsätze* (Berlin: Arani-Verlags-GmbH, 1955), 91-92.

40. Max Domarus, *Hitler, Reden und Proklamationen, 1932–1945* (Würzburg: Schmidt, 1962–63), II, 1058.

41. Domarus, *Hitler*, 1663.

42. Domarus, *Hitler*, 1828-29.

43. Quoted in A.I. Berndt and Oberst Wedel (eds.), *Deutschland im Kampf* 81 (January 1943), 45. As found in Norman Cohn, *Warrant for Genocide: The Myth of the Jewish World Conspiracy and the Protocols of the Elders of Zion* (London: Serif, 1996), 210.

44. Saul Friedländer is certainly right when he says that while there was no 'program' for extermination worked out, the hatred, and I would add the apocalyptic logic, was there. Moreover, he noted, 'a series of radical threats against the Jews were increasingly integrated into the vision of a redemptive final battle for the salvation of Aryan humanity'. Friedländer, *Nazi Germany and the Jews*, 314.

45. The theory of cognitive dissonance, and its application to a failed millennial prophecy, was first put forward by Leon Festinger, Henry W. Reiken, and Stanley Schachter, in *When Prophecy Fails: A Social and Psychological Study of a Modern Group that Predicted the Destruction of the World* (New York: Harper & Row, 1956). For a critique of the thesis see Walter P. Zenner, 'The Case of the Apostate Messiah: A Reconsideration of the "Failure of Prophecy"', *Archives de Sociologie des Religions* 21 (1966), 111-18. Zenner utilizes the case of Sabbatai Zvi, his apostasy, and the differing strategies used by followers to cope with their messiah's self-denial.

46. I first discussed the induced apocalypse in a brief essay written in response to the Heaven's Gate suicides. See David Redles, 'Heaven's Gate and the Induced Apocalypse', *Clio's Psyche* 4 (1997), 1-5. For more on millennial movements that have ended violently see the collection of essays in Catherine Wessinger (ed.), *Millennialism, Persecution, and Violence: Historical Cases* (Syracuse: Syracuse University Press, 2000).

47. I discuss Hitler's messianic revelations as well as his belief in his unimpeachable inner voice at length in *Hitler's Millennial Reich*, ch. 4.

48. Percy Ernst Schram (ed.), *Kriegstagebuch des Oberkommando der Wehrmacht (Wehrmachtführungstab) 1940–1945* (Frankfurt am Main: Bernard & Graefe, 1961–1965), II, Halder, 336-37.

49. Quoted in 'Deutschland zum Endkampf mit dem jüdisch-bolschewistisch Mordsystem angetreten'. National Archives Microfilm Collection, Records of the National Socialist German Labor Party, T81, serial 890, roll 672, pages 5, 34, 22 of this document. The pamphlet further notes that Bolshevism is not an 'idea' or 'Weltanschauung', but rather 'organized criminality' (22).

50. Quoted in Omer Bartov, *Hitler's Army: Soldier's, Nazis, and War in the Third Reich* (New York: Oxford University Press, 1992), 129. Similar orders, all apocalyptically rendered, would follow from General von Reichnau, commander of the 6th army, General von Mannstein, commander of the 11th army, and Colonel-General Hoth, commander of the 17th army. See Bartov, *Hitler's Army*, 129-31.

51. Quoted in Daniel Jonah Goldhagen, *Hitler's Willing Executioners; Ordinary Germans and the Holocaust* (New York: Knopf, 1996), 404. Goldhagen is certainly correct when he states that many German soldiers believed that they were engaged in an apocalyptic war for existence with Jewry, one which necessitated, if not demanded the extermination of all Jews. However, whether the 'Germans' as a collected body believed this, which Goldhagen argues, is not at all clear.

52. Quoted in Goldhagen, *Hitler's Willing Executioners*, 442. This explanation from this man's 1962 criminal investigation.

53. Goldhagen, *Hitler's Willing Executioners*, 593, n. 50. That *Einsatzgruppen* commandos believed they were engaged in an apocalyptic battle with Jewish-Bolsheviks was even argued by their post-war criminal defender. See Dr Reinhard Maurach, 'Expert Legal Opinion Presented on Behalf of the Defense', 'U.S. v. Ohlendorf et al.', *Trials of War Criminals before the Nüremberg Military Tribunals under Control Council Law No. 10. Nüremberg, October 1946–April, 1949* (Washington: U.S. Government Printing Office, 1949–1953), IV, 339-55. Ohlendorf, who commanded *Einsatzgruppe* D, continued to argue after the war that Jewry 'has continued to sow hate; and it reaps hate again. What else could we have done when confronted with demons at work, engaged in a struggle against us?' From a letter to his wife smuggled out of prison. Quoted in Goldhagen, *Hitler's Willing Executioners*, 393-94.

54. Letter 351, in Ortwin Buchbender and Reinhold Sterz (eds.), *Das andere Gesicht des Krieges: Deutsche Feldpostbriefe, 1939–1945* (Munich: C.H. Beck, 1982), 171.

Theorizing Radical Islam in Northern Nigeria

Rosalind I.J. Hackett

Introduction[1]

Despite the long and complex associations of religion and violence, several scholars have recently called for a critical revisiting of the subject. For example, Bruce Lincoln, in a 1997 essay on 'Conflict', lamented the dearth of scholarly analysis of religion by 'serious students of conflict' and the parallel neglect of conflict by scholars of religion.[2] Likewise, in the introduction to his new volume on *Religion and Violence*, Hent de Vries regrets the fact that protagonists in current debates surrounding multiculturalism, citizenship, immigration, and democracy 'seem unwilling to allow religion more than a marginal position in the constitution, definition and redefinition of the public sphere'.[3] He rightly states that '[t]o address violence in relation to religion and in all the further complexity of its origins, mediations, and effects seems a topical project'.

Certainly the tragic events of 11 September, 2001 gave rise to a host of publications on religiously-motivated violence,[4] notably with regard to radical or political Islam.[5] While the focus of these publications has generally been the Middle East, Nigeria has featured in some of these discussions because of its history of conflict between Muslims and Christians since the late 1970s. Most recently these inter-religious tensions have been sparked by moves to implement full Shari`a in several northern states. In this chapter I examine a particularly formative incident of religiously-related violence in Nigeria to reveal the panoply of theoretical interpretations adduced by 'insiders' and 'outsiders' to account for such unprecedented violence in a country previously known for its religious tolerance.

The radical northern Nigerian Islamic movement which serves as my empirical springboard for theoretical discussion forms part of my larger work on religious conflict in Nigeria.[6] I have also been exploring questions of religious freedom and conflict in Africa more generally.[7] My focus here was provoked in part by the current heightened attention to geo-religious realities,[8] and the undergraduate course on 'Religion, Violence and Conflict' that I unwittingly launched in Fall 2001. I could not have anticipated how relevant this course would turn out to be. I was also motivated by the outbreak of religiously-related communal riots which occurred in northern Nigeria just before 11 September. As I read vivid and heart-rending narratives of the fighting and destruction in Jos—a town where I have several colleagues in Religious Studies—my mind traveled back to the time when I had been living in southern Nigeria. One evening in 1980 the Muslim trader who used to come to our house and sell African art started recounting tales of mass killings in the north of the country. I shall always remember his throat-cutting gesture and the fear in his eyes when we asked him how serious it was. Within days news of a major uprising led by a mysterious figure known as 'Maitatsine' in the great northern Islamic city of Kano was flooding the front pages of our newspapers.

Of particular interest to me in my ongoing research on the Nigerian religious scene is the way that this millennialist Islamic or Islamist movement has assumed metonymic status in the psyche of Africa's most populous nation. In other words, the name 'Maitatsine' has come to stand for, at least in the popular imagination, religious extremism and violence on a more general scale. Notwithstanding the localized nature of the violence, and the eventual death of the leader in 1980, subsequent sporadic uprisings of Maitatsine followers in other parts of the country, with the attendant media spotlight, have sustained the fears of Nigerians regarding the explosive potential of religious violence. The development of a 'generalized concept' of Maitatsine was noted by Niels Kastefelt in an earlier piece examining the impact of rumors of 'invisible magical powers' on popular political culture in the early 1980s.[9] Even today, when communal clashes occur, for whatever reason, the name of Maitatsine is frequently invoked as historical memory and explanation. For example, a local ethnic conflict in 1998/1999 in Lagos between northerners and southerners was initially described in the press as a new outbreak of 'Maitatsine' even though this explanation was later challenged by the authorities. While the non-Nigerian origins and un-Islamic orientation of the movement's leader were underlined in the aftermath of the original crisis in 1980, for many southern (Christian) Nigerians this extremist movement evoked old and new concerns about Islamization. The movement's rejection of many worldly ways and modern accoutrements further reinforced ideas about Islamic resistance to Western-style education and development so integral to the southern part of the country.

In this vein, the Maitatsine movement can be viewed as one example of the wider, burgeoning phenomenon of radical religious expression or religious fundamentalism. This is underscored by Michael Watts, in his insightful study of Islamic modernities and civil society in the city of Kano, and of the Maitatsine movement in particular.[10] He shows how Maitatsine's reformist, even utopian, message inscribed itself into a dynamic, discursive tradition that dated back to colonial times of debating Muslim identity and correct practice. In that respect this controversial religious leader was not, in Watts' view, an 'isolated fanatic'.[11] Like other critics of the status quo he was in and out of jail, and deported on occasion.[12] This resonates with Jonathan Z. Smith's call to students of religion to treat extremist religious groups (he was using the example of Jonestown) not as 'unique' or 'utterly exotic' but 'to reduce [them] to the category of the known and the knowable'.[13] Naturally, this begs the question as to whether we always have the capacity to do this.

One of the primary hallmarks of these more radically oriented religious movements is their location at the fringes of modernity, and their condemnation of Western liberalism and modernism.[14] Birgit Meyer's work on Ghanaian Pentecostalism, for example, reveals the ambivalence toward modernity which characterizes many such religious groups situated at the post-colonialist, post-missionary juncture.[15] Watts also notes the ambiguity and contradiction in Maitatsine's critique of materialism and the West. This controversial Muslim leader promoted a simple disciplined life while also advocating the political control of modern institutions.[16] In line with this, Watts argues that much of Islamism is in fact new and modern because, rather than returning to some mythical past, it 'involved contesting some Islamic traditions and creating new ones by a direct engagement with capitalist modernity read through new scripturalist understandings of Islam'.[17] He describes the Maitatsine insurrection as a 'parochial sort of political Islam' and a 'powerful, if counterhegemonic reading and critique of the Nigerian oil boom and of the Nigerian ruling classes'.[18]

What follows is a (re)examination of the Maitatsine movement in light of the above-mentioned theories of religious violence, as well as more 'local' and contextual interpretations.[19] It is hoped that this brief excursus through this interpretive maze will not only explain the movement's paradigmatic status in the popular imagination and with regard to state power, but also lend support to John Hall's position that a *single theory linking religion and violence is inappropriate*.[20] As he appropriately states, 'religious violence is embedded in moments of history and structures of culture'. We turn now to the most formative moment of the Maitatsine narrative amidst all the complexities of the Nigerian religious and political scene.

Tales of Horror and Heroism

In December 1980 the city of Kano erupted virtually into civil war, as a result of violent clashes with the followers of a dissident religious teacher, Muhammad Marwa or 'Maitatsine' ('the one who damns') as he was known. The details of Maitatsine's life, the growth of the movement, and the 1980 revolt by his hundreds, if not thousands, of followers, which led to the death of more than 4,177 people (including Maitatsine himself),[21] and the subsequent uprisings in the early 1980s, and again in 1993, have been well documented by a number of authors.[22] Kano became the stage for an outbreak of violence on a scale not seen in Nigeria since the Civil War in 1967–1970. Many see this incident as a turning point in Nigeria's history when religious intolerance began to assume a more violent guise.[23]

Tales of horror and heroism abounded in the series of clashes between Maitatsine followers (or 'Yan Tatsine) and the security forces.[24] In late November, the governor, Abubakar Rimi, responding to complaints about property expropriation and indoctrination of young boys, and police harassment, by Maitatsine and his followers, ordered them to vacate the area they occupied in the city. Instead, the latter brought reinforcements from the countryside. For several months prior to that the police had claimed that it was too dangerous to enter the ward occupied by the group. There had also been failed efforts by some local government officials, legislators, and senior police officers to curb the abusive and illegal religious preaching.[25] However, it was the rumor that Maitatsine planned to take over the two principal *jumaat* mosques of the city that eventually propelled the governor to send in the police and the army. The resultant turmoil, which ceased around the end of December when the army was sent in and Maitatsine was killed, was graphically depicted in the media.[26]

The reactions of the state and its security agents raise another level of discussion among scholars of new religious movements, that of the role of 'perceptions' and 'interpretations' of each group of the other in a crisis situation. Known as the 'interpretive approach' it sees

> the orientations and behavior of problematic movements with apocalyptic worldviews as significantly influenced by the actions and perceived dispositions of groups in their environment, particularly groups and individuals who are perceived as distinctly *hostile* to the movement, such as state authorities, anti-movement activists, and recriminating apostates.[27]

It seeks to challenge analyses which essentialize such movements as inherently violent, directing more attention to the 'variable balance of internal and external influences underlying various episodes'.[28] In the case of Maitatsine, it would seem that the inaction rather than the over-reaction of the state is more notable, at least in the earlier stages. This is generally more the case in the Nigerian context, but as we shall see in the next section, the inefficacy of the security forces often fuels wider interpretations of conflict situations, as well as allowing local disorder to flourish. The data available on the Maitatsine incident do not provide the details of the dynamics of the escalating violence, as are available for other movements such as Aum Shinrikyo, the Peoples Temple, or the Branch Davidians.[29]

Discourses of Deviancy and Conspiracy

For nearly three weeks, Muhammad Marwa and his young recruits held the ancient walled city of Kano, renowned as a center of international trade from the mid-eighteenth century, under siege. The 'Yan Tatsine outnumbered the police, and even managed to commandeer many of their weapons. They occupied some buildings and destroyed others. Many Kano inhabitants fled the city as the economy ground to a halt, and the assaults and fatalities began to mount up. When the devastation was assessed, and the recriminations began, the movement was, not surprisingly, roundly condemned in most quarters. Many Nigerian Muslims sought every opportunity to disclaim the movement and its leader as Muslims.[30] Some even went as far as describing Maitatsine as satanic. Muslim leaders emphasized that their religion was one of peace, and urged the government to take the necessary action regarding the 'fanatics' and 'violators of the constitutional principle of religious tolerance'.[31]

Arjun Appadurai has written suggestively of the growing relationship between globalizing forces and a 'new order of uncertainty in social life', frequently countered by the certainty of violence, notably in relation to the body.[32] The presence of large numbers of West African immigrants, including Maitatsine himself who was from neighboring Cameroon, fomented a number of conspiracy theories in this regard.[33] These were readily fueled by journalistic accounts which picked up on the fears and rumors generated by this violent episode.[34] For example, Zahradeen, a journalist who was involved with the coverage of the incident, writes about the purported 'Jewish connection' of the Maitatsine movement, as even was publicly announced by then Governor Abubakar Rimi.[35] In fact, it was a university lecturer, Mallam Shehu Umar Abdullah, who informed the Aniagolu Tribunal that there was a link between Maitatsine and Zionist forces. The latter were purportedly angry at their failure to bring Nigeria under their influence, and used the 'Zionist-controlled Western media to launch a campaign of calumny against Nigeria'.[36] This was further endorsed by then Major Haliru Akilu of Military Intelligence, who, in his testimony to the tribunal, spoke of the manipulation of movements like Maitatsine by 'international intelligence firms'. Similarly, other conspiracy theories sprung up about the role of Qaddafi, the Saudis and the CIA, or at very least, the manipulation of events by power-hungry Nigerians.[37]

The Muslim Students Society (MSS), known for its militant activism, claimed in one of its publications that the 'Maitatsine phenomenon' was being exploited by anti-Islamic forces, notably the government.[38] They described it as a *fitna* or an extraneous movement aimed at destroying or undermining Islam, whose destructive activities remained unchecked by the police and armed forces.[39] The MSS objected to Maitatsine followers being referred to by government officials as 'Muslim religious fanatics' or 'Islamic fundamentalists' as they deemed the practices of the group to be deviant, non-interactionist, and un-Islamic (praying separately, facing north, and slandering the Sunna). Facing Jerusalem rather than Mecca was in their eyes due to the influence of the 'Israeli-based Baha'i Movement'.

Poverty and Politics

Socio-economic considerations predominated in the post-riot analysis. Increased migration in the north, higher unemployment, inadaptation of Qur'anic students, an ethnic and cultural reaction of poorly integrated non-Hausas in Hausa Muslim society were all cited as destabilizing factors.[40] A disaffected class, made up of both rural and urban followers, was ripe for the anti-modernist message of Maitatsine—symbolized in the ban on radios, buttons, watches, bicycles, and automobiles. For these reasons, political scientist Michael Watts argues that Maitatsine's controversial religious teachings—syncretist, prophetic, revivalist—should receive less attention than his 'anti-materialist, class-based reading of the moral superiority of the Qur'an which led him to attack decadence, profligacy, and moral decay'.[41] Similarly, Lubeck concentrates on the clash between pre-capitalist and capitalist networks as reflected in the worsening social and economic status of the *gardawa* or peripatetic students of a Qur'anic mallam or teacher during the oil boom.[42] He notes that Maitatsine's followers began appropriating private land prior to the main disturbances, claiming that plots of land and markets belonged to Allah and his people.[43]

Religious and political analyst Matthew Hassan Kukah lays more emphasis on the contemporary political climate, pointing to the pre-existing tensions between the Kano state governor, Alhaji Abubakar Rimi, and the Emir of Kano, as well as the internal divisions within the ruling party, the

People's Redemption Party.[44] Rimi's fraternizing with emissaries from Maitatsine—as potential political allies—meant that he could not call out the police. He saw the disturbances in Kano as a suitable irritant for his political opponents.[45] Peter Clarke notes, however, that it was not unusual for wealthy and powerful Muslims to ask 'clerics' to pray for them on the basis of their supposed mystical powers derived from their nomadic existence.[46]

Religion scholar Muhammed Sani Umar challenges the easy attribution of the movement's momentum to a revolt of the oppressed against the oppressor, despite its creative potential as an explanation.[47] The fact that the Maitatsine also attacked fellow members of the oppressed vitiates this interpretation, in his view. He also poses the trenchant question, '[W]hy is it that only the Northern part of the country shall provide [a] religious platform for revolting against the system that operates in the whole of the country?' In addition to these peculiarities, he points significantly to the lack of direct, voluntary and uncoerced information from the Maitatsine followers themselves about their beliefs and motivations. Lubeck also notes that the imprisoned *gardawa* refused to discuss their beliefs with the authorities, adding to the fear and mystique surrounding the movement.[48]

Watts offers a more nuanced, materialist analysis of this destructive religious movement by situating it within 'two locally constituted global force-fields', namely Islam and capitalism.[49] He lays important emphasis on the actual *experience* of the oil boom by Kano residents. This was mediated by the state in the form of corruption and violent, undisciplined security forces (the police were popularly referred to as *daggal* or the devil), the family and associational spheres of civil society, and the return to civilian party politics in 1979 after a long period of military rule. This latter development generated a political space more conducive to radical, populist critique of the Sufi brotherhoods associated with feudal elites.[50] Watts points not just to the 'anarchic and chaotic growth of Kano city' but also to the 'changing material basis of commoners' life and what it implied for the brute realities of urban living'.[51]

In an examination of new forms of territoriality and sovereignty in Africa, Achille Mbembe writes of the ways in which religious movements may reconfigure, even conquer, the urban space.[52] Maitatsine's efforts to create a zone of both refuge and protest in Kano are apposite here. South Asian specialist and political scientist Ashutosh Varshney has shown how, in the case of India, communally integrated associational life can serve as an agent of peace by restraining those, including powerful politicians, who would polarize religious groups along communal lines.[53] The isolationist tactics and exogenous (rural areas or neighboring countries) origins of many of the members of this Nigerian movement reinforce this analysis.

Mahdism and Millennialism

A rich body of literature is now available on millennialism and apocalypticism more generally that can offer fresh perspectives on Maitatsine as a religious movement.[54] For example, the recent work by sociologist John R. Hall et al., which explores the link between apocalyptic movements and violence, highlights not only internal dynamics and conflict with outsiders, but also the significance of historical memory.[55] The latter idea is particularly illuminating with regard to the Maitatsine movement and its mahdist connections, as well as its more contemporary 'manifestations' or 'reverberations'. The role played by the modern media in exacerbating public fears by recalling events and similarly infamous 'cults' around the world hardly needs emphasizing, particularly in the context of the current 'war on terrorism'.[56]

Several scholars choose to give more weighting to the religious, specifically millennialist, orientation of the movement. Central to the mahdist or messianic tradition in northern Nigeria, argues Clarke, is that 'the process of "redemption", the onset of the millennium involves a form of defensive "war" '.[57] There was, contemporaneously, a growing awareness of Ayatollah Khomeini's achievements in Iran, and this may have inspired more aggressive tactics in Maitatsine's movement.[58] Furthermore, it was the beginning of a new Muslim century—1400 or 1979/1980 CE was believed to be the end of the world for millennialist Muslims after which all the world would be converted to Islam.[59] Some of Kano's leading scholars indeed saw the crisis as evidence of 'Signs of the Hour' which in Islamic eschatological thought is related to the idea that at the end of every century a *mujaddid* or renewer may arise to restore order.[60] Christelow argues that there was a clear mahdist motif operating through 'Yan Tatsine.[61] He attributes this in part to the fact that Maitatsine came from Northern Cameroon where several mahdist movements had operated during the colonial period (from the late-nineteenth century until 1961). The 'Yan Tatsine, in his opinion, also bore resemblance to a branch of the Tijaniyya sufi order known as the Hamaliyya, in that they were reclusive. Lubeck disputes the mahdist element, referring to newspaper reports during the 1980 insurrection that his followers rather took Maitatsine to be a prophet for Africans.

The fact that Maitatsine rejected the Hadith and the Sunna, and arrogated to himself the role of prophet after downgrading the status of the

Prophet Muhammad to 'just another Arab' served to create an 'intense religious fervor' and, simultaneously, 'a frightening moral anarchy' among his followers.[62] It was this, suggests Christelow, that accounted for the distinctiveness of this movement and its appeal to those who, for reasons of youth and/or poverty, felt the need to be 'different and defiant'.[63] Religion scholar Matthews A. Ojo notes that there were other Islamic leaders and their groups operating in Kano at the time but which did not result in violence. The backlash came as an eventual response to Mai-tatsine's deviant teachings.[64] The controversial preacher based his pared-down reading of the Qur'an on local, pre-Islamic conditions.[65] Zahradeen also described how Maitatsine's appearance—he had a squint in one eye—contributed to the fear that he was the 'Dujal', the one-eyed Anti-christ, who would fight gallantly against the true faith of Islam at the beginning of the end of the world.[66] This underlines the importance of mythological memory in mediating contemporary crises.

Mahdism has a long history in Nigeria.[67] The belief in a form of crisis before the Last Days and the idea that the Mahdi has direct communi-cation with Allah had obvious revolutionary potential. Indeed, it was de-ployed by the jihadists of the nineteenth century in their anti-colonialist struggles. The reformer, Uthman dan Fodio, drew on mahdist ideas in his writings prior to the *jihad* in northern Nigeria, but denied his per-ceived status as a Mahdi after the *jihad* ended. His son perpetuated the mahdist tradition by prophesying the appearance of the Mahdi between 1882 and 1979. It is reported that many people abandoned their homes in pursuit of the Mahdi.

Historians Lovejoy and Hogendorn argue that the wave of revolu-tionary mahdism that swept through the Sokoto Caliphate in 1905–1906 needs to be distinguished from other forms of early-twentieth-century mahdism as it was characterized by strong divisions on the basis of class.[68] This particular revolt attracted 'disgruntled peasants, fugitive slaves and radical clerics' on a wide scale but not the local aristocracy. Had this revo-lutionary form of mahdism not been so weak in terms of military strategy and not relied so heavily on supernatural means, they might have 'altered the course of early colonial history'.[69] As it was, they served to entrench the relationship between the British and the indigenous rulers.

The quest for a Mahdi who could initiate a new order of peace, unity, and order took some Nigerians to Sudan where mahdist movements had challenged British colonial rule. Hayatu ibn Said, the great-great-grandson of Dan Fodio, was said to be influenced by the Sudanese Mahdi 'Abd al-Rahman al-Mahdi in his efforts to establish a mahdist nucleus in the Sokoto Caliphate in the early 1920s.[70] The Sudanese Mahdi wrote a letter to his would-be Khalifa in the West advising him that when 'the day' comes the guns of the Christians would not go off.[71] Two other mahdist states were established in northern Nigeria through cooperation between Nigerians and Sudanese, but they ended in failure.[72] That notwithstanding, militant mahdist elements persisted in battles against colonial rule in the early-twentieth century. Survivors of these battles migrated to the Sudan. The mahdist tradition was also sustained and propagated by the annual pilgrimage to Mecca as many Nigerians passed through the Sudan en route to Mecca. They brought back mahdist ideas and literature, illustrating the significance of social networks for the transmission of ideas and commodities.[73]

Maitatsine as Metonym

Despite the fact that the government cremated Maitatsine's body to prevent his tomb becoming a site of martyrdom and pilgrimage, and has since symbolically built a police station on the ruins of his home, there have been further outbreaks of violence linked to the Maitatsine movement in subsequent years. These occurred as surviving members of the group, discontented and poor, spread to other areas. Some were also released from prison in 1982—a highly unpopular decision by then President Shagari. The disturbances took place at Bullumkutu, Maiduguri (October, 1982), Rigassa/Tudun-wada, Kaduna State (October, 1982), Yola, Gongola State (February–March, 1984), and Gombe, Bauchi State (April, 1985). It was then not until 1993 that the *Citizen* magazine carried an article entitled, 'The Volcano Erupts Again' or 'Maitatsine–Act VI'.[74] It described how, between 19–22 January in Funtua, violence erupted between a variant of the `Yan Tatsine known as the Kalakato and the authorities. What purportedly began as a dispute between Islamic scholars turned into a rampage with reports of up to 400 deaths, as members of the movement attacked government buildings. The Sarkin Maska or district head of Funtua, Alhaji Idris Sambo, whose palace was also targeted, declared that the whole incident was politically motivated. But the report emphasizes that a body of opinion suggested that the movement was linked to an extreme form of Qur'anic recitation. Members of this movement were primarily hostile toward the police, but not toward the general populace (which was not the case with the original movement which attacked both Muslims and Christians).[75]

The original Maitatsine incident left an indelible mark on the Nigerian psyche, and certainly created long-lasting reverberations in neighboring countries, since it marked the first real incident of religiously-related violence on a large scale. It has become the metonym or paradigm for religious violence among Nigerians, despite the fact that it was primarily a local phenomenon and an intra-religious, rather than an inter-religious, conflict. It has also come to symbolize a challenge to authority, notably the police. Umar asked somewhat prophetically in the 1985 Academic Staff Union newspaper 'Is Maitatsine Here to Stay?'[76] In his recent account of religious violence in Nigeria, historian Toyin Falola claims that the movement proved especially archetypical as President Shagari's 1981 New Year's broadcast became a model of government reaction to all subsequent violent outbreaks of the 1980s and 1990s.[77] This comprised an expression of shock, an appeal for cooperation of the public, and a promise to investigate. Indeed, every major outbreak of violence has resulted in a panel of inquiry, similar to the 1981 Tribunal of Inquiry headed by Justice Anthony Aniagolu, to analyze the causes of the violence. Furthermore, the government sought to absolve itself of connection to the crisis, blaming the disturbances on external forces inimical to Nigeria's national interests. It tried to deny the interpretation of the crisis as a religious war, perhaps in order to avoid casting one religion (in this case, Islam) in a negative light, or harming inter-religious relations.

Muslim scholars themselves have been keen to dismiss Maitatsine's reformist claims, declaring him to be a heretical, self-proclaimed prophet and 'at best a Muslim deviant; at worst, a charlatan who took advantage of our societal weakness'.[78] His purported spiritual powers drew followers and patrons while eliciting accusations of excessive 'fetishism' from others.[79] One of his wives described him as a magician.[80] The 'riddle' of his political protests and close connections with a number of prominent politicians, businessmen, and civil servants will likely remain unsolved.[81]

Sources on Maitatsine's political and religious aspirations are indeed limited, and he will undoubtedly retain his enigmatic and controversial status. However, neither this nor the discursive strategies of religious leaders and politicians to deny his authenticity as a ('true') Muslim should prevent us from recognizing the religious dimensions of this conflict. As Bruce Lincoln aptly states, communities that define themselves in terms of their religion will wage their conflicts primarily around rival claims to material and non-material resources.[82] This is helpful in generating more relevant and nuanced interpretations, and problematizing those which tend to polarize the religious and the secular—a somewhat untenable perspective in the case of African Islam.[83] That notwithstanding, Lincoln's argument that religious collectivities or 'fractions' have often been the most effective in exploiting contradictions between nation and state in recent years also has strong resonance with the Nigerian context. He is less salutary when it comes to religious discourse and practice providing the resources for peace.

Indeed, Nigeria continues to experience outbreaks of religiously-motivated violence, notably in the northern and Middle Belt sections of the country. It is commonly stated that more than 10,000 people have lost their lives to ethnic and religious violence since President Obasanjo took office in 1999. Despite the rhetoric of tolerance from many government religious and community leaders, political corruption, economic frustrations, and infra-structural problems drive many Nigerians into newer and more activist religious groups that address these problems. Competition rather than cooperation currently defines the religious public sphere. Nigeria needs to draw inspiration from South Africa's feat of turning a country marred by racial conflict into a 'rainbow nation', and generate a new model of post-colonial religious pluralism, drawing on indigenous ideas of tolerance and global ideals of democracy and human rights.

References

Al-Karsani, Awad Al-Sid, 'Beyond Sufism: The Case of Millennial Islam in the Sudan', in L. Brenner (ed.), *Muslim Identity and Social Change in Sub-Saharan Africa* (London: Hurst, 1993), 135-53.

Appadurai, Arjun, 'Dead Certainty: Ethnic Violence in the Era of Globalization', *Public Culture* 10.2 (1998), 225-47.

Aravamudan, Srinivas, 'Ground Zero; or the Implosion of Church and State', in S. Hauerwas and F. Lentricchia (eds.), *Dissent from the Homeland: Essays After September 11* (Durham, NC: Duke University Press, 2003), 195-203.

Asad, Talal, 'Religion and Politics: An Introduction', *Social Research* 59.1 (1992), 1-16.

Barkindo, Barwuro M., 'Growing Islamism in Kano City Since 1970: Causes, Form and Implications', in L. Brenner (ed.), *Muslim Identity and Social Change in Sub-Saharan Africa* (London: Hurst & Company, 1993), 91-105.

Barkun, Michael (ed.), *Millennialism and Violence* (London: Frank Cass, 1996).

Birai, Umar M., 'Islamic Tajdid and the Political Process in Nigeria', in M.E. Marty and R.S. Appleby (eds.), *Fundamentalisms and the State: Remaking Polities, Economies, and Militance* (Chicago: University of Chicago Press, 1991), 184-203.

Christelow, Allan, 'Religious Protest and Dissent in Northern Nigeria: From Mahdism to Qur'anic Integralism', *Journal, Institute of Muslim Minority Affairs* 6 (1985), 375-93.

—'The 'Yan Tatsine Disturbances in Kano: A Search for Perspective', *The Muslim World* 75 (1985), 69-84.

Clarke, Peter, 'The Maitatsine Movement in Northern Nigeria in Historical and Current Perspective', in R.I.J. Hackett (ed.), *New Religious Movements in Nigeria* (Lewiston, NY: Edwin Mellen Press, 1987), 93-115.

Clarke, Peter B., and Ian Linden, *Islam in Modern Nigeria: A Study of a Muslim Community in a Post-Independence State 1960–1983* (Mainz: Grunewald, 1984).

Eck, Diana L., 'Dialogue and Method: Reconstructing the Study of Religion', in K.C. Patton and B.C. Ray (eds.), *A Magic Still Dwells: Comparative Religion in the Postmodern Age* (Los Angeles: University of California Press, 2000), 131-49.

Esposito, John L., *Unholy War: Terror in the Name of God* (New York: Oxford University Press, 2002).

Falola, Toyin, *Violence in Nigeria: The Crisis of Religious Politics and Secular Ideologies* (Rochester, NY: University of Rochester Press, 1998).

Hackett, Rosalind I.J., 'Religious Freedom and Religious Conflict in Africa', in M. Silk (ed.), *Religion on the International News Agenda* (Hartford, CT: The Leonard E. Greenberg Center for the Study of Religion in Public Life, 2000), 102-19.

—'Managing or Manipulating Religious Conflict in the Nigerian Media', in J. Mitchell and S. Marriage (eds.), *Mediating Religion: Conversations in Media, Religion and Culture* (Edinburgh: T & T Clark, 2003), 47-64.

—'Prophets, "False Prophets", and the African State: Emergent Issues of Religious Freedom and Conflict', in P. Lucas and T. Robbins (eds.), *New Religious Movements in the 21st Century: Legal, Political and Social Challenges in Global Perspective* (New York: Routledge, 2004), 151-78.

—*The Response of Scholars of Religion to Global Religious Violence*. Vol. 2003, *Occasional Paper (2003) Annual Lecture* (British Association for the Study of Religion, 2004).

—*Nigeria: Religion in the Balance* (Washington, DC: United States Institute of Peace, forthcoming).

Hall, John R., 'Religion and Violence: Social Processes in Comparative Perspective', in M. Dillon (ed.), *Handbook for the Sociology of Religion* (New York: Cambridge University Press, 2003), 359-81.

Hall, John R., Philip D. Schuyler and Sylvaine Trinh (eds.), *Apocalypse Observed: Religious Movements and Violence in North America, Europe, and Japan* (New York: Routledge, 2000).

Hiskett, Mervyn, 'The Maitatsine Riots in Kano 1980: An Assessment', *Journal of Religion in Africa* 17.3 (1987), 209-23.

Ibrahim, Hassan Ahmed, 'Imperialism and Neo-Mahdism in the Sudan: A Study of British Policy towards Neo Mahdism, 1924–1927', *International Journal of African Historical Studies* 13.2 (1980), 214-39.

Isichei, Elizabeth, 'The Maitatsine Risings in Nigeria in 1980–85: A Revolt of the Disinherited', *Journal of Religion in Africa* 17.3 (1987), 194-208.

Johnson, Paul Christopher, 'Death and Memory at Ground Zero: A Historian of Religion's Report', *Bulletin of the Council of Societies of the Study of Religion* 31.1 (2002), 3-7.

Kaplan, Jeffrey, 'Interpreting the Interpretive Approach: A Friendly Reply to Thomas Robbins', *Nova Religio* 1.1 (1997), 30-49.

Kapteijns, Lidwien, 'Mahdist Faith and the Legitimation of Popular Revolt in Western Sudan', *Africa* 55.4 (1985), 390-99.

Kastefelt, Niels, 'Rumours of Maitatsine: A Note on Political Culture in Northern Nigeria', *African Affairs* 88 (1989), 83-90.

Kingston, Paul, 'Reflections on Religion, Modernization, and Violence in the Islamic Middle East', *Method and Theory in the Study of Religion* 13.3 (2001), 293-309.

Kukah, Matthew Hassan, *Religion, Politics and Power in Northern Nigeria* (Ibadan: Spectrum, 1993).

Lawrence, Bruce, *Defenders of God: The Fundamentalist Revolt against the Modern Age* (Greenville, SC: University of South Carolina Press, 1995).

Light, Timothy, and Brian Wilson (eds.), *Religion as a Human Capacity: A Festschrift in Honor of E. Thomas Lawson* (Leiden; Boston, MA: Brill, 2004).

Lincoln, Bruce, 'Conflict', in M.C. Taylor (ed.), *Critical Terms for Religious Studies* (Chicago: University of Chicago Press, 1997), 55-69.

Loimeier, Roman, *Islamic Reform and Political Change in Northern Nigeria* (Evanston, IL: Northwestern University Press, 1997).

Lovejoy, Paul, and J.S. Hogendorn, 'Revolutionary Mahdism and Resistance to Colonial Rule in the Sokoto Caliphate, 1905–1906', *Journal of African History* 31 (1990), 217-44.

Lubeck, Paul, 'Islamic Protest under Semi-Industrial Capitalism: Yan Tatsine Explained', *Africa* 55.4 (1985), 369-89.

Mayer, Jean-Francois, 'Cults, Violence and Religious Terrorism: An International Perspective', *Conflict and Terrorism* 24 (2001), 361-76.

Mbembe, Achille, 'At the Edge of the World: Boundaries, Territoriality, and Sovereignty in Africa', *CODESRIA Bulletin* 3 and 4 (1999), 4-16.

Meyer, Birgit, *Translating the Devil: Religion and Modernity among the Ewe in Ghana* (Edinburgh: Edinburgh University Press, 1999).

Nicolas, Guy, 'Guerre Sainte à Kano', *Politique Africaine* 1 (1981), 47-70.

Ojo, M. Adeleye, 'The Maitatsine Revolution in Nigeria', *American Journal of Islamic Social Sciences* 2.2 (1985), 297-306.

Rashid, Ahmed, *Jihad: The Rise of Militant Islam in Central Asia* (New Haven, CT: Yale University Press, 2002).

Robbins, Thomas, 'Religious Movements and Violence: A Friendly Critique of the Interpretive Approach', *Nova Religio* 1 (1997), 17-33.

Robbins, Thomas, and Susan J. Palmer (eds.), *Millennium, Messiahs, and Mayhem: Contemporary Apocalyptic Movements* (New York: Routledge, 1997).

Smith, Jonathan Z., *Imagining Religion: From Babylon to Jonestown* (Chicago: University of Chicago Press, 1982).

Usman, Usufu Bala, *The Manipulation of Religion in Nigeria: 1977–1987* (Kaduna: Vanguard, 1987).

Varshney, Ashutosh, *Ethnic Conflict and Civic Life: Hindus and Muslims in India* (New Haven, CT: Yale University Press, 2001).

Vries, Hent de, *Religion and Violence: Philosophical Perspectives from Kant to Derrida* (Stanford, CA: Stanford University Press, 2002).

Watts, Michael, 'Islamic Modernities: Citizenship, Civil Society and Islamism in a Nigerian City', *Public Culture* 8 (1996): 251-89.

Wessinger, Catherine, *How the Millennium Comes Violently: From Jonestown to Heaven's Gate* (New York: Seven Bridges Press, 2000).

Williams, Pat, and Toyin Falola, *Religious Impact on the Nation State* (Aldershot, UK: Avebury, 1995).

Zahradeen, Nasir B., *The Maitatsine Saga* (Shanu: Hudahuda Publishing, 1988).

Notes

1.   The present chapter grew from a presentation made at the Center for Millennial Studies annual conference, 3–5 November, 2001. This is an amended version of an article 'Theorizing Religious Violence and the Religious Other' which appeared (in Portuguese and English) in a special issue of *Imaginario* (Sao Paulo, Brazil) 8, 461-78 (2002). It is reproduced with permission. Portions of this text also appear in Timothy Light and Brian Wilson (eds.), *Religion as a Human Capacity: A Festschrift in Honor of E. Thomas Lawson* (Leiden; Boston, MA: Brill, 2004), 193-206. Valuable suggestions were received from Richard Landes and David Cook. I am also grateful to Jonathan

Reynolds for supplementary sources, to Matthews A. Ojo for helpful additions, and to Ibrahim Ado-Kurawa for his critical comments.

2.   Bruce Lincoln, 'Conflict', in M.C. Taylor (ed.), *Critical Terms for Religious Studies* (Chicago: University of Chicago Press, 1997), 55-69.

3.   Hent de Vries, *Religion and Violence: Philosophical Perspectives from Kant to Derrida* (Stanford, CA: Stanford University Press, 2002).

4.   Rosalind I.J. Hackett, 'The Response of Scholars of Religion to Global Religious Violence', Vol. 2003, *Occasional Paper (2003) Annual Lecture: British Association for the Study of Religion* (British Association for the Study of Religion, 2004).

5.   Cf. Paul Kingston, 'Reflections on Religion, Modernization, and Violence in the Islamic Middle East', *Method and Theory in the Study of Religion* 13.3 (2001), 293-309, for a critique of the oversimplified links between Islam and violence. For more nuanced texts, see John L. Esposito, *Unholy War: Terror in the Name of God* (New York: Oxford University Press, 2002); and Ahmed Rashid, *Jihad: The Rise of Militant Islam in Central Asia* (New Haven, CT: Yale University Press, 2002).

6.   Rosalind I.J. Hackett, *Nigeria: Religion in the Balance* (Washington, DC: United States Institute of Peace, forthcoming).

7.   Rosalind I.J. Hackett, 'Religious Freedom and Religious Conflict in Africa', in M. Silk (ed.), *Religion on the International News Agenda* (Hartford, CT: The Leonard E. Greenberg Center for the Study of Religion in Public Life, 2000), 102-19; and Rosalind I.J. Hackett, 'Prophets, "False Prophets", and the African State: Emergent Issues of Religious Freedom and Conflict', in P. Lucas and T. Robbins (eds.), *New Religious Movements in the 21st Century: Legal, Political and Social Challenges in Global Perspective* (New York: Routledge, 2004), 151-78.

8.   Diana L. Eck, 'Dialogue and Method: Reconstructing the Study of Religion', in K.C. Patton and B.C. Ray (eds.), *A Magic Still Dwells: Comparative Religion in the Postmodern Age* (Los Angeles: University of California Press, 2000), 131-49.

9.   Niels Kastefelt, 'Rumours of Maitatsine: A Note on Political Culture in Northern Nigeria', *African Affairs* 88 (1989), 83-90; and Paul Lubeck, 'Islamic Protest under Semi-Industrial Capitalism: Yan Tatsine Explained', *Africa* 55.4 (1985), 369-389, here page 369.

10.   Michael Watts, 'Islamic Modernities: Citizenship, Civil Society and Islamism in a Nigerian City', *Public Culture* 8 (1996), 251-89 (279).

11.   Watts, 'Islamic Modernities', 279.

12.   Lubeck, 'Islamic Protest under Semi-Industrial Capitalism', 369.

13.   Jonathan Z. Smith, *Imagining Religion: From Babylon to Jonestown* (Chicago: University of Chicago Press, 1982), 111-12.

14.   Bruce Lawrence, *Defenders of God : The Fundamentalist Revolt against the Modern Age* (Greenville, SC: University of South Carolina Press, 1995).

15.   Birgit Meyer, *Translating the Devil: Religion and Modernity among the Ewe in Ghana* (Edinburgh: Edinburgh University Press, 1999).

16.   Watts, 'Islamic Modernities'.

17.   Watts, 'Islamic Modernities', 283-84.

18.   Watts, 'Islamic Modernities', 282.

19.   The variety of analytical perspectives is also noted by Lubeck, 'Islamic Protest under Semi-Industrial Capitalism', 370.

20. John R. Hall, 'Religion and Violence: Social Processes in Comparative Perspective', in M. Dillon (ed.), *Handbook for the Sociology of Religion* (New York: Cambridge University Press, 2003), 359-81.

21. According to the Aniagolu Commission of Inquiry, which was reprinted in thirty-five instalments in the *New Nigerian* from 13 November, 1981— 2 January, 1982. Unofficial estimates of deaths run as high as 10,000 (Kastefelt, 'Rumours of Maitatsine', 84).

22. Kastefelt, 'Rumours of Maitatsine'; Lubeck, 'Islamic Protest under Semi-Industrial Capitalism'; Mervyn Hiskett, 'The Maitatsine Riots in Kano 1980: An Assessment', *Journal of Religion in Africa* 17.3 (1987), 209-23; Guy Nicolas, 'Guerre Sainte à Kano', *Politique Africaine* 1 (1981), 47-70; Allan Christelow, 'The 'Yan Tatsine Disturbances in Kano: A Search for Perspective', *The Muslim World* 75 (1985), 69-84; Peter Clarke, 'The Maitatsine Movement in Northern Nigeria in Historical and Current Perspective', in R.I.J. Hackett (ed.), *New Religious Movements in Nigeria* (Lewiston, NY: Edwin Mellen Press, 1987), 93-115; Elizabeth Isichei, 'The Maitatsine Risings in Nigeria in 1980–85: A Revolt of the Disinherited', *Journal of Religion in Africa* 17.3 (1987), 194-208.

23. In fact, the Aniagolu Report (1981), 106, reports that a total of 34 clashes between rival religious groups in the Northern states had preceded the Maitatsine episode, in most cases requiring police intervention. The Report indicated that steps had been taken from 1979 by the government in the form of an Advisory Council on Hajj Affairs and an edict (from the Sokoto State government) to regulate Islamic religious preachers.

24. Christelow, 'The 'Yan Tatsine Disturbances in Kano', 71-72.

25. Permits are required (from the police) for outdoor preaching in Nigeria. Toyin Falola, *Violence in Nigeria: The Crisis of Religious Politics and Secular Ideologies* (Rochester, NY: University of Rochester Press, 1998), 151.

26. The Nigerian Television Authority produced a documentary entitled '55 Minutes of Maitatsine' which was first aired on 21 July, 1984. See the favorable review of it in the *Sunday New Nigerian* 2 September, 1984.

27. Thomas Robbins, 'Religious Movements and Violence: A Friendly Critique of the Interpretive Approach', *Nova Religio* 1 (1997), 17-33; see also Jeffrey Kaplan, 'Interpreting the Interpretive Approach: A Friendly Reply to Thomas Robbins', *Nova Religio* 1.1 (1997), 30-49.

28. Robbins, 'Religious Movements and Violence', 19.

29. John R. Hall, Philip D. Schuyler and Sylvaine Trinh (eds.), *Apocalypse Observed: Religious Movements and Violence in North America, Europe, and Japan* (New York: Routledge, 2000); and Catherine Wessinger, *How the Millennium Comes Violently: From Jonestown to Heaven's Gate* (New York: Seven Bridges Press, 2000).

30. See, for example, Ibrahim Sulaiman, 'The Kano Uprising—A Muslim View', *Sunday New Nigerian*, 6 June, 1982.

31. On the negative reaction of the main anti-Sufi group, `Yan Izala, to its being linked with `Yan Maitatsine see Roman Loimeier, *Islamic Reform and Political Change in Northern Nigeria* (Evanston, IL: Northwestern University Press, 1997).

32. Arjun Appadurai, 'Dead Certainty: Ethnic Violence in the Era of Globalization', *Public Culture* 10.2 (1998), 225-47.

33. Isichei, 'The Maitatsine Risings in Nigeria'; Christelow, 'The 'Yan Tatsine Disturbances in Kano', 83-84, points out that actual figures do not bear out the large numbers of foreigners in the movement, and that this popular perception was a defense mechanism.

34. Christelow, 'The 'Yan Tatsine Disturbances in Kano', 69.

35. Nasir B. Zahradeen, *The Maitatsine Saga* (Shanu: Hudahuda Publishing, 1988), 75.

36. Zahradeen, *The Maitatsine Saga*, 107.

37. Isichei, 'The Maitatsine Risings in Nigeria', nn. 76-78; M. Adeleye Ojo, 'The Maitatsine Revolution in Nigeria', *American Journal of Islamic Social Sciences* 2.2 (1985), 297-306 (303-304).

38. *Radiance* (Nigerian magazine in English, published in Kano, 1981–1982), 36-40.

39. 'Fitna' is defined as a 'burning with fire, a melting of (metals) in order to separate or distinguish the bad from the good, a means whereby the condition of a man is evinced in respect of good or evil, punishment, chastisement, conflict among people, faction and sedition, discord, dissension, difference of opinions, a misleading, causing to err, seduction, temptation' (E. Lane, *An Arabic-English Lexicon*). Information from David Cook, 7 November, 2001.

40. Barwuro M. Barkindo, 'Growing Islamism in Kano City since 1970: Causes, Form and Implications', in L. Brenner (ed.), *Muslim Identity and Social Change in Sub-Saharan Africa* (London: Hurst, 1993), 91-105; Hiskett, 'The Maitatsine Riots in Kano', 221-22; Lubeck, 'Islamic Protest under Semi-Industrial Capitalism'.

41. Watts, 'Islamic Modernities', 282.

42. Lubeck, 'Islamic Protest under Semi-Industrial Capitalism', 371-72.

43. Lubeck, 'Islamic Protest under Semi-Industrial Capitalism', 386-87.

44. Matthew Hassan Kukah, *Religion, Politics and Power in Northern Nigeria* (Ibadan: Spectrum, 1993); cf. also Lubeck, 'Islamic Protest under Semi-Industrial Capitalism'.

45. It should be noted that manipulationist theories of religious conflict are popular with several Nigerian scholars. (See, e.g., Usufu Bala Usman, *The Manipulation of Religion in Nigeria: 1977–1987* [Kaduna: Vanguard, 1987]).

46. Clarke, 'The Maitatsine Movement in Northern Nigeria', 120.

47. *Clarion* 1, 3 (Nigerian newspaper in English, October 1985).

48. Lubeck, 'Islamic Protest under Semi-Industrial Capitalism', 386.

49. Watts, 'Islamic Modernities'.

50. Talal Asad writes of the struggles for 'discursive dominance' and the difficulties of securing 'Orthodoxy' in conditions of radical change. Talal Asad, 'Religion and Politics: An Introduction', *Social Research* 59.1 (1992), 1-16. Cited in Watts, 'Islamic Modernities', 272-73.

51. Watts, 'Islamic Modernities', 271.

52. Achille Mbembe, 'At the Edge of the World: Boundaries, Territoriality, and Sovereignty in Africa', *CODESRIA Bulletin* 3 and 4 (1999), 4-16 (7-8).

53. Ashutosh Varshney, *Ethnic Conflict and Civic Life: Hindus and Muslims in India* (New Haven, CT: Yale University Press, 2001).

54. See, e.g., Michael Barkun (ed.), *Millennialism and Violence* (London: Frank

Cass, 1996); Jean-Francois Mayer, 'Cults, Violence and Religious Terrorism: An International Perspective', *Conflict and Terrorism* 24 (2001), 361-76; Thomas Robbins and Susan J. Palmer (eds.), *Millennium, Messiahs, and Mayhem: Contemporary Apocalyptic Movements* (New York: Routledge, 1997); and Catherine Wessinger, *How the Millennium Comes Violently* (New York: Seven Bridges Press, 2000).

55. Hall, Schuyler, and Trinh, *Apocalypse Observed*.

56. Rosalind I.J. Hackett, 'Managing or Manipulating Religious Conflict in the Nigerian Media', in J. Mitchell and S. Marriage (eds.), *Mediating Religion: Conversations in Media, Religion and Culture* (Edinburgh: T & T Clark, 2003), 47-64.

57. Clarke, 'The Maitatsine Movement in Northern Nigeria', 121.

58. Clarke, 'The Maitatsine Movement in Northern Nigeria', 121.

59. Awad Al-Sid Al-Karsani, 'Beyond Sufism: The Case of Millennial Islam in the Sudan', in L. Brenner (ed.), *Muslim Identity and Social Change in Sub-Saharan Africa* (London: Hurst, 1993), 135-53. Al-Karsani, in comparing Sudanese and Nigerian patterns of millennial Islam, shows that both used images and messages to express popular discontent and grievances, but that the Nigerian form tended toward more militant action (Al-Karsani, 'Beyond Sufism', 151).

60. Barkindo, 'Growing Islamism in Kano City since 1970'.

61. Christelow, 'The 'Yan Tatsine Disturbances in Kano'; see also Clarke, 'The Maitatsine Movement in Northern Nigeria'; and also, Allan Christelow, 'Religious Protest and Dissent in Northern Nigeria: From Mahdism to Qur'anic Integralism', *Journal, Institute of Muslim Minority Affairs* 6 (1985), 375-93.

62. Christelow, 'The 'Yan Tatsine Disturbances in Kano', 83.

63. Christelow, 'The 'Yan Tatsine Disturbances in Kano', 84. Barkindo, who is a historian of the region, also suggests that this movement should be seen against the increased militancy of Christians (notably the youth) from the late 1970s onwards. The numerous publications by the Christian Association of Nigeria (CAN) caused Muslims to think more critically about their religion (Barkindo, 'Growing Islamism in Kano City', 99). He also sees the overall trend in Kano during that period to employ Islamic solutions to urban problems, with the building of mosques, schools, and the creation of government committees involving both academics and leading `ulama, as influencing the growth of Islamism (Barkindo, 'Growing Islamism in Kano City', 100-105).

64. Matthews A. Ojo, personal communication, 4 April, 2002.

65. Watts, 'Islamic Modernities', 260.

66. Zahradeen, *The Maitatsine Saga*, 11.

67. Pat Williams and Toyin Falola, *Religious Impact on the Nation State* (Aldershot, UK: Avebury, 1995), 167-70.

68. Paul Lovejoy and J.S. Hogendorn, 'Revolutionary Mahdism and Resistance to Colonial Rule in the Sokoto Caliphate, 1905–1906', *Journal of African History* 31 (1990), 217-44.

69. Lovejoy and Hogendorn, 'Revolutionary Mahdism', 243.

70. Hassan Ahmed Ibrahim, 'Imperialism and Neo-Mahdism in the Sudan: A Study of British Policy towards Neo-Mahdism, 1924–1927', *International Journal of African Historical Studies* 13.2 (1980), 214-39.

71. Ibrahim, 'Imperialism and Neo-Mahdism in the Sudan', 218.

72. Williams and Falola, *Religious Impact on the Nation State,* 167-70.

73. On the rise of 'Prophet Jesus' movements in the Sudan at the end of the nineteenth century and the beginning of the twentieth, see Lidwien Kapteijns, 'Mahdist Faith and the Legitimation of Popular Revolt in Western Sudan', *Africa* 55.4 (1985), 390-99.

74. See the *Citizen*, (Nigerian magazine in English, published in Kaduna), 1 February, 1993.

75. Clashes occurred in a Lagos suburb, Abule-Taylor, Agege, in August 1997 and again a year later, between police and a group of 'Muslim fundamentalists'. *TheWeek*, (Nigerian magazine in English, published weekly), 6 August 1998. Following this the religious identity of those implicated was disputed. But again in December 1998 *P.M. News* reports that 'Maitatsine Fanatics Held in Lagos' (24 December, 1998) after the arrest of 18 of the 'zealots' by the Special Armed Robbery Squad and the confiscation of home-made guns, knives, machetes, charms and amulets, as well as 'inciting religious books and pamphlets'. Matthews A. Ojo notes that after 1980 it became common to identify any unkempt, lean Muslim zealot with Maitatsine just as it has become common since 11 September, 2001 to designate Muslims with beards as supporters of Osama bin Laden. Personal communication, 4 April, 2002.

76. *Clarion*, 1, 3 (October 1985).

77. Falola, *Violence in Nigeria*.

78. Jibril Aminu, *Observations* (Delta Publications, 1988), 64, cited in Birai, 'Islamic Tajdid and the Political Process in Nigeria', in M.E. Marty and R.S. Appleby (eds.), *Fundamentalisms and the State: Remaking Polities, Economies, and Militance* (Chicago: University of Chicago Press, 1991), 184-203, here 198.

79. *New Nigerian*, Kaduna, 21 February, 1982 cited in Birai, 'Islamic Tajdid and the Political Process in Nigeria', 198.

80. Birai, 'Islamic Tajdid and the Political Process in Nigeria', 197.

81. Birai, 'Islamic Tajdid and the Political Process in Nigeria', 197.

82. Lincoln, 'Conflict'.

83. For similar arguments pertaining to the terrorist attacks of 11 September in the US see Paul Christopher Johnson, 'Death and Memory at Ground Zero: A Historian of Religion's Report', *Bulletin of the Council of Societies of the Study of Religion* 31.1 (2002), 3-7; and Srinivas Aravamudan, 'Ground Zero; or the Implosion of Church and State', in S. Hauerwas and F. Lentricchia (eds.), *Dissent from the Homeland: Essays after September 11* (Durham, NC: Duke University Press, 2003), 195-203.

Postmodernity and the Imagination of the Apocalypse:
A Study of Genre

Marc Fonda

Introduction

When some people speak of our era as one that suffers the malaise of philosophical uncertainty causing a sense of urgency,[1] such people speak of a time that is considered ready for change. It is part of human nature to want to reduce tension and anxiety caused by uncertain and anxious situations as quickly as possible. There is no doubt that there is a range of possible responses to situations of increased tension, social or psychological. Most often the reduction of excessive stimulation appears in small, localized, and relatively uneventful reactions. However, the human drive to reduce anxiety also surfaces in dramatic and revolutionary ways: intellectual revolutions (in the form of paradigm shifts), on the one hand, and millennial movements, on the other.

In this article I propose to examine the uncertain postmodern[2] situation as it is illuminated by western culture's propensity to make myths about end times. I suggest that because it allows for no certain ground for speculation about a comprehensive world-view, the postmodern perspective reflects a millennial-styled deliberation about the end of the present order of existence and the emergence of another. I submit that our predilection to make myths, to imagine our world in mythic themes, understood to operate in relation to the undergirding apocalyptic character of the western ethos and the expiration of the second millennium, makes it imperative to investigate how the contemporary West reveals its attitudes toward the world.

In the following pages, I will take you on an ideational expedition into the theories of mythology, the history of ideas and literary criticism. This journey disembarks by contrasting Richard Tarnas' characterization of the postmodern genre with the necessary preconditions for millennialism as provided by Michael Barkun, in the light of Thomas Kuhn's description of paradigm shifts while examining the example of paradigm shifts in American university literature departments. We then will consider the prevalence of the preconditions of apocalypticism in North America since the 1960s. This will be followed by a brief side-trip with Robert Brockway into the mythic roots of apocalyptic thought as found in ancient Sumeria and ancient Israel and their implications for the contemporary world.

The Postmodern Apocalypse

I would like to begin by outlining several characteristics common to both millennial movements and postmodern thought. In general terms, both anticipate the role of a crisis or disaster as something that upsets the usual order of things and instigates change. Furthermore, both conclude that the traditional means of explaining the world are no longer adequate. Both also provide a new, revivalistic vision of the world; and, finally, adherents of both postmodernism and apocalypticism suffer from a specific degree of angst caused by the recognition of impending doom of civilization as they know it.

In *The Passion of the Western Mind* Richard Tarnas characterizes the postmodern condition as one that is 'subversive of all paradigms'.[3] He explains that we can find at the core of postmodernity's style of criticism the awareness that reality is 'at once multiple, local and temporal, and without demonstrable foundation'.[4] Because we now understand reality as consisting of a multitude of dimensions that are all constructs of human symbol usage and imaginative inclinations, we can no longer sustain any grand cosmological theories without producing 'empirical falsification and intellectual authoritarianism'.[5] The literalism of modernity is now being rejected as too narrow a perspective from which we can survey our ideational landscapes.

One consequence of such relativization of all thought is that we can no longer theorize without being suspicious of our complicity in reaffirming traditional world-views that institutionalize and codify our selves. Furthermore, we live in no small modicum of fear over accusations of racism, sexism, heterosexism, parochialism, elitism, and of being politically incorrect. This is to say that we live in a state of intellectual uncertainty, and this brings with it a strong sense of urgency to find a means of reducing anxiety.

Yet, as Tarnas points out, there is a strong re-emergence of Romanticism in the contemporary West. Such contemporary Romanticism appears in contrast to the postmodern disposition to deconstruct the roots of our thinking. According to Tarnas this postmodern style of Romanticism operates as a means to the 'radical integration and reconciliation' of contemporary culture.[6] 'Faced with such a problematic and difficult intellectual situation', Tarnas writes, 'thoughtful individuals engage the task of evolving a flexible set of premises and perspectives that would not reduce or suppress the complexity and multiplicity of human realities, yet could also serve to mediate, integrate and clarify.'[7] It has become the task of many contemporary thinkers to develop an intellectual vision that accounts for the profound diversity of the world and humanity. This romantic vision of cultural revitalization must also be capable of bringing some sense of coherence to the experience of fragmentation characteristic to postmodernity. There is the need of an intellectual revelation, an alternate paradigm that will provide sustainable and fertile ground for the 'generation of unanticipated new perspectives and possibilities in the future'.[8]

What I have been trying to do is to point out elements belonging to the postmodern intellectual situation that parallel those found in apocalyptic movements. To make the analogy more explicit, it is necessary to look at the conditions required for the emergence of apocalyptic visions which instigate millennial movements. Michael Barkun in *Disaster and the Millennium* presents the following as a nutshell definition of millenarian or chiliastic movements:

> [They] are social movements which expect immediate, collective, total, this worldly salvation. They anticipate the complete destruction of the existing social order, political, and economic order, which is to be superseded by a new and perfect society. They frequently couple this anticipation with an active desire to speed the inevitable result, often through violent, revolutionary means.[9]

This description sounds rather like the deconstructive method championed originally by Derrida. Deconstruction proceeds from the assumption that traditional ways of viewing the world are wrong or false; it then delegitimates such metanarratives insofar as they are considered totalizing. Consequently, space is left open for the postmodern Romantic impulse to speculate upon a brighter future (not that adherents of deconstruction often do more than tear things apart). Nonetheless, such challenges to the legitimation of traditional paradigms of thought must, at some level, invite social change in general.

The available means of social change, however, are not always violent in nature. As the title to Barkun's book suggests, disasters play a role in the onset of millennial thought and movements. Disasters upset social ordering of the world that surrounds a community. Furthermore, such communities need not be understood as merely rural in character. Urban expressions of millennialism have become more and more frequent with the appearance of mass communications, which allow us to vicariously experience disasters as well as enabling an unprecedented potential for the dissemination of the 'revealed truth' of a group's apocalyptic vision.

Moreover, we must keep in mind that disasters are not necessarily acts of god or of nature. Man-made disasters now proliferate and include: economic instability; nuclear war; environmental catastrophe; political unrest; as well as ethical and intellectual deprivation, to name a few instances. This is to say that we need not look to natural disasters to find highly destructive events. As Barkun puts it: 'Relatively non-destructive events can be characterized as disasters when onlookers regard them as confirming the existence of greater future dangers'.[10]

Other characteristics to millennial movements include: an intense emotional expression; the absolute condemnation of the existing political and social order, while denying its legitimacy; the transgression of accepted norms, laws, and taboos; and, unrealistic aims in regard to the work of revitalizing society.[11] In other words, a communal vision of revitalization is necessary: a vision of revitalization that will take place on this planet, whose appearance is imminent, which will involve the total reorganization of reality, and, finally, the belief that the millennium will be initiated by supernatural agencies.[12]

For Barkun 'revitalization lies in the need of a society under excessive stress to either reinforce itself or die'.[13] This is to say that revitalization movements emerge out of a need to reduce the stress and anxiety that confronts people when their society is no longer capable of providing an effective means of doing so. For Barkun, the twentieth century is 'particularly fertile' in its expression of millennialism. One of the things Barkun does in *Crucible of the Millennium*, is analyze American expressions of apocalypticism between 1960 and 1985. According to Barkun, the contemporary 'apocalyptic chic' has been accompanied by the emergence of political radicalism, a sense of ideological exhaustion,[14] the simultaneous emergence of a new form of leftism in American culture[15] as well as a resurgence of fundamentalist perspectives and practices, and, finally, the appearance of secular apocalyptic literature.[16]

Briefly, the ten years following Kennedy's assignation have been seen as a period in which one perceived disaster emerged after another: Martin Luther King's death and the resulting race riots; Viet Nam; the advent of the new left radicals and the hippy dropouts; the emergence of Southern fundamentalism, to name a few instances. Although there were not many significant natural disasters during this period, it was not a stable time. The heydays of counter-cultural radicalism profoundly upset traditionalists because radicals brought about what traditionalists considered to be assaults on the family, patriotism, and the work ethic. Furthermore, there were social and legal changes that

> helped prepare the way for a new millenarian ambience: the women's movement, with its challenge to traditional gender roles; the increasing frequency of sex before and outside of marriage; the visibility and activism of the gay community; and, Supreme Court decisions banning school prayer and permitting abortion.[17]

More traditional forms of apocalypticism other than the new left's utopia of Maslowian self-fulfillment have also emerged since the 1960s. Turning to dispensationalism, traditional millennial groups pushed prophesies of the millennium into the future upon realizing that the establishment of Israel as a state suggested that Biblical prophecies were being fulfilled in the contemporary world.[18] Furthermore, fundamentalist denominations in the Southern states saw a dramatic increase in attendance as mass media took the dispensationalist message further than it previously ever had gone. Moreover, there was a coinciding shift in political attitudes towards the right as well as an increase in population in the Bible-belt—both of which added to the prestige of the fundamentalists' new apocalyptic message.[19]

More interesting, however, is the concurrent rise in influence of secular apocalyptic literature among intellectuals, government officials, and business leaders. Examples of secular apocalypticism includes such challenges as feminist thought, a perceived environmental disaster, scenarios regarding planetary destruction, and certain Internet subcultures. According to Barkun, contemporary secular apocalypticism has lead to an unintentional buttressing of the authority of their less sophisticated premillennial counterparts (i.e., those who believe that Christ will come to initiate the millennium). 'This secular apocalyptic literature contended that because of the failure of individuals and nations to act wisely, decisions were being taken or were about to be taken which would destroy "civilization as we know it".'[20]

By reinforcing the authority of apocalyptic themes, secular intellectuals helped make apocalyptic thought more acceptable in western society as a whole. Furthermore, there has been a trend in recent scholarship to acknowledge that apocalypticism is increasingly becoming a global phenomenon. Apocalypticism is now understood to be a phenomenon that transcends historical periods and cultures, and encompasses 'the traditionally religious as well as the avowedly secular'.[21] Yet, as Barkun points out, there is also a romantic element in secular apocalypticism: the optimism that we will transcend '*Homo sapiens* and become *Homo humanus*'.[22] Just as religious apocalyptic visions anticipate a new, revitalized society emerging from the carcass of the past world, so too does contemporary secular apocalypticism anticipate the emergence of a pristine, more perfect society.

Statements like these lend credence to my earlier comment that there is a similarity between apocalyptic and postmodern styles of thought. The disasters and threats of disasters during the past 30 years such as natural calamities, abortion, the Gulf War, political correctness, the AIDS epidemic, 9/11 as well as political and economic instability throughout the world all contribute to our psychic condition as members of western society. Because of the uncertainty and anxiety caused by this perceived string of disastrous events, those of us in the West may be suffering from what is called disaster syndrome. This is a condition in which people become stunned, withdrawn, passive, suggestible, experience diminished mental capacity, and have difficulties in perceiving reality correctly[23] (witness the erosion of civil liberties in the USA after 9/11). All of these conditions contribute to a motive for speculating about a better future.

By establishing a motive for such speculation we might conclude that an obsession with disaster and the possibility of an ever-changing society has come home to roost in western thought. If we are not deconstructing the world and radically relativizing thought, we are anticipating a new synthesis, a new order that will alleviate all of our uncertainty, urgency, and anxiety. If we are not causing the complete subversion and destruction of the present order of things, we are petitioning for a revitalized society in which we can find worldly salvation. It is the frequency of perceived disasters, their intensification via mass media, the increasing acceptability of challenging and transgressing society's norms that places the postmodern perspective firmly in the Apocalyptic genre.

In Thomas Kuhn's *The Structure of Scientific Revolutions,* one can find similarities between paradigm shifts and millennial movements. First, let's characterize Kuhn's thought. A successful paradigm shift requires that an alternate idea must be present and seem to be able to solve some 'outstanding and generally recognized problem' and must 'promise to preserve a relatively large part of the concrete problem-solving ability' that the previous paradigm accrued to the field of study.[24] There are five further characteristics to paradigm shifts: (1) a community of thinkers must reject its 'time-honored theory' in favor of another approach incompatible with it; (2) this produces a consequent shift in the intellectual problems available to that community and the standards by which the community determines whether or not a problem is valid; (3) the alternate theory must be sufficiently unprecedented to attract an enduring group away from the competition; (4) the theory must be sufficiently open-ended so as to leave all sorts of problems for the redefined group of practitioners to resolve; and (5) ideational revolutions must transform the intellectual imagination in ways that needs be described as a 'transformation of the world within which the scientific work was done'.[25]

These sorts of paradigm change are not limited to the scientific side of academia. In the next few pages we look at how Michele Lamont's 'How to Become a Dominant French Philosopher: The Case of Jacques Derrida' and Mark A. Schneider's 'Social Dimensions of Epistemological Disputes: The Case of Literary Theory' characterize the institutional (academic) legitimation of Derrida's work in the USA. As the latter case builds on the former, both authors report on how Derrida's work was legitimated in American academia not only because it was, in part, related to its cultural context but that it found its inroads into American culture mainly via departments of literature. First, let us consider a touch of history.

New Criticism was one of the most influential theories in the field of American literary criticism from the 1940s to the end of the 1950s. When Northrop Frye wrote his *Anatomy of Criticism* (1957) he launched a powerful attack against the textual emphasis of New Criticism. In conjunction with other critiques published previously, Frye's critique caused a deep crisis in American literary criticism. The existing paradigm was rejected and new paradigms struggled to fill the void. French structuralism was introduced and it successfully prepared the ground for the arrival of deconstruction.[26]

Lamont considers that other factors have also contributed to the acceptance of deconstruction. These factors include pressures brought to the fore because American comparative literature departments did not have a long intellectual tradition and were in search of a paradigm. The French tradition had long enjoyed high status and influence in comparative literature. Moreover, structuralism itself offered an exciting style, as far as intellectual fashions go, that was ingenious, exotic, and subversive insofar as it was emancipatory or rejuvenating. These qualities offered hope of revitalization for a traditionally austere field, suffering crisis. In postmodern methodologies, American literary scholars saw an opportunity to build their own institutional and intellectual positions by promoting the importation of structuralism. This was a new paradigm that a new generation of scholars could adopt in order to secure a niche in the field[27] and along with structuralism came Derrida's deconstruction.

Other specific conditions leading to the ascension of Derrida's thought in American departments of literature include the fact that it was easily integrated into existing intellectual agendas and disseminated via prestigious institutions (e.g., Cornell, Johns Hopkins and Yale). Furthermore, the diffusion of Derrida's theories was aided by several journals that regularly published work on deconstruction, helping to create an audience and institutionalizing deconstruction as a legitimate theory. Further, there were several renowned scholars who incorporated deconstruction in their own work (Bloom, Hartman, de Man, Miller, the so-called 'Yale enclave' —whose influence ensured academic support in literature departments).[28]

What's more, Derrida's work was exported to the USA along with that of a number of other influential French scholars. He profited from that association. Deconstruction's diffusion was also facilitated because literary criticism had been a dominant sub-field within language departments since the 1950s and a hegemony of literary critics was well established. Finally, deconstruction was an answer to a disciplinary crisis that was in play in departments of literary criticism.[29] That is, the crisis caused by Frye and others included a debate on the validity of one of two different methodological approaches to literature: realist and relativist (as crude, ideal types).

Schneider points out that the debate between literary historians (realists) and New Critics (relativists) displays the instability endemic to literary inquiry. Historians assumed the mantel of experts with skills and knowledge that placed them well above amateurs. However, these very same features rendered the historians dry and pedantic. The interpreters of New Criticism had similar problems. They were most often faulted as procrustean and mechanically imitable. New Criticism had to present itself as distinctly scientific in order to claim authority, if it were to compete on a level field with the literary historians. Nevertheless, this exposed it to routinization or professionalization, a disconcerting possibility for the New Criticism's poet-creators, as art is often considered inventive and novel.[30]

The realist position argued that discrimination between valid and invalid interpretations of a text could only be established by discovering the authors' intentions through historical research. The relativist response after the 1960s, deconstruction, attacked realist forms of interpretations as 'totalizing systems'. Proponents argued that once released from a desire for knowledge, true close reading could expose the 'self-dissipation of any determinate meaning by texts caused by the texts themselves'. Yet, this ambition left deconstruction open to the same charge of tautological or pedantic analysis that had been leveled against New Criticism.[31]

The social organization proposed by deconstruction is more akin to the arts than it is to the sciences. While it was originally presented as a science that, inspired by Neitzsche, Heidegger and Saussure, would expose the excessive power of language to signify a thing and, thus, determine meaning, deconstruction relied heavily on art, especially insofar as it rejected the framework that made the claims to 'knowledge' possible. Deconstruction is not propositional but like poetry offers a style that is dense and playful. Like art, it rejects as misrepresentation all efforts to define it or turn it into a method. Although deconstruction uses close reading similarly to New Criticism, it presupposes significantly greater philosophical and cultural knowledge.[32]

According to Schneider, deconstruction is 'ambivalently emancipatory' in that it challenges hierarchies and distinctions, yet admits its inability to move beyond them. Yet, it rejects the entire framework of traditional scholarship (i.e., the model of 'objective historical truth') as a force of oppression. It allows practitioners to employ stylistic idiosyncrasy. Each develops a distinctive approach and values competitors insofar as they offer product differentiation. Mutual dependency is thus ignored and achieving adept status requires gigantic stores of cultural capital, a god-like tone, and the skill to avoid falling into arguments with the opposition, at least on their terms. This is not a stance that is easy to professionalize and because of its demanding nature, it is not something that is aimed at undergraduate markets (the main university market).[33] That is, the insulation from lay scrutiny brought by deconstruction's microscopic textual analyses, dense style, and theoretical sophistication came at the cost of pedagogical suitability and marketability outside of the university—where tolerance was never high for 'nihilistic obscurantism'.[34]

All of this sounds much like our former discussion on the shared generic characteristics between postmodernity and the apocalyptic imagination. The preceding discussion exposed certain similarities to what Kuhn has said about paradigm shifts in the context of departments of literature: a new method that does not radically change the field but ensures numerous problems remain to be solved. In so doing, it rejects other dominant theories and causes the community problems in determining its validity. Finally, it was sufficiently unprecedented theoretically and was easily able to convert American scholars to its perspective, who could then find their niches. It all sounds like a conversion experience (albeit to some sort of intellectual perspective).

At this point, I want to return to the observation that millennial movements are movements that are beset with similar pressures to those one finds in the characterization of Kuhnian paradigm shifts. Both provide theories about a perspective that is felt to better respond to the group's observations about their present condition than traditional models do. As it turns out, Barkun also makes a comparison between millenarian movements and Kuhnian notions about paradigm shift. Barkun proposes that in disaster situations, as with millennial thought and paradigm shifts, there is the emergence of an alternative system of explanation. The emergence of an alternative system of explanation reflects two requirements which Kuhn uses to characterize paradigm shifts: 'disconfirming evidence and an alternative explanation'.[35] Furthermore, like Kuhn,[36] Barkun notes that conversion experiences play a role in the acceptance of an alternative picture of reality. In both secular and religious conversion experiences, there is an abrupt and 'total reorientation, by the frequent surrender of beliefs once strongly held, and by the concurrent adoption of beliefs that once would have been rejected'.[37]

At the risk of sounding repetitive, I want to emphasize again what now may be obvious: Postmodern thought in many ways belongs to a genre which can be best described as apocalyptic. We may well wonder how this can be so, after all is not the academic ivory tower supposed to be objective and, hence, removed from the vulgarities of society? Well, as postmodern thinkers, we know that belief in objectivity is a modern myth that emerged during the Enlightenment. Moreover, the very notion that there was even an Age of Reason or an Enlightenment has mythic implications. Through deconstruction, we might say, the postmodern world is in the process of re-mythologizing the stories which have emerged out of the legacy of Cartesian-Newtonian thought and brought about the cosmology of modernity. It is developing a distinct, post-modern *Weltanschauung*.

As Robert Brockway informs us in *Myth from the Ice Age to Mickey Mouse*,

> 'Both the Enlightenment and deconstructionist positions are subjective interpretations rooted in the milieu of the times, the personalities and psychologies of historians, and many other factors. For these reasons they are more like the myths, legends, and story-telling of archaic times than they are not'.[38]

This is to say that like paradigms, myths are founded on the best available evidence at any given time, and 'are discredited when the evidence no longer sustains them'.[39] Brockway also suggests this: when a specific myth no longer functions as a efficient theory or cosmology for a society, new ones rise to attention. Like Kuhn, Brockway claims that these 'new' myths were already present as cultural artifacts because they emerged out of the old myths: '[F]irst as modifications and revisions, and ultimately as independent species, something new and different'.[40]

These considerations about myth suggest two things: first, myth-making is an inherent human activity. We make myths in the sense that we invent paradigms and the major change in the modern age has been in the style of mythic expression: 'the archaic myth is a metaphor; the modern myth is a theory. Both are models or paradigms.'[41] Second, the myths or paradigms that we invent are invariably based upon dominant themes of our society. For Brockway, the reason that the apocalyptic genre is present in postmodern thought is that the myths upon which messianism or apocalypticism, for instance, are based 'are detectable as the basic foundation on which [western] schemas are built'.[42]

The myths Brockway believes to constitute the foundation to western stories are the Eternal Return and the Hero who Slays the Dragon.[43] The myth of the Eternal Return is felt to be the older of the two and reflects a cyclical understanding of the passage of time, characterized as feminine. The myth of the Eternal Return is probably based upon the observation of the cyclical nature of time as reflected by such things as the seasons, cycles of sun and moon, menstruation cycles, the round of birth-life-death, and so on. According to the myth of Eternal Return, 'there is neither an absolute beginning nor terminus, but instead, infinite regression in the past and eternal recurrence for all time to come'.[44] It is a myth that is more characteristic of ancient Greece, India, and the East, than it is of the West since the onset of Judaism.

The myth of the Eternal Return is believed to have been challenged in Sumeria around 2500 BCE About this time an agrarian culture was supplanted by nomadic warriors, who conquered the Mesopotamian area and set up an alternate style of social order based on kingship, patriarchy, and patrilinearality of descent.[45] Along with such social changes, as the argument goes, came a transformation in how time was perceived: rather than reflecting femininity by its cyclical nature, time was now understood to be linear and masculine. For this reason, we could say that with the myth of the Hero who Slays the Dragon came an understanding of time as linear, as having a beginning and an end. Finding its literary prototype in the *Enuma Elish*, we encounter a story of the hero-warrior god Marduk, who does battle with chaos symbolized by his (great) grandmother, the dragoness, Tiamat. Marduk eventually defeats the dragon and, by creating the cosmos and all living beings out of Tiamat's shattered corpse, 'fulfils history'.[46] Yet, as is appropriate of a story emerging out of the myth of the Eternal Return, Tiamat or chaos is never ultimately defeated and must be fought again every year in an attempt to 'ensure the survival of the fragile cosmos'.[47]

According to Brockway, however, the Hebrews completely rejected the myth of the Eternal Return and conceived of history as the period between creation and the Judgment that ushers in an eternal divine order. Furthermore, 'This idea was emphasized by the early Christians who believed they were living in the last days'.[48] Consequently, we can conclude that the western, Christian world-view is one that is based, at least in part, on the apocalyptic vision symbolized by the hero who defeats chaos and recasts reality. Hence, we are enabled to understand what is meant when Brockway points out that

> most postmodern historical interpretations are variants of the Christian apocalyptic, since most are written in terms of future expectations, with the view in mind that the nations are moving towards some ultimate destiny. Moreover, since the expansion of Europe has created a single global village, global history itself is now written in terms of Christian sacred history. The myth provides the paradigm.[49]

We can, I believe, extend this assertion to all of western speculation, art, literature, and the like. That is, if we assume that the story of the hero slaying the dragon is one of the foundations of western thought, its sphere of influence can be expected to appear in all realms of western culture.

It is in the hero who slays the dragon, I propose, that we can find a reflection of both postmodern and apocalyptic styles of thought: that is, the tendency to do battle with past monsters, and the vision of creating a new and better world. The apocalyptic postmodern hero is one that would fight for the de-institutionalization of traditional social edifices, subvert traditional systems of authority, presumably to bring about a new and more perfect society. Consequently, we might say that the apocalyptic postmodern hero is optimistic and idealistic: faced with a disastrous contemporary situation, he or she is on the road to being converted to romanticism in the desire to help imagine a better world. The romanticism mentioned by Tarnas is characteristic of a felt need for revitalization, for a paradigm shift and we can say that this happened in departments of literature when they accepted deconstruction as a methodological and theoretical viewpoint. The apocalyptic postmodern hero is also idealistic in his or her anticipation of the defeat of chaos represented by the monster of modernity and the opportunity to radically recast the world—that is, to instigate a paradigm shift.

What the apocalyptic character of postmodern thought suggests is that the deconstructive project may have failed its mandate.[50] If it is the goal of deconstruction to unmask the background assumptions built into western thought, one of its tasks must necessarily be to demythologize, to unmask the apocalyptic basis of its own thought. Yet, deconstruction has not looked into its own motives and presuppositions to a satisfactory degree.[51] Even if deconstruction has failed itself, it is not the only epistemological perspective characteristic of postmodernity. Contemporary western romanticism as characterized by feminism, for example, not only questions and debunks traditional intellectual edifices, it also offers alternative perspectives that ultimately challenge the status of the apocalyptic hero—which has been the basis of the Modern West's imagination of selfhood.

There are several individuals who are writing about a selfhood that can be characterized as postmodern. I will look at one feminist's criticisms of the modern imagination of self as hero: Catherine Keller. In *From a Broken Web: Separation, Sexism, and Self*, Keller denies the primacy of the hero as a model for selfhood. As a feminist, Keller is extremely interested in deconstructing the traditional narrative of the self. In *From a Broken Web* Keller criticizes traditional philosophy, theology, and psychology's heroic attitude in regard to how self is constructed. She characterizes traditional concepts of self: it is separated, unemotional and rational, non-material, and normatively masculine.[52] Keller understands the heroic ego as constituting the basis of western thought.

Like Brockway, she finds roots of the hero paradigm in the *Enuma Elish*, which, as we know, is the Babylonian myth of genesis. To Keller, Marduk's act of slaying Tiamat represents the onset of patriarchy in the western tradition. It was the patriarchal warrior-hero that came to Mesopotamia, and defeated the matriarchal-based agrarian cultures already present. In such characterizations, we find suggestions of a paradigm shift: the paradigm of cyclical time as represented by the myth of the Eternal Return appearing in agrarian cultures was supplanted by a model of linear time represented by the Hero who Slayed the Dragon.

Keller, however, extends the metaphor to posit that the events in ancient Sumeria have become the prototype for a tradition of symbolic matricide in the western world.[53] Like Brockway, who claims that the Hebrews completely rejected the Eternal Return, Keller suggests that the *Enuma Elish* is at the roots of Jewish mythology. Jewish mythology, as we know, is in turn the basis of much of Christian myth and ultimately contemporary western theology, philosophy, science, and psychology. Arguing from a psychoanalytical critique of development based in the thoughts of Nancy Chodorow, Carol Gilligan, and Dorothy Dinnerstein, Keller claims that the Freudian Oedipal drama and Jungian notions of individuation reflect the matricidal impulse represented by the murder of Tiamat. That is, the impulse to violently free oneself from and slay the overwhelming mother is understood to constitute the basis of maturation in traditional forms of Jungian depth psychology.[54] Keller claims that the hero is not a good model for theorizing about self in general, and women's understanding of self in specific. Asserting that it is possible to reflect upon maturation using themes other than matricide, Keller argues for the idea of a connective self as a possible corrective to the traditional, separated self. She uses feminist insights to suggest an idea of self as interconnected to the surrounding world, a self that exists in community, a self that is in process, and a self that is diverse as well as multi-determined.[55]

In Keller's criticisms of traditional notions of selfhood, we once more find the paradox of the hero who slays the monster of modernity. On the first level, Keller takes on the role of the hero that instigates the postmodern apocalypse: a paradigm shift that, in slaughtering the monster of modernity, denies the primacy and legitimacy of the hero itself. It is the voice of the rational hero that is being employed to deconstruct itself. There is, however, another, paradoxical, level to this metaphor that needs to be considered. What I am referring to is Keller's charge that matricide is intrinsic to western culture. She finds in the *Enuma Elish* a literary representation of the defeat of matriarchy as represented by the myth of the Eternal Return, by the patriarchal Hero who Slayed the Dragon. Keller suggests that we can find in the destruction of Tiamat, the beginnings of the patriarchal, separated self that matures through a model which includes the symbolic or mythic act of matricide. Yet it is now the dragon, as represented by feminism for instance, that is rising up to slay the hero and set the world right.

Brockway inadvertently concurs with Keller over this point. Referring to Northrop Frye's *Anatomy of Criticism*, Brockway suggests that today we encounter little else than the ironic mode in contemporary myths or literature. According to Brockway

> the ironic version of the Hero and Dragon myth is a moral commentary on our age since it is the dragon who is really the hero. Only the dragon acts with courage and determination, but, of course, he [sic] is bound to lose as well since there are no winners or losers. The Hero and Dragon myth has been reabsorbed into the Myth of Eternal Return.[56]

This is to suggest that today it is the feminine principle, if you will, it is feminists, it is the dragon understood to represent women and not modernity, that is emerging as the protagonist at the end of the second and the beginning of the third millennia.

Richard Tarnas also agrees with the assessment that feminist thought is emerging as a protagonist of our times. To Tarnas the 'dynamic tension and interplay between the deconstructive and the integrative' is nowhere 'more dramatically in evidence than in the rapidly expanding body of work produced by women informed by feminism'.[57] Furthermore, Tarnas claims that the Western, masculine world-view has evolved through the repression of the feminine—on the repression of the undifferentiated unitary consciousness, of the *participation mystique* with nature: a progressive denial of the *anima mundi*, of the soul of the world, of the community of being, of the all-pervading, of mystery and ambiguity, of imagination, emotion, instinct, body nature, woman.[58]

Tarnas suggests that the masculine-hero paradigm has existed by feeding upon the repressed, vilified, and murdered feminine. He suggests that the days of the hero are numbered, because we are much more interested in hearing what the dragon, or the feminine, has to say in regard to how the world is constructed by our myths or paradigms.

The myth of the Eternal Return is coming back because the dragon was never truly defeated, as is suggested by the Babylonian New Year's ceremonies. With the resurgence of a style of thought based in the myth of Eternal Return may come a more realistic and less compulsive approach to self and society. For, as I suggested earlier, the Hero myth can be seen to be an idealistic praxis in regards to its optimism and romanticism, its fantasy of apocalyptic revitalization, its call for the de-institutionalization of self and society, and the story of dramatic events causing the end of time and bringing about a new and improved world. In contrast, the myth of the Eternal Return suggests that life is not a story but, instead, moves 'from anticlimax to anticlimax'.[59] There is to be no real sudden change for the better, for as much as the hero must slay the returning dragon every year, so, too, do radical and new ideas eventually become institutionalized and must then be nullified. To me, the myth of the Eternal Return represents a less idealistic more realistic view of things: it suggests that any dramatic change is not for all time, that things work in cycles, that there is no one way of representing the world, and that all things operate in conjunction.

Conclusion

Although the myth of Eternal Return may be re-emerging in contemporary western society, the Hero still maintains a large sphere of influence. The attitude represented by the Hero will be with us for a long time, insofar that it has penetrated all forms of western thought: the sciences, the arts, and the religious. I am not attempting to say that the attitudes represented by the myth of the Hero should be rejected outright, that would not fall within the purview of postmodernity, which employs myriad forms of expression to appreciate humanity's inherent diversity. Yet, we must keep in mind the human tendency to make myths and how this is reflected at the end of the second millennium. The battle between the dragon and the hero, or between cyclical and linear nature, between institutionalized and alternative paradigms will continue as we move beyond the millennial year, 2000.[60] The year 2000, Barkun predicted, 'once the symbol of a technological consummation, where human ills would yield to scientific solutions...is certain to revert to its chiliastic function, [as] a sign post on the road to some cosmic overturning'.[61]

How western society responded to the turn of the second millennium was not surprising: it anticipated an apocalypse (e.g., Y2K, the 'Left Behind' series, etc.). But the means of revitalizing society, of shifting paradigms, do not necessarily have to be climatic and violent. Even though the world will change, is changing faster and more profoundly than ever before, perhaps the re-emergence of the myth of Eternal Return can help to mitigate the dramatic chaos that might unfold as we enter the third millenium.

References

Barkun, Michael, *Disaster and the Millennium* (New Haven, CT: Yale University Press, 1974).

—*Crucible of the Millennium: The Burned-over District of New York in the 1840's* (Syracuse: Syracuse University Press, 1986).

Brockway, Robert W., *Myth from the Ice Age to Mickey Mouse* (Albany, NY: State University of New York Press, 1993).

Chodorow, Nancy, *The Reproduction of Mothering: Psychoanalysis and the Sociology of Gender* (Berkeley, CA: University of California Press, 1978).

Eisler, Riane, *The Chalice and the Blade: Our History, our Future* (San Francisco: HarperSanFrancisco, 1987).

Ellis, Richard, *Against Deconstruction* (Princeton, NJ: Princeton University Press, 1989).

Frye, Northrop, *Anatomy of Criticism: Four Essays* (Princeton, NJ: Princeton University Press, 1973 [1957]).

Keller, Catherine, *From a Broken Web: Separation, Sexism and Self* (Boston: Beacon Press, 1986).

Kuhn, Thomas, *The Structure of Scientific Revolutions* (Chicago: University of Chicago Press, 1962).

Lamont, Michele, 'How to Become a Dominant French Philosopher: The Case of Jacques Derrida', *American Journal of Sociology* 93.3 (November 1987), 584-622.

Lasch, Scott, *Sociology of Postmodernism* (New York: Routledge, 1989).

Lyotard, Jean-François, *The Postmodern Condition: A Report on Knowledge* (trans. Geoff Bennington and Brian Massumi; Minneapolis: University of Minnesota Press, 1984 [1979]).

Schneider, Mark A., 'Social Dimensions of Epistemological Disputes: The Case of Literary Theory', *Sociological Perspectives* 40.2 (1997), 243-63.

Starhawk, *The Spiral Dance: A Rebirth of the Ancient Religion of the Great Goddess* (San Francisco: Harper & Row, 1989 [1979]).

Tarnas, Richard, *The Passion of the Western Mind: Understanding the Ideas that Have Shaped our World View* (New York: Ballantine Books, 1991).

Notes

1.   Richard Tarnas, *The Passion of the Western Mind: Understanding the Ideas that Have Shaped our World View* (New York: Ballantine Books, 1991), 398.

2.   I understand postmodernity to be characterized by the following four points: it is (1) the radical relativization of western cultural practices, discourses, myths, and sciences (Lyotard); (2) the radical politicization of western cultural practices, mores, ideals, and norms; (3) a radical expression of the western ideal of democracy based in the metaphors of the individual, human freedom, human rights, access to information, and the right to self determination; and, (4) a radically informed romanticism reemerging in contemporary western thought with an apocalyptic vision which articulates and alternate imagination of subjectivity and cosmology.

3.   Tarnas, *The Passion of the Western Mind*, 401.

4.   Tarnas, *The Passion of the Western Mind*, 401.

5.   Tarnas, *The Passion of the Western Mind*, 401.

6.   Tarnas, *The Passion of the Western Mind*, 408.

7.   Tarnas, *The Passion of the Western Mind*, 409.

8.   Tarnas, *The Passion of the Western Mind*, 409.

9.   Michael Barkun, *Disaster and the Millennium* (New Haven: Yale University Press, 1974), 18.

10.   Michael Barkun, *Crucible of the Millennium: The Burned-over District of New York in the 1840's* (Syracuse: Syracuse University Press, 1986), 153. Disasters themselves may also be predominantly social constructions or interpretations of anomalous events and experiences.

11.   Barkun, *Crucible of the Millennium*, 18-19.

12.   Barkun, *Crucible of the Millennium*, 18.

13.   Barkun, *Disaster and the Millennium*, 38.

14.   Barkun characterizes such ideological exhaustion as appearing during the period between the 1930s and 1950s in which the right and the left had exhausted their ideologies which were ' "once the road to action, has come to a dead end" '. This exhaustion was 'compounded by disillusionment over ideologies in power abroad and the rise of a political consensus in the United States'. Hence the old means of speaking about a social utopia 'appeared neither desirable nor necessary' (*Crucible of the Millennium*, 154).

15.   Barkun characterizes this new form of leftism as one that merely re-emphasized the end of ideology thesis. 'This terminally ideological exhaustion was confirmed by the tendency of many in the New Left to migrate into non-political activities.' From radical political activity, to social interaction, and finally the commune of self discovery—the people dropped out! (*Crucible of the Millennium*, 155).

16.   Barkun, *Crucible of the Millennium*, 154-56.

17.   Barkun, *Crucible of the Millennium*, 155.

18.   Barkun informs us that the 1960s premillennial movement 'arose out of a system of Biblical interpretation developed by the English evangelical, John Nelson Darby'. Darby divided the world into religious significant periods or 'dispensations', and 'the effect of these new historical divisions was to push the fulfillment of Biblical prophecies into the future' (*Crucible of the Millennium*, 156).

19. Barkun, *Crucible of the Millennium*, 157-58.

20. Barkun, *Crucible of the Millennium*, 158.

21. Barkun, *Crucible of the Millennium*, 17.

22. Barkun, *Crucible of the Millennium*, 17.

23. Barkun, *Disaster and the Millennium*, 52.

24. Thomas Kuhn, *The Structure of Scientific Revolutions* (Chicago: University of Chicago Press, 1962), 168.

25. Kuhn, *The Structure of Scientific Revolutions*, 5-10.

26. Michele Lamont, 'How to Become a Dominant French Philosopher: The Case of Jacques Derrida', *American Journal of Sociology* 93.3 (1987), 609-10.

27. Lamont, 'How to Become a Dominant French Philosopher', 609-10.

28. Lamont, 'How to Become a Dominant French Philosopher', 609-10.

29. Lamont, 'How to Become a Dominant French Philosopher', 610-14.

30. Mark A. Schneider, 'Social Dimensions of Epistemological Disputes: The Case of Literary Theory', *Sociological Perspectives* 40.2 (1997), 249-50.

31. Schneider, 'Social Dimensions of Epistemological Disputes',250.

32. Schneider, 'Social Dimensions of Epistemological Disputes', 251-52.

33. Schneider, 'Social Dimensions of Epistemological Disputes', 251-52.

34. Schneider, 'Social Dimensions of Epistemological Disputes', 252.

35. Barkun, *Disaster and the Millennium*, 121.

36. Kuhn, *The Structure of Scientific Revolutions*, 149, 151.

37. Barkun, *Disaster and the Millennium*, 98.

38. Robert W. Brockway, *Myth from the Ice Age to Mickey Mouse* (Albany, NY: State University of New York Press, 1993), 79.

39. Brockway, *Myth*, 93.

40. Brockway, *Myth*, 93.

41. Brockway, *Myth*, 75.

42. Brockway, *Myth*, 80.

43. Brockway, *Myth*, 80.

44. Brockway, *Myth*, 53.

45. See Catherine Keller, *From a Broken Web: Separation, Sexism and Self* (Boston: Beacon Press, 1986) and Starhawk, *The Spiral Dance: A Rebirth of the Ancient Religion of the Great Goddess* (San Francisco: Harper & Row, 1989 [1979]).

46. Brockway, *Myth*, 51-52.

47. Brockway, *Myth*, 53-54.

48. Brockway, *Myth*, 54.

49. Brockway, *Myth*, 93.

50. Personal communication with Henry Leyenhorst, January 1994.

51. For an interesting and initial debate on the relative usefulness of deconstruction see Richard Ellis, *Against Deconstruction* (Princeton, NJ: Princeton University Press, 1989). Ellis argues, for instance, that the viewpoint espoused by deconstructionists is neither original nor coherent.

52. Keller, *From a Broken Web*, 1-111.

53. Keller, *From a Broken Web*, 81.

54. Keller, *From a Broken Web*, 61-67.

55. Keller, *From a Broken Web*, 151-54.

56. Brockway, *Myth*, 72.

57. Tarnas, *Passion of the Western Mind*, 407. Tarnas also has this to say: 'Considered as a whole, the feminist perspective and impulse has brought forth perhaps the most vigorous, subtle and radically critical analysis of conventional intellectual and cultural assumptions in all of contemporary scholarship' (408).

58. Tarnas, *Passion of the Western Mind*, 442.

59. Tarnas, *Passion of the Western Mind*, 71.

60. Barkun, *Crucible of the Millennium*, 160.

61. Barkun, *Crucible of the Millennium*, 160.

Part III

Millennial Hopes, Apocalyptic Disappointments

The Deflating Power of Progress:
A Nietzschean View of the Millennial Promise of Science

John R. Turner

Friedrich Nietzsche was a provocative and complex thinker who wrote some of the most delightful books in the Western philosophical canon. But for our purposes, the best choice will be to concentrate on the central feature of his thought, which can be stated fairly simply.

Western culture for quite a long time—for at least two millennia—has operated out of a delusion. We have believed that our minds, which are phenomena of this world, can somehow be brought into contact with realms and forces not of this world which inform us that what we commonly call reality is, in truth, neither real nor good and therefore that we should be devoting our lives to escaping it.

This, according to Nietzsche, is a pathological illogic. If the world is not real, then our minds, which are parts of the world, are not real either. And to pay attention to unreal minds is an absurdity.

The way out of this delusionary illogic lies in facing the truth that this is the only world we have and, in fact, that this is the only world which exists. With the truth of the world's reality in mind, we might then adopt perspectives that would allow us to live healthily within it. We probably cannot exaggerate the degree to which health was for Nietzsche the single intelligent goal of living. As he says in *Ecce Homo:* 'I turned my will to health into a philosophy'.[1]

Nietzsche has no illusions about how difficult escaping from this dominant delusion is going to be. We have been at it a long time. It is firmly ingrained in our mental habits. And even when we adopt modes of thought that are expressly designed to rid us of faith in a false reality, the wily power of habit finds ways to disguise the old mirage and insert it into the new system. This is true even of the brightest of modern faiths, the belief that science can lead us to a firmly grounded world of human mastery, and, therefore, of human triumph.

To grasp Nietzsche's assessment of science, one needs to remain constantly aware of another fundamental aspect of his thought: sound thinking on almost any subject is constituted by pervasive and unresolvable tensions. We are not limited to a single valid way of seeing a thing worth examination, because the world in which we find ourselves offers an uncountable number of legitimate perspectives. And just because two perspectives are in conflict we can't conclude that one of them has to be false or mistaken. This is the famous doctrine of Nietzschean *perspectivism* which has often been misread as either relativism or subjectivism. But to view it in those ways is to misunderstand Nietzsche's argument. Just because the world will bear multiple interpretations we can't assume that every interpretation is valid. There are many interpretations the world will not bear. And this is true whether we are speaking of the world as nature, or as nature plus all human artifacts.

Science—or at least science up till the advent of quantum mechanics—out of an unconscious loyalty to previous faiths, adopted belief in a single explanation, a unique set of effects and causes which can be traced back to a first cause. This, says Nietzsche, is to posit the world as something 'that can be mastered completely and forever with the aid of our square little reason'.[2] And then he goes on to ask, 'Do we really want to permit existence to be degraded for us like this—reduced to a mere exercise for a calculator and an indoor diversion for mathematicians?'

How is it that this impulse for self-degradation rules in the world of scientific scholarship? Nietzsche's answer is contained in the third of his four theses on the false reasoning of philosophers:

> To invent fables about a world 'other' than this one has no meaning at all, unless an instinct of slander, detraction, and suspicion against life has gained the upper hand in us: in that case we avenge ourselves against life with a phantasmagoria of 'another', a 'better' life.[3]

The term Nietzsche assigns to this instinct, which keeps us both miserable and pathetic, is *ascetic supernaturalism*. Since at least the time of Socrates and Plato, the Western world has set asceticism as an ideal because it has believed that the apparent world—the world that comes to us through our senses—is a false world, a tainted world, a low world which is, at best, a parody of the real world we should be working to attain. The purpose of life is to get out of the apparent world and into the real world. Consequently, we should involve ourselves in the apparent world as little as possible and reject the rewards it only seems to offer. Hence asceticism.

It might appear that such an attitude is the opposite of the scientific spirit which promises that, over time, we can learn to manipulate the apparent world to such a degree that it can be forced to do our bidding and usher us into a paradise where every desire we imagine can be fulfilled. This is the dream of unending progress, fueled by science, which for centuries has driven Western thought and effort. It has pointed towards an apocalypse of happiness as complete as anything religions have promised, and, in that sense, has become a religion itself.

So, what's ascetic about that?

Nietzsche's answer is that science, in wedding itself to mathematics, has brought forth a single perspective on reality that banishes the rich and satisfying views that ordinary people must employ as the basis of their existence. Though he does not frequently use the concept 'human nature', his arguments not only imply its existence but ground human misery in attempts to deny natural instincts. Some portions of his work seem almost to come from modern evolutionary psychology. A recent publication which is drawing extensive notice, Steven Pinker's *The Blank Slate,* is thoroughly Nietzschean in its premises, though Pinker's three references to Nietzsche in the book indicate that he is severely ignorant of what Nietzsche actually wrote.

Modern science, in proclaiming that the nature of the universe is mathematical and has no moral component whatsoever, introduces an existential problem which Nietzsche links to the monotheistic past:

> Why have morality at all when life, nature, and history are 'not moral'? No doubt, those who are truthful in that audacious and ultimate sense that is presupposed by the faith in science thus affirm another world than the world of life, nature and history, and insofar as they affirm this 'other world' —look, must they not by the same token negate its counterpart, this world, our world? But you will have gathered what I am driving at, namely, that it is still a metaphysical faith upon which our faith in science rests—that even we seekers after knowledge today, we godless metaphysicians still take our fire, too, from the flame lit by a faith that is thousands of years old, that Christian faith which was also the faith of Plato, that God is the truth, that truth is divine.[4]

The scientific divinity may, at first glance, strike observers as hard and cold. But human psychology is ingenious in directing emotion towards whatever happens to be the current delusion. Nietzsche, in effect, says that emotion has got to go somewhere and, in his judgment, the feeling that was forced out of religious life by the Enlightenment threw itself into science.[5]

Thus we fell into the grip of a scientific morality that exhibits the same asceticism that all Western moralities have been forced to display. The mechanism in each case is identical: 'In every ascetic morality people worship a part of themselves as god and therefore need to diabolize the remaining part'.[6]

It may seem a great leap from the coldness of a universe devoid of any moral principle and indifferent to human wellbeing to the rosy views of the scientific enterprise that are incessantly beamed at us by popular culture. But a moment's thought shows that the gap is not as great as it first appears. If, in fact, the universe does not care, then humans are free to indulge themselves in whatever manner science permits. And what science does permit is the control and manipulation of matter in ever-more complete and ingenious ways. Since this is all there is, why not make the best of it? After all, you only go round once, as we were told recently by flickering images of young men cavorting on beaches with plenty of beer and readily available and comely female flesh.

Though the priests of science offer a different heaven from the priests of Christianity, and though they posit different delusions as the work of the devil, they are still engaged, as all priests must be, in telling us to cleave to one feature of life at the expense of all other features.

We see the effectiveness of their message all around us. Right now, as we sit here in our rooms, there is probably playing on the television somewhere a commercial which depicts a young man finding a brass lamp on a beach. He rubs it, and who else appears but the genie, who, naturally enough, tells him he has three wishes. Without hesitation the young man wishes for a certain make and model of an automobile. When it pops into existence, he promptly hops in it and drives away, leaving the genie screaming, 'Wait, you have two more wishes!' But as the young man is racing down the road he is thinking to himself, 'I've got everything I could possibly want'.

It is some version, or another, of this situation which is constantly beamed at us as the end and purpose of life. It is the logical end product of the scientific faith. It is the sermon that issues forth every day from the mouths of politicians as the American dream. It is the essential promise of capitalism—that happiness can be insured unto eternity by getting new stuff.

Dreams, however, as we know, can transmogrify into nightmares, and rather quickly. And if the dream has been powerful enough, the accompanying nightmare can deliver apocalyptic disappointment.

In addition to idyllic images of people finding salvation through shiny cars, shimmering dresses, palatial houses on the beach and so forth, we have, also, every night on the television, a series of directives:

> Ask your doctor if Paxil is right for you.
> Ask your doctor if Nexium is right for you.
> Ask your doctor if Clarinex is right for you.
> Ask your doctor if Vioxx is right for you.[7]

> Ask your doctor if Zocor is right for you.
> Ask your doctor if Plavix is right for you.
> Ask your doctor if Procrit is right for you.

And so on.

These, obviously, are intended to raise anxiety to such excruciating levels it can be relieved only—and then only partially—by the expenditure of dollars. If one were to attempt to enumerate the media efforts designed to scare people out of their wits, he would soon see he could not get halfway done before death overtook him.

Fear cannot be induced in people who are not ripe for it. It is no accident that the business community has chosen it as its most potent sales technique. Just a moment's reflection on the preachments of the priests of science reveals why this is the case. Think of the young man who has in his ideal car everything he could ever want. What happens if his car is threatened?

A damnable feature of material objects is that they change, and when they're merely left alone they almost always change for the worse—or, at least, what we call the worse. The shiny finish on the perfect car fades, no matter how expensive a garage you construct to house it. The perfect face you buy from Oil of Olay, when you're 25-years old, sags. And not all the scientists that Oil of Olay can ever employ can stop it from sagging. The magnificent heart that you built with diet and exercise and supplements won't take you up the hill quite as well when you're 70-years old as it did when you were 30.

The heaven that the priests of science have promised you is a heaven of degeneration and decay. You can drive yourself crazy trying to stop the deterioration but the best you can achieve is a diminution of the rate. The process goes forward—perhaps a bit more slowly—but forward nonetheless.

As the truth about scientific progress dawns on greater numbers, and as they also realize they have nothing but that progress to hold onto, they begin to behave in socially pathological ways. The ABC News for 29 October 2002 had a segment titled 'The Worried Well', pointing out that the numbers of healthy but anxiety-driven people seeking medical tests is seriously overloading the medical system and driving the cost of procedures for people who need them beyond their ability to pay. One doctor interviewed said that half the people he saw had no significant symptoms but were simply worried that something might be wrong with them.

Anyone born before 1950 knows how fears about security have mushroomed. If children today did the things I and my friends did regularly when I was a boy, their parents would be facing investigations by social service agencies and a good many of them would be threatened with jail. The norms of 50 years ago have become horrific dangers today, and when a transformation of that magnitude takes place within two generations anxiety grows dramatically.

Nietzsche's argument is that it is impossible to escape degenerative anxiety as long as a single aspect of life, which is actually an attempt to escape life's reality, becomes obsessive. This always eventuates in an asceticism, and as Nietzsche says, science 'is not the opposite of the ascetic ideal but rather the latest and noblest form of it'.[8]

Nietzsche can speak of science as the noblest form of asceticism because it has within it an instinct of workmanship which he admires. There is much useful work that remains for science to do, and Nietzsche says explicitly that he has no desire to destroy the pleasure that scientists take in their craft. But that scientists can work contentedly and usefully does not prove that 'science as a whole possesses a goal, a will, an ideal, or the passion of a great faith'.[9]

In truth, Nietzsche claims, the average scientific man—and here he is speaking not just of natural scientists but of any scholar who employs scientific methodology—always resembles an old maid. Both will give up anything for respectability, which is simply another form of security. The scientist needs respectability in order to overcome the internal mistrust which is the sediment in the hearts of all dependent men and herd animals.[10]

The outcome of scientist, as scientist, is the famous 'last man' who, in an attempt to achieve perfect security, has surrendered everything that makes life worth living—or at least everything that humans previously believed made life worthwhile. The description of the last man is spun out contemptuously and in great detail in the prologue to *Thus Spoke Zarathustra*. The last man asks the questions that previous men have asked:

> What is love?
> What is creation?
> What is longing?
> What is a star?
> And then, in answer, the last man simply blinks.

The last man has become small. He doesn't want to do anything that requires too much exertion and certainly not anything that involves danger. The last men still quarrel but not vehemently because it might spoil their digestion. The last man wishes to be like everyone else and anyone who feels differently 'goes voluntarily into a madhouse'.[11]

The thing we must remember is that when Zarathustra has presented this scathing picture to the crowd in the marketplace, they are delighted and cry out:

'Give us this last man, O Zarathustra.'
'Turn us into these last men!'[12]

Zarathustra, feeling that he has been misunderstood, goes sadly away.

This is the dilemma Zarathustra, and ultimately Nietzsche, leave us with. How much is to be sacrificed to a scientifically-based security, which even in his own time Nietzsche said was 'now worshipped as the supreme divinity'?[13] He wanted people to understand that the price of such security was the abolition of the individual, and particularly of the individual spirit, which was being squandered in the interests of security.[14]

The entire body of his work is a detailed exposition of the features of this sacrifice which struck him as a great and ludicrous piece of insanity. He found it in the near worship of what we call work, which is little more than the fear of everything individual, which mightily hinders the development of reason, which functions primarily as a policeman.[15]

He found it in attitudes about punishment which he claims defile us more than the acts for which punishment is being inflicted, and reminds us to ask ourselves today why the modern world has seen fit to multiply the offenses demanding public disciplinary action far beyond the number our ancestors put into that category. Schoolyard scuffles now frequently trigger police investigations.[16]

He found it in moralists, who have no interest in knowledge, and operate only out the pleasure of causing pain.[17]

He found it in an impatience that is incapable of understanding that if a change is to be profound it must be achieved in small increments pursued over a long period of time, and pursued with a perspective that is unremitting.[18]

If one comes to Nietzsche's works in a certain frame of mind, they can appear to be magically prescient. Yet, if we accept Nietzsche's own argument that profound changes build gradually and become recognizable to most only as they approach their final stages, we can assume that an unusually perceptive observer in the nineteenth century would have discerned movements of thought and attitude which by now, a century and a quarter later, have had time to ripen.

These are speculative matters and are not amenable to what people who believe in single, objective perspective are fond of calling 'proof'. Yet, it seems to me they do at least raise the question whether the translation of science from a useful tool into a god-like avenue towards perfect happiness through perfect control and security may not, in truth, be leading us somewhere else, somewhere we won't particularly like when we get there.

References

Nietzsche, Friedrich, 'Thus Spoke Zarathustra', in *The Portable Nietzsche* (trans. Walter Kaufmann; New York: The Viking Press, 1954), 103-439.

—'Twilight of the Idols', in *idem*, *The Portable Nietzsche* (trans. Walter Kaufmann; New York: The Viking Press, 1954), 463-563.

—*The Gay Science* (trans. Walter Kaufmann; New York: Vintage Books, 1974).

—*On The Genealogy of Morals and Ecce Homo* (trans. Walter Kaufmann; New York: Vintage Books, 1989).

—*Beyond Good and Evil* (trans. R.J. Hollingdale; London: Penguin Books, 1990).

—*Human, All Too Human* (trans. Gary Handwerk; Stanford, CA: Stanford University Press, 1995).

—*Daybreak: Thoughts on the Prejudices of Morality* (trans. R.J. Hollingdale; Cambridge: Cambridge University Press, 1997).

Pinker, Steven, *The Blank Slate: The Modern Denial of Human Nature* (New York: Viking, 2002).

Notes

1. Friedrich Nietzsche, *On The Genealogy of Morals and Ecce Homo* (trans. Walter Kaufmann; New York: Vintage Books, 1989), 224; ('Why I Am So Wise', Sec. 2, *Ecce Homo*).

2. Friedrich Nietzsche, *The Gay Science* (trans. Walter Kaufmann; New York: Vintage Books, 1974), 335; (Book V, Sec. 373).

3. Friedrich Nietzsche, 'Twilight of the Idols', in *idem*, *The Portable Nietzsche* (trans. Walter Kaufmann; New York: The Viking Press, 1954), 463-563 (484); ('Reason' in Philosophy', Sec. 6).

4. Nietzsche, *Gay Science*, 282-83; (Book V, Sec. 344).

5. Friedrich Nietzsche, *Human, All Too Human* (trans. Gary Handwerk; Stanford, CA: Stanford University Press, 1995), 116-17; (ch. 4, Sec. 150).

6. Nietzsche, *Human*, 106; (ch. 4, Sec. 137).

7. Editor's note: During manuscript preparation, Merck & Company, the pharmaceutical firm, withdrew its blockbuster arthritis remedy from the market, citing increased risk of heart attack and stroke among its users, thus proving Turner's point.

8. Nietzsche, *Genealogy*, 147; ('Third Essay', Sec. 23).

9. Nietzsche, *Genealogy*, 147; ('Third Essay', Sec. 23).

10. Friedrich Nietzsche, *Beyond Good and Evil* (trans. R.J. Hollingdale; London: Penguin Books, 1990), 132-33; (Part 6, Sec. 206).

11. Nietzsche, 'Thus Spoke Zarathustra', in *idem*, *The Portable Nietzsche* (trans. Walter Kaufmann; New York: The Viking Press, 1954), 103-439 (129-30); (Part 1, Sec. 5).

12. Nietzsche, *Zarathustra*, 130; (Part 1, Sec. 5).

13. Friedrich Nietzsche, *Daybreak: Thoughts on the Prejudices of Morality* (trans.

R.J. Hollingdale; Cambridge: Cambridge University Press, 1997), 105; (Book III, Sec. 173).

    14. Nietzsche, *Daybreak,* 107-108; (Book III, Sec. 179).

    15. Nietzsche, *Daybreak*, 105; (Book III, Sec. 173).

    16. Nietzsche, *Daybreak,* 139; (Book IV, Sec. 236).

    17. Nietzsche, *Daybreak,* 166-67; (Book IV, Sec. 357).

    18. Nietzsche, *Daybreak,* 211; (Book V, Sec. 534).

A Cultural History of Dissonance Theory

Glen S. McGhee

'The test of a first-rate intelligence is the ability to hold two opposed ideas
in the mind at the same time, and still retain the ability to function.'

F. Scott Fitzgerald

The phrase 'cognitive dissonance' is certainly at the top of the list of loan-
words that have been borrowed from the technical vocabulary of psychology and applied to virtually every situation imaginable. Perhaps no
other phrase from psychology has been more greatly misused and misunderstood. But popular culture is as passionate in its indiscriminate embrace
of 'cognitive dissonance' as it has been ill-informed about dissonance
theory as a whole. Little sense of its origins and significance for experimental social psychology in America attends its everyday use.

On the other hand, the protean nature of Leon Festinger's most successful psychological theory, the theory of cognitive dissonance, is also
easily observed: it seems to mean something slightly different and nuanced for each experimental psychologist that sets out to confirm or
refute the hypothesis.[1] The theory itself can be easily described, and its
basic characteristics have appeared throughout the history of social psychology in various forms, none of which ever reached the acme of success attained by Festinger's theory of cognitive dissonance.[2] Cognitive
consistency theories in the 1940s, such as Fritz Heider's balance theory,
had earlier pointed to the need for internal consistency among beliefs,
behaviors and attitudes.[3]

In the cultural and historical exploration that follows, I want to review
what I take to be important contextual features that contributed to the
unprecedented diffusion of dissonance theory across American social psychology, as well as those factors that resulted in its gradual decline, and
the controversy it spawned outside social psychology. But first there is the
matter of the differing stories told about the origins of Festinger's theory
of cognitive dissonance that must be addressed, as well as a consideration
of *When Prophecy Fails* (1956) in its narrative contexts.

A Problem with Birth Narratives

In his explanatory foreword to *A Theory of Cognitive Dissonance* (1957), Leon Festinger associates the birth of his famous theory with an earlier literature review concerned with studies of the spread of rumors, begun late Fall of 1951. Festinger tells the story in his foreword, and repeats the same story on other occasions, as do others.[4]

> The first hunch that generated any amount of enthusiasm among us came from trying to understand some data, reported by Prasad[5] concerning rumors subsequent to the Indian earthquake of 1934... The fact reported by Prasad which puzzled us was that following the earthquake, the vast majority of the rumors that were widely circulated predicted even worse disasters to come in the very near future. Certainly the belief that horrible disasters were about to occur is not a very pleasant belief, and we may ask why rumors that were 'anxiety provoking' arose and were so widely accepted. Finally a possible answer to this question occurred to us—an answer that held promise of having rather general application: perhaps these rumors predicting even worse disasters to come were not 'anxiety provoking' at all but were rather 'anxiety justifying'. That is, as a result of the earthquake these people were already frightened, and the rumors served the function of giving them something to be frightened about. Perhaps these rumors provided people with information that fit with the way they already felt. From this start, and with the help of many discussions in which we attempted to pin the idea down and to formalize it somewhat, we arrived at the concept of dissonance and the hypotheses concerning dissonance reduction.[6]

There are interesting variations of this story, which is arguably the birth narrative of the most successful theory in the history of experimental social psychology. Almost 20 years later, for example, in an interview with David Cohn, Festinger identifies the Indian report that initially generated interest as being authored by 'an Indian named Singh'.[7] But a review of earlier work by Festinger, beginning at the time of his transition from 'level of aspiration' and decision-time studies to research on group dynamics, reveals a long history of prior interest in rumor. 'A Study of Rumor: Its Origin and Spread' (1948) is the earliest, and stems from work with improving social conditions through active intervention at a Weymouth housing project soon after World War II, work undertaken by Kurt Lewin's newly-founded Research Center for Group Dynamics at MIT. The Weymouth housing project was an early example of 'action research', which Lewin envisioned as a means of exploring social behavior.[8]

But things did not quite work out as planned. Rumor, gossip and discord soon stymied the researchers' efforts, much to their amazement, as it had previous attempts to organize community activities. The careful investigation that followed six months later examined how the group's efforts had unintentionally resulted in rumor and resistance, and led directly to the publication of 'A Study of Rumor' in 1948 by the investigators.[9]

This study, as well as various publications by the Research Center for Group Dynamics in 1950 and 1951, further generalized or otherwise recounted the results of the Weymouth housing rumor investigation, and points to a long gestation period for the mature version of the theory of cognitive dissonance that began to appear from the mid to late 1950s.[10]

'A Study of Rumor' exhibits many of the distinguishing characteristics found in the later *When Prophecy Fails* (1956) study that has proven so attractive to a wide audience of millennial scholars, social psychologists, sociologists, and other social scientists as well, and partially demonstrates the application of Kurt Lewin's 'field theory' to dynamic social situations. The 1948 rumor study is essentially a narrative description of events as they unfolded, interspersed with social communication and transaction analysis, and statistical tables. Theoretical commentary is sparse, the authors choosing instead a neutral, matter-of-fact narrative stance throughout the study, waiting until the conclusion to present theoretical reflections.

There emerge, in this early study of rumor, what Festinger calls psychological 'principles' that foreshadow important elements of his later theory of cognitive dissonance. There is, for example, the 'principle of cognitive unclarity':

> Rumors will tend to arise in situations where cognitive regions especially relevant to immediate behavior are largely unstructured… The result of this unclarity was insecurity. People could not confidently predict what was going to happen to them or what the consequences of their own actions would be. Any explanation giving an acceptable clarification of these matters would reduce insecurity by providing a basis for more confident action.[11]

The principle of cognitive unclarity makes its anticipatory appearance here as a cognitive motivational factor that will later become 'dissonance' and 'dissonance reduction' in Festinger's mature theory of cognitive dissonance. 'Many rumors arise in situations where the cognitive unclarity concerns, not the explanation of why things happen, but merely what will happen in the immediate future'.[12]

Related to this is a second principle to emerge, that of 'integrative explanation':

> Once the central theme of a rumor is accepted, there will be a tendency to reorganize and distort items so as to be consistent with the central theme…once accepted [the rumor] made it necessary to interpret events

> so that they fitted the conception people had... Thus, it was relatively easy
> to organize into an integrated explanation the many new events which had
> been taking place... It is apparent that this principle of integrative expla-
> nation operates both in the conception and the transmission of a rumor.[13]

As with the previous principle of cognitive unclarity, integrative explanation acts as a motivating factor influencing cognitive processes, and comes
close to Heider's balance or consistency theory (1946). Thus, the later
hypothesis regarding the Prasad report, that perhaps 'these rumors provided people with information that fit with the way they already felt', had
already been presented in 1948.

Lastly, the conclusion of the early rumor study also points—however
clumsily—to motives which later appear again in Festinger's unwavering
focus on 'proselyting' as a means of dissonance reduction in *When
Prophecy Fails*:

> If, upon hearing a rumor, a person's social behavior is to be modified by it,
> strong forces will be created to bring other people's thinking in line with his
> own. If this is not accomplished, his own behavior will not be understood
> or accepted by others, and joint social action will become difficult.[14]

The concluding theoretical remarks of 'A Study of Rumor' point tanta-
lizingly toward other group cohesion effects and dissonance reduction
functions of rumor, even though the bulk of the study focuses primarily
on sociometrically establishing the communication channels and social
structures through which the rumor spread, and the forces behind its
dissemination.[15]

The real mystery, of course, is how this exceedingly rich pre-history
came to be forgotten when the story of the birth of the theory of cognitive
dissonance was told. Perhaps it is not without a certain irony that the early
principle of 'integrative explanation' can now be called upon to address
the apparent discrepancy between Festinger's birth narrative and the chronology just recounted. By beginning the story where he does, Festinger
engages in a selective re-telling that starts with the 1951 literature search
on rumor and conveniently forgets the prior work in this area, as well as
its roots in Gestalt and experimental psychology. This is convenient because
it greatly simplifies the telling of an exceedingly complex tale, and provides a 'central theme', which once accepted, creates 'a tendency to reor-
ganize and to distort items so as to be consistent with the central theme'.[16]
Viewed this way, Festinger's story of the origin of his theory of cognitive
dissonance begins to look like a rumor itself.

This line of thinking can be extended, I think, to dissonance theory as
a whole by resorting to a phenomenological turn or shift in perspective in

which the theory itself can be viewed as a specialized kind of rumor, or meme, characterized by its extensive reach and penetration within the domain of American experimental psychology. Thus, rather than originating as a theory about 'rumors', dissonance theory figures as a rumor that is a psychological theory, with its own social channels and means of communication, and its own particular content. It even has its own intellectual and experimental lineage.[17]

Waiting for the Saucers

The channeling group that formed in 1954 around the automatic handwriting messages of Marian Dorothy Martin (aka Marion Keech) and the personalities of Dr Charles Laughead and his wife Lillian (aka Dr Thomas and Daisy Armstrong) became the subject of an innovative participant-observer investigation conducted by Festinger, Riecken, Schachter and their assistants at the Laboratory for Research in Social Relations of the University of Minnesota. *When Prophecy Fails* (1956) is the gripping narrative of this unfolding drama and its denouement, and aftermath. It is told from the perspective of impartial, completely objective, anonymous experimenters in a genuinely novel (and therefore unrepeatable) social psychology experiment.

The announced purpose of the study was to prove or disprove the validity of the theory of cognitive dissonance which stated that, given the right conditions, when confronted with unequivocal disconfirmations of their heart-felt beliefs, true believers acted in ways to reduce the discomfort or dissonance this created. That is, either the dissonance proved too great, and they abandoned these beliefs, or they grew more committed to their beliefs and they proselytized others, thereby seeking social support for their beliefs. However, even if the study had not confirmed the theory of cognitive dissonance (and there is some question that it did), the bizarre tale of the UFO channeling group was certainly worth telling in the 1950s.

As a human drama, the story is a compelling read, and, at times, painful. It is an intimate look into the lives of those that, for whatever reason, shed their skepticism and replaced it with varying degrees of blind acceptance. Making this all the more painful is the fact that the reader knows what the participants did not know, that is, how the story ends: in failed prophecy and disappointment.

But largely missing from the narrative is the emotional atmosphere of the 1950s that was created by numerous inexplicable (even to this day) sightings of flying saucers (UFOs), and the tumult of fear, anxiety and speculation concerning these apparitions. Individuals such as George Adamski were openly proclaiming their extraterrestrial encounters at the height of the Cold War and the 'Red scare' of McCarthyism, and the Soviets had just detonated their first hydrogen bomb. Without taking this *milieu* into account, the characters of *When Prophecy Fails* are reduced to mere puppets on a string being manipulated by unseen forces only hinted at by the authors.[18]

The writers' concern throughout *When Prophecy Fails* is to marshal evidence supportive of the theory of cognitive dissonance. Nothing, it seems, that can help to establish the centrality of Mrs Keech's prediction for the group of a flood on 21 December, and its dramatic disconfirmation, and the 'dissonance' this causes, escapes the authors. In fact, the imposition of these categories over the story of Mrs Keech's channeling group amounts to a re-telling of that story, albeit from a different point of view.

In the hands of the authors, the end-of-the-world prediction is established as a central cognition held by the group. But occurring as it does in the midst of Mrs Keech's interactions with the 'Guardians of the Earth', and another member's verbal incarnation of the 'Creator', and their steady support by Dr Armstrong and others, dissonance theory is transformed into a kind of invisible 'shadow narrator'. It is not, however, until the climax, when the prophecy actually fails, that this narrative viewpoint becomes more clearly apparent and the reader is reminded, in a final unveiling, that this was just a psychology experiment, after all.

When Prophecy Fails can be seen as one of many UFO 'close encounter' books flooding the market in the 1950s.[19] Part of the book's success, I suspect, came from the fact that it specifically targeted a well-educated and professional readership, as opposed to the general public. This reading audience was noticeably underserved during the height of the flying saucer sightings and publicity, and thus the book was able to quickly find a cultural niche with its blend of disinterested skepticism, and avowedly scientific orientation.[20] What made *When Prophecy Fails* interesting to these readers was how it was able to realistically present an extreme example of the saucer craze, intimately and truthfully, while at the same time maintaining a scientific focus throughout. In this unique way, it catered for the curiosity of cultured bystanders by giving them the inside story, but did so within the context of an objective psychological experiment.

This contrivance is indicative of a number of other, and less subtle, forms of deception running throughout the narrative itself. The most obvious deception is that of the social scientists themselves, who, along with their observers, present themselves as sympathetic to the beliefs of the group, and devise false stories by which to gain entry into it. Stanley

Schachter even presented himself initially to the Keech group as Leon Festinger, thereby effectively switching their identities over the months of the experiment![21]

The narrative account itself, as published, disguised the true identities of the channeling group participants, as well as those of the 'observers' and their younger assistants. Various hoaxers and jokers also appeared, including five men claiming to be 'spacemen' themselves, who were accepted as such by the group.[22]

The complexity of the interlocking narratives in and surrounding *When Prophecy Fails* makes it a veritable puzzle box. There is, for example, the original source material on which the book is based, both written and oral.

> In all, the reports of the observers filled approximately sixty-five reels of one-hour tapes, yielding almost one thousand pages of typescript when they were transcribed; in addition, we accumulated about one hundred typewritten pages of material that had been directly recorded.[23]

The fabricated stories or scripts used by the observers to gain initial acceptance by the group are also narrative 'texts'.[24] The notebooks filled with Mrs Keech's automatic handwriting ('the secret books'), and the role these writings played in the lives of the group also function as a kind of 'text'. Certainly, the prevailing rumors and beliefs at the height of the flying saucer craze form a distinct discursive background that also intersects with the other 'texts' as well.[25] Another such discursive background would be social psychology in general, and the specific praxis of participant-observer experiments. Lastly, there is the story of the reader's interaction with the published book, which forms yet another intersecting narrative. Textual-narrative analysis can proceed along each of these levels of narrative since they constitute their own forms of discourse that can be distinguished from the other modes of discourse.

It is also important to consider the role played by modern technology and technological innovation in the narrative, and attempt to assess its impact on the final account. Observers were equipped with the latest in midget tape recorders, which allowed them to record their interactions with the channeling group, usually within a few hours. Therefore, the researchers were very confident that this gave them a more accurate record than otherwise would have been possible. Tape recordings also linked some of the principals in the drama, allowing researchers to transcribe recorded telephone conversations and other recorded channeled messages. The completed narrative has been significantly shaped by these instruments, and can therefore be approached as a kind of instrumental artifact.[26]

The larger cultural context was clearly understood by the group itself in terms of an encounter with technologically advanced extraterrestrial civilizations, and the belief in flying saucers is itself a kind of inclusive techno-mythology within which the group acted out its drama and which Mrs Keech's automatic handwriting drew upon. Yet, even when all these intersecting narrative threads and discourses are taken into account, the intent of the authors is to 'tell a coherent story' and at the same time, 'to provide for firm [scientific] conclusions'. This is the meta-narrative that dominates *When Prophecy Fails* and serves to maintain its internal consistency.[27]

The Rise of Dissonance Theory

In a nutshell, Leon Festinger's theory of cognitive dissonance said that when any deeply held belief or conviction, which he called a 'cognition', was unequivocally contradicted or 'disconfirmed' by events, this created a situation of internal 'dissonance' for the one holding the belief. In Festinger's theory, dissonance functioned as a motivational state that resulted in cognitive and behavioral changes geared toward reducing this inner tension or dissonance, including changes in perception.

In hindsight, Festinger's hopes for dissonance theory, as it came to be called, were justified; but not even Festinger could have predicted the widespread controversy and excitement among psychologists and others that his theory produced. As already mentioned, the words 'cognitive dissonance' have even worked their way into our language to refer to disappointed expectations, disorientation, and other states of cognitive discomfort.

But I must now account for the theory's rapid, and in some ways, un-precedented rise to prominence, and to describe the various predispos-ing factors and contextual elements that contributed to its rapid diffusion throughout American psychology. It has been noted that as many as 1,000 psychology experiments have been conducted to test the disso-nance hypothesis, using numerous creative and inventive experimental scenarios to induce and measure 'cognitive dissonance' and, more impor-tantly, its reduction.[28]

Before the advent of dissonance theory, a widely accepted idea in psy-chology was that in order to change behavior it was first necessary to change the attitudes informing those behaviors. For example, in the 1950s and 1960s, racial discrimination was a topic of concern, as it continues to be, and it was thought that racism and racial prejudice had to be elimi-nated in the individual before discrimination would end. Needless to say, this was not good news for a nation attempting to address its racial problems, since racist attitudes were found to be notoriously difficult to eradicate.

But what dissonance theory clearly demonstrated in a number of carefully planned experiments—the so-called forced compliance experiments—was that attitudes need not be changed first in order to have desirable behaviors; indeed, dissonance theory established the reverse of this: that there were circumstances in which new behaviors induced attitudinal change. In this way, the implementation of a nationwide policy of desegregation in the 1950s and 1960s was seen (in part) as mute testimony to the validity of dissonance theory.[29]

What is noteworthy here is the extent to which the experimental findings amassed by dissonance theory were dramatically counter-intuitive: the data often seemed to contradict common sense, and even began to make human beings appear somewhat irrational. This feature is very important as an example of what Thomas Kuhn has referred to as a scientific anomaly. Anomalies are 'violations of expectation',[30] unexpected results that are a kind of Holy Grail for the scientific enterprise; that is, a scientific puzzle that generates interest and excitement, and cries out to the scientific community for solution. And it is primarily for this reason that a large body of literature now exists—in fact, a whole branch of cognitive social psychology has arisen to address and explore further the results first produced by dissonance theory.

These are just the kinds of intellectual puzzles that begin to generate what sociologist Randall Collins calls 'emotional energy', which he identifies as a necessary factor in the success of any line of intellectual inquiry or investigation.[31] Consider, if you will, the educational demographics of the post-World War II era. After the war and the passage of the G.I. Bill, droves of eager students went back to school. This coincided with a surge of institutional growth and expansion which drew along a whole new generation of social psychologists to fill newly available teaching positions. This new generation wanted to understand their wartime experiences on a broad social scale, and in terms of group and social dynamics, but the dominant school of American psychology at the time, behaviorism, could not meet this need. In this context, the 'emotional energy' of the dissonance approach, and its marked appeal to the younger generation, was enormous, especially when contrasted with the older generation's long-lived attachment to reinforcement psychology, which was now coming to an end.[32]

The new theory's frontal attack on behaviorism created excitement and controversy, and moved it to the center of what Collins calls psychology's 'attention space'. In a series of famous experiments, including the one conducted by Festinger and Carlsmith in 1959, experimental subjects acted in ways that clearly contradicted key tenets of reinforcement theory, which correlated behavior and rewards, and which predicted that greater rewards would correspond to greater cognitive or behavioral changes. But in the experiments of 1959, greater cognitive changes were induced by smaller rewards, and surprisingly, greater rewards tended to minimize cognitive changes altogether![33]

There are, of course, other contributing factors, but I think we need to recognize the extent to which the theory of cognitive dissonance represented a decisive break for the post-World War generation of psychologists from what Ernest Hilgard has called the 'stultifying influence of positivism and behaviorism'[34] that reigned unchallenged for decades in American Psychology; that is, until the advent of dissonance theory. It is in this break with the past, this emancipation from the shackles of behaviorism, that a re-invigorated social psychology emerged, with fresh perspectives, and new intellectual puzzles to solve, and, most of all, new theories to test. Dissonance theory emerged to dominate the attention space of American social psychology, and would continue to do so for the next couple of decades.[35]

One of the ways it was able to do this was through its experimental creativity, that was then modeled throughout the discipline to showcase a new kind of experimentalism for psychology, culminating in the famous obedience experiments of Stanley Milgram at Yale in the early 1960s, and Philip Zimbardo's later, but equally shocking, conformity experiments at Stanford.[36]

Dissonance theory also produced important data contradicting the catharsis theory of psychoanalysis, thereby opening another research-front that would generate interest and excitement. Psychoanalysis understood aggressive behavior in terms of the release of pent-up hostile emotion, which, according to the theory, once released leads to decreased aggressive behavior. But what dissonance theory found was that unleashed aggression resulted in more, not less, aggressive behavior, because the very act of aggression created a need to justify oneself cognitively, and the cognitive need for self-justification frequently resulted in the derogation of the victim which led, instead, to repeated acts of aggression.[37] Taking all these factors together it is little wonder that, in reflecting on this period, one of Festinger's key disciples, Elliot Aronson, would exclaim:

> It was an exciting time, when we were swashbuckling our way through the literature, doing a lot of very exciting experiments, challenging reinforcement theory, and generating annoyances and controversies in the litera-

ture. At the time, we *thought* we were on to something big, and we were. We *thought* we were opening up whole new areas, and we were. We *thought* we were being innovative methodologically, and *we* were.[38] (Emphasis in the original.)

Another key proximal cause has to do with the fact that dissonance theory was involved in the successful transmission of the intellectual assets that were part of the Gestaltist lineage that Festinger was heir to and was able to transform and deploy.[39] Festinger had direct access to Gestalt intellectual assets through his highly successful teacher, Kurt Lewin. One of the things Lewin did was to coin suggestive terms to describe his theories, such as 'field theory', 'topological psychology', and 'life-space'. Similarly, Festinger's use of the term 'cognitive dissonance' made the theory easier to popularize and disseminate, as well as easier to attack. This vulnerability, interestingly, can aid in the success of a new theory. In Randall Collins' sociology of knowledge, conflict plays an important role in successful diffusion: not too much conflict, but just the right kind of conflict with competing theories—the kind of conflict that succeeds in generating interest in the outcome, and drawing new players and new creativity into the competition.[40]

Gone, but Certainly Not Forgotten

If we have been thus far successful in recounting the ascendancy of the dissonance approach in post-World War II American psychology, then we must also be able to make an equally compelling case for its gradual decline. For this we must turn to what could surely be called the '3-Cs' of millennial studies—'context, context, context'—which puts us in a position to recognize that, in fact, a kind of millennial fervor had surrounded the advent of dissonance theory in the 1950s and 1960s, most notably because it carried the banner of emancipation into the battle with metaphysical and methodological behaviorism[41] and when, in effect, it blew the lid off the Skinner box. A lot of the initial excitement surrounding Festinger was generated by the expectations of a new, younger generation of eager experimenters and social psychologists just coming into the field, and this extended especially to those Festinger and his circle trained. Under these conditions, it was not only probable, but almost a certainty that there would be some kind of letdown from these high hopes; indeed, such disappointment is inevitable because bubbles of optimism generated by inflated hopes have a nasty habit of bursting.[42]

Thus, the insights of millennial studies (for example, what I referred to as the '3 Cs' of millennial studies) are more apt to shed light on dissonance theory, rather than the reverse. Rather then tell us all we want to know about the psychology of millennial groups—which I see as an unjustified expectation based on the widespread dissemination of Festinger's ideas—the history of dissonance theory can tell us why we might hold these expectations to begin with.

In the end, there were a number of factors that led to the gradual decline of dissonance theory. Those initially drawn to it went off in other directions and devoted their energy and attention to the newly emergent fields of motivational and cognitive psychology, which, ironically, dissonance theory had helped to create. Dissonance theory, then, became a victim of its own success. There was also a significant shift in the social awareness of ethical concerns regarding the use of deception and manipulation in high-impact experiments on unsuspecting human subjects. This was soon followed by growing restrictions and guidelines, and ethics committees to oversee these kinds of experiments, further bringing them into disfavor.[43]

Probably symptomatic of this situation, or perhaps even a contributing cause, Festinger himself left the field entirely in the 1960s—just as interest in dissonance theory was peaking—to pursue laboratory work relating to visual perception. Others have commented that, as the central charismatic figure for a generation of dissonance theorists and as Kurt Lewin's heir apparent, he took along with him some of the excitement and interest he was able to generate.[44]

Looking back, it has been almost 50 years since *When Prophecy Fails* was first published. The response to the book over the years by millennial scholars and social scientists has been decidedly mixed. A number of follow-up studies have been published, many of them unsuccessful attempts to replicate Festinger's initial findings. The overall sense of dissatisfaction with Festinger's theory can be seen in the title of one such study, 'When Festinger Fails'.[45]

In actual case studies similar to those found in *When Prophecy Fails*, most agree that dissonance does emerge when there are physical or empirical disconfirmations. However, the magnitude of that dissonance and the dissonance reduction efforts it generates are dependent—far more dependent—on the contexts in which each disconfirmation occurs than Festinger's theory allowed for. But an even greater problem is that dissonance theory has been shown to be a very poor predictor of when proselytizing occurs. By focusing so intently on proselytizing as the chief indicator of post-disconfirmation dissonance reduction, it has been charged that Festinger theoretically misunderstood the very broad range of dissonance reduction options available, including the ultimate collapse of the movement being studied.[46] Thus, the narrowness of his theoretical framework rendered the role and function of the group's spiritual-ideology, or what could be called its narrative frame, invisible to him, and led him to inaccurate conclusions. For example, successful dissonance reduction occurs in groups that are able to 'spiritualize' or absorb disconfirmations into their narrative frames, sometimes with such success that it is not even clear that dissonance followed the disconfirmation.[47]

Oddly enough, however, the experimental methodology of Festinger —and Kurt Lewin before him—has also proven to be extremely robust and adaptable outside the laboratory. One of Lewin's research assistants at Cornell was a man named Allan Funt, who adapted Lewin's one-way mirror techniques for entertainment, first in 'Candid Radio', and then in 'Candid Camera'. Funt has estimated that his shows have involved as many as one and a quarter million subjects, and to have been seen by countless viewers over the years and around the globe. No other 'experimental social psychologist' (which is what Philip Zimbardo calls Funt)[48] can claim to have had that many subjects, that kind of influence. This is just one transformation of the experimental protocol on which dissonance research was based, but shows that its use today is not only as an 'epistemology engine'[49] for the production of psychological knowledge, but also for the production of entertainment, where there are fewer restrictions against deception and manipulation to create dissonance, and where the Gestalt experimental tradition continues to have a life of its own, outside the laboratory.

When Cognitions Disappear (or Turf Wars)

As one would expect, it was not long before the intense anticipatory fervor that surrounded the advent of the theory of cognitive dissonance began to crest, especially outside the precincts of social psychology. Although it has fared far worse with non-psychologists, Festinger's theory continues to be frequently cited in psychology textbooks, and professional journal literature, and Festinger and his associates continue to be ranked among the very top eminent psychologists of the twentieth century.[50] This is no small achievement when you consider the competition includes S. Freud, J. Piaget, B. Skinner and W. James, to name a few.[51]

But if Festinger's prestigious status is well established in American psychology, and shows no sign of diminishing, how are we to account for quite the reverse among non-psychology based social scientists? The answer has to do, I think, with the fact that social scientists and religious historians are only familiar with Festinger's work through his field work project, *When Prophecy Fails*. It is only by focusing solely on this book, and its specification of proselytizing behavior as the dependent variable to be observed, that Jon Stone in *Expecting Armageddon* can compare it to 'an ocean liner that developed leaks soon after its first launch', adding that '[t]he strong criticisms leveled at the Festinger study…have all but scuttled its reliability for predicting responses to failed prophecy'.[52] The important question is, why has this kind of criticism not had an impact in the field of psychology? The answer lies, perhaps, in the isolation of these fields from one another, which results in these kinds of skirmishes at their borders.[53]

There is a kind of double irony in how Festinger's social science critics fasten onto this key characteristic—his failed prediction of increased proselytizing—to the exclusion of all else, thereby mirroring *in* this perceived failing their own radical reduction of Festinger and his work down to 'the Festinger thesis', or 'the Festinger study'. Which is the real 'Festinger'? Is it the highly regarded figure appearing in the pantheon of American psychology, or is it the whipping boy of the social scientists? The 'Festinger' that appears in *Expecting Armageddon* has been radically decontextualized and abstracted, shorn of all its connections to American psychology, the Gestalt tradition and Lewinian psychology, as well as Festinger's prior work at MIT with the Research Center for Group Dynamics. This, of course, is the same kind of 'decontextualizing' that Festinger's social science critics often accuse him of engaging in.

In 1960, while Festinger's theory was gaining importance, a pair of his students, Jane Allyn Hardyck and Marcia Braden, studied a Pentecostal sect that had retreated to bomb shelters for 42 days in anticipation of an impending nuclear attack. They were attempting to replicate the results of *When Prophecy Fails*, but were unable to do so. Festinger himself was rather blasé about this apparent disconfirmation of his theory.[54] Hardyck and Braden, moreover, understood their results as a *confirmation* of dissonance theory, since only minor adjustments were needed to accommodate their findings.[55] Of course, Festinger's social science critics did not take the Hardyck and Braden study this way, but rather saw it as an outright refutation of the 'Festinger thesis'.[56] This ambiguity, I hold, is indicative of the boundary-line disputes that dominate the inter-disciplinary discussion of these issues.

Genuine inter-disciplinary collaboration between the American social psychological traditions and those limited to studying new religious movements has been sorely lacking. While errors on both sides cannot be ignored, perhaps the time has come for these disciplines to enter into conversation.[57]

References

Aronson, Elliot, 'Whatever Happened to Dissonance?', *Contemporary Social Psychology* 11 (1985), 132-35.

—'Leon Festinger and the Art of Audacity', *Psychological Science* 2.4 (1991), 213-17.

—'The Return of the Repressed: Dissonance Theory Makes a Comeback', *Psychological Inquiry* 3 (1992), 303-11.

—'The Theory of Cognitive Dissonance: The Evolution and Vicissitudes of an Idea', in Craig McGarty and S. Alexander Haslam (eds.), *The Message of Social Psychology: Perspectives on Mind in Society* (Cambridge, MA: Blackwell Publishers, 1997), 20-35.

Ash, Mitchell G., 'Cultural Contexts and Scientific Change in Psychology: Kurt Lewin in Iowa', *American Psychologist* 47 (1992), 198-207.

—*Gestalt Psychology in German Culture, 1890–1967: Holism and the Quest for Objectivity* (Cambridge: Cambridge University Press, 1995).

Back, Kurt, Leon Festinger, B. Hymovitch, H. Kelley, S. Schachter, and J. Thibaut, 'The Methodology of Studying Rumor Transmission', *Human Relations* 3 (1950), 307-12.

Beauvois, Jean-Leon, and Robert Joule, *A Radical Dissonance Theory* (London: Taylor & Francis, 1996).

Ben-David, Joseph, and Randall Collins, 'Social Factors in the Origins of a New Science: The Case of Psychology', *American Sociological Review* 31.4 (1966), 451-65.

Billig, Otto, *Flying Saucers, Magic in the Skies: A Psychohistory* (Cambridge, MA: Schenkman, 1982).

Cialdini, Robert B., *Influence: The Psychology of Persuasion* (New York: William Morrow, 1993 [1984]).

Cohn, David, *Psychologists on Psychology: Modern Innovators Talk about their Work* (New York: Taplinger, 1977).

Collins, Randall, 'Temporal Summation of Intracranial Reinforcement' (Psychology MA thesis, Stanford University, 1964).

—'Why the Social Sciences Won't Become High-Consensus, Rapid-Discovery Science', *Sociological Forum* 9 (1994), 155-77.

—*The Sociology of Philosophies: A Global Theory of Intellectual Change* (Cambridge, MA: Harvard University Press, 1998).

—'Social Movements and the Focus of Emotional Attention', in Jeff Goodwin, James M. Jasper, and Francesca Polletta (eds.), *Passionate Politics: Emotions and Social Movements* (Chicago: University of Chicago Press, 2001), 27-44.

Coser, Lewis A., 'Kurt Lewin (1890–1947) and the Renaissance of Social Psychology', in *idem, Refugee Scholars in America: Their Impact and their Experiences* (New Haven, CT: Yale University Press, 1984), 22-27.

Danziger, Kurt, *Constructing the Subject: Historical Origins of Psychological Research* (New York: Cambridge University Press, 1990).

—'Making Social Psychology Experimental: A Conceptual History, 1920–1970', *Journal of the History of the Behavioral Sciences* 36.4 (2000), 329-47.

Danziger, Kurt, and Katalin Dzinas, 'How Psychology Got its Variables', *Canadian Psychology* 38.1 (1997), 43-48.

Fellman, Bruce, 'Under the Influence', *Yale Alumni Magazine* (May/June 2004), 28.

Festinger, Leon, 'The Role of Group Belongingness in a Voting Situation', *Human Relations* 1 (1947), 154-80.

—'A Theory of Social Comparison Processes', *Human Relations* 7 (1954), 117-40.

—*A Theory of Cognitive Dissonance* (Stanford, CA: Stanford University Press, 1957).

—'Cognitive Dissonance', *Scientific American* 207.4 (1962), 93-101.

—'Interview by David Cohen', in Cohn, *Psychologists on Psychology*, 126-44.

—'Reflections on Cognitive Dissonance: 30 Years Later', in Eddie Harmon-Jones, and Judson Mills (eds.), *Cognitive Dissonance: Progress on a Pivotal Theory in Social Psychology* (Washington, DC: American Psychological Association, 1999), 381-85.

Festinger, Leon, and James Carlsmith, 'Cognitive Consequences of Forced Compliance', *Journal of Abnormal and Social Psychology* 58 (1959), 203-211.

Festinger, Leon, Dorwin Cartwright, Kathleen Barber, Juliet Fleischl, Josephine Gottsdanker, Annette Keysen, and Gloria Leavit, 'A Study of Rumor: Its Origin and Spread', *Human Relations* 1 (1948), 464-86.

Festinger, Leon, and Harold H. Kelley, *Changing Attitudes through Social Contact* (Ann Arbor, MI: Institute for Social Research, University of Michigan, 1951).

Festinger, Leon, Henry W. Riecken, and Stanley Schachter, *When Prophecy Fails: A Social and Psychological Study of a Modern Group that Predicted the Destruction of the World* (New York: Harper Torchbooks, 1964 [1956]).

Festinger, Leon, Stanley Schachter, and Kurt Back, *Social Pressures in Informal Groups: A Study of Human Factors in Housing* (New York: Harper Brothers, 1950).

Friedman, Bruce Jason, 'An Historical Review of the Life and Works of an Important Man: Leon Festinger' (PsyD dissertation, Carlos Albizu University, 2000).

Gergen, Kenneth, 'Social Psychology as Social Construction: The Emerging Vision', in Craig McGarty and S. Alexander Haslam (eds.), *The Message of Social Psychology: Perspectives on Mind in Society* (Cambridge, MA: Publishers, 1997), 113-28.

Grayling, A.C., 'Family Feuds', review of Randall Collins, *The Sociology of Philosophies: A Global Theory of Intellectual Change* (*New York Times Book Review*, 27 September, 1998).

Green, Christopher D., Marlene Shore, and Thomas Teo (eds.), *The Transformation of Psychology: Influences of 19th Century Philosophy, Technology, and Natural Sciences* (Washington, DC: American Psychological Association, 2001).

Greenwald, A., and D. Ronis, 'Twenty Years of Cognitive Dissonance: Case Study of the Evolution of a Theory', *Psychological Review* 85 (1978), 53-57.

Grun, Bernard, *The Timetables of History* (New York: Simon & Schuster, 1979).

Grunberg, Neil E., *A Distinctive Approach to Psychological Research: The Influence of Stanley Schachter* (New Jersey: L. Erlbaum Associates, 1987).

Haggbloom, Steve J., S.R. Warnick, J.E. Warnick, G.L. Yarbrough, T.M. Russell, C.M. Borecky, V.K. Jones, R. McGahhey, J.L. Powell III, J. Beavers, and E. Monte, 'The 100 Most Eminent Psychologists of the 20th Century', *Review of General Psychology* 6 (2002), 139-52.

Harmon-Jones, Eddie, and Judson Mills (eds.), *Cognitive Dissonance: Progress on a Pivotal Theory in Social Psychology* (Washington, DC: American Psychological Association, 1999).

Hardyck, Jane Allyn, and Marcia Braden, 'Prophecy Fails Again: A Report of a Failure to Replicate', in Stone (ed.), *Expecting Armageddon*, 55-63.

Heider, Fritz, 'Attitudes and Cognitive Organization', *Journal of Psychology* 21 (1946), 107-12.

Hilgard, Ernest, *Psychology in America: A Historical Survey* (San Diego: Harcourt Brace Jovanovich, 1987).

Ihde, Don, 'Epistemology Engines', *Nature* 406 (6 July, 2000), 21.

Jung, C.G., *Flying Saucers: A Modern Myth of Things Seen in the Skies* (Trans. R.F.C. Hull;

Vol. 10 of *Collected Works*; Bollingen Series XX; Princeton, NJ: Princeton University Press, 1991 [1959]).

Katzko, Michael W., 'The Rhetoric of Psychological Research and the Problem of Unification in Psychology', *American Psychologist* 57.4 (2002), 262-70.

Korn, James H., *Illusions of Reality: A History of Deception in Social Psychology* (Albany, NY: State University of New York Press, 1997).

Krohn, Claus-Dieter, *Intellectuals in Exile* (Amherst, MA: University of Massachusetts Press, 1993).

Kuhn, Thomas S., *The Structure of Scientific Revolutions* (Chicago: University of Chicago, 2nd enlarged edn, 1970).

Lucanion, Patrick, *Them or Us: Archetypal Interpretations of Fifties Alien Invasion Films* (Indianapolis: Indiana University Press, 1987).

Marrow, A.F., *The Practical Theorist: The Life and Work of Kurt Lewin* (New York: Basic Books, 1969).

Melton, J. Gordon, 'Spiritualization and Reaffirmation: What Really Happens when Prophecy Fails', in Stone (ed.), *Expecting Armageddon*, 145-57.

Melton, J. Gordon, and George M. Eberhart, 'The Flying Saucer Contactee Movement, 1950–1994: A Bibliography', in James R. Lewis (ed.), *The Gods Have Landed: New Religions from Other Worlds* (Albany, NY: State University of New York Press, 1995), 251-32.

Morawski, Jill G. (ed.), *The Rise of Experimentation in American Psychology* (New Haven, CT: Yale University Press, 1987).

Prasad, J., 'A Comparative Study of Rumors and Reports in Earthquakes', *British J. Psychology* 41 (1950), 129-44.

Patnoe, Shelly, *A Narrative History of Experimental Social Psychology: The Lewin Tradition* (New York: Springer-Verlag, 1988).

Rudmin, Floyd, Ruediger M. Trimpop, Ilona-Patricia Kryl, and Pawel Boski, 'Gustav Ichheiser in the History of Social Psychology: An Early Phenomenology of Social Attribution', *British Journal of Social Psychology* 26 (1987), 165-80.

Schachter, Stanley, and M. Gazzaniga, *Extending Psychological Frontiers: Selected Works of Leon Festinger* (New York: Russell Sage Foundation, 1989).

Schmalz, Matthew N., 'When Festinger Fails: Prophecy and the Watchtower', in Stone (ed.), *Expecting Armageddon*, 233-50.

Simonton, Dean K., *Great Psychologists and their Times: Scientific Insights into Psychology's History* (Washington, DC: American Psychological Association, 2002).

Steiner, Ivan D., 'Whatever Happened to the Group in Social Psychology?', *Journal of Experimental Social Psychology* 10 (1974), 94-108.

Stone, Jon R., 'Introduction', in Stone (ed.), *Expecting Armageddon*, 1-29.

Stone (ed.), Jon R., *Expecting Armageddon: Essential Readings in Failed Prophecy* (New York: Routledge, 2000).

Tumminia, Diana, 'How Prophecy Never Fails: Interpretive Reason in a Flying Saucer Group', *Sociology of Religions* 59 (1998), 157-70.

Turner, Ralph H., 'Rumor as Intensified Information Seeking: Earthquake Rumors in China and the United States', in Russell R. Dynes and Kathleen J. Tierney (eds.), *Disasters, Collective Behavior, and Social Organization* (New Jersey: University of Delaware, 1994), 244-56.

Winston, Andrew S., 'Cause into Function: Ernst Mach and the Reconstruction of Explanation in Psychology', in Christopher D. Green, Marlene Shore, and Thomas Teo (eds.), *The Transformation of Psychology: Influences of 19th-Century Philosophy, Technology, and Natural Science* (Washington, DC: American Psychological Association, 2001), 107-31.

Zimbardo, Philip G., and Allen Funt, 'Laugh Where We Must, Be Candid Where We Can', *Psychology Today* 18 (1985), 42-47.

Notes

1.   See, for example, the discussion in the 'Introduction' to Jean-Leon Beauvois and Robert Joule, *A Radical Dissonance Theory* (London: Taylor & Francis, 1996), which is a plea to return to Festinger's original formulation. See also ch. 1, in Eddie Harmon-Jones and Judson Mills (eds.), *Cognitive Dissonance: Progress on a Pivotal Theory in Social Psychology* (Washington, DC: American Psychological Association, 1999). Even Leon Festinger comments on this issue in *A Theory of Cognitive Dissonance* (Stanford, CA: Stanford University Press, 1957), 278-79.

2.   Frequently overlooked in considerations of early examples of consistency theory is the work of an obscure Austrian social psychologist, Gustav Ichheiser (1897–1969). Ichheiser's earliest publications relating to personal dissonance and dissonance reduction measures in the context of his attribution theory date from 1928. See Floyd Rudmin, Ruediger M. Trimpop, Ilona-Patricia Kryl and Pawel Boski, 'Gustav Ichheiser in the History of Social Psychology: An Early Phenomenology of Social Attribution', *British Journal of Social Psychology* 26 (1987), 165-80.

3.   Fritz Heider, 'Attitudes and Cognitive Organization', *Journal of Psychology* 21 (1946), 107-12.

4.   Festinger, *A Theory of Cognitive Dissonance*, 'Foreword', pages v, vi-vii; and David Cohn, *Psychologists on Psychology* (New York: Taplinger Publishing, 1977), 134-35. See also Elliot Aronson, 'Leon Festinger and the Art of Audacity', *Psychological Science* 2.4 (1991), 214; Jerome Singer in Shelly Patnoe, *A Narrative History of Experimental Social Psychology: The Lewin Tradition* (New York: Springer-Verlag, 1988), 147-48; and James H. Korn, *Illusions of Reality: A History of Deception in Social Psychology* (Albany, NY: State University of New York Press, 1997), 85.

5.   J. Prasad, 'A Comparative Study of Rumors and Reports in Earthquakes', *British J. Psychology*, 41 (1950), 129-44. See the discussion in Festinger, *A Theory of Cognitive Dissonance* (1957), ch.10 and citation on page 284. For a more current approach to earthquake rumors, and rumors in general, see Ralph H. Turner, 'Rumor as Intensified Information Seeking: Earthquake Rumors in China and the United States', in Russell R. Dynes and Kathleen J. Tierney (eds.), *Disasters, Collective Behavior, and Social Organization* (New Jersey: University of Delaware, 1994), 244-56.

6.   Festinger, *A Theory of Cognitive Dissonance*, vi-vii.

7.   Cohn, *Psychologists on Psychology*, 134. The similarity between the names 'Singh' and 'Sinha'—the latter being the author of a 1952 post-earthquake study that Festinger also used at about the same time as the Prasad study—leads me to believe the confusion may be partially due to a conflation of the two studies by Festinger, a transcription error, or both. See the discussion in Festinger, *A Theory of Cognitive Dissonance*, 236-41, and 285.

8.   There are various excellent accounts of the life, work and legacy of Kurt Lewin. See Alfred J. Marrow, *The Practical Theorist: The Life and Work of Kurt Lewin* (New York: Basic Books, 1969). Also indispensible for access to the Lewin-Festinger legacy

and *milieu* is Patnoe, *A Narrative History*. See also: Lewis A. Coser, *Refugee Scholars in America: Their Impact and their Experiences* (New Haven, CT: Yale University Press, 1984); Mitchell G. Ash, 'Cultural Contexts and Scientific Change in Psychology: Kurt Lewin in Iowa', *American Psychologist* 47 (1992), 198-207, and his *Gestalt Psychology in German Culture, 1890–1967: Holism and the Quest for Objectivity* (Cambridge: Cambridge University Press, 1995); and Kurt Danziger, *Constructing the Subject: Historical Origins of Psychological Research* (Cambridge: Cambridge University Press, 1990), 173-78.

    9.   Leon Festinger, Dorwin Cartwright, Kathleen Barber, Juliet Fleischl, Josephine Gottsdanker, Annette Keysen and Gloria Leavitt, 'A Study of Rumor: Its Origin and Spread', *Human Relations* 1 (1948), 464-86.

    10. This is the view of Stanley Schachter: 'That particular study lead to Leon's whole theory of pressures to conformity and social influence, which in turn led to dissonance' (Patnoe, *A Narrative History*, 192). For the relevant publications from 1948 through 1951, see 'Published Works of Leon Festinger', in Stanley Schachter, and M. Gazzaniga, *Extending Psychological Frontiers: Selected Works of Leon Festinger* (New York: Russell Sage Foundation, 1989), 569-73. For example: Leon Festinger, Stanley Schachter and Kurt Back, *Social Pressures in Informal Groups: A Study of Human Factors in Housing* (New York: Harper Brothers, 1950); and Leon Festinger and Harold H. Kelley, *Changing Attitudes through Social Contact* (Ann Arbor, MI: Institute for Social Research, University of Michigan, 1951).

    11. Festinger, *et al.*, 'A Study of Rumor', 484.

    12. Festinger, *et al.*, 'A Study of Rumor', 484-85.

    13. Festinger, *et al.*, 'A Study of Rumor', 485.

    14. Festinger, *et al.*, 'A Study of Rumor', 486. Compare the work done by Festinger on group dynamics just prior to and after the Weymouth study: Leon Festinger, 'The Role of Group Belongingness in a Voting Situation', *Human Relations* 1 (1947), 154-80; and 'A Theory of Social Comparison Processes', *Human Relations* 7 (1954), 117-40.

    15. Festinger, *et al.*, 'A Study of Rumor', 478-83; Festinger, Schachter and Back, 'Social Pressures', 130.

    16. Festinger, *et al.*, 'A Study of Rumor' (1948), 485. When asked about this Elliot Aronson said that he had 'no idea about what might have been going on in Festinger's mind at the time he wrote the [1957] foreword'. Elliot Aronson, 'Re: Origins of Dissonance Theory', 20 May, 2003, personal e-mail (20 May, 2003).

    17. Cf. Joseph Ben-David and Randall Collins, 'Social Factors in the Origins of a New Science: The Case of Psychology', *American Sociological Review* 31.4 (1966), 451-65, concerning the application of the social network theory of intellectual history to the early development of psychology; and using the same approach later, see Randall Collins, *The Sociology of Philosophies: A Global Theory of Intellectual Change* (Cambridge, MA: Harvard University Press, 1998) in connection with the world's philosophical and early scientific traditions. Lewis Coser engages in a similar actor-network analysis of German émigré psychologists and their impact in America (*Refugee Scholars in America*). Coser as well as Collins have been faulted by their critics for telling the respective stories of psychology and philosophy, but without including the ideas themselves. Hence the philosopher A.C. Grayling's criticism of Collins in *New*

York Times Book Review (27 September, 1998) 'Family Feuds': 'The essential fault in Collins's account is that although he is discussing the history of ideas, he all but ignores the ideas themselves and has his eye only on the sociologist's legitimate prey—social structures and relationships'. Similarly Coser is accused of conducting 'a form of intellectual history with the ideas left out' by Wilfred M. McClay, 'Weimar in America', *American Scholar* (Winter 1985–1986), 126 (cited by Claus-Dieter Krohn, *Intellectuals in Exile* [Amherst, MA: University of Massachusetts Press, 1993], 213-14).

18. Contrast this general neglect of historical background with its careful delineation in Festinger, *et al.*, 'A Study of Rumor', 475-76. Leon Festinger, Henry W. Riecken and Stanley Schachter, *When Prophecy Fails: A Social and Psychological Study of a Modern Group that Predicted the Destruction of the World* (New York: Harper and Row, 1964 [1956]), 54-55. Contemporaneous events included: Flying Saucers first reported in the US (1947) and the beginning of the 'Nuclear Arms Race' with the Soviets; US exploded the first hydrogen bomb (1952), and the Soviets follow with theirs the next year (1953). Also, the hunt for Communist conspiracies and spies in the US starts, known as McCarthyism (1950–1954); the 'Cold War' turns hot with the North Korean invasion of South Korea, which results in the 'Korean War' (1950–1953). Billy Graham holds evangelical crusades in major cities across the western world (1954), and Samuel Beckett stages 'Waiting for Godot'. In a surprising reversal of the extraterrestrial invasion myth, Pope Pius XII proclaims the dogma of the bodily assumption of the Virgin Mary (1950). At this time, 29 million US homes have television access. (From Bernard Grun, *The Timetables of History* [New York: Simon & Schuster, 1979], 527-37.)

Concerning the correlation between the 'Red scare' and UFO sightings, see Otto Billig, *Flying Saucers, Magic in the Skies: A Psychohistory* (Cambridge, MA: Schenkman Publishing, 1982). Film makers capitalized on these fears, especially the Flying Saucer craze, with the release of numerous black and white science fiction films, for example: *The Day the Earth Stood Still* (1951), *Invaders from Mars* (1953, filmed in '3-D'); *It Came from Outer Space* (1953); and *The Man from Planet X* (1951). See Patrick Lucanion, *Them or Us: Archetypal Interpretations of Fifties Alien Invasion Films* (Indianapolis: Indiana University Press, 1987).

19. See J. Gordon Melton and George M. Eberhart, 'The Flying Saucer Contactee Movement, 1950–1994: A Bibliography', in James R. Lewis (ed.), *The Gods Have Landed: New Religions from Other Worlds* (Albany, NY: State University of New York Press, 1995), 251-332.

20. The same can probably be said of Carl Jung's *Flying Saucers: A Modern Myth of Things Seen in the Skies* (Trans. R.F.C. Hull; *Collected Works* Vol. 10; Bollingen Series XX; Princeton, NJ: Princeton University Press, 1991 [1959]). Of additional interest is the fact that Jung began his book by examining UFOs as a 'worldwide rumor'. See ch. 1, 'UFOs as Rumor', pages 8-23. If, as I argue here, Festinger's *When Prophecy Fails* has its roots in earlier work regarding rumors, it is interesting that, Carl Jung, working in a very different psychological context, has chosen to make explicit the nature of the flying saucer 'modern myth' as a 'visionary rumor'.

21. In *Illusions of Reality* Korn repeatedly draws attention to the themes of illusion and deception, and the roles they play in the development of modern experimental social psychology.

22. Festinger, Riecken and Schachter, *When Prophecy Fails*, 151-55, 178, 190-92.

23. Festinger, Riecken and Schachter, *When Prophecy Fails*, 248-49.

24. Festinger, Riecken and Schachter, *When Prophecy Fails*, 69-70, and 236-40.

25. Even the notion of benevolent 'Space Brothers' or 'Guardians' can be viewed as a modernization of the Ascended Masters found in Theosophy.

26. Festinger, Riecken and Schachter, *When Prophecy Fails* ends with a 'Methodological Appendix', 234-49, detailing all these aspects of the 'field project'.

27. Festinger, Riecken and Schachter, *When Prophecy Fails*, 249. See also, pages 31-2, 192, 243.

28. Aronson, 'Leon Festinger and the Art of Audacity', 215; Elliot Aronson, 'The Return of the Repressed: Dissonance Theory Makes a Comeback', *Psychological Inquiry* 3.4 (1992), 304.

29. Aronson, 'Leon Festinger and the Art of Audacity', 215; Aronson, 'The Return of the Repressed', 305.

30. Thomas S. Kuhn, *The Structure of Scientific Revolutions* (Chicago: University of Chicago, 2nd edn, 1970), ix.

31. Collins, *The Sociology of Philosophies*, 33-39 and 73-74. Regarding the importance of 'emotional energy' for the success of social and religious movements, which also concerns intellectual movements, see also Randall Collins, 'Social Movements and the Focus of Emotional Attention', in Jeff Goodwin, James M. Jasper, and Francesca Polletta (eds.), *Passionate Politics: Emotions and Social Movements* (Chicago: University of Chicago Press, 2001), 27-44. See also n. 39 below.

32. Patnoe, *A Narrative History*, 106, 194, and especially 261; Elliot Aronson, 'Whatever Happened to Dissonance?', *Contemporary Social Psychology* 11 (1985), 133; Aronson, 'Leon Festinger and the Art of Audacity', 215; Aronson, 'The Return of the Repressed', 303. Steiner reports that '...after World War II was far from serene. [It] spawned a very groupy social psychology...the late 40s and 50s brought a rediscovery and reformulation of the problem of group processes, and a "flight of young talent from the area of attitudes"... The political and social upheavals of the first third of the century had generated concerns that favored a new line of research and led to...a tenfold increase in the publication of research dealing with groups.' (Ivan D. Steiner, 'Whatever Happened to the Group in Social Psychology?', *Journal of Experimental Social Psychology* 10 [1974], 105.)

33. Leon Festinger and James Carlsmith, 'Cognitive Consequences of Forced Compliance', *Journal of Abnormal and Social Psychology* 58 (1959), 203-211. See also, Leon Festinger, 'Cognitive Dissonance', *Scientific American* 207.4 (1962): 93-101 (96-97).

34. Ernest Hilgard, *Psychology in America: A Historical Survey* (San Diego: Harcourt Brace Jovanovich, 1987), 222. Also Aronson, 'Leon Festinger and the Art of Audacity', 25.

35. I should also note that this was happening when social psychology was becoming a recognized sub-field within American psychology, and successfully negotiating its independence and establishing itself within the academy.

36. Shelly Patnoe's narrative history of the group that formed around Festinger, as it had earlier with Kurt Lewin, particularly emphasizes the prominent place given scientific rigor, and at the same time, innovative experimentation. See Patnoe, *A Nar-*

rative History, 112-13, 121-22, 128, 148, 154-55, 185, 228, 246, 267, 270 and especially 192. See also: Aronson, 'Leon Festinger and the Art of Audacity', 216; Aronson, 'The Return of the Repressed', 304. See Mitchell G. Ash, ('Kurt Lewin in Iowa'), and Kurt Danziger, (*Constructing the Subject*), regarding the distinctive experimental approach that emerged within the context of Lewinian social psychology, and Andrew S. Winston, 'Cause into Function: Ernst Mach and the Reconstruction of Explanation in Psychology', in Christopher D. Green, Marlene Shore, and Thomas Teo (eds.), *The Transformation of Psychology: Influences of 19th Century Philosophy, Technology, and Natural Science* (Washington DC: American Psychological Association, 2000), 107-31, regarding changes in American experimentalism occurring in the 1930s. The deep irony here is that the original 'philosophy of science on the basis of which Lewin constructed or justified his work in Iowa was either ignored or met with complete incomprehension. His experiments with groups were admired as effective manipulations, and Lewin himself was elevated to iconic status as the founder of experimental social psychology. However, some of his most prominent students rejected his model of procedure; instead, they reconstructed what they took to be Lewinian research on the basis of, by then standard, American experimental methodology, which prescribed the parceling out of independent and dependent variables and this presupposed the very elementalism [Lewin] criticized' (Ash, 'Kurt Lewin in Iowa', 205). As Kurt Danziger observes, the 'experimentalists who succeeded [Lewin] had a very different conception of what experiments were for. They were [now] for isolating specific manipulable elements and their directly denotable effects... Whereas Festinger had departed from the spirit of the Lewinian conception of experimentation in several significant respects, the generation of his followers took social psychology much further in this direction' (Kurt Danziger, 'Making Social Psychology Experimental: A Conceptual History, 1920–1970', *Journal of the History of the Behavioral Sciences* 36.4 (2000), 329-47, here 342-44.) As Ivan Steiner points out, this is about the same time that social psychology shifted its experimental focus away from studying the group as well (Steiner, 'Whatever Happened to the Group in Social Psychology?').

37. Aronson, 'Whatever Happened to Dissonance?', 133; Aronson, 'Leon Festinger and the Art of Audacity', 305.

38. Aronson, 'Whatever Happened to Dissonance?', 135.

39. Hilgard points to the untimely death of Kurt Lewin in 1947 at MIT of a heart-attack at age 56, and the leadership crisis this created for the field and the direction it was to take. Festinger, Hilgard says, was 'a temporary successor, both for the students trained and excitement generated'. Hilgard, *Psychology in America*, 610. As Collins states, both the students attracted, the networks they create, and the 'emotional energy' they carry, are important for later success (Collins, *The Sociology of Philosophies*). Cf. Patnoe, *A Narrative History*, 16-17, 20-21 and 24-25 regarding 'Quasselstrippe', Kurt Lewin's open-ended informal gatherings or seminars held in the evenings that kept the emotional energy high, which Festinger continued.

40. See Collins, *The Sociology of Philosophies*, 80-82 and 162-64, and *idem*, 'Social Movements and the Focus of Emotional Attention', 27-44, regarding the important role of counter-movements and conflict for the production of 'emotional energy'.

41. Metaphysical behaviorism holds that behavior is the essence of an organism,

the connection between stimuli and response. The extreme form of this view specifies that there are no other things, such as perception, memory, and consciousness, only behavior. Methodological behaviorism states that the approach to understanding organisms is through, and only through, what can be observed, and that is behavior.

42. In fact, instead of contributing to the unification or consolidation of social psychology around a paradigm or set of paradigms, dissonance theory only fueled the fragmentation of the discipline. Cf. Hilgard, *Psychology in America*, 606. Dean K. Simonton, *Great Psychologists and their Times: Scientific Insights into Psychology's History* (Washington, DC: American Psychological Association, 2002), 359-68, makes much the same complaint regarding psychology as a whole, suggesting the problem is the lack of a widely accepted paradigm. In 'Why the Social Sciences Won't Become High-Consensus, Rapid-Discovery Science', *Sociological Forum* 9 (1994), 155-77, Randall Collins goes further, citing the lack of 'a genealogy of research technology, whose manipulation reliably produces new phenomena and a rapidly moving research front' in the social sciences as a whole. 'Unless the social sciences invent new research hardware, they will likely never acquire much consensus or rapid discovery.' See also, Michael W. Katzko, 'The Rhetoric of Psychological Research and the Problem of Unification in Psychology', *American Psychologist* 57.4 (2002), 262-70.

43. Korn, *Illusions of Reality*, 143-57; Festinger in Cohn, *Psychologists on Psychology*, 140; Aronson, 'Whatever Happened to Dissonance?', 134; Aronson, 'The Return of the Repressed', 306.

44. Hilgard, *Psychology in America*, 610.

45. Matthew N. Schmalz, 'When Festinger Fails: Prophecy and the Watchtower', in Jon R. Stone (ed.), *Expecting Armageddon: Essential Readings in Failed Prophecy* (New York: Routledge, 2000), 233-50. Scholars owe Jon Stone a debt of gratitude for collecting and publishing the most important of these studies in his *Expecting Armageddon*. The anthology includes Stone's excellent overview, 'Introduction', and J. Gordon Melton's 1985 response to Festinger. Those interested in a full account of the vicissitudes of dissonance theory in the context of the study of new religious movements should consult this valuable volume.

46. Regarding the centrality of 'proselyting', see Festinger, Riecken and Schachter, *When Prophecy Fails*, 4, 28, 37, 38, 52, 3, 75, 100, 103, 114, 131, 134-35, 148-49, 182, 194, 208-15. However, the complete failure of the group to gain any new recruits (other than deeply uncommitted social psychologists and associated observers) raises the question of whether there was any proselytizing taking place at all. See Festinger, Riecken and Schachter, *When Prophecy Fails*, 89, 133, 174, 186. In this social or group setting, the inability to measure dissonance or its reduction is, in my view, a far greater problem than the theory's inability to predict responses to failed prophecy, since Festinger's theory of cognitive dissonance depends entirely upon the presence of dissonance to begin with. As Carl Jung pointed out many years ago, where strong feelings are involved, 'even in quite intelligent people who have considerable education and experience one can sometimes observe a real blindness, a true systematic anaesthesia', such that 'the strongest and most plausible arguments…make no impression; they simply bounce off, because emotional inhibitions are stronger than all logic' (*Collected Works* 3, par 90). In this situation, there would be no cognitive dissonance generated, because the logic upon which the dissonance depends doesn't

stand. For this reason, I think Festinger's cognitive focus overlooks the role of the affective realm when it comes to the presence of dissonance and dissonance reduction processes.

47. See, for example, Diana Tumminia, 'How Prophecy Never Fails: Interpretive Reason in a Flying Saucer Group', *Sociology of Religions* 59 (1998), 157-70. For decades, the Unarius Academy of Science has been setting dates without any problem for the arrival of messianic Space Brothers. I would be remiss if I did not at least mention that social constructivist critics of experimental psychology, such as Kenneth Gergen and others, view 'dissonance' and 'cognitions' as social constructs, or worse yet, artifacts of the Cartesian dualism that dominates modern psychology. The joke at the time was that if someone wanted to know whether 'X' is dissonant with 'Y', you had to 'Ask Leon!' (Aronson, 'The Return of the Repressed', 305, and Cohn, *Psychologists on Psychology*, 142.) Social constructivist critics of experimental psychology point out that since these phenomena are largely limited to experimental settings, they can be said to be 'experimentally constructed'. Cf. Collins, *The Sociology of Philosophies*, 1029-1030, on the ontological standing of thoughts and beliefs (i.e., 'cognitions'), generally corresponding with Cooley's Axiom in sociology. It is perhaps no accident that Randall Collins was a one-time graduate student of Leo Festinger at Stanford in 1963, but transferred the next year to study sociology at Berkeley, turning his attention instead to psychology's intellectual lineages (Randall Collins, 're: Sociological analysis of Lewin/Festinger?' 19 September, 2002, personal e-mail). See also, Ben David and Collins, 'The Case of Psychology'.

48. Cited by Korn, *Illusions of Reality*, 161. Philip Zimbardo, 'Laugh Where We Must, Be Candid Where We Can', *Psychology Today* 18 (June 1985), 44. Of Funt, Zimbardo says, 'You are really an experimental social psychologist. You share with some of my most creative colleagues, Leon Festinger, Stanley Schachter and Elliot Aronson, the ability to design and manipulate social situations that reveal much about the way we behave, alone and with others.'

49. The term was coined by the philosopher of technology, Don Ihde, who has described an epistemology engine as 'a technology or a set of technologies that, through use, frequently become explicit models for describing how knowledge is produced'. (Don Ihde, 'Epistemology Engine', *Nature* 406.6791 [6 July, 2000], 21.)

50. Even successful popularizations of social psychology continue to prominently include Festinger's work. See Robert B. Cialdini, *Influence: The Psychology of Persuasion* (New York: William Morrow, 1993 [1984]), 119-28, which begins a long chapter on 'Social Proof', 114-66, with a short positive account of Festinger, Riecken and Schachter, *When Prophesy Fails* that is well integrated into the rest of the chapter. Dissonance experiments continue at Yale (Bruce Fellman, 'Under the Influence', *Yale Alumni Magazine*, May/June 2004, 28). Thus, for psychologists, it is far from true that 'the Festinger thesis has been relegated to the place of an obligatory footnote', however true this may be for those studying new religious movements and millenarian groups (Jon R. Stone, 'Introduction', in *idem* [ed.], *Expecting Armageddon*, 16).

51. Steve J. Haggbloom, S.R. Warnick, J.E. Warnick, G.L. Yarbrough, T.M. Russell, C.M. Borecky, V.K. Jones, R. McGahhey, J.L. Powell III, J. Beavers and E. Monte, 'The 100 Most Eminent Psychologists of the 20th Century', *Review of General Psychology* 6 (2002), 139-52.

52. Stone (ed.), *Expecting Armageddon*, 23.

53. Social psychologists may not be aware of these attacks on dissonance theory due to the fact that existing academic networks cannot accommodate this kind of confrontation across interdisciplinary lines. For example, their bibliographic systems of citation are incompatible. It would appear that social psychologists made a hasty retreat to the laboratory and experimental psychology, abandoning any subsequent attempts to confirm Festinger's proselytizing hypothesis. In the waves of hundreds and hundreds of experiments confirming the presence of dissonance or dissonance-like phenomena in the laboratory, dissenting voices were effectively drowned out. Social psychologists, in marked contrast to the social scientists in Stone (ed.), *Expecting Armageddon*, never recognized a problem with the theory.

At one level, the problem is that there was never a connecting social network that brought social scientist dissenters into direct confrontation with experimental social psychologists. Even if that were to occur, there would not be any way for the dissenters to raise their concerns within the exclusively experimental context, that is, there would not be any way to translate their objections into the language of independent and dependent variables, and laboratory protocol. Those I am calling the dissenters also had no real access to the journals and conferences for experimental social psychologists precisely at the time that the enthusiasm for dissonance theory was at its height. Choosing instead American studies, religion and sociology journals, the dissenters were unable to create a presence in the attention space of experimental psychology, nor were they able to reformulate their objections in theoretical terminology, or come up with a way to test them experimentally.

54. Festinger in Cohn, *Psychologists on Psychology*, 136-37. Jane Allyn Hardyck and Marcia Braden, 'Prophecy Fails Again: A Report of a Failure to Replicate', in Stone (ed.), *Expecting Armageddon*, 55-63.

55. Hardyck and Braden in Stone, *Expecting Armageddon*, 60-63.

56. J. Gordon Melton, 'Spiritualization and Reaffirmation: What Really Happens when Prophecy Fails', in Stone (ed.), *Expecting Armageddon*, 154-55.

57. Use the words 'brainwashing' and 'cults' with social psychologists, for example, and you will probably get an entirely different response than you would from those that study new religious movements. This is another fault line between the disciplines that badly needs to be addressed.

A Cusp Catastrophe Model of Cult Conversions

Leslie L. Downing

Ideological conversion has been the subject of extensive inquiry in recent decades.[1] One of many areas of confusion regarding this topic involves the often reported radical, stepwise, nature of some conversions, subjectively experienced as 'snapping'.[2] Such conversions stand in contrast to others which are reported to be gradual transitions, sometimes occurring so slowly that no specific experience of conversion occurs at all.[3] On reviewing extensive written reports of conversions from autobiographies,[4] from therapists,[5] and from sociologists, social psychologists, and others,[6] the frequent occurrence of both types of conversions seems incontrovertible. This paper attempts to delineate the conditions under which one or the other type of conversion is to be expected.

The nature of the problem can be readily couched in terms of mathematical catastrophe theory.[7] Catastrophe theory was developed as a means for better understanding nonlinear transitions in biology and in other sciences. The term catastrophe is potentially confusing, as it has nothing to do with the importance, magnitude, or devastating consequences of the event, such as is often implied in non-mathematical uses of the term. In mathematics, all that is meant by a catastrophe is a nonlinear transition from one state to another. Consider, for example, opening a stuck lid on a pickle jar. As increasing pressure is applied, nothing happens, the lid remains stuck. But at some point, a minuscule increase in pressure will cause the lid to become unstuck. This transition, from stuck to unstuck, is a catastrophe. It is a change of state from stuck to unstuck, which does not occur as a linear gradual change induced by gradual increases in pressure, but as a radical transformation of state, a catastrophe. Many disasters are catastrophes in this sense. An avalanche, for example, is a radical change of state induced by an accumulating weight of new snow. A fire may be started by spontaneous combustion resulting from increasing heat. Many physical transitions can be described in these terms.

Of the various types of catastrophes, the one that has been most useful for describing nonlinear relationships has been what is known as the 'cusp' catastrophe. Abraham Tesser, for example, makes a plausible case for a cusp catastrophe interpretation of the sometimes gradual and some-times discontinuous and bi-modal relationship between dispositional forces and environmental forces in studies of social influence.[8]

The cusp catastrophe model describes how changes in a dependent variable, 'Behavior', are related to the levels of two independent variables, called 'Control Factor I', and 'Control Factor II', (see Figure 1).

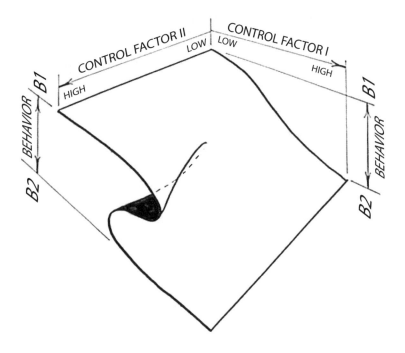

Figure 1. *The 'Cusp Catastrophe' Surface, with Control Factor I, Control Factor II (the Splitting Factor), and Behavior (B1 or B2).*

The folded shape depicted in Figure 1 is called the 'Behavior Surface'. The only stable locations for Behavior are assumed to be on this surface. If we take a horizontal plane, defined by the two Control Factors, that plane is referred to as the 'Control Surface' (not shown). At most points on that plane, defined by the levels of the two Control Factors, a vertical line projected perpendicular to the plane will intersect with the Behavior Surface at one and only one point on the vertical Behavior dimension, between B1 at the top, and B2, at the bottom. This indicates the level of Behavior that will occur for those Control Factors. Where the vertical line encounters the 'fold' in the Behavior Surface, however, it will intersect that surface at three points, one of which is on the underside of the fold. A projection down onto the horizontal Control Surface of all possible three-point locations will define a cusp-shaped area, wide at the front edge of the space, and receding to a sharp point somewhere prior to reaching the back edge. Although vertical projections from the areas defined by the cusp intersect the Behavior Surface in two places, Behavior cannot be at two levels at the same time, so it is assumed that Behavior is not possible on the underside of the fold. Hence the name, the 'cusp catastrophe' model.

The dynamics of the model allow that 'history counts'. If Control Factor I is low, and Control Factor II is high, the intersection with the Behavior Surface is to the left on the top surface, near the front edge. As increases in Control Factor I forces move the point to the right, it will enter the area of the fold, the cusp. When the cusp is encountered Behavior will persist on the top surface until it reaches the far right side of the cusp, at which point no more top surface exists. Behavior will then make a radical transition to the lower surface. But if Behavior starts on the lower surface, and moves into the cusp area from the right to the left, it will persist on the bottom surface until, at the far left edge of the cusp, that surface no longer exists. At that point Behavior will jump to the top surface. This phenomenon, of having two different points at which the transition occurs depending upon prior history or the path taken, is called 'Hysteresis'.

Assume a low level of Control Factor II, and we see that increases in Control Factor I move us along the back edge of the Behavior Surface from left to right. In so doing, the position of the surface on the vertical 'Behavior' dimension has gradually gone from B1 at the top, to B2 at the bottom. This is a linear transition with no discontinuities.

Conversion and Catastrophe.

The continuous transition from B1 to B2 at low levels of Control Factor II, is similar to the gradual transition to a new ideology described in some accounts. The abrupt transition at high levels of Control Factor II is similar to the sometimes reported 'snapping' from one ideology or set of beliefs to acceptance of an incompatible ideology. For the cusp catastrophe model to be useful in understanding the differences between these two types of conversion, it is necessary to operationally define the two Control Factors, Factor I, and Factor II, and the Behavior Factor, which are relevant to ideological conversion (see Figure 2).

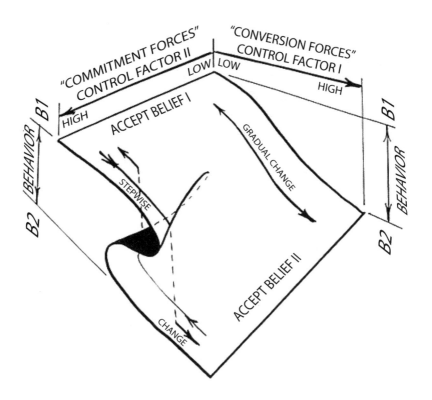

Figure 2. *The Ideological Conversion Model, with Control Factor I as Degree of Conversion Forces, Control Factor II as Degree of Commitment Forces, and Behavior (B1), as Total Non-Acceptance of the NewIdeology, and Behavior (B2) as Total Acceptance of the New Ideology.*

The dependent 'Behavior' of interest, at one extreme, indicated at the top of the vertical dimension by state B1, is *non-acceptance of the new ideology*. At the other extreme, indicated at the bottom by state B2, is *total acceptance of the new ideology*. Our use of the term Behavior is not to imply actual overt behavioral compliance, or public acceptance of the ideology. The term Behavior as used here reflects common usage of that term to indicate the dependent variable. In our model, the dependent variable is internal acceptance of the validity of the ideology. Also, it is assumed, in the definition of ideological conversion, that B2 is perceived to be incompatible with B1, such that the two could not reasonably be accepted at the same time. In a gradual transition from B1 to B2, at the back edge of the surface, one would encounter intermediate beliefs as well, such as partial acceptance of B2, or uncertainty about the validity of

B2. But at the front edge of the surface, the transition would be discontinuous, changing in a stepwise fashion from non-acceptance of B2, at the top, to a catastrophic change resulting in acceptance of B2, with no intermediate beliefs intervening.

Control Factor I

In the model as illustrated in Figure 2, Control Factor I, 'Conversion Forces', contains all of the forces disposing one to accept as valid the beliefs or ideology constituting the original position, B1, as well as all of the forces disposing one to accept the new ideology, B2. In describing change from B1 to B2, the magnitude of conversion forces is enhanced by forces favoring B2, and is reduced by forces favoring B1. The more that B2 forces outweigh B1 forces, the further to the right one would be on the left to right dimension of the Behavior Surface.

In principle, the meaning of Control Factor I, Conversion Forces, is fairly straightforward. In practice, however, it becomes necessary to develop a comprehensive theory about what these various force are and how they operate. I have in fact developed such a theory.[9] At the heart of the theory is a Six-Component Model of Ideological Conversion, which is based upon a review and analysis of relevant research and theory in social psychology. The first three components describe an interdependent set of social psychological processes which combine to undermine acceptance of the original belief system. The last three of the six components describe an interdependent set of social psychological processes which combine to promote acceptance of the new ideology. In terms of the catastrophe model, the first three components contribute to weakening acceptance of the B1 position, and the last three components contribute to strengthening acceptance of the B2 position. Combined these constitute what we have labeled 'Conversion Forces' (see Figure 3).

Control Factor II

In the model described in Figure 2, the back to front dimension of the control surface, Control Factor II, is sometimes called the 'Splitting Factor'. It is the strength of the Splitting Factor that determines whether or not transitions on the Behavior dimension will be continuous or discontinuous, whether they will form a unimodal distribution of possible locations, or will be split into a bimodal distribution. In our model, this Splitting Factor, Control Factor II, is level of 'Commitment' to one's original position. Where Commitment is low, at the back edge of the Behavior Surface, as Conversion Forces increase from left to right, the transition of

Behavior changes continuously and gradually from B1 to B2. But as Commitment increases, moving toward the front of the surface, at some level of Commitment the Cusp Catastrophe Behavior Surface begins to fold such that the transition from left to right (with increases in Conversion Forces) ceases to be continuous, resulting in a jump from near the top of the Behavior dimension, acceptance of B1, to near the bottom on that dimension, acceptance of B2. The concept of Commitment Forces, like that of Conversion Forces, needs to be further developed as a social psychological construct. In previous work I have made some efforts to do exactly that.[10]

STAGE ONE:	Impairment of the Ability of the Original Belief System to Adequately Function.
Component 1:	Threat to Functioning of the Original Belief System. Selection for or Inducement of a Weakened or Threatened Original Belief System.
Component 2:	Undermining Internal Resources for Coping with Threat. Reduced Potential for Using One's Own Internal Resources for Coping with Threat.
Component 3:	Undermining External Resources for Coping with Threat. Loss of, Separation from, or Disparagement of Original Social Support System.
STAGE TWO:	Provision of Conditions in Which a New Ideology is Made Available and Is Perceived to Be Functional.
Component 4:	Provision of a New Social Support System: 'Lovebombing', or Other Means of Supplying the Potential Convert with a New Emotionally Accepting, Loving, and Caring Group.
Component 5:	Provision of a New Ideology: The New Ideology Is Made Available to the Potential Recruit.
Component 6:	Provision of Conditions Promoting Commitment to and Consolidation of the New Ideology: Living Day to Day in Terms of the New Ideology, Making Sacrifices on Behalf of It, and Participating in the Recruitment and Conversion of Others, All Aid in This Process.

Figure 3. *The Six-Component Model of Conversion Forces.*

Commitment is defined as that which makes one persist, in acceptance of beliefs or in continuation of behavior, in spite of good reasons to do otherwise. Many of the forces that induce such resistance to change have been developed through systematic research in social psychology, and at least a good start can be made to delineate those forces. Very basically, Commitment Forces constitute the combinations of factors that induce persistence or resistance to change from the originally accepted position. A Three-Category Model of Commitment, which encompasses most of the established influences on commitment, is shown in Figure 4.

	Three Categories of Ideological Commitment
Category 1	Commitment Resulting from Pain, Loss, Suffering, Investment, or Sacrifice.
Category 2	Commitment Due to Integration with a Larger Belief System.
Category 3	Commitment Due to Absence, Unawareness, or Disparagement of Alternatives.

Figure 4: *The Three-Category Model of Commitment Forces*

Commitment Category 1

Commitment to a position will be high to the extent that one has endured irreversible loss, pain, or suffering on its behalf. Considerable research has supported this idea, from the experimental laboratory studies of Leon Festinger and others on predictions from the Theory of Cognitive Dissonance,[11] to the archival studies of nineteenth-century Utopian communities studied by the sociologist, Rosabeth Moss Kanter.[12] The power of such forces to increase commitment was also convincingly developed in Brickman.[13] It was Brickman's work which led to the definition of Commitment as 'persistence of a belief or action in spite of good reasons to do otherwise'. In a perverse sense, one's commitment to a belief, ideology, or course of action, is likely to be inversely related to the extent that one has good reasons to accept it. One does not make a commitment to believe what is obviously true, but does make commitments, as concerning religious beliefs, to exactly those ideas that are most lacking in objective support. In religious terms, one is likely to refer to commitment to believe as having faith. The extreme of Brickman's idea is expressed succinctly, in an anonymously attributed quote, 'Faith is believing in what you know to be not true'.

Commitment Category 2

Commitment to a position will be high to the extent that it is integrated with a larger and still functional belief system. In particular, integration with a major organizing schema of the belief system, such as the self-schema, will promote commitment. Recall that commitment is about persistence. The more tied one's beliefs become to stable features of the larger system, the more resistant to change they will be. It is clear for example that if one has personally espoused a position, especially publicly, or if one has practiced developing counter-arguments in defense of one's position,[14] one will become more resistant to changing even in the face of good reasons to change.[15] Beliefs are also resistant to change to the extent that they are consistent with views of highly credible groups,[16] or groups with which one has developed a sense of shared identity, as in Groupthink.[17]

Commitment Category 3

Commitment to a position is dependent not only on the reasons for accepting it, but on the absence of viable alternatives. Persistence in accepting a clearly deficient or flawed position may occur because no better alternative is known to be available. These ideas are supported by work on Social Exchange Theory,[18] and are consistent with Becker's notion of commitment based upon what he called 'Side Bets'.[19] If every week for 20 years one has put money into a retirement account which can only be collected if they retire after 25 or more years with the company, they may persist in staying with that company in spite of dissatisfying working conditions. They are committed, not because they value the company, but because they view the alternative of leaving it and losing all that money as even worse. But suppose you believe your prophet's prediction of the end of the world next year, and hoping to improve your standing in heaven, give all of your money to the poor. Then your prophet appears to show signs of being psychotic and delusional. Do you give up belief in him? You cannot get your money back. You have in a sense burned your bridges to the life you had before you accepted the prophet. Also, there is still some possibility that he is a true prophet, and if you have faith in him your faith and generosity will be rewarded. Having given away all of your money will increase the persistence of your belief in the prophet, to the extent that options and alternatives to holding that belief have been eliminated or devalued, even when objective evidence suggests he is only a false prophet.

The relationships between these three Categories of Commitment Forces are complex, and are only partially understood at present. Their relationship to Conversion Forces is also potentially confusing, especially the third Category concerning viability of alternatives. Nevertheless, enough has been established that, in many particular circumstances, one can be reasonably certain of the effects that changes occurring in these Categories will have on the strength of Commitment.

Implications of the Catastrophe Model

If the cusp catastrophe model of conversion and commitment is valid, two major effects are predictable, 'Hysteresis' and 'Discontinuity'.

Hysteresis

The hysteresis effect refers to the predicted tendency for Behavior to resist change in spite of the existence of substantial Control Factor I Conversion Forces. On the front portion of the Behavior Surface, in the area of the cusp, where the vertical line intersects both the upper and lower surface, hysteresis relates to the tendency for Behavior *to persist on whatever surface it has started on, until there is no more surface at that level, before making the radical transition to the other level.* We might call this the strong hysteresis effect. Even at lower levels of Commitment, the extent to which hysteresis will occur is directly related to the strength of Commitment Forces. This weaker version of hysteresis relates to the fact that persistence at the original level will start to occur even prior to the point where commitment is high enough to produce discontinuity. Thus even where Behavior change is gradual, the higher that Commitment is, the more Behavior will *resist* change in the face of Conversion Forces. When substantial change to the other level does occur, it occurs without discontinuity. Where commitment is high enough to produce discontinuity, a persistent high level of acceptance of B1 will occur before the fold, and after that point an exaggerated acceptance of B2 will occur. In more ordinary language, this means that commitment to an original position will produce resistance to change in that position, even in the face of good reasons (Conversion Forces) to do otherwise. To put it another way, the amount of change in Belief acceptance induced by Conversion Forces will be *less* than would otherwise be expected and the extent of this effect will increase with increasing commitment.

Laboratory experiments offer some support for the hysteresis prediction. For example, in decision-making research, when objective evidence in favor of acceptance of an alternative hypothesis accumulates slowly, confidence in the originally accepted hypothesis remains much higher than would be objectively warranted. This has been labeled the 'Inertia Effect'.[20] Also in such research, when the originally accepted hypothesis is rejected, and the alternative hypothesis is accepted, the transition is often abrupt, suggesting the discontinuity predicted for high levels of commitment. While commitment to the original position was not usually manipulated in this research, the fact is that early public declarations (about which hypothesis seemed most likely to be correct) were routinely part of the procedure, and have been shown to enhance commitment.[21]

In social psychology, the phenomenon has been often demonstrated and is usually called 'Belief Perseverance'. Failure to relinquish belief even in the face of discrediting evidence is most likely when people have previously generated a rationale for that belief.[22] Doing so embeds the belief more fully in a system of related beliefs, which is one of the factors promoting commitment. In fact, nearly all of the research on commitment can be interpreted as evidence of what catastrophe theory calls hysteresis.

Discontinuity

One interesting set of predictions is that initial conversion to religious cults, coming as it usually does from weak commitment to original beliefs, is likely to be gradual. But rejection of the cult position, as might occur in cases of 'deprogramming', which usually occurs after the building of strong commitment to it, is expected to be abrupt or discontinuous. Anecdotal case history reports of ex-cult members are largely consistent with this set of expectations.[23] In many reports of being converted into religious cults, the process is so gradual that no specific choice, decision, or even experience marks a clear point at which the new ideology was accepted. In most of these cases, no strong commitment to an earlier ideology or belief system seems to have existed, thus the gradual nature of conversion from B1 to B2 is predicted. Months or years of believing in the cult's ideology, B2, and sacrificing for it, living it, preaching it, raising money for it, and converting others to it, all commitment building forces, should produce high levels of commitment. According to the model, at high commitment, any conversion to another set of beliefs, B1, would be expected to be discontinuous or abrupt. Applying Conversion Forces to return the cult follower to the original belief system (B1) is now expected to have little effect on acceptance (the hysteresis effect), until those forces are strong enough to reach the fold in the cusp catastrophe Behavior Surface, at which point transition to the B1 position will be abrupt. In the cult literature, the experience of 'snapping' from one ideological position to another is most prominent in reports of 'deprogramming'. This is a process of intentionally producing sufficient Conversion Forces to induce the highly committed cult member to relinquish acceptance of the cult ideology and return to a previously held set of beliefs.

The idea that high commitment, that which induces resistance to change, is what characterizes those situations in which rapid, stepwise, conversions take place may sound initially to be counter-intuitive. I believe that the confusion lies in a commonsense notion that to be highly committed means to have many good reasons to support one's belief. If this were so, it seems unlikely that one would give up the belief precipitously, but would require accumulated reasons for gradually losing confidence in it, and hence a gradual change to another position. The error lies in a misunderstanding of commitment. Commitment is not associated with having 'many good reasons to support one's belief', but with persisting in believing 'in spite of good reasons to believe otherwise'. The strong commitment to a belief is like a house of cards. It ought not to be standing at all, for that which supports it is very weak. When it does collapse, the bigger it is, the faster it will fall.

But why would one become committed in the first place to that which is most likely not true? Because one wants to believe it is true, for social or personal reasons, and in the absence of good and sufficient reasons for believing it, commitment is the necessary mechanism for *allowing* such belief to exist and to persist.

People do not make commitments to believe what is obviously true based upon objective evidence, experience, or the straightforward uses of logic. My belief that the sun will come up tomorrow is strong, but I do not have to make a commitment to believe it, for the evidence based upon my own experience is enough. Belief in a particular idea about the nature of God, about the efficacy of prayer, or about the afterlife, may also be strong, but lacking a sufficient factual basis for acceptance of these beliefs, rather than the numerous alternatives posed and accepted by millions of others, may require commitment, or in religious terms, faith. Lack of good reasons for beliefs, and strong commitments to them, go hand in hand. Not only are they correlated, but evidence suggests they are causally connected.[24] Lack of good reasons for beliefs *enhances* commitment to them. Once one has come to accept the belief that Jim Jones is God's messenger, the more one discovers about his infidelities, abuses of children, fraud, or even psychosis, the more committed one becomes.

Conclusions

The relationship between ideological conversion processes and ideological commitment processes has seldom been clearly articulated. In fact, even acknowledging that these are in fact separate processes is seldom done. Considering forces that induce conversion, and other forces that induce commitment, as Control Factors in a cusp catastrophe model makes clear several specific predictions of how these variables are interrelated. Whether or not the cusp catastrophe Behavior Surface accurately describes these relationships is an empirical matter. In this paper I have attempted to show how the available evidence, mostly from research in social psychology, and from case studies and autobiographical reports of converts to religious cults, is largely consistent with what would be predicted from the cusp catastrophe model developed.

Such support, while generally consistent with the model, has severe limitations. The experimental studies are never actually about major ideological issues or about extreme levels of commitment. For both practical and ethical reasons, such experiments are not likely ever to be done on real world ideological conversions. Real world ideological conversions can be studied through the use of case study materials and self-reports of actual converts, but this research is not experimental, and in addition is usually subject to problems of biased reporting, low validity, or inadequate specificity concerning the variables in question. In spite of these limitations, however, it is hoped that framing the important issues in terms of a conceptual model, the cusp catastrophe model, will be helpful in future research development.

Perhaps for social scientists this model will help field researchers in their choices about what variables are most important to try to assess; and it may help experimental researchers in the design of research capable of testing more precise predictions about the dynamic relationships between conversion and commitment forces. Hopefully historians, religious studies scholars, and others will also find here some conceptual tools for better understanding the effects of millennial movements, messianic prophecies, and religious and political extremism. That these are issues of great importance is not in doubt, nor, I believe is there any doubt that we have much yet to learn. More interdisciplinary efforts toward furthering our knowledge about such issues are clearly needed.

References

Anderson, Craig A., 'Inoculation and Counter-Explanation: Debiasing Techniques in the Perseverance of Social Theories', *Social Cognition* 1 (1982), 126-39.

Anderson, Craig A., Mark R. Lepper, and Lee Ross. 'Perseverance of Social Theories: The Role of Explanation in Persistence of Discredited Information', *Journal of Personality and Social Psychology* 39 (1 Supp. 6, 1980), 1037-1049.

Aronson, Elliot, and Judson Mills, 'The Effects of Severity of Initiation on Liking for a Group', *Journal of Abnormal and Social Psychology* 59 (1959), 177-81.

Asch, Solomon E., 'Effects of Group Pressure upon the Modification and Distortion of Judgments', in Harold Guetzkow (ed.), *Groups, Leadership, and Men: Research in Human Relations* (Pittsburgh, PA: Carnegie Press, 1951), 177-90.

Becker, H.S., 'Notes on the Concept of Commitment', *American Journal of Sociology* 66 (1960), 32-40.

Brickman, Philip, *Commitment, Conflict, and Caring* (ed. Richard Sorrentino and Camille Wortman; New York: Prentice Hall, 1987).

Conway, Flo, and Jim Siegelman, *Snapping: America's Epidemic of Sudden Personality Change* (New York: Dell Publishing, 1978).

Downing, Leslie L., 'Cults: Psychological and Legal Issues of Ideological Conversion', (Paper presented at the New England Social Psychological Association Convention; University of Rhode Island, 17 November, 1979).

—'Conversion to Religious Cults', (Paper presented at the New York Conference on Asian Studies; New Paltz, New York, October, 1986).

—'On Being Committed: Theories and Speculations', (Paper presented to the Social Psychology Association of the University of Georgia: Athens, Georgia, 13 February, 1998).

—'Fragile Realities: Conversion and Commitment in Cults and Other Powerful Groups' (Unpublished manuscript, 2000).

Edwards, Christopher, *Crazy for God: The Nightmare of Cult Life* (Englewood Cliff, NJ: Prentice Hall, 1979).

Festinger, Leon, *A Theory of Cognitive Dissonance* (Stanford, CA: Stanford University Press, 1957).

Festinger, Leon, Henry Riecken, and Stanley Schachter, *When Prophesy Fails: A Social and Psychological Study of a Modern Group that Predicted the Destruction of the World* (Minneapolis: University of Minnesota Press, 1956).

Flay, Brian R., 'Catastrophe Theory in Social Psychology: Some Applications to Attitudes and Social Behavior', Behavioral Science 23 (1978), 335-50.

Galanter, Marc, *Cults: Faith, Healing, and Coercion* (New York: Oxford University Press, 1989).

Hearst, Patricia, and Alvin Moscow, *Every Secret Thing* (Garden City, NY: Doubleday, 1982).

Janis, Irving L., *Groupthink* (Boston: Houghton Mifflin, 2nd edn, 1982).

Kanter, Rosabeth Moss, *Commitment and Community: Communes and Utopias in Sociological Perspective* (Cambridge, MA: Harvard University Press, 1972).

Kiesler, Charles A., *The Psychology of Commitment: Experiments Linking Behavior to Belief* (New York: Academic Press, 1971).

Levine, Saul V., *Radical Departures: Desperate Detours to Growing Up* (New York: Harcourt Brace Jovanovich, 1984).

Lifton, Robert J., *Thought Reform and the Psychology of Totalism* (New York: Norton, 1961).

McGuire, William J., 'Inducing Resistance to Persuasion', in L. Berkowitz (ed.), *Advances in Experimental Social Psychology* (New York: Academic Press, 1964), I, 192-229.

Melton, J. Gordon, *Encyclopedic Handbook of Cults in America* (New York: Garland, 1986).

Mosatche, Harriet S., *Searching: Practices and Beliefs of the Religious Cults and Human Potential Groups* (New York: Stavron, 1983).

Pitz, Gordon F., and Leslie L. Downing, 'Optimum Behavior in a Decision-making Task as a Function of Instructions and Payoffs', *Journal of Experimental Psychology* 73 (1967), 549-55.

Ross, Lee, and Craig A. Anderson, 'Shortcomings in the Attribution Process: On the Origins and Maintenance of Erroneous Social Assessments', in D. Kahneman, P. Slovic, and A. Tversky (eds.), *Judgment under Uncertainty: Heuristics and Biases* (New York: Cambridge University Press, 1982).

Rusbult, C.E., J.M. Martz, and C.R. Agnew, 'The Investment Model Scale: Measuring Commitment Level, Satisfaction Level, Quality of Alternatives, and Investment Size', *Personal Relationships* 5 (1998), 357-591.

Streiker, L.D., *Mindbending: Brainwashing, Cults, and Deprogramming in the 80's* (Garden City, NY: Doubleday, 1984).

Tesser, Abraham, 'When Individual Dispositions and Social Pressure Conflict: A Catastrophe', *Human Relations* 33 (1980), 393-407.
Thibaut, John W., and Harold H. Kelley, *The Social Psychology of Groups* (New York: Wiley, 1959).
Thom, René, *Structural Stability and Morphogenesis* (trans. D.H. Fowler; New York: Benjamin, 1975).
Woodcock, A., and M. Davis, *Catastrophe Theory* (New York: Avon, 1978).
Zeeman, E.C., 'Catastrophe Theory', *Scientific American* (April 1976), 65-70, 75-83.

Notes

1. For example, J. Gordon Melton, *Encyclopedic Handbook of Cults in America* (New York: Garland, 1986).

2. Flo Conway and Jim Siegelman, *Snapping: America's Epidemic of Sudden Personality Change* (New York: Dell Publishing, 1978).

3. L.D. Streiker, *Mindbending: Brainwashing, Cults, and Deprogramming in the 80's* (Garden City, NY: Doubleday, 1984).

4. Christopher Edwards, *Crazy for God: The Nightmare of Cult Life* (Englewood Cliff, NJ: Prentice Hall, 1979); and Patricia Hearst and Alvin Moscow, *Every Secret Thing* (Garden City, NY: Doubleday, 1982).

5. Marc Galanter, *Cults: Faith, Healing, and Coercion* (New York: Oxford University Press, 1989); Saul V. Levine, *Radical Departures: Desperate Detours to Growing Up* (New York: Harcourt Brace Jovanovich, 1984); and Robert J. Lifton, *Thought Reform and the Psychology of Totalism* (New York: Norton, 1961).

6. Leon Festinger, Henry Riecken and Stanley Schachter, *When Prophesy Fails: A Social and Psychological Study of a Modern Group that Predicted the Destruction of the World* (Minneapolis: University of Minnesota Press, 1956); and Harriet S. Mosatche, *Searching: Practices and Beliefs of the Religious Cults and Human Potential Groups* (New York: Stavron, 1983).

7. René Thom, *Structural Stability and Morphogenesis* (trans. D.H. Fowler; New York: Benjamin, 1975); E.C. Zeeman, 'Catastrophe Theory', *Scientific American* (April 1976), 65-83; and A. Woodcock and M. Davis, *Catastrophe Theory* (New York: Avon, 1978).

8. Abraham Tesser, 'When Individual Dispositions and Social Pressure Conflict: A Catastrophe', *Human Relations* 33 (1980), 393-407; and Brian R. Flay, 'Catastrophe Theory in Social Psychology: Some Applications to Attitudes and Social Behavior', *Behavioral Science* 23 (1978): 335-50.

9. Leslie L. Downing, 'Cults: Psychological and Legal Issues of Ideological Conversion', (Paper presented at the New England Social Psychological Association Convention; University of Rhode Island, 17 November, 1979); and *idem*, 'Conversion to Religious Cults', (Paper presented at the New York Conference on Asian Studies; New Paltz, New York, October, 1986); *idem*, *Fragile Realities: Conversion and Commitment in Cults and Other Powerful Groups* (Unpublished manuscript, 2000).

10. Leslie L. Downing, 'On Being Committed: Theories and Speculations', (Presented to the Social Psychology Association of the University of Georgia; Athens, Georgia, 13 February, 1998), and Downing, *Fragile Realities*.

11. Leon Festinger, *A Theory of Cognitive Dissonance* (Stanford, CA: Stanford University Press, 1957); and Elliot Aronson and Judson Mills, 'The Effects of Severity of Initiation on Liking for a Group', *Journal of Abnormal and Social Psychology* 59 (1959), 177-81.

12. Rosabeth Moss Kanter, *Commitment and Community: Communes and Utopias in Sociological Perspective* (Cambridge, MA: Harvard University Press, 1972).

13. Philip Brickman, *Commitment, Conflict, and Caring* (ed. Richard Sorrentino and Camille Wortman; New York: Prentice Hall, 1987).

14. Charles A. Kiesler, *The Psychology of Commitment: Experiments Linking Behavior to Belief* (New York: Academic Press, 1971).

15. William J. McGuire, 'Inducing Resistance to Persuasion', in L. Berkowitz (ed.), *Advances in Experimental Social Psychology* (New York: Academic Press, 1964), I, 192-229.

16. Solomon E. Asch, 'Effects of Group Pressure upon the Modification and Distortion of Judgments', in Harold Guetzkow (ed.), *Groups, Leadership, and Men: Research in Human Relations* (Pittsburgh, PA: Carnegie Press, 1951), 177-90.

17. Irving L. Janis, *Groupthink* (Boston: Houghton Mifflin, 2nd edn, 1982).

18. John W. Thibaut and Harold H. Kelley, *The Social Psychology of Groups* (New York: Wiley, 1959); and C.E. Rusbult, J.M. Martz and C.R. Agnew, 'The Investment Model Scale: Measuring Commitment Level, Satisfaction Level, Quality of Alternatives, and Investment Size', *Personal Relationships* 5 (1998), 357-591.

19. H.S. Becker, 'Notes on the Concept of Commitment', *American Journal of Sociology* 66 (1960), 32-40.

20. Gordon F. Pitz and Leslie L. Downing, 'Optimum Behavior in a Decision-making Task as a Function of Instructions and Payoffs', *Journal of Experimental Psychology* 73 (1967), 549-55.

21. Kiesler, *The Psychology of Commitment*.

22. Craig A. Anderson, Mark R. Lepper and Lee Ross, 'Perseverance of Social Theories: The Role of Explanation in Persistence of Discredited Information', *Journal of Personality and Social Psychology* 39 (1 Supp. 6, 1980), 1037-1049; and Lee Ross and Craig A. Anderson, 'Shortcomings in the Attribution Process: On the Origins and Maintenance of Erroneous Social Assessments', in D. Kahneman, P. Slovic and A. Tversky (eds.), *Judgment under Uncertainty: Heuristics and Biases* (New York: Cambridge University Press, 1982).

23. Edwards, *Crazy for God*; and Levine, *Radical Departures*.

24. Brickman, *Commitment, Conflict, and Caring*.

The Retreat of the Millennium

Damian Thompson

Introduction

Is millenarianism spreading or becoming marginalized in Western society? On the one hand, technological and social changes have lent new vitality to apocalyptic images of Antichrist, Armageddon and conspiracy, and have carved out fresh audiences for them. On the other, the malleability and detachability of these images points to a certain shallowness: apocalyptic theology is increasingly being turned into entertainment, thereby losing much of its social impact. This article will suggest that, by studying the marginalization of millenarian belief, we can better understand the effect of secularization on religious ideas in general. Modernity fragments the social support that millenarian prophecies require in order to remain plausible; and this helps explain why the dawn of the third Christian millennium, a moment supposedly pregnant with apocalyptic significance, passed so uneventfully.

Millenarianism, Charisma, and Subcultural Deviance

Scholars of millenarianism have tended to stress its remarkable ideological power. Norman Cohn, writing about the revolutionary millenarians of the later Middle Ages, describes the effect of apocalyptic prophets on the rootless and disorientated masses:

> For what the *propheta* offered his followers was not simply a chance to improve their lot and escape from pressing anxieties—it was also, and above all, the prospect of carrying out a divinely ordained mission of stupendous, unique importance. This fantasy performed a real function for them, both as an escape from their isolated and atomized condition and as an emotional compensation for their abject status; so it quickly came to enthrall them in their turn. And what emerged was a new group—a restlessly dynamic and utterly ruthless group which, obsessed by the apocalyptic fantasy and filled with the conviction of its own infallibility, set itself infinitely above the rest of humanity and recognized no claims save that of its own supposed mission.[1]

Cohn's descriptions of crazed medieval millenarians have strongly colored what one might call the ideal type of the millenarian movement—

that is, a movement whose members, thanks to its ideology, undergo the most remarkable social and psychological transformation. In the last 2,000 years, hundreds of such radical movements have taken root in the most diverse soil: their participants have included early Christian heretics, medieval Bohemian peasants, North-West frontier tribesmen, Islamic scholars, Chinese merchants, Plains Indians, Japanese university students and the followers of Melanesian cargo cults. Many of these groups have indulged in extremes of behavior, such as taking up arms against the secular state, which arise from their belief in imminent apocalyptic catastrophe leading to the dawn of a new world; as a result, scholars and other commentators have tended to present the formation of dynamic millennial movements (including violently-inclined millennial cults) as a likely consequence of the spread of apocalyptic ideas.

Such a view is misleading. Millenarian ideology, defined by Cohn as belief in salvation that is collective, terrestrial, imminent, total and miraculous,[2] is a necessary but certainly not sufficient condition for the emergence of such movements. Historically, the proportion of apocalyptic prophets who have succeeded in attracting a vigorous following, as opposed to a mere audience, is relatively small. Of the 3,482 millenarian documents listed by Tom McIver in his annotated bibliography,[3] only a few are associated with the sort of movement described by Cohn. The vast majority of this literature is the work of freelance authors whose attempts to demonstrate that the world is coming to an end are—despite their rhetorical exhortations—not seriously intended as a spur to radical social action.

Not only do people consume millenarian literature without resorting to behavior that is in any way millenarian, but even religions that proclaim the end of the world do not necessarily allow those teachings to overshadow their daily activities. As J. Gordon Melton points out:

> Though one or more prophecies may be important to a group, they will be set within a complex set of beliefs and interpersonal relationships. They may serve as one of several important sources determining group activity, but the prediction is only one support device for the group, not the essential rafter. The belief that prophecy is the organizing or determining principle for millennial groups is common among media representatives, nonmillennial religious rivals, and scholars. In their eagerness to isolate what they see as a decisive or interesting fact, they ignore or pay only passing attention to the larger belief structure of the group and the role that structure plays in the life of believers.[4]

Indeed, prophecy often gradually ceases to be the organizing principle of religious movements. Several important religions, including mainstream

Christianity, have first marginalized and then effectively abandoned the millenarian elements in their heritage, and one can see this process at work in many contemporary sects and denominations, such as the Seventh-Day Adventists and the Unification Church.

How can we account for the lack of excitement within supposedly apocalyptic groups, and their willingness to tone down doctrines relating to the end of the world? As I have argued elsewhere,[5] the special fragility of millenarianism arises from the nature of its claims to charismatic authority. For Max Weber, the distinguishing feature of this type of authority was that it was rooted in 'specific gifts of the body and spirit'; typically, it revolved around war leaders, prophets or magicians whose special powers persuaded others to grant them authority.[6] This makes charismatic authority fragile by definition. In Weber's words:

> The charismatic leader gains and maintains authority solely by proving his strength in life. If he wants to be a prophet, he must perform miracles; if he wants to be a war lord, he must perform heroic deeds. Above all, however, his divine mission must 'prove' itself in that those who faithfully surrender to him must fare well. If they do not fare well, he is obviously not the master sent by the gods.[7]

The need for proof is the Achilles' heel of charismatic authority and, especially, of the peculiarly concentrated variety of it associated with millenarianism. Many millenarian prophecies can be fulfilled only by a global catastrophe taking place at the appointed hour; and even those that are less time-specific require current events to proceed according to an apocalyptic script. Small wonder that those millenarian prophets who aspire to a mass following are forced to develop complicated rhetorical strategies in order to prevent themselves being proved wrong. These strategies—some of which are adopted before disconfirmation, as an insurance policy—usually represent a retreat from the prophet's original position; as Jon R. Stone observes, 'the empirical elements of a prophecy are quickly discarded in favor of a nonempirical understanding of its meaning and import to the group'.[8] The proposition that the world will end (or begin to end) in a specific way at a specific time is replaced by vague apocalyptic assertions presented in the broader context of the prophet's spiritual teachings.[9]

This move away from the empirical realm is also a move away from the purest form of charismatic authority, which aspires to direct power over the empirical world. Every time a religious leader manages to tone down the apocalyptic elements in a belief system, charisma is routinized, and this is true irrespective of whether the original author of the prophecies is still alive or not. Weber's original concept of routinization involved the transmission of a leader's special powers to his followers, thereby losing some of their magic and becoming less vulnerable to disconfirmation. But Ralph Schroeder, in his study of Weber, makes the point that charisma can be attributed to ideas as well as to people. This sort of charisma can be understood as the novel impact of doctrines on social life; it is routinized by 'the systematization of a belief system by a stratum of religious virtuosi, or through the accommodation of this belief system to the predispositions of a certain strata of believers'.[10]

Seen from the perspective of the host society, the claims of millenarianism are so extreme that, if accepted unquestioningly, they are bound to have a devastating impact on social life; at the same time, they are so intensely vulnerable to being proved wrong that they invite (and have often produced) crushing disappointment and mockery. In the long term, the costs of millenarian belief usually outweigh the benefits. But the balance of costs and benefits is different if the rough edges can be knocked off millenarian teachings by religious virtuosi—if, for example, apocalyptic ideas can be turned into tools for analyzing geopolitical change. This is what happened in the European Middle Ages, when the predictive millenarianism of the early Christians was routinized into the explanatory variety favored by theologians and political polemicists.[11] But such systematization is often only a step on the road to the safest option of all: effective banishment of apocalypticism from institutional theology. In short, the marginalization of millenarian belief is, like other forms of routinization, the outcome of rational choices; it is not inevitable, but it is likely to happen.

This routinization of millenarian charisma can also be understood as a response to the pressure that minority groups come under to reduce the tension between themselves and society—what Rodney Stark and Roger Finke (2000) call their 'subcultural deviance'.[12] All religious groups can be placed on a spectrum of subcultural deviance, which will often be determined by the extent to which they make claims about the empirical world that society rejects: cults that believe (say) that the world is ruled by satanic lizards will be towards one end, churches that practice therapeutic healing will be towards the other.

The more deviant a group, the higher the costs of belonging to it; but the benefits of belonging to it, subjectively assessed, may also be high. Likewise, routinized religion is attractively easy to subscribe to, but offers only moderate rewards. The challenge for religious groups is to find the right level of deviance or, put differently, a way of preserving the charisma that inspired its founders without offering too many hostages to fortune in the shape of dissonance-inviting claims. Sometimes, a movement's degree of subcultural deviance will increase sharply in response to events; but the gravitational pull of the societal consensus is difficult to resist, and the general trend is downwards. The history of millenarianism offers many clear-cut examples of this tendency: for every group that retreats to the wilderness to do battle with the forces of the state there are dozens that retreat from their own apocalyptic heritage. (Unfortunately for law enforcement bodies, there is no simple formula for determining in advance which group will lurch towards violent millenarianism; it is easy to read too much into bloodthirsty rhetoric.)

Secularization and Entertainment

The reduction of subcultural deviance by religious organizations is analogous to, and often forms part of, secularization. Every time a group abandons claims that intellectual orthodoxy rejects—whether it be the Catholic Church distancing itself from reports of weeping statues at a Marian shrine, or the Church of Scientology de-emphasizing the quasi-magical claims of Dianetics—society's rational world-view is reinforced. The demythologization of religion lies at the heart of secularization, though it is important to stress that secularization in this context does not mean the inevitable withering-away of religious belief envisaged by the founding fathers of sociology, including Weber. A more modest and useful definition is that of Bryan Wilson, for whom the social significance of religion has declined as its functions have been taken over by secular agencies; as a result, religious consciousness has been replaced by 'an empirical, rational, instrumental orientation'.[13] Another proponent of secularization theory, Steve Bruce, puts it as follows: 'Science and technology have not made us atheists, but underlying "rationality" has made us less likely than our forebears to entertain the notion of the divine'.[14]

Bruce's point is a valid one, but I would question his use of the word 'entertain'. Scientific rationality has certainly made modern people less likely to *accept* supposed evidence of the divine and the miraculous: the ease with which most charismatic claims can be subjected to empirical testing means that we demand a far higher standard of proof than previous generations did. But our willingness to *entertain* bizarre, countercultural and counterintuitive ideas is not greatly reduced by the spread of rationality. Religious institutions may have followed the example of the secular world in reducing the number and significance of the dissonance-inviting supernatural claims they make; but similar claims are still being made. Reports of miracles and conspiracies have been pushed to the margins of Western society, in the sense that their plausibility is no longer reinforced by the ideological support of churches and governments in the developed world. Yet, paradoxically, the revolution in information technology makes them more accessible than ever before.

The Internet has contributed to a flourishing of what Colin Campbell calls the 'cultic milieu', a vast pool of unorthodox ideas whose shared feature is that its propositions—which include belief in lost civilizations, alien invasion, Nazi racial science, astrology, Creationism, and apocalyptic conspiracies—are rejected by society, mostly on empirical grounds; in other words, they make claims to charismatic authority that are not recognized by the majority.[15] The motifs circulating and combining in the cultic milieu lack what Peter Berger and Thomas Luckmann called 'plausibility structures'—that is, significant social support that makes it easy for the individual to sustain belief in them over a long period of time.[16] Although it is true that literal belief in deviant propositions can be nurtured within the confines of a tightly knit sect, the vast majority of people who encounter the products of the cultic milieu do not wish to place themselves in a state of high tension with their environment. For example, we were told during the 1990s that millions of Americans believed in alien abduction—but such a 'belief' had a negligible effect on American society. This was because millions of people only ever *entertained* the notion, meaning that they consumed books and films about alien abduction. Sometimes these products emanated from small groups of 'true believers' for whom the concept was deadly serious; sometimes they were put together by speculative entrepreneurs who knew their audience; often it was difficult to tell the difference.

The political scientist Michael Barkun, in his recent book *A Culture of Conspiracy*, draws attention to an important paradox. On the one hand, the nature and influence of what he calls 'stigmatized knowledge' has increased dramatically: 'Motifs, theories and truth claims that once existed in hermetically sealed subcultures have begun to be recycled, often with great rapidity, into popular culture'.[17] On the other hand, the appropriation of countercultural (and especially conspiratorial) themes by the mass media can reduce their potency. The reports of 'black helicopters' circulating on the Far Right in the mid-1990s became less believable once they had been tweaked by Hollywood; very few of the cultic motifs reworked by *The X-Files* survived with their dignity intact. Their charisma had undergone routinization by entertainment.

The free-floating, fast-morphing character of ideas in the cultic milieu lends them a sort of shallow vitality that is ideally suited to the fragmented plausibility structures of modernity. But it is not only stigmatized ideas that are detached from the imaginations of true believers and recycled for a mass market. As James Beckford argues, the deregulation of the religious marketplace means that religious organizations lose control over their historic symbols; religion becomes less a social institution and more of a cultural resource susceptible to many different uses.[18] Catwalk models clutch rosaries; Hollywood celebrities adopt their own version of the Kabbalah; footballers cross themselves; millions of people hover over religious traditions like cultural magpies, appropriating ideas and imageries as they customize their personal cosmologies. One could argue that the dissemination of these motifs points to a residual religiosity. I see it as an aspect of secularization, since this cultural trend does not inspire significant social action and the motifs themselves are denuded of much of their original charismatic power.

Marginalizing the Apocalypse

The retreat of Doomsday from the consciousness of modern men and women tells us a lot about the way dissonance-inviting charismatic claims have been routinized in Western society. Few beliefs require such concentrated social support as millenarianism: there is no precedent for the world ending but there are countless precedents for apocalyptic prophets being proved humiliatingly wrong. 'Mainstream' Christianity in America and Europe is no longer millenarian, in the sense that its adherents expect Jesus to return in their lifetimes; indeed, the absence of such a belief is one of the things that makes it mainstream. Many of the impulses of Christian millenarianism were transferred to secular utopianism; but the ideological disasters of the twentieth century produced their own brand of apocalyptic disappointment and there are now only small islands of secular millenarianism in the modern world.[19] Millenarianism has suffered not only from its own failure to fulfill its promises, but also from the multiplication of choices described by Peter Berger in his book *The Heretical Imperative*. Any single doomsday scenario represents just one option among an almost infinite range of possibilities; and in this respect millenarianism is like any other variety of supernatural belief. Although technology has enormously expanded the range and reach of the religious ideas available to the individual, it has reduced their taken-for-granted quality; the existence of so many alternative beliefs has inevitably shrunk plausibility structures.[20]

That said, the worldwide flourishing of conservative evangelical Christianity in the late-twentieth century appears to invalidate the argument that belief systems are invariably fragmented by modernity, and to demonstrate the continued vitality of the Christian apocalyptic tradition. There are around 200 million conservative Protestants in the world,[21] a high proportion of whom believe in the inerrancy if not the literal truth of the Bible's apocalyptic narrative: that is, the rise of Antichrist, leading to the Rapture and the Tribulation (not necessarily in that order), followed by Armageddon and the millennial reign of Jesus. There are, however, no reliable data establishing the intensity with which these doctrines are held, and it must be stressed that the multiplication of religious choices described by Berger has fragmented Protestant apocalyptic belief into hundreds of rival theories about the timing, order and significance of the Last Days.

The anthropologist Susan Harding has described how, within the conservative evangelical world, discrete traditions have given way to an eschatological free market:

> The old-fashioned dispensationalist scheme is still spoken in sermons on the Rapture, the Tribulation, and the Second Coming, in self-declared pretribulational, premillennial churches (see ads in the Yellow Pages), and in books by (older) Dallas Theological Seminary professors. But believers are routinely exposed to an undifferentiated array of variations in other sermons by their preachers, in other books (the prophecy sections in most Christian bookstores contain a hodgepodge of millennial texts), in television, audio and video tapes, in conversations among Christian friends from other churches.[22]

One could hardly ask for a clearer description of the progressive splintering of plausibility structures—and Harding was writing in 1994, before the heyday of the Internet. Since the advent of the World Wide Web, variations on apocalyptic belief have taken on an even more free-ranging quality. Barkun's *Culture of Conspiracy* shows how cyberspace has provided a laboratory for the conspiratorial theories of the cultic milieu, many of them explicitly apocalyptic and inspired by real events. Within weeks of 11 September, 2001, for example, hundreds of improbable explanations for the attack on the Twin Towers had sprung ready-formed into the public domain, pinning the blame variously on the Federal Government, the Jews, the Masons and reptilian aliens; many Internet authors unmasked Osama bin Laden as the Antichrist of Revelation.[23] While some of these theories could be combined into mega-conspiracies, they mostly contradicted each other. This did not matter very much, however, since (with a few exceptions) the authors were asking the audience to entertain their ideas rather than to head for the hills to await the End.

Barkun refers to this technology-driven variety of apocalypticism as 'improvisational millennialism'. He argues that, despite the undisciplined fashion in which its motifs circulate and combine, they are increasingly being held together by the ideological glue of belief in a New World Order.[24] I agree with him that this is a cause for concern, since shared beliefs about the encroachment of a Satanic one-world government can inspire acts of terrorism (though whether 11 September falls into this category is open to question). But the point I want to stress is that fringe beliefs in a New World Order, however scary, are what is left after Christian millenarianism has atrophied to such a degree that even Bible-believing Protestants invoke the return of Christ as a rhetorical device rather than as a looming inevitability.

When today's born-again Christians employ apocalyptic rhetoric, much of it has an improvisational quality. Furthermore, to a much greater extent than in the past, they often choose to encounter concepts such as Rapture and Tribulation in the form of fiction. The bestselling *Left Behind* thrillers by Tim LaHaye and Jerry Jenkins, which conjure up the horrors of the reign of Antichrist, and which by 2004 had sold over 50 million copies, are intended by their fundamentalist authors to introduce a skeptical audience to the truth of Bible prophecy. Equally, however, one could see them as a means of repackaging End Times doctrines in a way that does not force evangelical Christians to subscribe to their literal truth. Fiction cannot be disconfirmed: no one is embarrassed if an airport thriller is overtaken by events in the real world. In short, the *Left Behind* sequence offers a variety of millenarianism that has been routinized by entertainment. Millions of people have been introduced to the figure of the Antichrist who would never otherwise have heard of him; but they might as well have been introduced to Superman for all the difference it will make to their lives, or to society.

From 1997 to 2003, during the height of the *Left Behind* phenomenon, I conducted fieldwork at Kensington Temple, a large, multi-ethnic Pentecostal church in London. 'KT', as it is known, was founded by the once strongly apocalyptic Elim denomination and is effectively fundamentalist in its theology. Many worshippers had read and enjoyed the *Left Behind* Books; even more had read non-fiction Christian conspiracy tracts about the New World Order. My questionnaire of 2,973 KT members revealed relatively high levels of conspiracy belief: 38 percent of respondents thought that the proposed single European currency was a sign of the Antichrist; 27 percent thought supermarket barcodes were Satanic. But worshippers put the study of the End Times at the bottom of their lists of spiritual priorities, and only 17 percent expected to witness the return of Christ within the first half of the twenty-first century.[25] Moreover, in face-to-face interviews, church members manifested little interest in prophecy, beyond vague assertions that Jesus would return one day 'as the Bible says'.

It is, of course, impossible to generalize from this sample: Britain, unlike America, lacks a strong apocalyptic tradition, and this may have influenced responses, even though over 100 nationalities were represented in the KT congregation. But I felt that my findings were consistent with those of the sociologist James Davison Hunter, who argues that American born-again Christians are subtly de-emphasizing teachings that secular society finds bizarre or distasteful—are, in fact, lowering their subcultural deviance.[26] At KT, people were painfully aware of the mockery that attends prophecies of the end of the world. Looking around the prophecy shelves of their own church bookshop, they found it hard to decide which, if any, of the detailed but contradictory prophetic timetables they should endorse. And so they moved on to what they regarded as the more appealing and relevant subjects of prosperity teaching, prayer and spiritual warfare.

The Year 2000: The Dog That Did Not Bark

Early in the 1990s, academics working in several disciplines came to believe that the approach of the year 2000 would bring about convulsive changes in religion and society. Many books were written pointing out the eschatological significance attached to the third Christian millennium by previous generations; the suggestion was that its actual arrival would stimulate fantasies of the return of Christ and other apocalyptic events, and with them dangerous outbreaks of religious fervor.[27] In the event, with the exception of a handful of cult deaths whose connection to 2000 was never fully established, nothing dramatic happened; even the prospect of secular catastrophe brought about by the Y2K computer glitch evaporated. Like the apocalyptic prophets they studied, 'millennial scholars' found themselves confronted by cognitive dissonance, and were forced to employ rhetorical strategies to explain the non-fulfillment of their prophecies. Some of them felt that the non-event of the year 2000 was in itself mysterious, like the dog in the Sherlock Holmes story that did not bark in the night time.

In fact, there was no mystery, and the non-event should have been anticipated. Amid the tangle of competing interpretations of the year 2000 circulating in the media, no single millenarian scenario could be expected to predominate: the necessary plausibility structures were simply lacking, even within relatively homogenous communities. Evangelical Christians, identified by scholars as the likeliest victims of 'millennial fever', found it hard to agree whether the year 2000 possessed apocalyptic significance—or, if it did, what that might be. The closer the anniversary, the more uncertain they became. The late 1980s had witnessed the launch of ambitious projects to evangelize the world's 'unreached' peoples by 2000, and some of these plans undoubtedly possessed millenarian overtones: the (usually unspoken) implication was that Jesus would return once the Gospel had been spread to the whole world. By the late 1990s, however, these schemes had been drastically scaled down, and leading evangelical preachers made only tentative references to the importance of 2000. My fieldwork at Kensington Temple suggested that church members were aware of media predictions that they would succumb to millennial fever and were determined to prove them wrong: many interviewees were as insistent as any secular commentator that 2000 was 'just a date'.[28] In other words, evangelical Christians, some of whom had once entertained vague apocalyptic expectations of 2000, sensibly abandoned those expectations as the likelihood of disconfirmation increased.

Most mainstream church leaders, meanwhile, had never given much thought to the anniversary; Pope John Paul II was an exception to this, but his vision of 2000 as the beginning of a new springtime for Christianity failed to energize his own bishops, let alone Catholic lay people. In Britain, an ecumenical attempt to persuade the entire population to light candles just before midnight proved comically ill-conceived.[29] Yet this confusion only reflected the experience of secular society. By the time it finally materialized, the long-awaited anniversary exerted less of a grip on the popular imagination than it had a few years earlier, when it was still a peg on which to hang futuristic expectations. Indeed, there was an interesting symmetry between the way secular and evangelical expectations of 2000 were gradually lowered during the 1990s. As the millennial moment rolled around the globe, hundreds of millions of people took part in spectacular celebrations; but, in the absence of any consensus about the special meaning of the date, these were essentially New Year's Eve parties writ large—in other words, pure entertainment. The millennium had been routinized.

Conclusion

This article has argued that complex modern society both circulates and destroys claims to charismatic authority, of which millenarianism is a classic example. As I have suggested elsewhere,[30] secularization weakens millenarianism in an even more direct way than it weakens other forms of religious consensus. The bewildering expansion of the spiritual supermarket, coupled with the ancient susceptibility of apocalyptic prophecy to disconfirmation and the ever more rapid circulation of the information

that disconfirms prophecies, makes it hard to envisage a large-scale outbreak of classic millenarian excitement in the West; we should certainly
not be surprised that the year 2000 failed to produce one. The situation
in the developing world is less clear, admittedly. The rise of the semi-
apocalyptic Falun Gong sect has changed the political landscape of
China in ways that no observer predicted; there is also an unmistakable
apocalyptic edge to the rhetoric of some (though by no means all) radical
Islamists.[31] Perhaps the impact of globalization on developing societies
will give rise to large-scale millenarian movements. That seems unlikely,
however, because the more such societies are integrated into the knowledge economy of the West, the more their charismatic claims will become
vulnerable to the same sort of disconfirmation that has helped to bring
about Western secularization. As a result, millenarianism is likely to
retreat even further towards the intellectual fringe, where its potential for
attracting mockery will be at least as great as its threat to public order.

References

Adherents.com, *Religion Statistics*, May 2003, <http://www.adherents.com> (October 15,
    2004).
Barkun, Michael, *A Culture of Conspiracy: Apocalyptic Visions in Contemporary America*
    (Berkeley, Los Angeles, and London: University of California Press, 2003).
Barna, George, *The Barna Group*, <http://www.Barna.org> (October 15, 2004).
Berger, Peter L., *The Heretical Imperative: Contemporary Possibilities of Religious Affir-
    mation* (London: Collins, 1980 [1979]).
Berger, Peter L., and Thomas Luckmann, *The Social Construction of Reality: A Treatise in
    the Sociology of Knowledge* (Harmondsworth: Penguin, 1971 [1966]).
Beckford, James A., 'Social Movements as Free-floating Religious Phenomena', in Richard
    K. Fenn (ed.), *The Blackwell Companion to Sociology of Religion* (Oxford: Basil
    Blackwell, 2001), 232-33.
Bruce, Steve, 'The Social Process of Secularization', in Richard K. Fenn (ed.), *The Blackwell
    Companion to Sociology of Religion* (Oxford: Basil Blackwell, 2001), 249-63.
Campbell, Colin, 'The Cult, the Cultic Milieu and Secularisation', in Jeffrey Kaplan and
    Heléne Lööw (eds.), *The Cultic Milieu: Oppositional Subcultures in an Age of
    Globalization* (Walnut Creek, CA: Altamira Press, 2002), 12-25.
Cohn, Norman, *The Pursuit of the Millennium: Revolutionary Millenarians and Mystical
    Anarchists of the Middle Ages* (London: Pimlico, rev. edn 1993 [1970]).
Cook, David, 'Muslim Apocalyptic and Jihad', *Jerusalem Studies in Arabic and Islam* 20
    (1996), 66-104.
Csordas, Thomas J., *Language, Charisma, and Creativity: The Ritual Life of a Religious Move-
    ment* (Berkeley, Los Angeles and London: University of California Press, 1997).
Harding, Susan, 'Imagining the Last Days: The Politics of Apocalyptic Language', in Martin
    E. Marty and R. Scott Appleby (eds.), *Accounting for Fundamentalisms: The Dynamic
    Character of Movements* (The Fundamentalism Project, 4; Chicago and London:
    University of Chicago Press, 1994).

Hunter, James Davison, *American Evangelicalism: Conservative Religion and the Quandary of Modernity* (New Brunswick, NJ: Rutgers University Press, 1983).

—*Evangelicalism: The Coming Generation* (Chicago: University of Chicago Press, 1987).

Lofland, John, *Doomsday Cult: A Study of Conversion, Proselytization, and Maintenance of Faith* (New York: Irvington, enlarged edn, 1977).

Lynas, Stephen, *Challenging Time: The Churches' Millennium Experience* (London: Churches Together in England, 2001).

McGinn, Bernard, *Visions of the End: Apocalyptic Traditions in the Middle Ages* (New York: Columbia University Press, 1998 [1979]).

McIver, Tom, *The End of the World: An Annotated Bibliography* (Jefferson, NC, and London: McFarland, 1999).

Melton, J. Gordon, 'Spiritualization and Reaffirmation: What Really Happens When Prophecy Fails', in Stone (ed.), *Expecting Armageddon*, 145-57.

Mills, Watson E. (ed.), *Lutterworth Dictionary of the Bible* (Cambridge: Lutterworth Press, 1990).

Schroeder, Ralph, *Max Weber and the Sociology of Culture* (London: SAGE Publications, 1992).

Stark, Rodney, and Roger Finke, *Acts of Faith: Explaining the Human Side of Religion* (Berkeley, Los Angeles, and London: University of California Press, 2000).

Stone, Jon R., 'Introduction', in Stone (ed.), *Expecting Armageddon*, 1-29.

Stone, Jon R. (ed.), *Expecting Armageddon: Essential Readings in Failed Prophecy* (London and New York: Routledge, 2000).

Thompson, Damian, *The End of Time: Faith and Fear in the Shadow of the Millennium* (London: Sinclair-Stevenson, 1996).

—'Fundamentally Wrong,' in the *Spectator* (29 September, 2001).

—*Waiting for Antichrist: Charisma and Apocalypse in a Pentecostal Church* (New York and London: Oxford University Press, 2005).

Weber, Max, *From Max Weber: Essays in Sociology* (trans., ed. and with an 'Introduction' by H.H. Gerth and C. Wright Mills; London: Routledge and Kegan Paul, 1970 [1948]).

Wilson, Bryan R., *Religion in Sociological Perspective* (Oxford: Oxford University Press, 1982).

Notes

1.   Norman Cohn, *The Pursuit of the Millennium: Revolutionary Millenarians and Mystical Anarchists of the Middle Ages* (London: Pimlico, rev. edn, 1993 [1970]), 285.

2.   Cohn, *The Pursuit of the Millennium*, 13. Any attempt to distinguish between apocalyptic and millenarian ideas is fraught with definitional problems, since different scholars employ the terms in different ways. Biblical scholars recognize a specific genre of works known as apocalypses, in which heavily symbolic dreams and visions prophesy a clash of cosmic forces leading to the imminent end of history. (See the *Lutterworth Dictionary of the Bible*, edited by Watson E. Mills [Cambridge: Lutterworth Press, 1990], 36-37.) The earliest surviving example of this genre, the Book of Daniel, is a Jewish document dating to the second century BC, though it and other apocalypses are influenced by older Zoroastrian traditions. The earliest religious movements that can be described as millenarian according to Cohn's definition, such as the early Christian Montanists, drew heavily on the theology of the apocalyptic genre; millenarian visions typically envisage a cosmic struggle or catastrophe that can be described

as apocalyptic, and in common usage the adjectives 'apocalyptic' and 'millenarian' are virtually interchangeable. My own approach is to employ 'apocalyptic' and 'apocalypticism' as occasional synonyms for 'millenarian' and 'millenarianism', and to distinguish instead between varieties of millenarianism.

3. Tom McIver, *The End of the World: An Annotated Bibliography* (Jefferson, NC, and London: McFarland, 1999).

4. J. Gordon Melton, 'Spiritualization and Reaffirmation: What Really Happens When Prophecy Fails', in Jon R. Stone (ed.), *Expecting Armageddon: Essential Readings in Failed Prophecy* (London and New York: Routledge, 2000), 147.

5. Damian Thompson, *Waiting for Antichrist: Charisma and Apocalypse in a Pentecostal Church* (New York and London: Oxford University Press, 2005).

6. Max Weber, *From Max Weber: Essays in Sociology* (trans., ed. and with an Introduction by H.H. Gerth and C. Wright Mills; London: Routledge and Kegan Paul, 1970 [1948]), 245.

7. Weber, *From Max Weber*, 249.

8. Jon R. Stone, 'Introduction' to Stone (ed.), *Expecting Armageddon*, 25.

9. A good example of this process is provided by the Unification Church of the Revd Sun Myung Moon, which during the 1960s taught that the millennium would begin in 1967. In the 1970s, Moon moved away from date-setting and, while still teaching that the millennium was imminent, adopted a more flexible timetable. See John Lofland, *Doomsday Cult: A Study of Conversion, Proselytization, and Maintenance of Faith* (New York: Irvington, enlarged edn, 1977), 281-82.

10. Ralph Schroeder, *Max Weber and the Sociology of Culture* (London: SAGE Publications, 1992), 17-18. Schroeder's argument seems to me compatible with recent perspectives of charismatic authority that emphasize its socially constructed and rhetorical character, and place the locus of charisma in social interaction; see, for example, Thomas J. Csordas, *Language, Charisma, and Creativity: The Ritual Life of a Religious Movement* (Berkeley, Los Angeles and London: University of California Press, 1997), 133-40.

11. Bernard McGinn, *Visions of the End: Apocalyptic Traditions in the Middle Ages* (New York: Columbia University Press, 1998 [1979]), 35. For a discussion of the distinction between predictive and explanatory millenarianism, see Damian Thompson, *Waiting for Antichrist*, ch. 2.

12. Rodney Stark and Roger Finke, *Acts of Faith: Explaining the Human Side of Religion* (Berkeley, Los Angeles, and London: University of California Press, 2000), 14.

13. Bryan R. Wilson, *Religion in Sociological Perspective* (Oxford: Oxford University Press, 1982), 149.

14. Steve Bruce, 'The Social Process of Secularization', in Richard K. Fenn (ed.), *The Blackwell Companion to Sociology of Religion* (Oxford: Basil Blackwell, 2001), 253.

15. Colin Campbell, 'The Cult, the Cultic Milieu and Secularization', in Jeffrey Kaplan and Heléne Lööw (eds.), *The Cultic Milieu: Oppositional Subcultures in an Age of Globalization* (Walnut Creek, CA: Altamira Press, 2002), 12-25.

16. Peter L. Berger and Thomas Luckmann, *The Social Construction of Reality: A Treatise in the Sociology of Knowledge* (Harmondsworth: Penguin, 1971 [1966]), 174.

17. Michael Barkun, *A Culture of Conspiracy: Apocalyptic Visions in Contemporary America* (Berkeley, Los Angeles, and London: University of California Press, 2003), 33.

18. James A. Beckford, 'Social Movements as Free-floating Religious Phenomena', in Richard K. Fenn (ed.), *The Blackwell Companion to Sociology of Religion* (Oxford: Basil Blackwell, 2001), 232-33.

19. Michael Barkun, *A Culture of Conspiracy*, 18.

20. For a discussion of this point, see Peter L. Berger, *The Heretical Imperative: Contemporary Possibilities of Religious Affirmation* (London: Collins, 1980 [1979]), ch. 1.

21. Source: *Adherents.com*, a leading Internet database of religious statistics, updated May 2003.

22. Susan Harding, 'Imagining the Last Days: The Politics of Apocalyptic Language', in Martin E. Marty and R. Scott Appleby (eds.), *Accounting for Fundamentalisms: The Dynamic Character of Movements* (The Fundamentalism Project, 4; Chicago and London: University of Chicago Press, 1994), 66.

23. Michael Barkun, *A Culture of Conspiracy*, 158-69.

24. Michael Barkun, *A Culture of Conspiracy*, 184.

25. Thompson, *Waiting for Antichrist*, ch. 6.

26. James Davison Hunter, *American Evangelicalism: Conservative Religion and the Quandary of Modernity* (New Brunswick, NJ: Rutgers University Press, 1983); *idem*, *Evangelicalism: The Coming Generation* (Chicago: University of Chicago Press, 1987). For more recent data, see various surveys by the evangelical pollster George Barna at www.barna.org, which suggest that the lifestyles of evangelicals and non-evangelicals are not as sharply differentiated as one might imagine.

27. For a particularly painful example of year 2000 hype, see Damian Thompson, *The End of Time: Faith and Fear in the Shadow of the Millennium* (London: Sinclair-Stevenson, 1996).

28. Thompson, *Waiting for Antichrist*, ch. 7.

29. A good account of the failure of the English Churches to agree on the significance of the millennium can be found in Stephen Lynas, *Challenging Time: The Churches' Millennium Experience* (London: Churches Together in England, 2001).

30. Thompson, *Waiting for Antichrist*, ch. 8.

31. See, for example David Cook, 'Muslim Apocalyptic and Jihad', *Jerusalem Studies in Arabic and Islam* 20 (1996), 66-104. Not only does jihadist Islam possess its own millenarian eschatology, but it also borrows from some of the prophecy writings of fundamentalist Christians: see my article, 'Fundamentally Wrong', in the *Spectator* (29 September, 2001). Some of the American-inspired Islamic apocalyptic literature may have influenced the actions of terrorists; however, many of its consumers treat it as a form of spiritual entertainment, in which respect they resemble Christian prophecy enthusiasts.

The Menace of Media-driven Public Credulity:
Will a Distorted Faith Now Win out?

Daniel C. Noel

When Paul Tillich wrote *Dynamics of Faith* in 1957, Wilfred Cantwell Smith, the historian of religions, had yet to publish his two books on belief, which did not appear until the late 1970s.

Still, it was Tillich, in *Dynamics of Faith*, who identified the problem which Cantwell Smith was to trace to its historical sources and which the visual media since the 1950s, I will argue, have exacerbated to an extreme state. In my brief article I will be exploring the deep roots of this problem with Cantwell Smith's help and its strange fruits by consulting several interpreters of the media, for my contention is that it is a besetting dilemma for the future of public religion in America.

Tillich's name for it is still apt: he called it 'the distortion of faith'—and I am stressing in particular what he termed the 'intellectualistic' distortion of faith. He described it tersely: this distortion involves misconstruing faith as 'an act of knowledge with a low degree of evidence'.[1] Such a misconstrual, said Tillich, confuses faith with 'belief', which differs importantly from it, although he did not closely examine this crucial difference or its historical construction in his little book. Wilfred Cantwell Smith did, however, to our great benefit.

It is the clear finding of his research that belief has only come to be widely—publicly—meant as a cognitive claim about empirical reality under the impetus of modernity, notwithstanding possible prefigurations in Greek thought. That is, it has only acquired this meaning under the impetus of the reforming of Western Christendom in the sixteenth century, the emergence of natural science in the seventeenth, and the rationalism of the eighteenth.

Cantwell Smith's two books, reissued in 1998 as *Believing: An Historical Perspective* and *Faith and Belief: The Difference between Them*, make this major point in painstaking detail (though they are importantly supplemented by Peter Harrison's study, *The Bible, Protestantism, and the Rise of Natural Science*, also from 1998).[2]

Cantwell Smith's groundbreaking investigation resulted in the remarkable, largely because remarkably overlooked, discovery that the etymology of the word 'belief' reveals it to be cognate with the German *beliebe* and the Latin *libido*, rooting it in the original sense of loving and desiring. Indeed, until its transformation beginning in the sixteenth century it in no way designated a propositional or literalistic claim about matters of fact, but rather a heartfelt cherishing or loving trust and loyalty, a devotion or, indeed, a 'faith' in the broadest possible sense (as also intended by the Bible's *pistis* and the early Church's *credo*).

Although philosophers in recent decades have distinguished between 'belief-that' and 'belief-in'—and Cantwell Smith acknowledges that the latter, belief-in, retains something of the pre-modern etymology of belief —it is just as clear that belief-that, the cognitive claim, is the main sense given us by five centuries of modernity.

This momentous redefinition of an absolutely pivotal term in the understanding and self-understanding of religion has served well the necessary skepticism of science, operating in collusion with the *sola scriptura* literalism of the Protestant Reformers.

Unfortunately, this collusion, Cantwell Smith shows, has been in many ways disastrous not only for our retrospective assessments of the medieval Church but also for the thought and practice of modern Christianity, despite mitigating accommodations and adjustments.

At all events, it served the hermeneutical needs of modernity, the literalistic needs of scientific *and* a certain kind of biblical interpretation in particular, as Harrison brilliantly demonstrates, for this crucial word and concept to be so sharply re-conceived.

Admittedly 'faith', in the fuller sense of heartfelt commitment (Tillich's 'ultimate concern'), has continued to function in a fashion, but it has too often been confused, to its detriment, as Tillich made plain, with narrow believing—or credulity—by modern observers and religious participants alike.

However, the situation with belief, and therefore with faith, is even more beleaguered than this, because another factor aggravates the history—in this case the recent history—of believing.

I refer to the rise to cultural dominance of the mass media, more particularly the visual media of film and television, along with the increasingly image-laden Internet. These forces of, mainly, the past 50 years are, as Marshall McLuhan proclaimed, far more than neutral conveyers of content. Their mediating processes are themselves, he famously insisted, 'the message'. Years later, when his views are debated as to their postmodern applicability, we can point to *both* content and process as the media's messages, although the techniques of mediation have indeed become more and more sophisticated, and I will be focusing on them in much of what follows.

In fact, so sophisticated have such processes become that they have overwhelmed our educated knowledge, hard-won since the advent of still photography, that seeing under the auspices of these media is hardly reliable enough to be believing. In our visual culture, truth has become a kind of 'special effect'. But we believe the manufactured images anyway.

This is perhaps the crux of what is building toward an epistemological crisis for public religion: 'media credulity'—or 'media-driven public credulity', the full name used by anthropologists Benson Saler and Charles Zeigler, extrapolating from a book on television entitled *Prime Time*. The three authors of that volume, writing in 1994, point out that 'today, the merger of information and entertainment has become so rapid and widespread as to threaten the very distinction between fact and fiction'.[3]

Obviously it is easier to be driven into credulousness when that distinction has been blurred, so that the situation thus described raises at least one central question at the outset: how did the technological mediation of images come to assume such control over the credulity our believing had been forced to serve under the conditions of modernity? We shall see that it is not only television's 'video verité products', as Saler and Ziegler characterize the infotainment contents *Prime Time* decries, but the processes of mediation as well that contribute to this situation.

Moreover, the media-blurring of the fact-fiction distinction was being discussed by writers on the media well before 1994, as ever-more-effective credulity-driving techniques of mediation to achieve such confusion were emerging. From the special effects of early movies to the digital cinematography and videography of the 1990s and beyond, seeing has been seduced into believing in increasingly 'effective' ways.

A sampling of testimonies, one each from the 1970s and 1980s, as well as another from the 1990s, can help me elaborate this point.

In 1977 former advertising executive Jerry Mander published his book, *Four Arguments for the Elimination of Television*. In a section called 'The Inherent Believability of All Images', Mander argues that TV images are superceding in our minds the images we have from outside of television. And this centrally involves, he says, our believing:

> Seeing is believing... Only since the ascendancy of the media has this been opened to question. Throughout the hundreds of thousands of generations of human existence, whatever we saw with our eyes was concrete and reliable. Experience was directly between us and the natural environment. Nonmediated. Nonprocessed. Not altered by other humans.[4]

Notwithstanding mirages in the desert or camouflaged animals in the jungle, we could usually trust our eyes—but, problematically, we still do so in the artificial environment of the media, exclusively made up, as it were, of mirage and camouflage. 'The media, all media but particularly moving-image media, which present data so nearly natural, effectively convert our naive and automatic trust in the reliability of images into their own authority.'[5]

Mander is quick to back up these large accusations with empirical studies of 'television and social behavior'.[6] He then elaborates that

> we assume that our rational processes protect us from implantation, or brainwashing. What we fail to realize is the difference between fact and image. Our objective processes can help us resist only one kind of implantation. There is no rejection of images.[7]

Thus, for Jerry Mander, writing three decades ago, televisual images are irresistible to belief because, as he entitles another section, 'All Television Is Real'.[8]

Certainly television has not been eliminated, has instead proliferated, since 1977, and Mander's arguments have been denounced by Neil Postman as a 'straight Luddite position'[9] in his own critique, *Amusing Ourselves to Death: Public Discourse in the Age of Show Business*, published eight years later. It is noteworthy, however, that Postman neglects to respond to Mander's points about the problematic credibility of TV images while describing something very close to this same threat himself.

Early on in Postman's book, in fact, we find a chapter entitled 'Media as Epistemology' which contains the following observation:

> 'Seeing is believing' has always had a preeminent status as an epistemological axiom, but 'saying is believing', 'reading is believing', 'counting is believing', 'deducing is believing', and 'feeling is believing' are others that have risen or fallen in importance as cultures have undergone media change. As a culture moves from orality to writing to printing to televising, its ideas of truth move with it...every epistemology is the epistemology of a stage of media development.[10]

This thoughtfully complexifies Mander's condemnation; nevertheless, Postman does end up particularly denouncing television as a distorting epistemology, pernicious to public discourse. He insists that 'television not only is inferior to a print-based epistemology but is dangerous and absurdist'.[11]

Although Postman is an avowed champion of typography he allows that it 'made modern science possible but transformed religious sensibility into mere superstition',[12] interestingly echoing Wilfred Cantwell Smith's findings about the redefinition of belief which consigned medieval devotion to the category of discredited knowledge. A few pages later, Postman actually says that 'beginning in the sixteenth century, a great epistemological shift had taken place',[13] but he is referring to the impact of Gutenberg, not the semantic distortion of belief. With the advantage of both perspectives, of course, we can see that these developments must certainly have been mutually reinforcing. Furthermore, it seems that if typography can be made to serve a distorted faith, we are now learning that the mass-mediation of images cannot help but do so.

Postman implies as much in saying of the advent of photographs in newspapers that by the end of the nineteenth century, 'for countless Americans, seeing, not reading, became the basis for believing'.[14] And soon enough, sounding even more like Mander, he once again indicts the epistemology of television very specifically:

> Television has achieved the status of 'meta-medium'—an instrument that directs not only our knowledge of the world, but our knowledge of *ways of knowing* as well… Its ecology, which includes not only its physical characteristics and symbolic code but the conditions in which we normally attend to it, is taken for granted, accepted as natural…its epistemology goes largely unnoticed.[15]

I shall be returning to this hidden quality of television epistemology.

Amusing Ourselves to Death, for its part, closes with a discussion of religion on TV—which is to say, televangelism. Here Postman concludes that 'most of the religion available to us on television is "fundamentalist", which explicitly disdains ritual and theology in favor of direct communication with the Bible itself, that is, with God'.[16] Lamentably, he never connects the biblical literalism of fundamentalist belief with the epistemological issues raised by his investigation of show-business-driven media beyond pointing out that the visual image of the televangelist, not the cogency of the claims made in the sermon, is the determinant of credibility. Postman never asks *why* fundamentalism should dominate religious offerings on American TV.

A more recent work of media criticism does deal with this question in its way, while casting another vote for the claim that the visual media have credulity-driving effects.

Jeffrey Scheuer's 1999 book, *The Sound Bite Society: Television and the American Mind*, in mounting an argument that TV is an intellectually-simplifying force in the service of political conservatism, and in drawing on assorted media studies writers including both Mander and Postman, does also discuss important aspects of television's incitement to belief.

For instance, Scheuer sounds a note very much like Mander's discussion of 'seeing is believing' when he writes that:

> Just as we are conditioned to trust our senses in apprehending our immediate environment, we are culturally conditioned to regard visual images—photographic, cinematic, or televisual—as faithful renderings of the world beyond the pinpoint we occupy in space and time.[17]

A page later he continues this point: 'This superficial fidelity to the human senses imparts a strong simplifying bias: in appearance, TV images are indisputably truthful and familiar'.[18] He later reiterates his appraisal by commenting that 'television is so pervasively and visually credible that in many ways it effectively merges with the rest of experience... If we give up TV entirely...at least at first, it doesn't seem normal. Television is the norm.'[19] If television is the norm for living and knowing in our culture—and Scheuer's book is only a few years old—what does that say about the force and inescapability of the literal belief, the credulity, which this medium is driving in/to the public mind?

In a section entitled 'Teleconsciousness: The Synthetic Revolution', Scheuer goes on to emphasize that 'the camera doesn't question the completeness or veracity of what it sees: it doesn't recognize, much less examine, its own mediating effects'.[20]

This strikes me as another very significant consideration, hinted at by Postman: these visual media automatically *mask* their processes of mediation—which is to say, in part, that they hide the methods by which they are inducing credulity in the viewer. Consequently, viewers are unaware of and without choice in the matter of their own indoctrination as believers. Or, as Scheuer puts it regarding 'teleconsciousness', 'we cannot fully differentiate what we know from TV and what we know from direct experience or reflection; the distinction itself loses meaning, and we don't even try'.[21] Indeed, he concludes, 'television, in most genres...invades reality by stealth and displaces the real, both in our minds and in our daily lives'.[22]

It is perhaps this 'stealth' of TV's epistemology that should particularly concern us. How can we adjust our understanding of public religion, or the meaning of faith in public life, in a media culture of credulity when the effects of the latter on our perceiving and thinking are so effectively surreptitious in nature?

Furthermore, following through on another earlier point, it is indubitable that onrushing technological innovations in media evolution will only strengthen this stealth, will only, as Scheuer states, 'enhance television's ability to subvert, *and camouflage its subversions of*, the real'[23] (emphasis added). Mediated images, more and more, will become 'perceptually credible but factually impossible',[24] and we will not, in many cases, care that they are.

And, finally, this is where, from his political direction, Scheuer hints at a reason for the domination of television's religious programming by fundamentalism. He places fundamentalism with two other true-believing 'orthodoxies' in American culture:

> Two orthodoxies have historically served as the great sea anchors of American culture, blunting and deferring its collisions with modernity. One is religious fundamentalism; the other is market fundamentalism, the simple, uncritical gospel of unlimited enterprise, growth, and consumption. They are forces of tradition and moral certainty, each rooted in radical simplicity… A third American orthodoxy, more subtly reactionary in its implications, and linked to faith in the market, is scientism, a blind faith in technology… Television, without intent or design, has failed to challenge, and in important ways has advanced each of these orthodoxies…[25]

While 'market fundamentalism' is a new term for me, I should like to underscore the linkage of the more familiar religious form of fundamentalism with *scientism* here at my paper's end in order to recall Wilfred Cantwell Smith's indictment of early modern scientists as well as Protestant Reformers in the fateful re-definition of belief. Scheuer helps us see this redefinition as the necessary pre-condition for the credulous fundamentalisms which he is confirming as massively influential in contemporary life—including religious life—through these social orthodoxies.

And Jeffrey Scheuer, we should note, is also identifying his three fundamentalist orthodoxies as beneficiaries of the subtle credulity fostered—as Jerry Mander and Neil Postman have argued for several decades—by the visual media whose images are everywhere in our midst and our minds today, and whose processes cannot but be shaping our public as well as our private religion. This menace of a distorted faith cannot be dealt with unless we understand its complex history and its contemporary exacerbation.

References

Harrison, Peter, *The Bible, Protestantism, and the Rise of Natural Science* (Cambridge: Cambridge University Press, 1998).

Ihde, Don, *Expanding Hermeneutics: Visualism in Science* (Evanston, IL: Northwestern University Press, 1998).

Kubey, Robert, and Mihaly Csikszentmihalyi, 'Television Addiction Is No Mere Metaphor', *Scientific American* (February 2002), 74-80.

Lichter, S. Peter, Linda S. Lichter, and Stanley Rothman, *Prime Time* (Washington, DC: Regnery Publishing, 1994).

Mander, Jerry, *Four Arguments for the Elimination of Television* (New York: William Morrow and Company, 1978).

Postman, Neil, *Amusing Ourselves to Death: Public Discourse in the Age of Show Business* (New York: Viking Press, 1985).

Saler, Benson, Charles A. Ziegler, and Charles B. Moore, *UFO Crash at Roswell: The Genesis of a Modern Myth* (Washington, DC: Smithsonian Institution Press, 1997).

Scheuer, Jeffrey, *The Sound Bite Society: Television and the American Mind* (New York: Four Walls Eight Windows, 1999).

Smith, Wilfred Cantwell, *Believing: An Historical Perspective* (Oxford: Oneworld Publications, 1998 [1977]).

—*Faith and Belief: The Difference between Them* (Oxford: Oneworld Publications, 1998 [1979]).

Sommerville, C., John, *How the News Makes Us Dumb: The Death of Wisdom in an Information Society* (Downers Grove, IL: InterVarsity Press, 1999).

Tillich, Paul, *Dynamics of Faith* (New York: Harper Torchbooks, 1958).

Weimann, Gabriel, *Communicating Unreality: Modern Media and the Reconstruction of Reality* (Thousand Oaks: Sage Publications, 2000).

Notes

1.   Paul Tillich, *Dynamics of Faith* (New York: Harper Torchbooks, 1958), 33.

2.   Wilfred Cantwell Smith, *Believing: An Historical Perspective* (Oxford: Oneworld Publications, 1998 [1977]), and *idem, Faith and Belief: The Difference between Them* (Oxford: Oneworld Publications, 1998 [1979]). Peter Harrison, *The Bible, Protestantism, and the Rise of Natural Science* (Cambridge: Cambridge University Press, 1998).

3.   S. Peter Lichter, Linda S. Lichter, and Stanley Rothman, *Prime Time* (Washington, DC: Regnery Publishing, 1994). See Benson Saler, Charles A. Ziegler, and Charles B. Moore, *UFO Crash at Roswell: The Genesis of a Modern Myth* (Washington, DC: Smithsonian Institution Press, 1997), ch. 5, regarding 'media-driven public credulity'.

4.   Jerry Mander, *Four Arguments for the Elimination of Television* (New York: William Morrow and Company, 1978), 246.

5.   Mander, *Four Arguments*, 249-50.

6.   Mander, *Four Arguments*, 253-55.

7.   Mander, *Four Arguments*, 258.

8.   Mander, *Four Arguments*, 250.

9.   Neil Postman, *Amusing Ourselves to Death: Public Discourse in the Age of Show Business* (New York: Viking Press, 1985), 158.

10.   Postman, *Amusing Ourselves to Death*, 24.

11.   Postman, *Amusing Ourselves to Death*, 27.

12.   Postman, *Amusing Ourselves to Death*, 29.

13.   Postman, *Amusing Ourselves to Death*, 31.

14.   Postman, *Amusing Ourselves to Death*, 74.

15.   Postman, *Amusing Ourselves to Death*, 78-79.

16.   Postman, *Amusing Ourselves to Death*, 122.

17.   Jeffrey Scheuer, *The Sound Bite Society: Television and the American Mind* (New York: Four Walls Eight Windows,1999), 94. [Editorial Note: According to Robert Kubey and Mihaly Csikszentmihalyi, our instinctual responses to 'any sudden or novel

stimulus' renders viewers especially vulnerable to this medium. Robert Kubey and Mihaly Csikszentmihalyi, 'Television Addiction Is No Mere Metaphor,' *Scientific American* (February 2002), 74-80. The philosopher of technology, Don Ihde, has written extensively regarding the visual aspects of what he calls 'instrumental realism', that is, technologically mediated reality, and the rise of visualism in the modern world. See, for example, *Expanding Hermeneutics: Visualism in Science* (Evanston, IL: Northwestern University Press, 1998).]

18. Scheuer, *Sound Bite Society*, 95.
19. Scheuer, *Sound Bite Society*, 101.
20. Scheuer, *Sound Bite Society*, 103-104.
21. Scheuer, *Sound Bite Society*, 104.
22. Scheuer, *Sound Bite Society*, 105.
23. Scheuer, *Sound Bite Society*, 115.
24. Scheuer, *Sound Bite Society*, 116.
25. Scheuer, *Sound Bite Society*, 182-83.

From Ground Zero:
Thoughts on Apocalyptic Violence and the New Terrorism

Charles B. Strozier

It is altogether appropriate to place the World Trade Center disaster at the center of any inquiry into the meaning of collective trauma in the contemporary age. The disaster symbolizes the new violence of the twenty-first century. Some mutter snidely that it is hype to say the World Trade Center disaster changed everything. They are wrong, in part because of the scale of the death that occurred, in part due to the form of the dying, and in part due to the psychological shock of the experience.

The scale of the death is gripping. 2,749[1] people died in the towers in New York (not counting 10 hijackers), 179 at the Pentagon (not including 5 hijackers), and 40 in the plane in Pennsylvania (not including 4 hijackers). We live with that horror, though the accurate counting of victims was for many months a moving target with confusing consequences. On 9/11 itself the media assumed the death toll would reach 20,000, given the number of those who might have been expected to be in the towers. That number quickly dropped to about 6,000, where it remained for nearly a month, because in the chaos of the rescue and recovery operations at Ground Zero and the general confusion in the city,[2] no one was comparing overlapping lists. Each month or so after that another thousand was shaved off the total. It was nearly six months before what seemed to be a final figure for the number of those who perished was reached, though even that number was decreased by three as late as 13 December, 2002. That radical process of decline in the number of victims during the first half a year, and the more gradual falling off after that, was wrenching for family members, and for the culture. The dread was that at some completely unknown point the number would become psychologically insignificant. It is fair to say that point was never reached, but something happened to our grasp of the event when it became no longer bloodier than Pearl Harbor (2,403 killed in action but 640 never accounted for) and a good deal less so than Antietam (3,650 killed and 17,300 wounded).

The form of the dying, however, never altered and remained psychologically confusing and painful.[3] The issue is the radical dismemberment of bodies that occurred in the disaster. The dying was not natural. It left us all bereft. For no group was this more important than for the observant Jewish community. It is a tenet of Judaism that when someone dies the body must be escorted from the moment of death to burial (the ritual of the shmira). Psalms are customarily chanted during this process. A corollary of this ritual is that the entire body must be together upon burial. Terrorism in Israel has profoundly disrupted the ability to gather the body together, which is why after any attack one sees a volunteer task force, organized by fervently Orthodox Jews, called Zaka, combing the streets for even the smallest body parts of victims. At the World Trade Center there was at best a vast number of often minute body parts. But those were precious. After the disaster, a Jewish group in the city emerged very quickly to do the best that was humanly possible under the circumstances to carry out the familiar ritual. They called themselves the Shomrim, or guardians, conducting the shmira. From very soon after the disaster volunteers gathered at the city morgue on 30th Street and First Avenue next to Bellevue Hospital for four-hour shifts of prayer as the vans with body parts arrived from Ground Zero, on the rationale that whatever was being recovered had to include substantial parts of Jewish bodies. Normally the shmira last 24 to 48 hours until burial. But since a quick burial was not possible, this shmira lasted seven months. At least one member of the Shomrim remained at the morgue to pray every minute of the day until May of 2002, as Uri Heilman did on 21 September, 2001:

> The site where the dead were kept was bustling with activity when I arrived, even in the pouring rain at four in the morning. New York police officers and state troopers stood guard as police, firemen, FBI agents, federal investigators, and other officials made their way in and out of the cordoned off area. I picked up my clergy tags from the previous volunteer and entered the scene.
>
> Eight or so simple white trucks, each draped with the American flag, each containing bags filled with countless body parts of the unidentified dead– victims of being in the wrong place at the fatally wrong time. A small American flag bound to the pole of the tent in which forensic investigators waited for the next truck to come in was drenched by the lashing rain, and even the flags adorning the trucks were curled up inside themselves.[4]

But the lack of whole bodies of the victims, or anything resembling whole bodies, affected everyone. Even the few firemen, among the 343 who perished, who were recovered more or less intact in their protective suits, were crushed beyond recognition. For the rest a body part was recovered, a hand here, part of a leg there, a piece of a spleen, sometimes little more than a fingernail. With DNA analysis these fragments that eventually numbered in the thousands were carefully assembled for detailed forensic investigation that as of the end of 2002 had led to the identification of 1,439 victims. Otherwise, victims simply disappeared into the air as they were incinerated in the fiery inferno. They left only the smell of death, of singed hair, as one respondent in an interview study I am conducting put it.[5]

The form of the dying radically impaired mourning. I had a very personal reaction to this dimension of the disaster. The trauma of my childhood was when my father died suddenly of a heart attack just after I turned 16. We had him cremated, and along with my brother, I picked up the ashes the next day at the funeral home. I was handed an innocuous tin can filled with white and grey ashes that were partly in clumps. Later that day, I stood in ocean water up to my knees near a cottage off the coast of Florida that our family had treasured, pried open the top of the can, peered for a long time at the clumps of ashes, and then tossed them out into the water where they sank slowly and disappeared.

In a similar way, many respondents in my study commented on their weird, desiccated, and fragmented death encounters. Henry T. was walking to work south of the World Trade Center that exquisitely beautiful Tuesday morning.

Henry T.:   I work on the corner of Rector Street and West. Ahm, and I walked all the way down and I was right in front of my office kind of getting ready to turn into the doors to go in my building, and heard an explosion, really loud explosion, and almost simultaneously saw a, ahm—about a six-feet-long piece of lamppost fly kind of onto Rector Street in front about 10-12 feet in front of me. And a couple of other large pieces of metal, ahm, landed like in front of me, too, and so I didn't—I kind of didn't know what was goin' on, obviously, and I smelled a little.

Strozier: At that point you're on the southwest corner of the [World Trade Center] complex?

Henry T.:   Yes, but I'm not—I'm still a few blocks away, right. As I started walking up West Street towards the World Trade Center, I walked up West Street a little bit, I could see that there were pieces of debris and there were, ahm, pieces of bodies on West Street. And this is still a couple hundred yards away [from the towers themselves]. So either—I initially felt that those people had got hit by the flying debris and it killed them, but, ahm, now I'm thinking maybe that somehow they—they could have got…like thrown out of the building that far or something. So I saw essentially what was like a torso, like the torso of somebody laying there, ahm, a head, and then one other large like piece of flesh.

Miranda M. began to exit from her office on the sixty-seventh floor of the south tower the minute she saw the fire in the other building. She did not understand what was happening but had been hyperalert to the threat of terrorism at the World Trade Center since 1993. As she descended the crowded staircase, she had no idea what was happening outside, only that it was bad. Her fear became panic when her building was hit by the second plane while she was halfway down. The entire 100-floor structure wavered and rumbled, then smoke was everywhere. She finally made it to the bottom of the stairs only to discover the door was locked. At that point she seems to have dissociated in ways that left her filled with trauma and PTSD symptoms six months later when I interviewed her. Somehow, she stumbled back up two flights of stairs and, rather miraculously, found an open door and walked out onto a plaza, unsure where she was or what was going on.

Miranda M.: I saw all chunks of metal and paper. There was a lot of paper. And then for a little way of running, like for one second I'm looking and I said, 'This is weird. It's so stupid. This is weird. Stuff is'—I don't even know how I had time to think of it. 'Is there a butcher that stuff's blowing out of?'

Strozier: A butcher?

Miranda M.: Yeah. I know I said that to myself and then like a couple of feet later, I was like, 'Holy heavens, it was pieces of people'. But like the first ones, like I guess the small stuff I saw, 'cause it looked like from a butcher like. And I'm like—'cause like you don't know what you do when you're running and then you see that and like you're stepping and I'm like, 'Is there stuff blowin' out of a butcher?' And then that's when I knew—then like I saw stuff, then I knew what it was. And then like then you knew like—and we still—I—like by then, I was alone and then I got to a street…

Strozier: Was there a lot of it, a lot of body parts?

Miranda M.: Yeah. I mean I ran—I don't know if I had the bad luck of being in a— yeah. I mean I—there was like…like if you looked down, you'd see a chunk there, a chunk—like, to me, I thought it was meat, which I'm not saying that to be cruel. Like I just couldn't figure out—like I'm like…

Strozier: You still didn't know what had happened.

Miranda M.: No. No. By then, I still thought it was a bomb, 'cause—no, I didn't know.

Strozier: (Overlap) (Unintell.)

Miranda M.:   Oh, yeah. No, I didn't look up, but that's right. I saw—yeah. Oh,
              God. I saw stuff falling, so I was runnin' like this and that's why I had
              to see everything down. I never looked up, but you could see in front
              of you stuff falling.

Many respondents in my study, as well, watched helplessly as people
jumped. Deirdre L. had a day job catering meetings with a business in 7
World Trade Center just to the north of the towers (that would itself collapse at 5.20 pm that day). She was in a room on the thirty-ninth of 50
floors when the first plane hit the north tower but had almost no idea of
the magnitude of what was happening. In a few minutes, however, she
and the others were told to evacuate the building. The long walk down
the stairs without windows or knowledge of the terror outside was eerie,
though mostly peaceful. The one moment of dread came when the
second plane hit the south tower and the whole building she was in
shook. No one knew what was happening but there was collective terror.
When Deirdre finally reached the street and relative safety, she stood for
a few minutes to watch the burning buildings. A man hung from a sheet
or tablecloth outside a window some 90 stories up, then gave up the
struggle and fell back with his arms outstretched. He seemed to fall in
slow motion. Crying now, Deirdre sensed the terrible danger of the scene
and felt she had to escape. With a friend she walked quickly up West
Broadway to Greenwich Street, fleeing north. On the way her progress
was slowed by crowds going toward the burning buildings, including three
women with babies, two in strollers and one with an infant so young it
was in her arms. Deirdre shook that woman by the shoulders and said she
should not be going that way, that it was dangerous and she was going the
wrong way, that she should turn around. The woman ignored her and
pushed on. For weeks afterwards Deirdre had nightmares of these women
with their children getting buried by the collapsing buildings.

These complex reactions to the form of the dying took shape within
'zones of sadness', a term first used by my colleague, Michael Flynn[6] and
one I have written about extensively, that radiated out from Ground
Zero.[7] The issue of trauma and impairment of mourning depended in
large part on one's proximity to the actual scene of the destruction. Many
factors influenced the reaction of the witness, the pain suffered, even the
trauma endured, but it did matter enormously how far one was from the
epicenter of death. The zones can even be mapped, and include, first,
those between the Hudson River and the Brooklyn Bridge, and below
Chambers Street as far as Battery Park, who directly witnessed the death;
second, those in Greenwich Village below 14th Street who saw the disaster directly but could not see people jumping; third, those in metropolitan

New York but without a clear line of vision of what was happening (or from such a great distance as to make the image of the buildings burning surreal); and, fourth, those outside New York and in the world who watched the disaster on television.

The difference between zones three and four is worth some comment. To observe the disaster through the medium of television had the contradictory psychological effect of intensifying the experience of horror through endless repetition while simultaneously numbing the viewer to its real meaning, in part because of the repetition as well but also because it was watched in protected spaces, there was commentary to contextualize what one saw, and the direct experience of death was leeched out of the images. The New York experience of the disaster, even outside the radius of death, was full of confusion and chaos, with people being evacuated from tall buildings and a mass exodus across the bridges, and much general fear. There was also the smell and taste of death, for in that cloud of incinerated computers and rugs and drapes and tons of cement were all the people whom we breathed into our lungs, into our souls.

Finally, there was the shock of what was experienced in the World Trade Center disaster. History had not prepared us for such a disaster. We were much too convinced of what has been called the American sense of exceptionalism that blessed, or cursed, us with a sense of entitlement and special security. We never feared attacks from foreign shores. The most important document in our political history about the danger of tyranny, Lincoln's 'Young Man Lyceum Speech', in 1838 argues that because we face no threat of foreign invasion the danger is that domestic unrest (the mobocratic spirit) will loosen our attachment to our democratic institutions and cause the emergence of a dictator.[8] There are other aspects of American exceptionalism. Ours was the first and greatest democratic republic. We had the richest soil and best institutions. Our military became the strongest. That sense of invincibility reached its zenith in our history, I would say, in the 1990s. America then had reached a pinnacle of absolute power and confidence. There was serious talk the new economy would never collapse and we would simply continue to get richer. American culture completely suffocated global heterogeneity. And American power after our so-called victory in the cold war left us with absolute dominance and what Robert Jay Lifton has called a 'superpower syndrome'.[9] Our arrogance was supreme, and nowhere was that sense of invincibility more supremely centered than New York, and no single image more concretely symbolized American power and authority and dominance than those giant towers reaching into the heavens.

To attack and actually crumble those towers was to demolish in a heart beat all that security. It literally rocked the ground of our being. We could not have been less prepared psychologically. It is fair to say that before 9/11 we lacked an appropriate level of fear of the apocalyptic. Now we are in a state of panic and hysteria. Perhaps the issue, touching as it does collective death, only invites extremes.

Nuclear Weapons and Apocalyptic Violence

The twin towers were still burning, but standing, when commentators began to draw the parallel between the World Trade Center and Pearl Harbor. It is quite obvious how Pearl Harbor and the World Trade Center are alike. What distinguishes them is that Pearl Harbor occurred in a world without nuclear weapons. In that difference lies the main conceptual point I want to make.

People have thought about the end of the world since its beginning. Such imaginings have stirred much creativity in religion and the arts and been an essential ingredient in the making of culture. But images of the end of human life itself also involve great violence and collective death. The apocalyptic is not benign. It is seductive, because such narratives involve the death of all evil and redemption for the saved.

One might say there are three dimensions of the apocalyptic. First, there is the ontological. Because we all die, we know of collective death, and that knowledge may, in fact, be what separates us from the higher primates. Second, there is the cultural and religious dimension to the apocalyptic. Images of our collective end lie very deeply embedded and their protean expressions in culture and religion are carried forward by mystics, artists, and psychotics. These three marginal groups played a critical role in keeping alive for everyone that image of an apocalyptic future which makes an ethical present more urgently necessary. But finally there is a historical or psychohistorical dimension to the apocalyptic. Something shifted in our consciousness in the middle of the twentieth century that was directly associated with the presence of nuclear weapons in the world. We don't need God any longer to end it all. The power is entirely within us and in our arsenals. We alone possess it.

This new psychology of weapons of mass destruction (and of course one now has to include biological and chemical weapons in what is an ever-more fearsome expansion of ultimate weapons in human hands) was not that apparent for the first few decades of the nuclear age because it seemed only states could possess the weapons. Technology has altered that limitation, and in retrospect it seems the 1990s was the hugely significant turning point in that historical process. You can not quite make a nuclear bomb in your bathtub yet, but nor do you need the mobilization of resources that was represented by, say, the Manhattan Project to imagine having the ability to kill not just hundreds, or thousands, but millions.

There is no question it is a huge threat to us all that apocalyptic groups may well very soon, if they don't already, have access to weapons of mass destruction. The respondents in my study report the generalized dread that if Osama bin Laden had had access to nuclear weapons he would have placed them on the planes flying into the towers on 9/11. But I want to turn this question around and stress its more general and psychological aspects, namely that the mere existence of the weapons themselves play what is perhaps the central role in evoking the new violence of the contemporary age.[10]

Why?

1. Nuclear weapons totalize politics, religion and, indeed, the self. They make possible the most extreme reach of violence and stir the worst devils, rather than what Abraham Lincoln called the better angels, of our nature. Richard Falk in this regard has written extensively about the way the weapons 'deform' our politics.[11]
2. Nuclear weapons totalize death itself, and change what Kurt Vonnegut called plain old ordinary death into absurd death.[12] Robert Jay Lifton has said that nuclear weapons bring about a 'pointless apocalypse'.[13] At least the fundamentalists get their Messiah (or get him back). Nuclear weapons bring back nothing.
3. Nuclear weapons open up new possibilities for violence, because the new power of God in human hands makes possible, and therefore affirms, the sinister workings of the paranoid mindset.

Paranoia may be the heart of the matter. There is a psychological synergy between the survivor's sense of endangerment and the more extreme imagery of victimization for the paranoid. The experience of suffering can ennoble and expand empathy. But victimization is not always or even mostly ennobling. It stirs rage and fury and the call for revenge.[14] The trauma gets imbedded.[15] All is false and counterfeit in the world. No one can be trusted. Evil is everywhere and the world a malevolent, threatening, dangerous place. In time such collective feelings get institutionalized and built into politics and culture. A paranoid style takes shape that merges self and world in ways that privilege the experience of victimization.[16]

Because paranoia is essentially at the border of psychosis, when it enters politics its forms can be sometimes quite amusing. The John

Birchers of the 1950s, for example, were terribly worried about Communism but the most immediate policy issue in the country they fiercely opposed was the eminently sensible public health move to fluoridate the water. The movie, *Dr. Strangelove*, from the late 1960s makes funny parody of this fear in the obsessions of the mad General Mandrake who rants about the 'Commies trying to get at our precious bodily fluids'.

But paranoia in politics is no laughing matter. Our wake-up call was, of course, McVeigh's bombing of the Federal building in Oklahoma City on 19 April, 1995. The most important question to ask about McVeigh is what he hoped to accomplish by his act of terrorism. Just because actions are apocalyptic does not mean they are without meaning, crazy and nuts and should simply be dismissed. I would say we have to keep our moral sights in focus and never stop condemning such violence but that we will never figure how to make ourselves safe if we don't enter into the mind of the terrorist. It is thus almost certainly the case that McVeigh was a disturbed young man. But he also fitted into an ideological movement that had been taking shape since the end of the Vietnam War, a movement that saw the government as uniquely malicious (and FEMA, for them, is the direct agent of the ZOG or Zionist Occupied Government, flying the black helicopters that took the true patriots to the hidden concentration camps, etc.), and which drew particular energy from the tragedy at Waco.[17] That movement also had its sacred texts in two novels, *The Turner Diaries* that McVeigh slept with under his pillow, and to a lesser degree, *Hunter*. I would conclude that McVeigh, because he was basically working with just one other person, only had access to the most primitive of bombs, but that his goals were to initiate a mystical, world-ending process. Thankfully, his means of destruction failed to match the extraordinary reach of his aspirations.

We also had another wake-up call in the 1990s that we mostly slept through in the wildly apocalyptic cult in Japan, Aum Shinrikyo, led by Shoko Asaharo. In Lifton's book on Aum, *Destroying the World to Save It*,[18] he shows in great detail how really peculiar Asaharo was (he sold his bath water to followers and rented out at $10,000 a month a device you wore on your head to coordinate your brain waves with those of the guru); but much more interestingly how Aum explicitly wanted to create Armageddon. That is why they were manufacturing sarin gas and botulinus toxin in their secret factory outside of Tokyo and why, most terrifyingly, they were negotiating with some of their 20,000 Russian followers to import plutonium. In the end, their plans were rushed because the police were closing in on them so they only managed a basically botched release of sarin gas in the subway system on 22 March, 1995. Their goal, how-

ever, with their full array of weapons of mass destruction they either had
or actively sought, was to kill many millions of Japanese, who would then
assume the Americans had attacked, which would then spark a Japanese
bombing of America, and that would in turn lead to an American nuclear
attack, once again, on Japan. Out of this Armageddon, this vast blood-
letting and destruction, the followers of Aum would magically survive and
remake the world in their own image.

And, of course, I end this sequence with Osama bin Laden, the malevolent and mysterious figure who has wreaked such havoc in our city and
made our world such an unsafe place. At some level we understood completely the apocalyptic dangers he represented. The respondents in my
study, for example, repeatedly expressed their belief that if bin Laden had
had access to nuclear weapons he would have placed them on one or
more of the planes in the attacks. Nor are such views mere hype. The
remarkable report of the 9/11 commission, headed by Thomas Kean and
co-chaired by Lee Hamilton, notes that in the latter 1990s the CIA knew
that bin Laden had 'been heard to speak of wanting a "Hiroshima" and
at least 10,000 casualties' from some kind of WMD (weapons of mass
destruction) attack on the United States.[19]

But who is this Osama bin Laden? And what does he want? On the
personal side, he is all the more dangerous because he is not as schizoid
as McVeigh or as openly psychotic as Asaharo. He does warmly embrace
the apocalyptic. As it has been said, he is like the president of terrorism
university, a charismatic figure with money who can inspire others to act.
He does not lead a cult but rather a movement. Though he issues fatwas,
which he has no right to, he is not a cleric. He is instead a curious blend
of political and religious leader and plays an important role vitalizing
Islamists who see the downfall of their faith and their lands the result of
outside western corrupting influences. Bin Laden has wrapped himself
around the Palestinian cause, mainly for pragmatic reasons in his effort to
gain support in Arab lands and unify the struggle, but he hardly cares
about the PLO or Israel. What he does care about is the presence of US
troops in Saudi Arabia during and after the Gulf War, which he sees as a
desecration, an affront to his faith, the presence of the evil other in holy
land.[20] Here I would note that the difference between his pragmatic
appropriation of PLO goals and his real feelings about American infidels in
Saudi Arabia is exactly the difference between the old and new terrorism.
Bin Laden was moving toward radical action in the late 1980s, but his Al
Qaeda organization came in the wake of the Gulf War and was its direct
consequence.

So what does he want? He wants to destroy America and its culture, and out of such a victory make a purified Islam. It seems the attack on our majestic towers in his eyes was both real and symbolic *and* succeeded beyond his wildest dreams. He also fits snugly into the paranoid style. He has made his fight a *jihad*, or crusade, which puts God on his side. There is an urgency to the struggle and it has to happen now, as time is running out. The end is at hand which is both fateful but offers the powerful appeal of transformation and redemption. Furthermore, the malice Americans create in the world is the motive force in history. He has special knowledge of that evil, which lends him the right to act by bending the rules about issuing fatwas, organize terrorist training camps, carry out actions that have ranged from the first bombing of the World Trade Center (which he seems to have had some relation to), to the America Embassy bombings in 1998, to the attack on the USS Cole, and of course the attacks on 9/11.

Conclusion

We live in a state of chronic fear and paranoia. It is not altogether inappropriate. There are those in the world with a grim determination to destroy us, and increasingly these new terrorists have access to means of annihilation that can realize their most extravagant dreams. Such threats, and a keen awareness of the dangers, have long been a part of our psyches. In my World Trade Center interviews, for example, I have been struck by how many people imposed pre-existing nuclear ideas onto their experience of the disaster. Many saw the plume of smoke from the burning buildings as a mushroom cloud. Miranda M., after her escape when she was entrapped by the dark cloud from the collapsed tower, jumped into a bush and passed out for she was sure it was nuclear and meant the end of the world. This sequence suggests the heart of my argument. We are all unsteady in the nuclear age. Something profound shifted when humans came to possess weapons with the destructive power of God. The new terrorists embrace that power with alacrity and seek to employ it. To fend off such dangers we first need to recognize its centrality in our souls and then find concrete ways to mitigate the threat.

These are issues we can think about if we are open to the psychological significance of nuclear weapons. In a seminar some years ago, a psychoanalytic colleague gave a clinical example to disprove my thesis about the centrality of nuclear weapons in our souls. He reported the dream of an 11 year-old boy whose parents were in the middle of an angry divorce. In the dream the boy woke in terror to the image of a mushroom cloud as a bomb exploded. Obviously, my colleague said, the boy had borrowed a powerful metaphor to convey his inner sense of the chaos and violence he felt about his exploding family. That was the sequence, he said, and the way to understand the dream. I responded that, of course, the dream has that meaning, and it probably would make the most sense in a clinical setting at least to begin the analysis of the boy's feelings about the divorce from within the image of the mushroom cloud. But the dream is incompletely interpreted if we stay only in its personal context. As I told my colleague, what this troubled but insightful boy has done from within his misery over his fragmenting family is to open himself to the meaning of totalized death in the world that we face with nuclear weapons. In that process of connecting the personal and the political, the boy grew and deepened. The most significant level of the dream, I feel, is the way it suggests the workings of history in the boy's psyche, not the other way around. This precocious boy took in the existential reality of our lives that we ignore at our own peril. It is entirely false to live as if there is a secure human future. What we can do is move through the doubt and fear and dread into cautious hope. In a dark time the eye begins to see.

References

Caruth, Cathy, *Trauma: Explorations in Memory* (Baltimore: The Johns Hopkins University Press, 1995).

Heilman, Uri, 'Personal and Unpublished Statement', 21 September, 2001.

—'Interview', 19 December, 2002.

—'Dept. of Remembrance, Praying for the Dead, Personal and Unpublished Statement', 2002.

Herman, Judith, *Trauma and Recovery* (New York: Basic Books, 1992).

Hill, Michael Ortiz, *Dreaming the End of the World: Apocalypse as a Rite of Passage* (Dallas: Spring Publications, 1994).

Hoffman, Bruce, 'The Leadership Secrets of Osama bin Laden: The Terrorist as CEO', *The Atlantic Monthly* (2003), 83-91.

Hofstadter, Richard, 'The Paranoid Style in American Politics', in *idem*, *The Paranoid Style in American Politics and Other Essays* (Chicago: The University of Chicago Press, 1964), ch. 1.

Kohut, Heinz, 'Thoughts on Narcissism and Narcissistic Rage', in *idem*, *The Search for the Self: Selected Writings of Heinz Kohut: 1950–1978* (ed. Paul Ornstein; New York: International Universities Press, 1978), II, 615-58.

Lifton, Robert Jay, *The Broken Connection: On Death and the Continuity of Life* (New York: Basic Books, 1979).

—*Destroying the World to Save It: Aum Shinrikyo, Apocalyptic Violence, and the New Terrorism* (New York: Metropolitan Books, 1999).

—*The Superpower Syndrome: America's Apocalyptic Confrontation with the World* (New York: Thunder Mouth Press/Nation Institute, 2003).

Lifton, Robert Jay, and Richard Falk, *Indefensible Weapons* (New York: Basic Books, 1985).

Lincoln, Abraham, *The Collected Works of Abraham Lincoln*, I (ed. Roy Basler, *et al.*; New Brunswick, NJ: Rutgers University Press, 1953).

Macdonald, Andrew [William L. Pierce], *The Turner Diaries* (Hillsboro,WV: National Vanguard Books, 1978).

—*Hunter* (Hillsboro,WV: National Vanguard Books, 1989).

Stern, Jessica, 'The Protean Enemy', *Foreign Affairs* 84 (2003), 14-27.

Strozier, Charles B., *Apocalypse: On the Psychology of Fundamentalism in America* (Boston: Beacon Press, 1994).

—'Apocalyptic Violence and the Politics of Waco', in Charles Strozier and Michael Flynn (eds.), *The Year 2000: Essays on the End* (New York: New York University Press, 1997), 97-111.

—'The World Trade Center Disaster and the Apocalyptic', *Psychoanalytic Dialogues* 12 (2002), 361-80.

—'From Ground Zero: Apocalyptic Violence and the World Trade Center Disaster', in *Dialogues on Terror: Patients and their Psychoanalysts* 20.2, (Special Issue *Psycho-analysis and Psychotherapy, Fall 2003*) (reprinted with changes in Samuel Heilman [ed.], *Death, Bereavement, and Mourning* [New Brunswick, NJ: Transaction Publishers, 2005]).

—'Trauma and Poetry: On the World Trade Center Disaster', in Yael Danieli and Robert Dingman (eds.), *On the Ground after September 11: Mental Health Responses and Practical Knowledge Gained* (Binghampton, NY: The Haworth Press, 2004).

Strozier, Charles B., and Michael Flynn (eds.), *Trauma and Self and Genocide, War, and Human Survival* (Lanham, MD: Rowman & Littlefield, 1996).

—*The Year 2000: Essays on the End* (New York: New York University Press, 1997)

Strozier, Charles B., and Katie Gentile, 'The Mental Health Response to the World Trade Center Disaster', in Daniella Knafo (ed.), *Living with Terror, Working with Trauma: A Clinician's Handbook* (Lanham, MD: Jason Aronson, 2004), ch. 20.

US Commission on Terrorist Attacks, *The 9/11 Commission Report: Final Report of the National Commission on Terrorist Attacks upon the United States* (New York: Norton, 2004).

van der Kolk, Bessel, *Psychological Trauma* (Washington, DC: American Psychiatric Press, 1987).

van der Kolk, Bessel, Alexander C. McFarlane, Lars Weisaeth, (eds.), *Traumatic Stress: The Effects of Overwhelming Experience on Mind, Body, and Society* (New York: Guilford, 1996).

Vonnegut, Kurt, *Slaughterhouse Five* (New York: Delacourt, 1969).

Notes

1.   The previous number of 2,792 that had become etched in everyone's mind was reduced by 40 on October 28, 2003, when New York City found it could no longer account for some of the victims.

2.   Charles B. Strozier and Katie Gentile, 'The Mental Health Response to the World Trade Center Disaster', in Daniella Knafo (ed.), *Living with Terror, Working with Trauma: A Clinician's Handbook* (Lanham, MD: Jason Aronson, 2004), ch. 20.

3.   On Thursday, 13 September, 2001, The *New York Times* showed a man who had jumped or fallen from the top floors of one of the towers descending to earth head first. That picture prompted a coordination of media executives to curtail the showing of any more images of people jumping or falling out of the towers (Personal

communication, Bill Blakemore of ABC, 18 July, 2001). The first documentary to break this self-imposed taboo was that of the Naudet Brothers, Jules and Gedeon, broadcast on CBS, 10 March, 2002. Others followed, and it seems such images are gradually entering the culture—and peoples' imagination.

4.   Uri Heilman, 'Personal and unpublished statement', 21 September, 2001, and 'Interview', 19 December, 2002. Note also Heilman's 'Dept. of Remembrance, Praying for the Dead, Personal and unpublished statement', from 2002 (but otherwise undated).

5.   A study of survivors and victims that I began the first weekend. See Charles B. Strozier, 'The World Trade Center Disaster and the Apocalyptic', *Psychoanalytic Dialogues* 12 (2002), 361-80.

6.   Michael Flynn, Personal communication, 8 October, 2001.

7.   Besides Strozier, 2002, note Strozier, 'Trauma and Poetry: On the World Trade Center Disaster', in Yael Danieli and Robert Dingman (eds.), *On the Ground after September 11: Mental Health Responses and Practical Knowledge Gained* (Binghampton, NY: The Haworth Press, 2004); *idem*, 'From Ground Zero: Apocalyptic Violence and the World Trade Center Disaster', *Dialogues on Terror: Patients and Their Psychoanalysts* 20.2 (Special Issue *Psychoanalysis and Psychotherapy, Fall 2003*) (reprinted with changes in Samuel Heilman [ed.], *Death, Bereavement, and Mourning* [New Brunswick, NJ: Transaction Publishers, 2005]).

8.   Abraham Lincoln, in Roy Basler, *et al.* (eds.), *The Collected Works of Abraham Lincoln*, (New Brunswick, NJ: Rutgers University Press, 1953), I, 109.

9.   Robert Jay Lifton, *The Superpower Syndrome: America's Apocalyptic Confrontation with the World* (New York: Thunder Mouth Press/Nation Institute, 2003).

10.   See Redles' essay in this volume that talks about 'induced apocalypse'. I mean something a little different, though certainly in the same psychological arena, and more that the apocalyptic exists as a human potential in the self before nuclear weapons and required the agency of God to actualize. Once God becomes irrelevant, I am arguing, we change in ways we are just beginning to understand. Compare Michael Ortiz Hill, *Dreaming the End of the World: Apocalypse as a Rite of Passage* (Dallas: Spring Publications, 1994), 10-46 and 159-65, where he talks of the contemporary 'nuclearized soul'.

11.   Robert Jay Lifton and Richard Falk, *Indefensible Weapons* (New York: Basic Books, 1985).

12.   Kurt Vonnegut, *Slaughterhouse Five* (New York: Delacourt, 1969). Robert Jay Lifton has shared this idea of his that nuclear weapons totalize death in numerous conversations over the years, in the many courses we taught together at John Jay College, but especially in connection with the analysis of the data that led to my *Apocalypse: On the Psychology of Fundamentalism in America* (Boston: Beacon Press, 1994).

13.   Robert Jay Lifton, *The Broken Connection: On Death and the Continuity of Life* (New York: Basic Books, 1979).

14.   Heinz Kohut, 'Thoughts on Narcissism and Narcissistic Rage', in Paul Ornstein (ed.), *The Search for the Self: Selected Writings of Heinz Kohut: 1950–1978* (ed. Paul Ornstein; New York: International Universities Press, 1978).

15.   Cathy Caruth, *Trauma: Explorations in Memory* (Baltimore: The Johns Hopkins

University Press, 1995); Judith Herman, *Trauma and Recovery* (New York: Basic Books, 1992); Bessel van der Kolk, *Psychological Trauma* (Washington, DC: American Psychiatric Press, 1987) and Bessel van der Kolk, Alexander C. McFarlane, Lars Weisaeth (eds.), *Traumatic Stress: The Effects of Overwhelming Experience on Mind, Body, and Society* (New York: Guilford, 1996); Charles B. Strozier and Michael Flynn (eds.), *Trauma and Self* and *Genocide, War, and Human Survival* (Lanham, MD: Rowman & Littlefield, 1996) and their, *The Year 2000: Essays on the End* (New York: New York University Press, 1997).

16. Richard Hofstadter, 'The Paranoid Style in American Politics', *The Paranoid Style in American Politics and Other Essays* (Chicago: The University of Chicago Press, 1964).

17. See my article that specifically develops this idea, Charles B. Strozier, 'Apocalyptic Violence and the Politics of Waco', *The Year 2000*, 97-111.

18. Robert Jay Lifton, *Destroying the World to Save It: Aum Shinrikyo, Apocalyptic Violence, and the New Terrorism* (New York: Metropolitan Books, 1999).

19. *The 9/11 Commission Report: Final Report of the National Commission on Terrorist Attacks Upon the United States* (New York: Norton, 2004), 116.

20. See his fatwa issued in 1998, available on numerous websites in translation, in which he declared war on the United States and called on all Muslims to join in the jihad. In that fatwa he lists the sources of his discontent. Compare Jessica Stern, 'The Protean Enemy', *Foreign Affairs* 84 (2003), 14-27 and Bruce Hoffman, 'The Leadership Secrets of Osama bin Laden: The Terrorist as CEO', *The Atlantic Monthly* (2003), 83-91.

Index